Fodor's 06

SAN DIEGO

Where to Stay and Eat for All Budgets

Must-See Sights and Local Secrets

Ratings You Can Trust

Fodor's Travel Publications   New York, Toronto, London, Sydney, Auckland
www.fodors.com

FODOR'S SAN DIEGO 2006
Editor: Kristin Moehlmann

Editorial Production: Bethany Cassin Beckerlegge
Editorial Contributors: Andrew Collins, Lenore Greiner, Maribeth Mellin, David Nelson, Tina Randall, Bobbi Zane
Maps: David Lindroth, *cartographer*; Rebecca Baer and Bob Blake, *map editors*
Design: Fabrizio La Rocca, *creative director*; Guido Caroti, *art director*; Moon Sun Kim, *cover designer*; Melanie Marin, *senior picture editor*
Production/Manufacturing: Angela L. McLean
Cover Photo (Mission Beach): Giovanni Simeone/Fototeca 9x12

COPYRIGHT

ISBN 1–4000–1595–2

ISSN 1053–5950

SPECIAL SALES

This book is available for special discounts for bulk purchases for sales promotions or premiums. Special editions, including personalized covers, excerpts of existing books, and corporate imprints, can be created in large quantities for special needs. For more information, write to Special Markets/Premium Sales, 1745 Broadway, MD 6-2, New York, New York 10019, or e-mail specialmarkets@randomhouse.com.

AN IMPORTANT TIP & AN INVITATION

Although all prices, opening times, and other details in this book are based on information supplied to us at press time, changes occur all the time in the travel world, and Fodor's cannot accept responsibility for facts that become outdated or for inadvertent errors or omissions. So **always confirm information when it matters,** especially if you're making a detour to visit a specific place. Your experiences—positive and negative—matter to us. If we have missed or misstated something, **please write to us.** We follow up on all suggestions. Contact the San Diego editor at editors@fodors.com or c/o Fodor's at 1745 Broadway, New York, NY 10019.

PRINTED IN THE UNITED STATES OF AMERICA

10 9 8 7 6 5 4 3 2 1

Be a Fodor's Correspondent

Your opinion matters. It matters to us. It matters to your fellow Fodor's travelers, too. And we'd like to hear it. In fact, we *need* to hear it.

When you share your experiences and opinions, you become an active member of the Fodor's community. That means we'll not only use your feedback to make our books better, but we'll publish your names and comments whenever possible. Throughout our guides, look for "Word of Mouth," excerpts of your unvarnished feedback.

Here's how you can help improve Fodor's for all of us.

Tell us when we're right. We rely on local writers to give you an insider's perspective. But our writers and staff editors—who are the best in the business—depend on you. Your positive feedback is a vote to renew our recommendations for the next edition.

Tell us when we're wrong. We're proud that we update most of our guides every year. But we're not perfect. Things change. Hotels cut services. Museums change hours. Charming cafés lose charm. If our writer didn't quite capture the essence of a place, tell us how you'd do it differently. If any of our descriptions are inaccurate or inadequate, we'll incorporate your changes in the next edition and will correct factual errors at fodors.com *immediately.*

Tell us what to include. You probably have had fantastic travel experiences that aren't yet in Fodor's. Why not share them with a community of like-minded travelers? Maybe you chanced upon a beach or bistro or B&B that you don't want to keep to yourself. Tell us why we should include it. And share your discoveries and experiences with everyone directly at fodors.com. Your input may lead us to add a new listing or highlight a place we cover with a "Highly Recommended" star or with our highest rating, "Fodor's Choice."

Give us your opinion instantly at our feedback center at www.fodors.com/feedback. You may also e-mail editors@fodors.com with the subject line "San Diego Editor." Or send your nominations, comments, and complaints by mail to San Diego Editor, Fodor's, 1745 Broadway, New York, NY 10019.

You and travelers like you are the heart of the Fodor's community. Make our community richer by sharing your experiences. Be a Fodor's correspondent.

Happy traveling!

Tim Jarrell, Publisher

CONTENTS

ABOUT THIS BOOK

Our Ratings

Sometimes you find terrific travel experiences and sometimes they just find you. But usually the burden is on you to select the right combination of experiences. That's where our ratings come in.

As travelers we've all discovered a place so wonderful that its worthiness is obvious. And sometimes that place is so unique that superlatives don't do it justice: you just have to be there to know. These sights, properties, and experiences get our highest rating, Fodor's Choice, indicated by orange stars throughout this book.

Black stars highlight sights and properties we deem Highly Recommended, places that our writers, editors, and readers praise again and again for consistency and excellence.

By default, there's another category: any place we include in this book is by definition worth your time, unless we say otherwise. And we will.

Disagree with any of our choices? Care to nominate a place or suggest that we rate one more highly? Visit our feedback center at www. fodors.com.

Budget Well

Hotel and restaurant price categories from ¢ to $$$$ are defined in the opening pages of each chapter. For attractions, we always give standard adult admission fees; reductions are usually available for children, students, and senior citizens. Want to pay with plastic? AE, D, DC, MC, V following restaurant and hotel listings indicate if American Express, Discover, Diner's Club, MasterCard, and Visa are accepted.

Restaurants

Unless we state otherwise, restaurants are open for lunch and dinner daily. We mention dress only when there's a specific requirement and reservations only when they're essential or not accepted—it's always best to book ahead.

Hotels

Hotels have private bath, phone, TV, and air-conditioning and operate on the European Plan (a.k.a. EP, meaning without meals), unless we specify that they use the Continental Plan (CP, with a Continental breakfast), Breakfast Plan (BP, with a full breakfast), or Modified American Plan (MAP, with breakfast and dinner) or are all-inclusive (including all meals and most activities). We always

list facilities but not whether you'll be charged an extra fee to use them, so when pricing accommodations, find out what's included.

Many Listings

- ★ Fodor's Choice
- ★ Highly recommended
- ✉ Physical address
- ✛ Directions
- ⌂ Mailing address
- ☎ Telephone
- 🖷 Fax
- ⊕ On the Web
- ✍ E-mail
- ✒ Admission fee
- ☉ Open/closed times
- ► Start of walk/itinerary
- Ⓜ Metro stations
- ▭ Credit cards

Hotels & Restaurants

- 🏨 Hotel
- ⟟ Number of rooms
- ♨ Facilities
- ❗ Meal plans
- ✕ Restaurant
- ⌂ Reservations
- 𝄞 Dress code
- ✎ Smoking
- ⛾ BYOB
- ✕🏨 Hotel with restaurant that warrants a visit

Outdoors

- ⚐ Golf
- ⛺ Camping

Other

- ☾ Family-friendly
- 🛈 Contact information
- ⇨ See also
- ✉ Branch address
- ☞ Take note

WHAT'S WHERE

BALBOA PARK	
	Even without the most alluring and impressive collection of museums and cultural institutions on the West Coast, and one of the world's most incredible zoos, leafy—and enormous—Balboa Park would qualify unequivocally as spectacular. It's San Diego's green lung. It's the city's arts mecca. And from this 1,200-acre patch of lush greenery, it's easy to reach all of the city's core neighborhoods of interest. You can't understand San Diego without at least a quick drive, or better yet a leisurely stroll or bike ride, through dynamic Balboa Park, which sits at the geographic heart of the city, just northeast of downtown. In short, before turning your attention to the rest of San Diego, pay a visit here.
HILLCREST AND NORTH PARK	
	These two trendy neighborhoods that form the northern border of Balboa Park (with Hillcrest to the west, North Park to the east) are bereft of museums and attractions—the usual touristy draws. But they're alive with slick nightspots, both sexy and simple restaurants, bookish coffeehouses, and oddball shops and boutiques along with a fairly typical splash of upscale franchise stores and eateries. Hillcrest, the heart of the city's gay and lesbian community, caters to a hip, upscale crowd and also has a few inns and small hotels of note. Funkier and less expensive North Park is better for antiques and vintage-clothing shopping. Throughout both neighborhoods, you can count on great people-watching.
DOWNTOWN	
	But for the bustling harborfront, downtown San Diego could have been any-dull-city U.S.A. as recently as 15 or 20 years ago, with a fairly banal blend of office towers and empty sidewalks at night and on weekends. Now, preservationists and entrepreneurs have turned the once-seedy but historic Gaslamp Quarter into a happening warren of restaurants, nightclubs, and shops. The downtown hub, Horton Plaza, has emerged into a fashionable shopping and dining complex spanning some six city blocks. South of the Embarcadero on Harbor Drive 14-acre Seaport Village buzzes with shopping plazas designed to reflect the architectural styles of early California. And 2004 saw the opening of Petco Park, home to baseball's Padres, an event that has spurred a wealth of mixed residential and com-

	mercial developments in this waterfront area just east of the Gaslamp Quarter. This is a bona fide thriving downtown that's busy 24/7.
CORONADO	
	Historic Coronado, an islandlike peninsula across the bay from San Diego's waterfront, came of age as a Victorian resort community during the late 19th century, developed around the ornate Hotel Del Coronado, which to this day remains a favorite haunt of celebs, A-listers, and—well—ghosts (if you believe the stories). You reach this dignified, graceful community either via the San Diego–Coronado Bridge or the San Diego–Coronado Ferry. Wealthy suburbanites and the Coronado naval base, which includes the Naval Air Station North Island and the Naval Amphibious Base Coronado, also make their home here. Boutiques and restaurants line Orange Avenue, and you can catch some rays and splash in the surf at Silver Strand State Beach and Imperial Beach, which extend in a long arc to the south.
HARBOR ISLAND & SHELTER ISLAND	
	A man-made strip of land in the bay directly across from San Diego International Airport and a short drive from downtown, Harbor Island has several hotels and restaurants and makes a good base for a visit to San Diego. You'll find a few more hotels and restaurants on Shelter Island, known for its yacht-building and sport fishing industries and also a short drive from downtown, just west of Harbor Island. From either locale, you're smack in the middle of the bay, with great views of downtown skyscrapers in one direction, and Point Loma and Coronado in the other.
POINT LOMA	
	Standing as a buffer against the temperamental Pacific Ocean, Point Loma curves almost crescentlike along San Diego Bay and extends south into the sea. Beyond its main drags, which contain a few too many fast-food restaurants and bland motels, Point Loma contains several well-to-do neighborhoods and bay-side estates (it's a favorite retirement spot for naval officers). From the bay side you can enjoy a terrific view of downtown, and from Sunset Cliffs, between Point Loma and Ocean Beach, you're treated to incomparable views of the Pacific. To this end, it's a great place to cap off a day of exploring as the sun sets.

LA JOLLA	
	There may not be a more charmed setting in San Diego County than the luxe, bluff-top enclave of La Jolla. Artsy and upscale, the village abounds with showcase Spanish Colonial and Mediterranean Revival homes. Posh inns, boutiques, and restaurants on or near the main thoroughfare, Prospect Street, cater to the affluent local gentry, but a surprising number of mid-range options please visitors on tighter budgets. Fortunately, the largely unspoiled scenery of its coast, coves, and verdant hillsides is still free. Although it feels like a separate entity, La Jolla is officially a section of the city of San Diego—it sits at the top of the city's string of beach neighborhoods, immediately north of Pacific Beach.
MISSION BAY & THE BEACHES	
	The coastal and unabashedly commercial Mission Bay area, a 15-minute drive northwest of downtown, sits between the airport and La Jolla. At its fringes are the lively Mission Beach and Pacific Beach communities, which are rife with surf shops, ice-cream stands, and beach bars. Just inland is one of Southern California's leading attractions, SeaWorld, but the area also serves as a 4,600-acre aquatic park teeming with scenic coves, crystalline beaches, and plenty of great turf for boating, jet skiing, sunning, running, swimming, and fishing. Terrestrial types can jog, bike, rollerblade, play basketball, or fly a kite on the bay's peninsulas and two main islands, Vacation Island and Fiesta Island.
OLD TOWN	
	Although this tourist-driven area a few miles north of downtown can be experienced in an afternoon, set aside at least a couple of hours to explore what is essentially a collection of remnants from the original San Diego, the first European settlement in California. The former pueblo of San Diego is now preserved as a state historic park and contains several original and reconstructed buildings, along with a handful of popular Mexican restaurants, souvenir stands, and art galleries. The historic sites are clustered around Old Town Plaza, which you can explore easily on foot.
MISSION VALLEY	
	Every city needs an area like Mission Valley, even if it lacks history and charm. This stretch of modern commercial development along the I–8 corridor contains dozens of cookie-

	cutter chain hotels in all price ranges, plus myriad glass-and-steel office towers, soulless condos, big-box stores, and brand-name shops at megamalls like the Fashion Valley shopping center and Westfield Shoppingtown Mission Valley. Hotel Circle holds the bulk of the area's lodging options; football's San Diego Chargers play at nearby Qualcomm Stadium.
COASTAL SAN DIEGO NORTH COUNTY	The seaside towns north of La Jolla developed separately from San Diego. Along the ocean, Del Mar contains natty golf and spa resorts, exclusive boutiques, and fancy restaurants. Small and mellow Solana Beach has evolved into a hip art and design center rife with home-furnishings shops. Encinitas is known for its fabulous fields of flowers and gardens, and for excellent surfing. Carlsbad, once known for its healing waters, now lures families to Legoland California, and Oceanside shows off its harbor and Mission San Luis Rey. It's easiest to reach the area via Interstate 5, but take slower Route S21 (old U.S. 101) to gain a better sense of the differences among the communities.
INTERIOR SAN DIEGO	You'll find a varied landscape, both physically and culturally, a short drive inland from the North County coast. The snazzy resort and retirement town of Rancho Bernardo, the quiet lakes of Escondido, the avocado-growing country surrounding Fallbrook, the former gold-mining town of Julian, and the vineyards of Temecula all have their charms. Home to old missions, San Diego Wild Animal Park, the Welk Resort Center, and innumerable three-generation California families, inland North County feels less rushed and densely populated than the rest of the county.
TIJUANA, PLAYAS DE ROSARITO & ENSENADA	From San Diego, it's incredibly easy and quite rewarding to venture a bit south of the border into Mexico's Baja California peninsula. Tijuana has grown during the past 20 years from a border town of 700,000 to a city of almost 2 million inhabitants; it continues to attract hordes of "yanquis" with its designer boutiques, souvenir shops, sports events, and great Mexican dining. Laid-back Playas de Rosarito (Rosarito Beach), farther south, has become something of a weekend hangout for Southern Californians. Ensenada is one of Mexico's largest seaports.

QUINTESSENTIAL SAN DIEGO

The Surf Bar

No activity captures the essence of San Diego more than surfing, which has influenced everything in Southern California from fashion to moviemaking to music. Although surfing is a rigorous, demanding sport, anybody can at least soak up the surf culture by hanging out around some of the top surfing beaches (Swami's in Encinitas, Windansea in La Jolla, and Mission Beach), watching young guys and gals take to the waves. Even better, drop by virtually any of the laidback surfer hangouts near the beaches and you'll hear seasoned, hard-bodied aficionados swapping stories about their exploits. Moondoggies, a top bar for surfers in Pacific Beach, pulls them in by airing surf and skate videos on the tube and hosting live bands on the patio. At RT's Longboard Grill, vintage photos, boards, and other surfing equipment line the walls—you feel like you've entered a surfing museum.

The Fish Taco

San Diego, one of the country's most innovative food cities, is above all a place to savor outstanding seafood—and you can do so on any budget. No matter what your finances, for example, you can probably afford that definitive regional delectable, the humble fish taco. Simple storefront restaurants and even simpler open-air take-out windows and mobile taco stands dispense these treats filled traditionally with mahimahi or wahoo (but any firm white fish fillet works), and locals love to debate where to get the best and the freshest. Some folks prefer them beer-battered and lightly fried, others grilled. One ardent fan likes his topped with salsa, another swears by mayo-based white sauces. And then there's the debate over whether fish tacos are best served with coleslaw or shredded lettuce. There seem to be a thousand ways to make great fish tacos, and just as many ways to enjoy them!

San Diego's sunlit, seafront setting prompts the city's take on the Southern California lifestyle. The locals have more than a few ways to make the best of a good thing, and there's nothing stopping you from joining them.

A Picnic in the Park

Balboa Park occupies a singular place in the hearts and minds of San Diegans. Although its museums, performance spaces, playing fields, gardens, trails, and attractions (notably the San Diego Zoo) are a huge tourist draw, locals frequent the park every chance they can. We've covered its highlights throughout the book, from great rambles through the Rose and Cactus gardens to memorable tours of the museums. But perhaps the simplest way to experience Balboa Park is to flop down along a patch of grass (try entering somewhere around 6th Avenue and Laurel Street) and enjoy a picnic. In the nearby Hillcrest neighborhood, just north, you'll find plenty of spots to stock up on picnic supplies. Noshing on fine food, soaking up the Southern California sun, listening to birds chirp, and admiring lush flora—there's arguably no better way to appreciate the joys of San Diego.

A Game at the Ballpark

You don't have to be a baseball fan to respond to the infectious buzz of a San Diego Padres game at the city's stunning new Petco Park. The fun lies as much in watching the fans and enjoying the scenery as in catching the action on the field—although if the beloved Padres are taking on one of their major rivals, such as the L.A. Dodgers or San Francisco Giants, the game itself can get pretty exciting. With its Spanish Mission–style exterior and artful landscaping, Petco is more open than the typical ballpark, with ample room to stroll around and catch the game from different vantage points. The once-dreary neighborhood surrounding the park has blossomed since it opened in 2004, so be sure to join the fans after the game for continued revelry at the many bars, cafés, and restaurants outside. The Padres play about 80 games at Petco, from early April through early October.

WHEN TO GO

For the most part, **any time of the year is the right time** for a trip to San Diego. The climate is generally close to perfect. Typical days are sunny and mild, with low humidity—ideal for sightseeing and for almost any sport that does not require snow and ice. From mid-December through mid-March gray whales can be seen migrating along the coast. In early spring wildflowers transform the mountainsides and desert into a rainbow of colors. In fall these same mountains present one of the most impressive displays of fall color to be found in Southern California.

Climate

The annual high temperature averages 70°F with a low of 55°F, and the annual rainfall is usually less than 10 inches. Most of the rain occurs in January and February, but precipitation usually lasts for only part of the day or for a day or two at most.

The chart shows the average high and low temperatures for San Diego.

 Forecasts **Weather Channel** ⊕ www.weather.com.

Fun in the Sun

In a city with easy access to beaches and parks and an eminently civilized climate, it would be hard not to do as the San Diegans do and venture outdoors. You'll find dozens of great beaches up and down the coastline. Some, like the Silver Strand on Coronado, are wide and sandy; others, like Sunset Cliffs on Point Loma, are narrow and rocky. At many beaches and marinas, you can rent water-sports equipment and take everything from surfing to kayaking lessons.

But away from the beach, there's plenty more to get you outdoors. Head out to the region's inland hills, and you'll find sweeping desert parks laced with hiking, mountain biking, and horseback riding trails. Then you'll find excellent fishing throughout the area, both saltwater and freshwater. In North County, you might even opt for a hot-air balloon ride. Here are a few of our favorite suggestions for getting outdoors in and around San Diego.

- Hit the beaches in La Jolla, which has some of the most magnificent sands on the West Coast. Investigate the shellfish-filled tidal pools at La Jolla Cove, which is also excellent for snorkeling or diving; watch the sunset at Black's Beach; or swim the gentle surf at La Jolla Shores.

- Ride a bike up scenic Route S21, from La Jolla to Oceanside—it stays close to the beach the whole way.

- Hike the trails at Tijuana Estuary in Imperial Beach—it's one of the top spots around for observing migrant and resident waterfowl.

The Stage

San Diego makes such a perfect outdoorsy getaway that visitors—and even some residents—overlook the fact it's a truly first-rate performing arts center. We don't just mean that, like all major cities, it has a fair share of theaters and music halls. San Diego truly shines in this regard. For specific listings, definitely check out the cool sandiegoartandSol.com Web site, which lists what's on and even sells tickets to many shows.

The city's most vaunted attribute is its theater scene, which draws a fair share of top-name actors down I–5 from L.A. You'll find about two-dozen theaters around the area, from smaller, avant-garde spaces to major venues hosting top national touring shows. Always be on the lookout for performances by the esteemed San Diego Symphony Orchestra, San Diego Opera, and San Diego Ballet.

Some venues we love:

- It's worth visiting Copley Symphony Hall just to see its ornate Spanish Baroque interior; the 1920s performing arts center hosts the San Diego Symphony Orchestra as well as major touring musicians.

- If you're up for unusual filmmaking, check out what's playing at the Ken Cinema, a superb art-house theater.

- La Jolla Playhouse often presents Broadway-bound shows before they head to the East Coast and can always be counted on for first-rate acting and direction.

- The Old Globe, the oldest professional theater in the state, occupies a handsome building in the heart of Balboa

Park and hosts a world-renowned Shakespeare Festival each summer.

Bicultural History

As the site of California's earliest European settlement, San Diego occupies a special place in U.S. history. The city's well-preserved and reconstructed historic sites help you to imagine what the area was like when Spanish and Portuguese explorers and missionaries arrived, usually by sea, in the 16th and 17th centuries. San Diego was the birthplace of California, claimed for Spain by Juan Rodríguez Cabrillo, in 1542. About 220 years later, another Spaniard, Franciscan missionary Father Junípero Serra, established the first of 21 California missions here. And the Spanish influence didn't stop with California's admission into the Union in 1850 as America's 31st state—it's continued to support a thriving, dynamic Latin American community, as evidenced by restaurants, arts center, museums, and music clubs that proliferate throughout the city to this day.

Although it doesn't date back so far, the Anglo side of U.S. history is also alive and well in San Diego, much of it revolving around the city's role as a major U.S. navy center since the turn-of-the-20th-century.

Here are some of the best ways to enhance your understanding of San Diego's heritage:

- See where explorer Juan Rodríguez Cabrillo landed in 1542 at **Cabrillo National Monument,** a 144-acre preserve perched on a dramatic bluff with fantastic views of the harbor and downtown.

- Tour the historic buildings, mostly from the 19th-century and including

some original adobes, preserved at **Old Town San Diego State Historic Park,** a living-history compound.

- Visit the beautifully preserved **Mission San Luis Rey,** in nearby Oceanside, the 18th of California's missions to be established and one of the most spectacular.

Charging It

You expect to find fancy megamalls in San Diego—it's Southern California, after all. But this city offers a far more distinctive retail experience than the mere national-chain shopping you can find anywhere. Your best bet is to head for some of the more engaging neighborhoods around San Diego, from Coronado—with its blocks of fancy boutiques and galleries—to Old Town, where, at Plaza del Pasado, you can browse goods reminiscent of those that might have been on offer back when Old Town San Diego *was* San Diego, and, at Bazaar del Mundo Shops, you can pick up arts and crafts from Mexico as well as other international goods, toys, and souvenirs. (For that matter, head just over the border to Tijuana for Mexican crafts and souvenirs.)

Farther afield, La Jolla has a collection of trendy designer boutiques and galleries along Prospect Street and Girard Avenue. Discounted designer fashions can also be found at the popular Carlsbad Company Stores.

Here are a few of the best overall shopping destinations in metro San Diego:

- **Horton Plaza,** in the heart of downtown, is the place to go for department stores, mall shops, and one-of-a-kind boutiques.

- Downtown's funky and historic **Gaslamp Quarter** is chock-full of art galleries, antiques shops, and specialty stores—and it's a great place to grab a bite to eat afterward.

- **Seaport Village** on the waterfront is thick with theme shops and arts-and-crafts galleries.

- Artsy **Hillcrest** is the place to go for vintage clothing, furnishings, and accessories.

- Finally, for a marvelous off-the-beaten-path shopping trek, head up the coast to **Solana Beach**, whose downtown **Cedros Design District** bustles with some of the hippest home-furnishing and design shops in the state. It's a real find, still unknown to many tourists.

GREAT ITINERARY

SAN DIEGO: CULTURE MEETS THE SAND

Day 1

Start with the San Diego Zoo in Balboa Park in the morning. You could easily knock off the entire day (and even a couple of more days) checking out the thousands of animals, but even if you've got kids along and they're nagging you to stay, plan to end the day with at least a stroll down El Prado, an easy walk or five-minute drive south of the zoo. This is the cultural heart of San Diego, with a feast of fabulous museums set in ornate Spanish colonial revival buildings. If you have time for just one museum, make it the distinctive Mingei International Museum of Folk Art. (With kids along, the Reuben H. Fleet Science Center may be a better bet.)

Day 2

It's time to check out San Diego's booming and bustling downtown, beginning with a shopping scramble through both Seaport Village and Horton Plaza, both of which have numerous lunch options. Next, stroll north on the Embarcadero, setting aside some time to tour the Maritime Museum or the San Diego Aircraft Carrier Museum. As early evening sets in, continue into downtown's lively Gaslamp Quarter, which pulses with hip bars, music clubs, and restaurants. Adults will find plenty to keep them busy here for hours. If you've got kids in tow, head for the festive Ghirardelli Soda Fountain & Chocolate Shop for some of the richest and prettiest desserts around.

Day 3

If you set out early enough, you might get a parking spot near La Jolla Cove. Watch the sea lions lounging on the beach at the Children's Pool and then head inland one block to Prospect Street, where you'll see the pink La Valencia hotel along with dozens of tony shops and galleries; this is also a good spot for an ocean-view lunch. Walk east on Prospect for a spin through the Museum of Contemporary Art, and then retrieve your car and head north to Torrey Pines City Park Beach and the adjacent Glider Port—this is an especially beautiful spot to watch the sun set. As dinner approaches, you'll find plenty of great restaurants back in La Jolla, or you might try one of the classic beach restaurants south of La Jolla, down Mission Boulevard, such as Hodad's.

Day 4

Begin with a morning visit to Cabrillo National Monument. Have lunch down near Shelter Island at one of the seafood restaurants on Scott Street, and then head over to Old Town (take Rosecrans Street north to San Diego Avenue) to see portions of San Diego's earliest history brought to life. If the daily schedule lists low tide for the afternoon, reverse the order to catch the tide pools at Cabrillo.

Day 5

Spend your final day heading into some of the communities nearby. If you're traveling with young children, make Legoland California in Carlsbad your main destination. En route to North County stop off at Torrey Pines State Beach and Reserve. If you're not going to Legoland, take Interstate 5 north to Del Mar for lunch, shopping, and sea views. A visit to Mission San Luis Rey, slightly inland from Oceanside on Route 76, will infuse some history and culture into the tour.

ALTERNATIVES:

You can make Day 2, when you're exploring downtown, more of a seafaring than a shopping experience by catching the ferry from the Broadway Pier (near Seaport Village) to Coronado. Then from Coronado's Ferry Landing Marketplace, board a bus down Orange Avenue to see the town's Victorian extravaganza, the Hotel Del Coronado. If it's whale-watching season, skip the trip to Coronado, tour the Embarcadero in the late morning, have lunch, and book an afternoon excursion boat from the Broadway Pier.

If hopping over to Mexico interests you, set aside Day 5 for a trip to Tijuana rather than an exploration of the towns north and east of San Diego. It's extremely easy to make this trip, as the border crossing is only a 15-mi drive down I-5. Once there, you shoppers can easily pass a couple of hours exploring the garish but exuberant Avenida Revolución. Also be sure to visit Centro Cultural Tijuana (CECUT), with its Omnimax Theater and excellent exhibits on Baja's history, flora, and fauna.

TIPS

① Watch the weather forecast prior to planning your itinerary. Try to save the downtown museums and shopping for the day with the least-promising weather. Balboa Park isn't too bad during mild rain either, as you can still tour the zoo, and the park's many museums make for pleasant rainy-day diversions. Visiting either SeaWorld or Legoland are similarly prudent rainy-day plans.

② Sure, it's fun to dip those toes in the sand and saunter through one of the world's most incredible zoos. But don't overlook San Diego's somewhat underrated performing arts scene. It's extremely easy to add a theater performance or a concert to any of the five days described above. Some of the city's top performance venues are in Balboa Park (Day 1), downtown (Day 2), and La Jolla (Day 3).

③ If you plan to tour more than a couple of museums in Balboa Park, buy the Passport to Balboa Park, which gets you into 13 attractions for just $30, or the Best of Balboa Park Combo Pass, which also gets you into the zoo (it costs $55). You can buy these at the Balboa Park Visitors Center (619/239–0512, www.balboapark.org).

ON THE CALENDAR

WINTER	San Diego has perfect Southern California weather that is the envy of all who live in less pleasant climes, but it still has seasons, and with them come festivals and special events. Plan well in advance if you hope to be in town for any of these celebrations.
Dec.	**Balboa Park December Nights** (☎ 619/239–0512 ⊕ www.balboapark. org) draws 100,000 guests on the first Friday and Saturday of December. Attractions include carolers, holiday food, music, dance, handmade crafts for sale, a visit from Saint Nick, a candlelight procession, and free admission to all the museums.
	During **Christmas in the Village** (☎ 619/462–3000 ⊕ www.lmvma. com), La Mesa takes on an old-fashioned look, with caroling, horse-drawn carriage rides, an outdoor market, and a visit from Santa Claus.
	The **Ocean Beach Parade and Tree Festival** (☎ 619/226–8613) takes place on Newport Avenue, generally the second weekend in December. The Ocean Beach Geriatric Surf Club tops any entry in any parade, anywhere.
	Old Town Holiday in the Park (☎ 619/220–5422) includes candlelight tours of historic homes and other buildings in Old Town by costumed docents; reservations are recommended.
	The **Port of San Diego Bay Parade of Lights** (☎ 619/224–2240, Oct.–Dec. only ⊕ www.sdparadeoflights.org) fills the harbor with lighted boats cruising in a procession that begins at Shelter Island and ends at the Coronado Ferry Landing Marketplace.
	The **Wild Animal Park Festival of Lights** (☎ 760/796–5621) includes free children's activities, Christmas caroling, live-animal presentations, and real snow.
Jan.	The **Buick Invitational** (☎ 800/888–2842 ⊕ www.buickinvitational. com), a major golf event since the 1950s, attracts more than 100,000 people, including local and national celebrities, to the Torrey Pines Municipal Golf Course.
Feb.	The **Borrego Springs Grapefruit Festival** (☎ 760/767–5555) celebrates the ruby-red grapefruit, which is grown in the desert. Music, food, arts, crafts, and games are part of the event.
SPRING	
Feb.–Mar.	**Mardi Gras in the Gaslamp Quarter** (☎ 619/233–5227 ⊕ www. gaslamp.org). This Fat Tuesday celebration features live music on several outdoor stages and traditional cajun food and drink.

Feb.–Apr.	**Wildflowers at Anza-Borrego Desert State Park** (☎ 760/767–5311, 760/767–4684 wildflower hotline ⊕ www.anzaborrego.statepark.org) are in bloom during these months. They are at their peak only for a two-week period, which varies according to winter rainfall. Phone the hotline for information.
Mar.	The **Kiwanis Ocean Beach Kite Festival** (☎ 619/531–1527) features a kite-making, decorating, and flying contest, plus a craft fair, food, and entertainment.
Mar. to mid-May	Tiptoe through fields of brilliantly colored ranunculuses. They're arranged rainbow-fashion on a hillside at **Flower Fields at Carlsbad Ranch** (☎ 760/431–0352 ⊕ www.theflowerfields.com) in Carlsbad.
Apr.	The **ArtWalk Festival** (☎ 619/615–1090 ⊕ www.artwalkinfo.com) showcases visual and performing artists in their studios and in staged areas; self-guided tours start downtown in Little Italy.
	The **San Diego Crew Classic** (☎ 858/488–0700 ⊕ www.crewclassic.org) brings together more than 3,000 high school, college, and masters athletes from across the United States for a rowing competition at Crown Point Shores in Mission Bay.
Apr.–May	Humming along for more than 30 years, the **Adams Avenue Roots Festival** (☎ 619/282-7329 ⊕ www.gothere.com/adamsave) is a free weekend festival of vintage blues, folk, jazz, country, cowboy, and international music on six outdoor stages.
	The **Del Mar National Horse Show** (☎ 858/792–4288 ⊕ www.sdfair.com) at the Del Mar Fairgrounds showcases national and international championship riders and horses in western week, dressage week, and hunter–jumper week competitions.
May	**Julian Wildflower Show** (☎ 760/765–1857 ⊕ www.julianca.com) is an annual display of wildflowers gathered within a 15-mi radius of the mountain town, and usually includes desert blooms.
	Old Town Fiesta Cinco de Mayo (☎ 619/296–3236 ⊕ www.fiestacincodemayo.com), at Old Town San Diego State Historic Park, commemorates Mexico's defeat of Napoleon's cavalry during the Battle of Puebla on May 5, 1862. Besides a historic reenactment, there's plenty of food and music and dance events celebrating Latino culture.
SUMMER	
June	The **Annual Inter-Tribal Pow Pow** (☎ 760/724–8505), held at Mission San Luis Rey in Oceanside, features dancing, Native Ameri-

	can arts and crafts, food booths, and games, and draws participants from all over the United States.
	A Taste of the Gaslamp (☎ 619/233–5227 ⊕ www.gaslamp.org) is a weekend of gastronomy; pick up your ticket and a map of participating restaurants and go from door to door sampling the house specialties of the Gaslamp Quarter's best chefs.
	At the **Threshing Bee & Antique Engine Show** (☎ 760/941–1791 ⊕ www.agsem.com), which takes place at the Antique Gas & Steam Engine Museum in Vista twice a year (it also takes place in October and is also known as the Harvest Fair), you can see threshing demonstrations and antique tractors on parade, as well as demonstrations of early American crafts, farming, and blacksmithing.
June–July	The **San Diego County Fair** (☎ 858/793–5555 ⊕ www.sdfair.com) is a classic county fair at the Del Mar Fairgrounds, with live entertainment, flower and garden shows, a carnival, livestock shows, and Fourth of July fireworks.
June–Aug.	**Carlsbad Jazz-in-the-Parks** (☎ 760/434–2904) series features free live performances at various parks in the Carlsbad area; call for a schedule.
	During the **Summer Organ Festival** (☎619/702–8138), enjoy free Monday-evening concerts under the stars at Balboa Park's Spreckels Organ Pavilion, in addition to the free year-round Sunday afternoon concerts.
June–Sept.	The **Nighttime Zoo** (☎ 619/234–3153 ⊕ www.sandiegozoo.org) at the San Diego Zoo and the **Park at Dark** (☎ 760/796–5621 ⊕ www.wildanimalpark.com) at the San Diego Wild Animal Park are wild ways to spend the evening, with extended evening hours and additional entertainment through the beginning of September.
	The Globe's **Summer Shakespeare Festival** (☎619/239–2255 ⊕www.theoldglobe.org), at the outdoor Lowell Davies Festival Theatre in Balboa Park, features works of Shakespeare in repertory with other classic and contemporary plays.
July	Patriots observe the July 4th **Coronado Independence Day** (☎ 619/437–8788) with a 15-km run, a 5-km run/walk, a parade, U.S. Navy air–sea demonstrations, and fireworks over Glorietta Bay.

		Julian Independence Day Celebration (☎ 760/765–1857 ⊕ www.julianca.com) is a small-town July 4 celebration with a parade of animals, women dressed as floozies, and bands; there's also a classic car show, vintage airplane fly-over, old-west shoot-out, barbecue, and quilt show.
		The annual lesbian and gay **Pride Parade, Rally, and Festival** (☎ 619/297–7683 ⊕ www.sdpride.org) is a weekend of entertainment in Hillcrest and Balboa Park.
		U.S. Open Sandcastle Competition (☎ 619/424–6663) at Imperial Beach Pier brings together sand sculptors of all ages for one of the largest castle-building events in the United States.
		The **World Championship Over-the-Line Tournament** (☎ 619/688–0817 ⊕ www.ombac.org) is a rowdy party, with 1,200 three-person teams competing in a sport that's a cross between softball and stickball; it takes place during two weekends on Fiesta Island in Mission Bay.
July–Sept.		The **San Diego Symphony Summer Pops** series (☎ 619/235–0804 ⊕ www.sandiegosymphony.com), with occasional fireworks, swings Friday and Saturday nights at Embarcadero Marina Park South.
Aug.		The **La Jolla SummerFest** (☎ 858/459–3728 ⊕ www.lajollamusicsociety.org) chamber music festival includes concerts, lectures, master classes, and open rehearsals, mainly in La Jolla but also in downtown San Diego.
		Street Scene (☎ 800/260–9985 ⊕ www.street-scene.com), a three-day urban music festival with food, rollicks with 100 bands from around the world performing on 10 stages near Petco Park.
		The **World Body Surfing Championships** (☎ 760/685–1992 ⊕ www.worldbodysurfing.org) pits more than 200 of California's top competitors against one another; viewing is from Oceanside Pier and Beach.
FALL		
Sept.		The free annual **Adams Avenue Street Fair** (☎ 619/282–7329 ⊕ www.gothere.com/adamsave) attracts 50,000 jazz, blues, and rock fans to the Normal Heights neighborhood for concerts on five stages, food, games, and a carnival. The largest event of its type in Southern California, it's popular with families.
		The **Cabrillo Festival** (☎ 619/557–5450 ⊕ www.nps.gov/cabrat) Cabrillo National Monument in Point Loma commemorates Juan

		Rodríquez Cabrillo's exploration of the West Coast with a week's worth of activities.
		The **Thunderboat Regatta** (☎ 619/225–9160 ⊕ www.thunderboats. net) draws hydroplane enthusiasts to Mission Bay for an exhilarating, deafening weekend of racing.
	Oct.	**Oktoberfest in La Mesa** (☎ 619/440–6161 ⊕ www.eastcountychamber. org) is a traditional celebration featuring German sausages, Bavarian brass oompah bands, dancing, and arts and crafts.
	Nov.	**Holiday of Lights** (☎ 858/793–5555 ⊕ www.sdfair.com) showcases more than 350 animated and lighted holiday displays in a drive-through setting at the Del Mar Fairgrounds.
		El Cajon's **Mother Goose Parade** (☎ 619/444–8712 ⊕ www. mothergooseparade.com) is a two-hour nationally televised spectacular with 200 floats, bands, horses, and clowns. It takes place the Sunday before Thanksgiving.

SMART TRAVEL TIPS

Finding out about your destination before you leave home means you won't spend time organizing everyday minutiae once you've arrived. You'll be more streetwise when you hit the ground as well, better prepared to explore the aspects of San Diego that drew you here in the first place. The organizations discussed in this section can provide information to supplement this guide; contact them for up-to-the-minute details, and consult the A to Z sections in the North County chapter for facts on the various topics as they relate to the areas around San Diego. Happy landings!

ADDRESSES

Downtown San Diego streets are on a grid. Avenues and streets running north–south are numbered. East–west streets are alphabetical. North of A Street, streets continue as Ash, Beech, Cedar, and Date, through Upas Street. Below C Street are a few streets with names in place of letters.

AIR TRAVEL TO & FROM SAN DIEGO

BOOKING

When you book, look for nonstop flights and remember that "direct" flights stop at least once. Try to avoid connecting flights, which require a change of plane. Two airlines may operate a connecting flight jointly, so ask whether your airline operates every segment of the trip; you may find that the carrier you prefer flies you only part of the way. To find more booking tips and to check prices and make flight reservations online, log on to www.fodors.com.

CARRIERS

All major and some regional U.S. carriers serve San Diego International Airport. Aero Mexico is the only international carrier to San Diego. All others require a connecting flight, usually in Los Angeles. Other connection points are Chicago, Dallas, and San Francisco.

🛪 Major Airlines **AeroMexico** ☎ 800/237-6639 🌐 www.aeromexico.com. **American/American Eagle** ☎ 800/433-7300, 0845/7789-789 in U.K.

⊕ www.aa.com. **British Airways** ☎ 800/247–9397 ⊕ www.britishairways.com. **Continental Airlines/ Continental Express** ☎ 800/525–0280 ⊕ www. continental.com. **Delta Airlines/Delta Connection** ☎ 800/221–1212, 0800/414767 in U.K. ⊕ www.delta. com. **Northwest Airlines/Northwest Airlink** ☎ 800/225–2525 ⊕ www.nwa.com. **Southwest** ☎ 800/435–9792 ⊕ www.southwest.com. **United/ United Express** ☎ 800/864–8331, 0800/888555 in U.K. ⊕ www.united.com. **US Airways** ☎ 800/428– 4322 ⊕ www.usairways.com.

🚩 Regional & Smaller Airlines Alaska Airlines/ Alaska Commuter ☎ 800/252–7522 ⊕ www. alaskaair.com. **Aloha Airlines** ☎ 800/367–5250 ⊕ www.alohaairlines.com. **America West/America West Express** ☎ 800/235–9292 ⊕ www. americawest.com. **Frontier/Frontier JetExpress** ☎ 800/432–1359 ⊕ www.frontierairlines.com. **Hawaiian Airlines** ☎ 800/367–5320 ⊕ www. hawaiianair.com. **JetBlue** ☎ 800/538–2583 ⊕ www.jetblue.com. **Sun Country** ☎ 800/359– 6786 ⊕ www.suncountry.com.

CHECK-IN & BOARDING

Coastal fog at San Diego International Airport can delay landings and takeoffs, and a delayed flight or two can jam the small boarding areas. During inclement weather **call your airline** or visit www.san. org to see if there are delays.

Always **find out your carrier's check-in policy.** Plan to arrive at the airport about two hours before your scheduled departure time for domestic flights and 2½ to 3 hours before international flights. You may need to arrive earlier if you're flying from one of the busier airports or during peak air-traffic times. To avoid delays at airport-security checkpoints, try not to wear any metal. Jewelry, belt and other buckles, steel-toe shoes, barrettes, and underwire bras are among the items that can set off detectors.

Assuming that not everyone who has bought a ticket will actually show up for the flight, airlines routinely overbook planes. When everyone does show up, airlines ask for volunteers to give up their seats. In return, these volunteers usually receive a flight voucher worth several hundred dollars applicable toward the purchase of another ticket and are rebooked on the next available flight out. If there are not enough volunteers, the airline must choose who will be denied boarding. The first to be bumped are passengers who checked in late and those flying on discounted tickets, so check in and get to the gate as early as possible, especially during peak periods.

Always **bring a government-issued photo ID** to the airport; even when it's not required, a passport is best.

CUTTING COSTS

The least expensive airfares to San Diego are priced for round-trip travel on most airlines and must usually be purchased a set number of days in advance of the flight. Airlines generally allow you to change your return date for a fee; most low-fare tickets, however, are nonrefundable.

It's smart to call a number of airlines and check the Internet; when you are quoted a good price, book it on the spot—the same fare may not be available the next day, or even the next hour. Always check different routings and look into using alternate airports. Also, price off-peak and red-eye (late night or overnight) flights, which may be significantly less expensive than others. Travel agents, especially low-fare specialists (⇨ Discounts & Deals), are helpful.

Consolidators are another good source. They buy tickets for scheduled flights at reduced rates from the airlines, then sell them at prices that beat the best fare available directly from the airlines. (Many also offer reduced car-rental and hotel rates.) Sometimes you can even get your money back if you need to return the ticket. Read the fine print detailing penalties for changes and cancellations carefully, purchase the ticket with a credit card, and confirm your consolidator reservation with the airline.

When you fly as a courier, you trade your checked-luggage space for a ticket deeply subsidized by a courier service. There are restrictions on when you can book and how long you can stay. Some courier companies list flights with organizations such as the Air Courier Association and the International Association of Air Travel

Couriers; these require you to become a member before you can book a flight.

✈ Consolidators AirlineConsolidator.com ☎ 888/468-5385 ⊕ www.airlineconsolidator.com, for international tickets. **Best Fares** ☎ 800/880-1234 ⊕ www.bestfares.com; $59.90 annual membership. **Cheap Tickets** ☎ 800/377-1000 or 800/652-4327 ⊕ www.cheaptickets.com. **Expedia** ☎ 800/397-3342 or 404/728-8787 ⊕ www.expedia.com. **Hotwire** ☎ 866/468-9473 or 920/330-9418 ⊕ www.hotwire.com. **Now Voyager Travel** ⊠ 1717 Ave. M, Brooklyn, NY 11230 ☎ 212/459-1616 ⊟ 718/504-4762 ⊕ www.nowvoyagertravel.com. **One-travel.com** ⊕ www.onetravel.com. **Orbitz** ☎ 888/656-4546 ⊕ www.orbitz.com. **Priceline.com** ⊕ www.priceline.com. **Travelocity** ☎ 888/709-5983, 877/282-2925 in Canada, 0870/111-7061 in U.K. ⊕ www.travelocity.com.

✈ Courier Resources Air Courier Association/Cheaptrips.com ☎ 800/211-5119 ⊕ www.aircourier.org or www.cheaptrips.com; $49 annual membership. **Courier Travel** ☎ 303/570-7586 ⊟ 313/625-6106 ⊕ www.couriertravel.org; $50 annual membership. **International Association of Air Travel Couriers** ☎ 308/632-3273 ⊟ 308/632-8267 ⊕ www.courier.org; $45 annual membership. **Now Voyager Travel** ⊠ 1717 Ave. M, Brooklyn, NY 11230 ☎ 212/459-1616 ⊟ 718/504-4762 ⊕ www.nowvoyagertravel.com.

ENJOYING THE FLIGHT

State your seat preference when purchasing your ticket, and then repeat it when you confirm and when you check in. For more legroom, you can request a seat in one of the emergency exit rows at check-in, if you're capable of moving obstacles comparable in weight to an airplane exit door (usually between 35 pounds and 60 pounds)—a Federal Aviation Administration requirement of passengers in these seats. Seats behind a bulkhead separator also offer more legroom, but because they have no seats in front of them they don't have under-seat storage. Don't sit in the row in front of a bulkhead, because those seats may not recline. SeatGuru.com has more information about specific seat configurations, which vary by aircraft.

Ask the airline whether a snack or meal is served on the flight. If you have dietary concerns, request special meals when booking. These can be vegetarian, low-cholesterol, or kosher, for example. It's a good idea to pack some healthful snacks and a small (plastic) bottle of water in your carry-on bag. On long flights, try to maintain a normal routine, to help fight jet lag. At night, get some sleep. By day, eat light meals, drink water (not alcohol), and **move around the cabin** to stretch your legs. For additional jet-lag tips consult *Fodor's FYI: Travel Fit & Healthy* (available at bookstores everywhere).

U.S. government rules prohibit smoking on all scheduled-service domestic flights within the United States, except for flights of longer than six hours to or from Alaska or Hawaii. The ban applies also to domestic portions of international flights, on both U.S. and foreign airlines (but not to nonstop international flights while they are in U.S. airspace). Most airlines prohibit smoking on all of their flights, even where these rules do not pertain; others allow smoking only on certain routes or certain departures. Ask your carrier about its policy.

FLYING TIMES

Flying time to San Diego is 5 hours from New York, 3½ hours from Chicago, 3½ hours from Dallas, 45 minutes from Los Angeles, 10–11 hours from London. Travelers from London who transfer at Los Angeles should expect to reach San Diego about two to three hours after landing in Los Angeles.

HOW TO COMPLAIN

If your baggage goes astray or your flight goes awry, complain right away. Most carriers require that you **file a claim immediately.** The Aviation Consumer Protection Division of the Department of Transportation publishes *Fly-Rights,* which discusses airlines and consumer issues and is available online. You can also find articles and information on mytravelrights.com, the Web site of the nonprofit Consumer Travel Rights Center.

✈ Airline Complaints Aviation Consumer Protection Division ⊠ U.S. Department of Transportation, Office of Aviation Enforcement and Proceedings, C-75, Room 4107, 400 7th St. SW, Washington, DC 20590 ☎ 202/366-2220 ⊕ airconsumer.ost.dot.gov. **Federal Aviation Administration Consumer Hot-**

line ✉ For inquiries: FAA, 800 Independence Ave. SW, Washington, DC 20591 ☎ 800/322-7873 🌐 www.faa.gov.

RECONFIRMING

Check the status of your flight before you leave for the airport. You can do this on your carrier's Web site, by linking to a flight-status checker (many Web booking services offer these), or by calling your carrier or travel agent.

AIRPORTS & TRANSFERS

The major airport is **San Diego International Airport,** called Lindbergh Field locally. The airport's three-letter code is SAN. Major airlines depart and arrive at Terminal 1 (east) and Terminal 2 (west); commuter flights identified on your ticket with a 3000 sequence flight number depart from a third terminal, the commuter terminal. A red shuttle bus provides free transportation between terminals.

With only one runway serving two main terminals, San Diego's airport remains too small to accommodate traffic during busy travel periods. Small problems including weather can cause congested terminals and flight delays. Delays of 20–30 minutes in baggage claim are not unusual.

If you need travel assistance at the airport, Travelers Aid has two information booths, one in Terminal 1 and one in Terminal 2, open daily 8 AM–11 PM.

Most international flights depart from and arrive at the Los Angeles International Airport (LAX); both American Eagle and United Express have frequent flights between LAX and San Diego. Ground shuttle service is available between LAX and San Diego.

🚺 Airport Information San Diego International Airport ☎ 619/400-2400 🌐 www.san.org.

AIRPORT TRANSFERS

San Diego International Airport is 3 mi from downtown. Ground transportation services include shuttle vans, buses, and taxis. All services operate from the Transportation Plaza, reached via the skybridges from Terminals 1 and 2. The cheapest and sometimes most convenient shuttle is the Metropolitan Transit System's Flyer Route

992, red- and blue-stripe buses that serve the terminals at 10- to 15-minute intervals between 5 AM and 1 AM. These buses have luggage racks and make a loop from the airport to downtown along Broadway to 9th Avenue and back, stopping frequently within walking distance of many hotels; they also connect with the San Diego Trolley, Amtrak, and the Coaster. The fare is $2.25, including transfer to local transit buses and the trolley, and you should **have exact fare handy.** If you're heading to North County, the Flyer can drop you off at the Santa Fe Depot, from where you can take the Coaster commuter train as far north as Oceanside for $3.75–$4.75. Of the various airport shuttles, only Cloud 9 has tie-downs for wheelchairs; however Access Shuttle can provide curbside service if requested in advance.

Limousine rates vary and are per hour, per mile, or both, with some minimums established.

Taxi fare is $10 plus tip to most downtown hotels. Fare to Coronado runs about $16 plus tip.

Major car rental agencies have outlets near the airport; use the courtesy phones in the baggage claim areas of Terminals 1 and 2. Agency shuttles cruise the airport continuously and pick you up at the islands outside the terminals to take you to their rental locations. If you rent a car at the airport, take Harbor Drive east to reach downtown, or west to reach Shelter Island and Point Loma. To access I–5 and I–8, take Harbor Drive west to Nimitz Boulevard, then right on Rosecrans Street. You can reach La Jolla and North County via I–5 North. Interstate 8 East leads to Hotel Circle, Fashion Valley, Mission Valley, and Qualcomm Stadium. To reach Mission Bay continue on Nimitz Boulevard, which intersects with Sunset Cliffs Boulevard. To get to Coronado, take Harbor Drive east and turn left on Grape Street to reach I–5 South. Take the Highway 75 exit to cross the San Diego–Coronado Bridge.

🚺 Limousines & Shuttles Access Shuttle ☎ 619/282-1515 or 800/690-9090 🌐 www.access-shuttle. com. **Cloud 9 Shuttle** ☎ 800/974-8885 🌐 www. cloud9shuttle.com. **Coronado Livery** ☎ 619/435-

6310. **Five Star** ☎ 619/294-3300 or 866/281-4288 ⊕ www.fivestarshuttle.com. **Metropolitan Transit System** ☎ 800/266-6883 ⊕ www.sdcommute.com.

BOAT & FERRY TRAVEL

If you're arriving in San Diego by private boat, keep in mind that many hotels, marinas, and yacht clubs rent slips short-term. Call ahead as available space is limited. The San Diego and Southwestern yacht clubs have reciprocal arrangements with other yacht clubs.

The small Coronado ferry ($2.25 one-way fare and 50¢ per bicycle), is a reminder of the pre-San Diego–Coronado Bridge days when ferries provided regular transportation between Coronado and downtown. Now it's a small excursion service that is fun to ride, but not often used as a practical transportation method.

FARES & SCHEDULES

🚹 Boat & Ferry Information **San Diego-Coronado Ferry** ☎ 619/234-4111.

🚹 Marinas **Best Western Island Palms Hotel & Marina** ✉ 2051 Shelter Island Dr. ☎ 619/223-0301. **Dana Inn & Marina** ✉ 1710 W. Mission Bay Dr. ☎ 619/222-6440. **Hyatt Regency Islandia** ✉ 1441 Quivira Rd. ☎ 619/221-4858. **Shelter Pointe Hotel and Marina** ✉ 1551 Shelter Island Dr. ☎ 619/224-7547. **San Diego Marriott Hotel and Marina** ✉ 333 W. Harbor Dr. ☎ 619/230-8955. **San Diego Yacht Club** ✉ 1011 Anchorage La. ☎ 619/221-8400. **Southwestern Yacht Club** ✉ 2702 Qualtrough St. ☎ 619/222-0438.

BUSINESS HOURS

Most banks are open weekdays 10 AM–6 PM. Some open for several hours on Saturday. Most other businesses are open Monday–Saturday from 9 or 10 AM to 6 or 9 PM. Many others are also open Sunday from noon to 5 or 6.

MUSEUMS & SIGHTS

Most museums are open Tuesday through Sunday 10 to 5. Major attractions are open daily 9 to 5, later in summer and during the Christmas holidays.

SHOPS

Mall and shopping center stores are open daily from 9 or 10 AM to 9 PM; some close at 6 PM on Sunday. Shops and boutiques in neighborhoods such as Hillcrest and La Jolla keep somewhat erratic hours, so it's a good idea to call first. Shops and restaurants in rural areas such as Julian and Descanso may close mid-week.

BUS TRAVEL TO & FROM SAN DIEGO

Greyhound operates 16 buses a day between San Diego and Los Angeles, connecting with buses to all major U.S. cities. Many buses are express or nonstop; others make stops at coastal towns en route.

Small bus companies connect San Diego to cities such as Chula Vista, National City, and Campo. Laidlaw Transit operates the Rural Bus that connects rural and backcountry communities such as Ramona, Jamul, Campo, Julian, and Borrego Springs. Service and schedules vary.

FARES & SCHEDULES

One-way fare to Los Angeles is $16, round-trip is $27. You can buy Greyhound tickets at the depot or in advance by phone.

Community and rural bus routes charge from $1 to $3.75 depending on location and destination.

RESERVATIONS

Boarding is on a first-come, first-served basis.

🚹 Bus Information **Chula Vista Transit** ☎ 619/233-3004 ⊕ www.sdcommute.com. **Greyhound** ✉ 120 W. Broadway ☎ 619/239-3266 or 800/231-2222. **National City Transit** ☎ 619/474-7505. **Rural Bus** ☎ 760/788-4995 or 800/858-0291 ⊕ www.sdcommute.com.

BUS TRAVEL WITHIN SAN DIEGO

Also see *Trolley Travel*.

San Diego County is served by a coordinated, efficient network of bus and rail routes that includes service to Oceanside in the north, the Mexican border at San Ysidro, and points east to the Anza-Borrego Desert. Under the umbrella of the Metropolitan Transit System, there are two major transit agencies: San Diego Transit and North County Transit District (NCTD). The staff at the downtown Transit Store sells passes and can help plan your travel.

Almost all stops on the San Diego Trolley light rail system connect with a San Diego Transit bus route. NCTD routes connect with Coaster commuter train routes between Oceanside and the Santa Fe Station in San Diego. They serve from Del Mar North to San Clemente, inland to Fallbrook, Pauma Valley, Valley Center, Ramona, and Escondido, with transfer points within the city of San Diego. NCTD also offers special express-bus service to Qualcomm Stadium for select major sporting events.

In Coronado the ATV Van Co. operates a bus service.

FARES & SCHEDULES
San Diego Transit fares range from $1 to $4; NCTD fares are $1.75. Discounted fares of $1 (San Diego Transit) and 75¢ (NCTD) are available for seniors and for people with disabilities. The Transit Store and NCTD transit centers sell packets of discounted universal tokens that can be used interchangeably on buses and the trolley. Most transfers are free; request one when boarding. Schedules are posted at each stop, and the buses usually are on time.

◪ Bus Information **North County Transit District** ☎ 800/266-6883 ⊕ www.sdcommute.com. **San Diego Transit** ☎ 619/233-3004, 619/234-5005 TTY, TDD ⊕ www.sdcommute.com. **Transit Store** ✉ 102 Broadway, Downtown ☎ 619/234-1060.

PAYING
You must have exact change in coins and/or bills. Pay upon boarding.

CAMERAS & PHOTOGRAPHY
The most popular San Diego residents to capture on film are Shamu the whale at SeaWorld and the San Diego Zoo's giant pandas. The most dramatic views are the harbor from the Coronado Bridge and the ocean from the bluffs at La Jolla Cove. The *Kodak Guide to Shooting Great Travel Pictures* (available at bookstores everywhere) is loaded with tips.

◪ Photo Help **Kodak Information Center** ☎ 800/242-2424 ⊕ www.kodak.com.

EQUIPMENT PRECAUTIONS
Do not pack film or equipment in luggage that you intend to check. The X-ray machines used to view checked baggage are extremely powerful and therefore likely to ruin your film. Ask for hand inspection of film, which becomes clouded after repeated exposure to airport X-ray machines, and keep videotapes and computer disks away from metal detectors. Always keep film, tape, and computer disks out of the sun. Carry an extra supply of batteries, and be prepared to turn on your camera, camcorder, or laptop to prove to airport security personnel that the device is real.

CAR RENTAL
A car is essential for San Diego's sprawling freeway system and comes in handy for touring Baja California (though the trolley serves the border at Tijuana). Rates in San Diego fluctuate with seasons and demand, but generally begin at $39 a day and $250 a week for an economy car with air-conditioning, automatic transmission, and unlimited mileage. This does not include tax on car rentals, which is 7.5%.

◪ Major Agencies **Alamo** ☎ 800/327-9633 ⊕ www.alamo.com. **Avis** ☎ 800/331-1212, 800/879-2847 or 800/272-5871 in Canada, 0870/606-0100 in U.K., 02/9353-9000 in Australia, 09/526-2847 in New Zealand ⊕ www.avis.com. **Budget** ☎ 800/527-0700 ⊕ www.budget.com. **Dollar** ☎ 800/800-4000, 0800/085-4578 in U.K. ⊕ www.dollar.com. **Hertz** ☎ 800/654-3131, 800/263-0600 in Canada, 0870/844-8844 in U.K., 02/9669-2444 in Australia, 09/256-8690 in New Zealand ⊕ www.hertz.com. **National Car Rental** ☎ 800/227-7368 ⊕ www.nationalcar.com.

CUTTING COSTS
For a good deal, book through a travel agent who will shop around. Also, price local car-rental companies—whose prices may be lower still, although their service and maintenance may not be as good as those of major rental agencies—and research rates on the Internet. Consolidators that specialize in air travel can offer good rates on cars as well (⇨ Air Travel). Remember to ask about required deposits, cancellation penalties, and drop-off charges if you're planning to pick up the car in one city and leave it in another. If you're traveling during a holiday period, also make sure that a confirmed reservation guarantees you a car.

Do look into wholesalers, which are companies that do not own fleets but rent in bulk from those that do and often offer better rates than traditional car-rental operations. Prices are best during off-peak periods. Rentals booked through wholesalers often must be paid for before you leave home.

🔃 **Local Agencies Advantage Rent-A-Car** ✉ 3180 N. Harbor Dr. ☎ 619/685-1660 and **Enterprise** ✉ 1691 Hancock St. ☎ 619/225-2281 pick up at area hotels.

INSURANCE

When driving a rented car you are generally responsible for any damage to or loss of the vehicle. You also may be liable for any property damage or personal injury that you may cause while driving. Before you rent, see what coverage you already have under the terms of your personal auto-insurance policy and credit cards.

For about $9 to $25 a day, rental companies sell protection, known as a collision- or loss-damage waiver (CDW or LDW), that eliminates your liability for damage to the car; it's always optional and should never be automatically added to your bill. In most states you don't need a CDW if you have personal auto insurance or other liability insurance. Some states, including California, have capped the price of the CDW and LDW. However, **make sure you have enough coverage to pay for the car.** If you do not have auto insurance or an umbrella policy that covers damage to third parties, purchasing liability insurance and a CDW or LDW is highly recommended.

REQUIREMENTS & RESTRICTIONS

In California you must be 21 to rent a car, and rates may be higher if you're under 25. Some agencies will not rent to those under 25; check when you book. Children up to age six or 60 pounds must be placed in safety or booster seats. Non–U.S. residents must have a license whose text is in the Roman alphabet, though it need not be in English. An international license is recommended but not required.

SURCHARGES

Before you pick up a car in one city and leave it in another, ask about drop-off charges or one-way service fees, which can be substantial. Also inquire about early-return policies; some rental agencies charge extra if you return the car before the time specified in your contract while others give you a refund for the days not used. Most agencies note the tank's fuel level on your contract; to avoid a hefty refueling fee, return the car with the same tank level. If the tank was full, refill it just before you turn in the car, but be aware that gas stations near the rental outlet may overcharge. It's almost never a deal to buy a tank of gas with the car when you rent it; the understanding is that you'll return it empty, but some fuel usually remains. Surcharges may apply if you're under 25 or if you take the car outside the area approved by the rental agency. You'll pay extra for child seats (about $8 a day) and usually for additional drivers (up to $25 a day, depending on location).

CAR TRAVEL

When traveling in the San Diego area, it pays to consider the big picture to avoid getting lost. Water lies to the west of the city. To the east and north, mountains separate the urban areas from the desert. Interstate 5, which stretches from Canada to the Mexican border, bisects San Diego. Interstate 8 provides access from Yuma, Arizona, and points east. Drivers coming from Nevada and the mountain regions beyond can reach San Diego on I–15. During rush hour there are jams on I–5 and on I–15 between I–805 and Escondido.

EMERGENCY SERVICES

Dial 911 to report accidents on the road and to reach police, the highway patrol, or the fire department. Emergency phone boxes can be found along most Interstate highways.

GASOLINE

The cost of gas varies widely depending on location, oil company, and whether you use the full-serve or self-serve aisle. Prices on the West Coast tend to be higher than those in the rest of the country, and in San Diego prices run about 15% higher than in many other California cities.

PARKING

Balboa Park and Mission Bay have huge free parking lots and it's rare not to find a space, though it may seem as if you've parked miles from your destination. The once-plentiful lots downtown have disappeared as a result of the opening of Petco Park in 2004 and the ongoing construction of hotels surrounding the ball field. On game day, expect to pay $17 or more for a short walk to the stadium, less for a longer one. Other downtown lots cost $5–$35 per day. The Web site of the Gaslamp Quarter Association maps currently open lots and shares parking secrets (www. gaslamp.org). Old Town has large lots surrounding the Transit Center. Parking is more of a problem in La Jolla and Coronado, where you generally need to rely on hard-to-find street spots or expensive by-the-hour parking lots.

Parking at meters costs $2 an hour; enforcement is 8 AM–6 PM except Sunday. Be extra careful around rush hour, when certain street-parking areas become tow-away zones. In the evenings and during events it can be difficult to locate parking spaces downtown. Parking violations in congested areas can cost you $25 or more. Car renters are liable for parking tickets and towing charges incurred.

ROAD CONDITIONS

Highways are generally in good condition in the San Diego area. Traffic is particularly heavy on I–5, I–8, I–805, and I–15 during morning and afternoon rush hours, 6–8:30 AM and 3:30–6 PM. Before venturing into the mountains, check on road conditions; mountain driving can be dangerous. Listen to radio traffic reports for information on the lines waiting to cross the border into Mexico.

⁊ Maps **AAA San Diego** ⊠ 2365 Northside Dr., Suite 120 ☎ 619/233-1000 ⊕ www.aaa.com.

RULES OF THE ROAD

Speed limits are 35 mph on city streets and 65 mph on freeways, unless otherwise indicated. Speed may be checked by radar or aircraft. Unless otherwise indicated, right turns are permitted at red lights, after you've come to a full stop. In San Diego, be alert for one-way streets, "no left turn"

intersections, and blocks closed to car traffic. Driving with a blood-alcohol level higher than 0.08 will result in arrest and seizure of your driver's license. The law is strictly enforced, and fines are severe.

Seat belts are required at all times and tickets are given for failing to comply. California law requires that children ride in the back seat of the car strapped into safety or booster seats until they are at least six years old or weigh 60 pounds.

Many California freeways have High Occupancy Vehicle lanes, usually restricted to vehicles carrying two or more persons.

CHILDREN IN SAN DIEGO

San Diego is a family-oriented destination, with many attractions geared to kids. You'll find strollers for rent, diaper-changing facilities, kids' menus, and special activities for kids at most major attractions.

The monthly *San Diego Family Magazine* is filled with listings of events and resources; it's available by mail for $3.50, which covers postage and handling, or free in San Diego at Longs Drug Stores, Blockbuster, MacDonald's, and local libraries.

If you're renting a car, don't forget to arrange for a car seat when you reserve. For general advice about traveling with children, consult *Fodor's FYI: Travel with Your Baby* (available in bookstores everywhere).

⁊ Local Information *San Diego Family Magazine* ⓕ Box 23960, San Diego 92193 ☎ 619/685-6970 ⊕ www.sandiegofamily.com.

BABYSITTING

Many agencies specialize in on- and off-site group and individual child care for conventions, tourists, and special events. They are licensed, bonded, and insured. Hotel concierges can usually recommend a reliable babysitting service.

⁊ Agencies **Panda Services** ⊠ 4655 Ruffner St., No. 100, San Diego 92111 ☎ 858/292-5503 ⊕ www. sandiegobabysitters.com. **Marion's Child Care** ⊠ 10491 Pine Grove Ave., Spring Valley 91978 ☎ 619/303-4379 ⊕ www.hotelchildcare.com.

FLYING

Experts agree that it's a good idea to use safety seats aloft for children weighing less than 40 pounds. Airlines set their own policies: if you use a safety seat, U.S. carriers usually require that the child be ticketed, even if he or she is young enough to ride free, because the seats must be strapped into regular seats. And even if you pay the full adult fare for the seat, it may be worth it, especially on longer trips. Do **check your airline's policy about using safety seats during takeoff and landing.** Safety seats are not allowed everywhere in the plane, so get your seat assignments as early as possible.

When reserving, request children's meals or a freestanding bassinet (not available at all airlines) if you need them. But note that bulkhead seats, where you must sit to use the bassinet, may lack an overhead bin or storage space on the floor.

FOOD

Most San Diego restaurants make at least some accommodation for kids: child-size portions, seats for children, amusements such as crayons and coloring paper, or, at a minimum, friendliness. The Gaslamp Quarter and La Jolla both have a Hard Rock Cafe, which is a big hit with kids and teenagers. Of the places reviewed in the Where to Eat chapter, the Cheesecake Factory, Fish Market, Ghirardelli Soda Fountain & Chocolate Shop, Hob Nob Hill, and Ricky's Family Restaurant are particularly suited to families; your children's din will blend right in.

LODGING

Most hotels in San Diego allow children under a certain age to stay in their parents' room at no extra charge, but others charge for them as extra adults; be sure to **find out the cutoff age for children's discounts.** Kids will find plenty to keep them busy at any of San Diego's waterfront hotels, including the Hotel Del Coronado and the Dana Inn and the Bahia Resort Hotel on Mission Bay.

🗷 **Best Choices Bahia Resort Hotel** ✉ 998 W. Mission Bay Dr., Mission Bay ☎ 858/488-0551. **Dana Inn & Marina** ✉ 1710 W. Mission Bay Dr., Mission Bay ☎ 619/222-6440. **Hotel Del Coronado** ✉ 1500 Orange Ave., Coronado ☎ 619/435-6611.

SIGHTS & ATTRACTIONS

All of San Diego's top attractions are designed for family entertainment. In this book, places that are especially appealing to children are indicated by a rubber-duckie icon (🦆) in the margin.

The San Diego Zoo has a 30-exhibit Children's Zoo filled with pettable goats, lambs, and miniature horses, Bugtown, and a zany science show hosted by Dr. Zoolittle. SeaWorld San Diego always makes a big splash with the kids, many of whom race for front-row seats at the Shamu show. Hands-on activities include Shamu's Happy Harbor, Forbidden Reef, and the California Tide Pool.

Walking the decks of the Maritime Museum's *Star of India* and HMS *Surprise* recalls visions of real and imaginary seafarers. The sailing ships are berthed along the Embarcadero in the shadow of San Diego's newest attraction, the San Diego Aircraft Carrier Museum on the USS *Midway.*

At Legoland California colorful plastic building blocks are climb-on or crawl-through. Interactive exhibits have been added including Dig Those Dinos and the Fun Town Fire Academy. Expect long lines at the driving school, the pedal boats, and the power tower.

CONCIERGES

Concierges, found in many hotels, can help you with theater tickets and dinner reservations: A good one with connections may be able to get you seats for a hot show or prime-time dinner reservations at the restaurant of the moment. You can also turn to your hotel's concierge for help with travel arrangements, sightseeing plans, services ranging from aromatherapy to zipper repair, and emergencies. **Always tip** a concierge who has been of assistance (⇨ Tipping).

CONSUMER PROTECTION

Whether you're shopping for gifts or purchasing travel services, **pay with a major credit card** whenever possible, so you can cancel payment or get reimbursed if there's a problem (and you can provide documentation). If you're doing business with a particular company for the first time, contact your local Better Business Bureau and the attorney general's offices in your state and (for U.S. businesses) the company's home state as well. Have any complaints been filed? Finally, if you're buying a package or tour, always consider travel insurance that includes default coverage (⇨ Insurance).

⑦ BBBs Council of Better Business Bureaus ✉ 4200 Wilson Blvd., Suite 800, Arlington, VA 22203 ☎ 703/276-0100 🖷 703/525-8277 ⊕ www.bbb.org.

CRUISE TRAVEL

Several cruise-ship lines make San Diego a port of call. Holland America and Royal Caribbean use San Diego as a regular point of embarkation for seasonal cruises to Alaska, the Mexican Riviera, and the Panama Canal. Other lines including Princess and Celebrity originate repositioning cruises in San Diego throughout the year. The San Diego cruise ship terminal is on the downtown waterfront just steps from the San Diego Maritime Museum and Midway Museum. The terminal is a short taxi ride to Balboa Park, Little Italy, and the Gaslamp Quarter.

To learn how to plan, choose, and book a cruise-ship voyage, check out Cruise How-to's on ⊕ www.fodors.com, and consult *Fodor's FYI: Plan & Enjoy Your Cruise* (available in bookstores everywhere).

⑦ Cruise Lines Carnival ☎ 888/227-6482 ⊕ www.carnival.com. **Celebrity** ☎ 800/437-3111 ⊕ www.celebrity.com. **Holland America** ☎ 800/ 426-0327 ⊕ www.hollandamerica.com. **Princess** ☎ 800/774-6237 ⊕ www.princess.com. **Royal Caribbean International** ☎ 800/398-9819 ⊕ www.royalcaribbean.com.

CUSTOMS & DUTIES

If you make a shopping trip to Mexico, keep receipts for all purchases. Upon reentering the country, **be ready to show customs officials what you've bought.** Pack purchases together in an easily accessible place. If you think a duty is incorrect, appeal the assessment. If you object to the way your clearance was handled, note the inspector's badge number. In either case, first ask to see a supervisor. If the problem isn't resolved, write to the appropriate authorities, beginning with the port director at your point of entry.

Customs officers operate at the San Ysidro border crossing, San Diego International Airport, and in the bay at Shelter Island.

IN AUSTRALIA

Australian residents who are 18 or older may bring home A$900 worth of souvenirs and gifts (including jewelry), 250 cigarettes or 250 grams of cigars or other tobacco products, and 2.25 liters of alcohol (including wine, beer, and spirits). Residents under 18 may bring back A$450 worth of goods. If any of these individual allowances are exceeded, you must pay duty for the entire amount (of the group of products in which the allowance was exceeded). Members of the same family traveling together may pool their allowances. Prohibited items include meat products. Seeds, plants, and fruits need to be declared upon arrival.

⑦ Australian Customs Service ✇ Locked Bag 3000, Sydney International Airport, Sydney, NSW 2020 ☎ 02/6275-6666 or 1300/363263, 02/ 8334-7444 or 1800/020-504 quarantine-inquiry line 🖷 02/8339-6714 ⊕ www.customs.gov.au.

IN CANADA

Canadian residents who have been out of Canada for at least seven days may bring in C$750 worth of goods duty-free. If you've been away fewer than seven days but more than 48 hours, the duty-free allowance drops to C$200. If your trip lasts 24 to 48 hours, the allowance is C$50; if the goods are worth more than C$50, you must pay full duty on all of the goods. You may not pool allowances with family members. Goods claimed under the C$750 exemption may follow you by mail; those claimed under the lesser exemptions must accompany you. Alcohol and tobacco products may be included in the seven-day and 48-hour exemptions but not in the 24-hour exemption. If you meet the age requirements of the province or territory through which you reenter Canada, you may bring in, duty-free, 1.5 liters of wine *or* 1.14 liters (40 imperial ounces) of liquor *or* 24 12-ounce cans or bottles of beer or ale. Also, if you meet the local age requirement for tobacco products, you may bring in, duty-free, 200 cigarettes, 50 cigars or cigarillos, and 200 grams of tobacco. You may have to pay a minimum duty on tobacco products, regardless of whether or not you exceed your personal exemption. Check ahead of time with the Canada Border Services Agency or the Department of Agriculture for policies regarding meat products, seeds, plants, and fruits.

You may send an unlimited number of gifts (only one gift per recipient, however) worth up to C$60 each duty-free to Canada. Label the package UNSOLICITED GIFT—VALUE UNDER $60. Alcohol and tobacco are excluded.

🚩 **Canada Border Services Agency** ⊠ Customs Information Services, 191 Laurier Ave. W, 15th fl., Ottawa, Ontario K1A 0L5 ☎ 800/461-9999 in Canada, 204/983-3500 or 506/636-5064 ⊕ www.cbsa.gc.ca.

IN NEW ZEALAND

All homeward-bound residents may bring back NZ$700 worth of souvenirs and gifts; passengers may not pool their allowances, and children can claim the concession only on goods intended for their own use. For those 17 or older, the duty-free allowance also includes 4.5 liters of wine or beer; one 1,125-ml bottle of spirits; and either 200 cigarettes, 250 grams of tobacco, 50 cigars, *or* a combination of the three up to 250 grams. Meat products, seeds, plants, and fruits must be declared upon arrival to the Agricultural Services Department.

🚩 **New Zealand Customs** ⊠ Head office: The Customhouse, 17-21 Whitmore St., Box 2218, Wellington ☎ 09/300-5399 or 0800/428-786 ⊕ www.customs.govt.nz.

IN THE U.K.

From countries outside the European Union, including the United States, you may bring home, duty-free, 200 cigarettes, 50 cigars, 100 cigarillos, or 250 grams of tobacco; 1 liter of spirits or 2 liters of fortified or sparkling wine or liqueurs; 2 liters of still table wine; 60 ml of perfume; 250 ml of toilet water; plus £145 worth of other goods, including gifts and souvenirs. Prohibited items include meat and dairy products, seeds, plants, and fruits.

🚩 **HM Customs and Excise** ⊠ Portcullis House, 21 Cowbridge Rd. E, Cardiff CF11 9SS ☎ 0845/010- 9000 or 0208/929-0152 advice service, 0208/929-6731 or 0208/910-3602 complaints ⊕ www.hmce.gov.uk.

IN THE U.S.

U.S. residents who have been out of the country for at least 48 hours may bring home, for personal use, $800 worth of foreign goods duty-free, as long as they haven't used the $800 allowance or any part of it in the past 30 days. This exemption may include 1 liter of alcohol (for travelers 21 and older), 200 cigarettes, and 100 non-Cuban cigars. Family members from the same household who are traveling together may pool their $800 personal exemptions. For fewer than 48 hours, the duty-free allowance drops to $200, which may include 50 cigarettes, 10 non-Cuban cigars, and 150 ml of alcohol (or 150 ml of perfume containing alcohol). The $200 allowance cannot be combined with other individuals' exemptions, and if you exceed it, the full value of all the goods will be taxed. Antiques, which U.S. Customs and Border Protection defines as objects more than 100 years old, enter duty-free, as do original works of art done entirely by hand, including paintings, drawings, and sculptures. This doesn't apply to folk art or handicrafts, which are in general dutiable.

You may also send packages home duty-free, with a limit of one parcel per addressee per day (except alcohol or tobacco products or perfume worth more than $5). You can mail up to $200 worth of goods for personal use; label the package PERSONAL USE and attach a list of its contents and their retail value. If the package contains your used personal belongings, mark it AMERICAN GOODS RETURNED to avoid paying duties. You may send up to $100 worth of goods as a gift; mark the package UNSOLICITED GIFT. Mailed items do not affect your duty-free allowance on your return.

To avoid paying duty on foreign-made high-ticket items you already own and will take on your trip, register them with a local customs office before you leave the country. Consider filing a Certificate of Registration for laptops, cameras, watches, and other digital devices identified with serial numbers or other permanent markings; you can keep the certificate for other trips. Otherwise, bring a sales receipt or insurance form to show that you owned the item before you left the United States.

For more about duties, restricted items, and other information about international travel, read the U.S. Customs and Border Protection's *Know Before You Go* brochure, available online at the agency's Web site, listed below. You can file complaints online at the same Web site.
🛂 **U.S. Customs and Border Protection** ⊠ For inquiries and complaints, 1300 Pennsylvania Ave. NW, Washington, DC 20229 ⊕ www.cbp.gov ☎ 877/227-5551 or 202/354-1000.

DISABILITIES & ACCESSIBILITY

San Diego ranks as one of the most accessible cities in the United States for people using wheelchairs. Although the Old Town district has some moderately uneven streets, curb cuts and smooth sidewalks are decidedly the rule rather than the exception for the city as a whole. The extensive network of walkways in Balboa Park affords views that are both lovely and negotiable. Most major attractions, shopping malls, tour services, and casinos are accessible. Special beach wheelchairs are available at the lifeguard station in Pacific Beach; make reservations 48 hours in advance. Accessible San Diego has a visitor information center and telephone hotline, makes hotel referrals, provides guides to San Diego's attractions for visitors with mobility problems, and can arrange for powered beach wheelchairs during the summer season.
🛂 **Local Resources Access Center of San Diego** ⊠ Information and Referrals, 1295 University Ave., Suite 10, San Diego 92103 ☎ 619/293-3500, 619/293-7757 TDD ⊕ www.accesscentersd.org. **Accessible San Diego** ⊠ 2850 6th Ave., Suite 311, San Diego 92103 ☎ 858/279-0704 ⊕ www.accessandiego.org. **MTS Access** ⊠ 4970 Market St., San Diego 92102 ☎ 888/517-9627 ⊕ www.sdcommute.com.

LODGING

Despite the Americans with Disabilities Act, the definition of accessibility seems to differ from hotel to hotel. Some properties may be accessible by ADA standards for people with mobility problems but not for people with hearing or vision impairments, for example.

If you have mobility problems, ask for the lowest floor on which accessible services are offered. If you have a hearing impairment, check whether the hotel has devices to alert you visually to the ring of the telephone, a knock at the door, and a fire/emergency alarm. Some hotels provide these devices without charge. Discuss your needs with hotel personnel if this equipment isn't available, so that a staff member can personally alert you in the event of an emergency.

If you're bringing a guide dog, get authorization ahead of time and write down the name of the person with whom you spoke.
🛂 **Best Choices Holiday Inn San Diego on the Bay** ⊠ 1355 N. Harbor Dr. ☎ 619/232-3861 ⊕ www.holiday-inn.com. **Manchester Grand Hyatt San Diego** ⊠ 1 Market Pl. ☎ 619/232-1234 ⊕ www.hyatt.com. **Town and Country Resort** ⊠ 500 Hotel Circle N ☎ 619/239-2200 ⊕ www.towncountry.com.

RESERVATIONS

When discussing accessibility with an operator or reservations agent, ask hard questions. Are there any stairs, inside *or* out? Are there grab bars next to the toilet *and* in the shower/tub? How wide is the doorway to the room? To the bathroom? For the most extensive facilities meeting the latest legal specifications, opt for newer accommodations. If you reserve through a toll-free number, consider also calling the hotel's local number to confirm the information from the central reservations office. Get confirmation in writing when you can.

SIGHTS & ATTRACTIONS

Most attractions have accessible restrooms, ramps, and parking spaces near the entrances reserved for people with disabilities. Travelers who use wheelchairs can see much of the San Diego Zoo via tram and get an overview of the Wild Animal Park from the monorail. SeaWorld San Diego has sign language interpreters, assistive listening devices, and wheelchairs for rent. Cabrillo National Monument waives admission fees for those with disability placards and has text telephones. Most attractions at Legoland have ramps and the park has wheelchairs for rent. Hornblower Cruises has an accessible gangway ramp and restroom.

TRANSPORTATION
Most public buses and the San Diego Trolley are equipped with lifts. About one-third of the bus lines are served by buses with elevator ramps. Call San Diego Transit (⇨ Bus Travel within San Diego) for detailed information. MTS Access (⇨ Disabilities & Accessibility) provides curb-to-curb transportation for those with restricted mobility; advance reservations are required. Car rental agencies can provide vehicles with hand controls, usually with 24 hours advance notice. The U.S. Department of Transportation Aviation Consumer Protection Division's online publication *New Horizons: Information for the Air Traveler with a Disability* offers advice for travelers with a disability and outlines basic rights. Visit DisabilityInfo.gov for general information.

🔳 **Information & Complaints Aviation Consumer Protection Division** (⇨ Air Travel) for airline-related problems; ⊕ airconsumer.ost.dot.gov/publications/horizons.htm for airline travel advice and rights. **Departmental Office of Civil Rights** ✉ For general inquiries, U.S. Department of Transportation, S-30, 400 7th St. SW, Room 10215, Washington, DC 20590 ☎ 202/366-4648, 202/366-8538 TTY 🖷 202/366-9371 ⊕ www.dotcr.ost.dot.gov. **Disability Rights Section** ✉ NYAV, U.S. Department of Justice, Civil Rights Division, 950 Pennsylvania Ave. NW, Washington, DC 20530 ☎ ADA information line 202/514-0301, 800/514-0301, 202/514-0383 TTY, 800/514-0383 TTY ⊕ www.ada.gov. **U.S. Department of Transportation Hotline** ☎ 800/778-4838 for disability-related air-travel problems, 800/455-9880 TTY.

TRAVEL AGENCIES
In the United States, the Americans with Disabilities Act requires that travel firms serve the needs of all travelers. Some agencies specialize in working with people with disabilities.

🔳 **Travelers with Mobility Problems Access Adventures/B. Roberts Travel** ✉ 1876 East Ave., Rochester, NY 14610 ☎ 800/444-6540 ⊕ www.

brobertstravel.com, run by a former physical-rehabilitation counselor. **Accessible Vans of America** ✉ 37 Daniel Rd. W, Fairfield, NJ 07004 ☎ 877/282-8267or 888/282-8267, 973/808-9709 reservations 🖷 973/808-9713 ⊕ www.accessiblevans.com. **CareVacations** ✉ No. 5, 5110-50 Ave., Leduc, Alberta, Canada, T9E 6V4 ☎ 780/986-6404 or 877/478-7827 🖷 780/986-8332 ⊕ www.carevacations.com, for group tours and cruise vacations. **Flying Wheels Travel** ✉ 143 W. Bridge St., Box 382, Owatonna, MN 55060 ☎ 507/451-5005 🖷 507/451-1685 ⊕ www.flyingwheelstravel.com.

🔳 **Travelers with Developmental Disabilities New Directions** ✉ 5276 Hollister Ave., Suite 207, Santa Barbara, CA 93111 ☎ 805/967-2841 or 888/967-2841 🖷 805/964-7344 ⊕ www.newdirectionstravel.com.

DISCOUNTS & DEALS
The International Visitor Information Center (⇨ Visitor Information) has a free coupon book, *San Diego Travel Values,* that contains a list of 25 free activities in San Diego plus discount coupons to attractions, hotels, and restaurants. Multiday passes to SeaWorld and Legoland are available from some Mission Bay area hotels. Arts Tix sells half-price, same-day tickets for performances.

Some of the best San Diego attractions are as free as the air. Balboa Park offers several free tours of historic buildings and gardens. Most museums in the park are free on one Tuesday a month, on a rotating schedule. The Spreckels Organ Pavilion presents free concerts on Sunday afternoons. Some of the best views to be seen without paying a cent include La Jolla Cove, waves crashing against more than 70 mi of public beaches, and spectacular, sweeping city and ocean views from the tops of Mt. Soledad and Mt. Helix. The Maritime Museum offers free admission for kids on Sundays from time to time. Free tours include the Arco Olympic Training Center in Chula Vista, a walking tour of the Stuart Sculpture Collection at the University of California at San Diego, and monthly sky-tours using portable telescopes at the Reuben H. Fleet Science Center in Balboa Park.

The Passport to Balboa Park, available at the visitor center in the House of Hospitality and at many of the park's museums, grants admission to 12 museums (plus the Japanese Friendship Garden) for a reduced price. It can be used over a number of days. The Best of Balboa Park Combo Pass includes the 13 attractions and a deluxe tour of the San Diego Zoo including a 40-minute bus tour and a Skyfari Aerial Tram ride. The San Diego 3-for-1 Pass is good for unlimited admission to the zoo, the San Diego Wild Animal Park, and Sea-World for five consecutive days. During October, zoo admission is free for kids, so be prepared for crowds. Both SeaWorld and Legoland offer multiday tickets that may end up saving you money. The San Diego Passport, available through the Old Town Trolley, bundles admissions to some of San Diego's most popular attractions at significant savings. You can print discount coupons for 50 area restaurants at the Web site of the San Diego Convention & Visitors Bureau (www.sandiego.org).

7 Discount Arts Tickets Arts Tix ⊠ Horton Plaza, Downtown ☎ 619/497-5000 ⊕ www. sandiegoperforms.com ⏱ Tues.-Thurs. 11-6, Fri. and Sat. 10-6, Sun. 10-5

DISCOUNT RESERVATIONS

To save money, look for discount reservations services that use their buying power to get a better price on hotels, airline tickets (⇨ Air Travel), even car rentals. When booking a room, always **call the hotel's local toll-free number** (if one is available) rather than the central reservations number—you'll often get a better price. Always ask about special packages or corporate rates.

7 Hotel Rooms Accommodations Express ☎ 800/444-7666 or 800/277-1064. **Hotels.com** ☎ 800/246-8357 ⊕ www.hotels.com. **Quikbook** ☎ 800/789-9887 ⊕ www.quikbook.com. **Turbotrip.com** ☎ 800/473-7829 ⊕ w3.turbotrip.com.

PACKAGE DEALS

Don't confuse packages and guided tours. When you buy a package, you travel on your own, just as though you had planned the trip yourself. Fly/drive packages, which combine airfare and car rental, are often a good deal. Packages combining lodging, dining, theater tickets, and museum admission within San Diego County are available through San Diego Art + Sol, a collaboration of the City of San Diego Commission for Arts and Culture, the San Diego Convention & Visitors Bureau, and their member organizations. Their offerings change frequently; you can order a brochure, but allow four to six weeks for delivery.

7 Packagers San Diego Art + Sol ☎ 800/236-1212 ⊕ www.sandiegoartandsol.com.

GAY & LESBIAN TRAVEL

With a large and visible gay community, San Diego is earning points as one of the country's most gay-friendly destinations. Hillcrest is the main gay neighborhood and retail district, with many bars, cafés, and shops. *Update,* a weekly gay paper, is available in Hillcrest and at a few locations downtown; the gay-lesbian bookstore Obelisk, in Hillcrest, is an excellent resource and hangout. The annual Pride Parade, Rally, and Festival takes place in Balboa Park over a weekend in July. The Rainbow Guide at www.sandiego.org lists other gay events, plus restaurants and nightclubs.

For details about the gay and lesbian scene, consult *Fodor's Gay Guide to the USA* (available in bookstores everywhere).

7 Gay- & Lesbian-Friendly Travel Agencies Different Roads Travel ⊠ 1017 N. LaCienega Blvd., Suite 308, West Hollywood, CA 90069 ☎ 310/289-6000 or 800/429-8747 (Ext. 14 for both) 🖷 310/855-0323 ✉ lgernert@tzell.com. **Kennedy Travel** ⊠ 130 W. 42nd St., Suite 401, New York, NY 10036 ☎ 800/237-7433 or 212/840-8659 🖷 212/730-2269 ⊕ www.kennedytravel.com. **Now, Voyager** ⊠ 4406 18th St., San Francisco, CA 94114 ☎ 415/626-1169 or 800/255-6951 🖷 415/626-8626 ⊕ www. nowvoyager.com. **Skylink Travel/Flying Dutchmen Travel** ⊠ 1455 N. Dutton Ave., Suite A, Santa Rosa, CA 95401 ☎ 707/546-9888 or 800/225-5759 🖷 707/636-0951, serving lesbian travelers.

7 Local Resources Lesbian and Gay Men's Community Center ⊠ 3909 Centre St., San Diego 92103 ☎ 619/692-2077 ⊕ www.thecentersd.org. *Update* ☎ 619/299-0500 ⊕ www.sandiegogaynews.com. **Obelisk** ⊠ 1029 University Ave., Hillcrest ☎ 619/297-4171.

HEALTH

DIVERS' ALERT

Do not fly within 24 hours of scuba diving.

HOLIDAYS

Major national holidays are New Year's Day (Jan. 1); Martin Luther King Day (3rd Mon. in Jan.); Presidents' Day (3rd Mon. in Feb.); Memorial Day (last Mon. in May); Independence Day (July 4); Labor Day (1st Mon. in Sept.); Columbus Day (2nd Mon. in Oct.); Thanksgiving Day (4th Thurs. in Nov.); Christmas Eve and Christmas Day (Dec. 24 and 25); and New Year's Eve (Dec. 31).

INSURANCE

The most useful travel-insurance plan is a comprehensive policy that includes coverage for trip cancellation and interruption, default, trip delay, and medical expenses (with a waiver for preexisting conditions).

Without insurance you'll lose all or most of your money if you cancel your trip, regardless of the reason. Default insurance covers you if your tour operator, airline, or cruise line goes out of business—the chances of which have been increasing. Trip-delay covers expenses that arise because of bad weather or mechanical delays. Study the fine print when comparing policies.

U.K. residents can buy a travel-insurance policy valid for most vacations taken during the year in which it's purchased (but check preexisting-condition coverage).

Always **buy travel policies directly from the insurance company**; if you buy them from a cruise line, airline, or tour operator that goes out of business you probably won't be covered for the agency or operator's default, a major risk. Before making any purchase, review your existing health and home-owner's policies to find what they cover away from home.

🛈 Travel Insurers In the U.S.: **Access America** ✉ 2805 N. Parham Rd., Richmond, VA 23294 ☎ 800/284-8300 🖷 804/673-1469 or 800/346-9265 ⊕ www.accessamerica.com. **Travel Guard International** ✉ 1145 Clark St., Stevens Point, WI 54481 ☎ 800/826-1300 or 715/345-1041 🖷 800/955-8785 or 715/345-1990 ⊕ www.travelguard.com.

FOR INTERNATIONAL TRAVELERS

For information on customs restrictions, *see* Customs & Duties.

CAR RENTAL

When picking up a rental car, non-U.S. residents need a reservation voucher for any prepaid reservations that were made in the traveler's home country, a passport, a driver's license, and a travel policy that covers each driver.

CAR TRAVEL

Highways in the United States are well paved. Interstate highways—limited-access, multilane highways whose numbers are prefixed by "I–"—are the fastest routes (although they may be heavily congested during rush hours in the San Diego area). Interstates with three-digit numbers encircle urban areas, which may have other limited-access expressways, freeways, and parkways as well. Tolls may be levied on limited-access highways. So-called U.S. highways and state highways are not necessarily limited-access but may have several lanes.

Along larger highways, roadside stops with rest rooms, fast-food restaurants, and sundries stores are well spaced. State police and tow trucks patrol major highways and lend assistance. If your car breaks down on an interstate, pull onto the shoulder and wait for help, or have your passengers wait while you walk to an emergency phone (available in most states). If you carry a cell phone, dial 911, noting your location on the small green roadside mileage markers.

Driving in the United States is on the right. Do obey the speed limits posted along roads and highways. Watch for lower limits in small towns and on back roads. On weekdays between 6 and 10 AM and again between 4 and 7 PM expect heavy traffic. To encourage carpooling, some freeways have special lanes for so-called high-occupancy vehicles (HOV)—cars carrying more than one passenger.

Bookstores, gas stations, convenience stores, and rest stops sell maps (about $3) and multiregion road atlases (about $10). Gas stations are plentiful. Most stay open late (24 hours along main highways and in big cities), except in rural areas, where Sunday hours may be limited and where you may drive long stretches without a re-fueling opportunity.

There are Border Inspection stations along the major highways in San Diego County. For this reason, it's best to travel with your passport in case you are asked to pull into one.

CONSULATES & EMBASSIES

🛂 Canada **Canada** ⊠ 300 S. Grand Ave., Los Angeles ☎ 213/346-2700.

🛂 New Zealand **Honorary Counsel** ⊠ Gray Cary, Ware & Freidenrich, 4365 Executive Dr., Suite 1100, San Diego ☎ 858/677-1485.

🛂 United Kingdom **United Kingdom** ⊠ 11766 Wilshire Blvd., No. 400, Los Angeles ☎ 310/477-3322.

CURRENCY

The dollar is the basic unit of U.S. currency. It has 100 cents. Coins are the copper penny (1¢); the silvery nickel (5¢), dime (10¢), quarter (25¢), and half-dollar (50¢); and the golden $1 coin, replacing a now-rare silver dollar. Bills are denominated $1, $5, $10, $20, $50, and $100, all mostly green and identical in size; designs and background tints vary. In addition, you may come across a $2 bill, but the chances are slim. The exchange rate at this writing is US$1.82 per British pound, 80¢ per Canadian dollar, 77¢ per Australian dollar, and 72¢ per New Zealand dollar.

ELECTRICITY

The U.S. standard is AC, 110 volts/60 cycles. Plugs have two flat pins set parallel to each other.

EMERGENCIES

For police, fire, or ambulance, **dial 911** ("0" in rural areas).

INSURANCE

Britons and Australians need extra medical coverage when traveling overseas.

🛂 Insurance Information In the U.K.: **Association of British Insurers** ⊠ 51 Gresham St., London EC2V 7HQ ☎ 020/7600-3333 📠 020/7696-8999 🌐 www.abi.org.uk. In Australia: **Insurance Council of Australia** ⊠ Level 3, 56 Pitt St., Sydney, NSW 2000 ☎ 02/9253-5100 📠 02/9253-5111 🌐 www.ica.com.au. In Canada: **RBC Insurance** ⊠ 6880 Financial Dr., Mississauga, Ontario L5N 7Y5 ☎ 800/387-4357

or 905/816-2559 📠 888/298-6458 🌐 www.rbcinsurance.com. In New Zealand: **Insurance Council of New Zealand** ⊠ Level 7, 111-115 Customhouse Quay, Box 474, Wellington ☎ 04/472-5230 📠 04/473-3011 🌐 www.icnz.org.nz.

MAIL & SHIPPING

You can buy stamps and aerograms and send letters and parcels in post offices. Stamp-dispensing machines can occasionally be found in airports, bus and train stations, office buildings, drugstores, and the like. You can also deposit mail in the stout, dark blue, steel bins at strategic locations everywhere and in the mail chutes of large buildings; pickup schedules are posted. You can deposit packages at public collection boxes as long as the parcels are affixed with proper postage and weigh less than one pound. Packages weighing one or more pounds must be taken to a post office or handed to a postal carrier.

For mail addressed to a destination within the United States, you need a 37¢ stamp for first-class letters weighing 1 ounce or less (23¢ for each additional ounce) and 23¢ for postcards. Mail sent to Canada or Mexico requires a 60¢ stamp for a 1-ounce letter and 50¢ for a postcard. Postage to most other countries is 80¢ for 1-ounce airmail letters and 70¢ for airmail postcards. An aerogram—a single sheet of lightweight blue paper that folds into its own envelope, stamped for overseas airmail—costs 70¢.

Staff at most U.S. post offices are efficient and helpful. Letters headed overseas take 10 days to two weeks to reach their destination. Private mailing services such as Mail Boxes, Etc. will pack and ship items for you. Most are authorized shippers for United Parcel Service (UPS), Federal Express (FedEx), and the U.S. Postal Service.

To receive mail on the road, have it sent c/o General Delivery at your destination's main post office (use the correct five-digit ZIP code). You must pick up mail in person within 30 days and show a driver's license or passport.

PASSPORTS & VISAS

When traveling internationally, carry your passport even if you don't need one (it's always the best form of ID) and **make two photocopies of the data page** (one for someone at home and another for yourself, to be carried separately from your passport). If you lose your passport, promptly call the nearest embassy or consulate and the local police.

Canadian and European Union citizens do not need a visa to visit the United States, nor do citizens of Australia who are staying fewer than 90 days.

🛂 Australian Citizens **Passports Australia** ☎ 131-232 ⊕ www.passports.gov.au. **United States Consulate General** ✉ MLC Centre, Level 59, 19-29 Martin Pl., Sydney, NSW 2000 ☎ 02/9373-9200, 1902/941-641 fee-based visa-inquiry line ⊕ usembassy-australia.state.gov/sydney.

🛂 Canadian Citizens **Passport Office** ✉ To mail in applications: 70 Cremazie St., Gatineau, Québec J8Y 3P2 ☎ 800/567-6868, 866/255-7655 TTY ⊕ www.ppt.gc.ca.

🛂 New Zealand Citizens **New Zealand Passports Office** ✉ For applications and information, Level 3, Boulcott House, 47 Boulcott St., Wellington ☎ 0800/22-5050 or 04/474-8100 ⊕ www.passports.govt.nz. **Embassy of the United States** ✉ 29 Fitzherbert Terr., Thorndon, Wellington ☎ 04/462-6000 ⊕ usembassy.org.nz. **U.S. Consulate General** ✉ Citibank Bldg., 3rd fl., 23 Customs St. E, Auckland ☎ 09/303-2724 ⊕ usembassy.org.nz.

🛂 U.K. Citizens **U.K. Passport Service** ☎ 0870/521-0410 ⊕ www.passport.gov.uk. **American Consulate General** ✉ Danesfort House, 223 Stranmillis Rd., Belfast, Northern Ireland BT9 5GR ☎ 028/9038-6100 🖷 028/9068-1301 ⊕ www.usembassy.org.uk. **American Embassy** ✉ For visa and immigration information or to submit a visa application via mail (enclose an SASE), Consular Information Unit, 24 Grosvenor Sq., London W1A 2LQ ☎ 090/5544-4546 or 090/6820-0290 for visa information (per-minute charges), 0207/499-9000 main switchboard ⊕ www.usembassy.org.uk.

TELEPHONES

All U.S. telephone numbers consist of a three-digit area code and a seven-digit local number. Within many local calling areas, you dial only the seven-digit number. Within some area codes, you must dial "1" first for calls outside the local area. To call between area-code regions, dial "1"

then all 10 digits; the same goes for calls to numbers prefixed by "800," "888," "866," and "877"—all toll free. For calls to numbers preceded by "900" you must pay—usually dearly.

For international calls, dial "011" followed by the country code and the local number. For help, dial "0" and ask for an overseas operator. The country code is 61 for Australia, 64 for New Zealand, 44 for the United Kingdom. Calling Canada is the same as calling within the United States, although you might not be able to get through on some toll-free numbers. Most local phone books list country codes and U.S. area codes. The country code for the United States is 1.

For operator assistance, dial "0." To obtain someone's phone number, call directory assistance at 555-1212 or occasionally 411 (free at many public phones). To have the person you're calling foot the bill, phone collect; dial "0" instead of "1" before the 10-digit number.

At pay phones, instructions often are posted. Usually you insert coins in a slot (usually 25¢-50¢ for local calls) and wait for a steady tone before dialing. When you call long-distance, the operator tells you how much to insert; prepaid phone cards, widely available in various denominations, are easier. Call the number on the back, punch in the card's personal identification number when prompted, then dial your number.

MAIL & SHIPPING

📮 Post Offices **San Diego Downtown** ✉ 815 E St. ☎ 619/232-8612 ⏱ Weekdays 8:30-5 📮 **La Jolla Main** ✉ 1140 Wall St. ☎ 858/459-5476 ⏱ Mon. 7:30-5, Tues.-Fri. 8:30-5, Sat. 9-1 📮 **Coronado Branch** ✉ 1320 Ynez Pl. ☎ 619/435-1160 ⏱ Weekdays 8:30-5, Sat. 8:30-noon.

OVERNIGHT SERVICES

Drop boxes for Federal Express and United Parcel Service can be found throughout the downtown area and at other locations in the county.

📦 Major Services **Federal Express** ☎ 800/463-3339 ⊕ www.fedex.com. **United Parcel Service** ☎ 800/742-5877 ⊕ www.ups.com.

MEDIA

NEWSPAPERS & MAGAZINES

San Diego's major daily newspaper is the *San Diego Union-Tribune,* and locals also read the *Los Angeles Times.* The leading weekly newspaper is the *San Diego Reader,* available free in sidewalk racks around town. *San Diego Magazine* carries monthly entertainment listings.

RADIO & TELEVISION

All the major television networks have local affiliates in San Diego including **KGTV** Channel 10, ABC; **KFMB** Channel 8, CBS; **KNSD** Channel 39, NBC; and **KPBS** Channel 15, PBS. There are also local affiliates of UPN, WB, Fox, PAX, and the Spanish-language network. Check the *San Diego Union-Tribune* for listings. Los Angeles television and radio stations can be received in many areas of the county.

Major radio stations include **KOGO-AM** 600, news–talk; **KFMB-AM** 760, CBS talk–sports; **KLSS**1360, Air America; **KPBS-FM** 89.5, National Public Radio; **XLTN-FM** 104.5, Spanish; and **STAR-FM** 100.7, adult contemporary.

MEXICO

If you're planning a side trip to nearby Mexico, **note the entry requirements** detailed in Chapter 8 (⇨ Tijuana, Playas de Rosarito & Ensenada A to Z) and customs information under For International Travelers.

MONEY MATTERS

Average prices for accommodations and food are comparable with those in Los Angeles. Expect to pay $1 to $2.50 for coffee, $6.95 for a sandwich, $4 for a beer, and $1.80 per mile for a taxi. Prices throughout this guide are given for adults. Substantially reduced fees are almost always available for children, students, and senior citizens. For information on taxes, *see* Taxes.

ATMS

Most ATMs in the San Diego area are linked to national networks that let you withdraw money from your checking account or take a cash advance from your credit card account for an additional fee. ATMs can be found at all banks and in many grocery and convenience stores. For more information on ATM locations that can be accessed with your particular account, call the phone number found on the back of your ATM or debit card.

CREDIT CARDS

Throughout this guide, the following abbreviations are used: **AE**, American Express; **D**, Discover; **DC**, Diners Club; **MC**, MasterCard; and **V**, Visa.

📶 **Reporting Lost Cards American Express** ☎ 800/992-3404. **Diners Club** ☎ 800/234-6377. **Discover** ☎ 800/347-2683. **MasterCard** ☎ 800/622-7747. **Visa** ☎ 800/ 847-2911.

NATIONAL PARKS

Look into discount passes to save money on park entrance fees. For $50, the National Parks Pass admits you (and any passengers in your private vehicle) to all national parks, monuments, and recreation areas, as well as other sites run by the National Park Service, for a year. (In parks that charge per person, the pass admits you, your spouse and children, and your parents, when you arrive together.) Camping and parking are extra. The $15 Golden Eagle Pass, a hologram you affix to your National Parks Pass, functions as an upgrade, granting entry to all sites run by the NPS, the U.S. Fish and Wildlife Service, the U.S. Forest Service, and the Bureau of Land Management. The upgrade, which expires with the parks pass, is sold by most national-park, Fish-and-Wildlife, and BLM fee stations. A major percentage of the proceeds from pass sales funds National Parks projects.

Both the Golden Age Passport ($10), for U.S. citizens or permanent residents who are 62 and older, and the Golden Access Passport (free), for persons with disabilities, entitle holders (and any passengers in their private vehicles) to lifetime free entry to all national parks, plus 50% off fees for the use of many park facilities and services. (The discount doesn't always apply to companions.) To obtain them, you must show proof of age and of U.S. citizenship or permanent residency—such as a U.S. passport, driver's license, or birth certificate—and, if requesting Golden Access, proof of disability. The Golden Age and Golden Access passes are available only at NPS-run sites that charge an entrance fee. The National Parks Pass is also available by mail and via the Internet.

�**National Park Foundation** ✉ 11 Dupont Circle NW, 6th fl., Washington, DC 20036 ☎ 202/238-4200 ⊕ www.nationalparks.org. **National Park Service** ✉ National Park Service–Department of Interior, 1849 C St. NW, Washington, DC 20240 ☎ 202/208-6843 ⊕ www.nps.gov. **National Parks Conservation Association** ✉ 1300 19th St. NW, Suite 300, Washington, DC 20036 ☎ 202/223-6722 ⊕ www.npca.org.

�**Passes by Mail & Online National Park Foundation** ⊕ www.nationalparks.org. **National Parks Pass** National Park Foundation 🕮 Box 34108, Washington, DC 20043 ☎ 888/467-2757 ⊕ www.nationalparks.org; include a check or money order payable to the National Park Service, plus $3.95 for shipping and handling (allow 8 to 13 business days from date of receipt for pass delivery), or call for passes.

PACKING

San Diego's casual lifestyle and year-round mild climate set the parameters for what to pack. You can leave formal clothes and cold-weather gear behind.

Plan on warm weather at any time of the year. Cottons, walking shorts, jeans, and T-shirts are the norm. Pack bathing suits and shorts regardless of the season. Few restaurants require a jacket and tie for men. Women may want to bring something a little dressier than their sightseeing garb.

Evenings are cool, even in summer, so be sure to bring a sweater or a light jacket. Rainfall in San Diego is not usually heavy; you won't need a raincoat except during the winter months, and even then, an umbrella may be sufficient protection. Be sure you have **comfortable walking shoes.** Even if you don't walk much at home, you'll find yourself covering miles while sightseeing on your vacation.

Sunglasses are a must in San Diego. Binoculars can also come in handy, especially if you're in town during whale-watching season from December through March.

In your carry-on luggage, pack an extra pair of eyeglasses or contact lenses and enough of any medication you take to last a few days longer than the entire trip. You may also ask your doctor to write a spare prescription (using the drug's generic name, as brand names may vary from country to country). **Never pack prescription drugs, valuables, or undeveloped film** in luggage that you intend to check. And don't forget to carry with you the addresses of offices that handle refunds of lost traveler's checks. Check *Fodor's How to Pack* (available at online retailers and bookstores everywhere) for more tips.

To avoid customs and security delays, carry medications in their original packaging. Don't pack any sharp objects in your carry-on luggage, including knives of any size or material, scissors, nail clippers, and corkscrews, or anything else that might arouse suspicion.

To avoid having your checked luggage chosen for hand inspection, don't cram bags full. The U.S. Transportation Security Administration suggests packing shoes on top and placing personal items you don't want touched in clear plastic bags.

CHECKING LUGGAGE

You're allowed to carry aboard one bag and one personal article, such as a purse or a laptop computer. Your carry-on bag must fit under the seat in front of you or be placed in an overhead bin. Get to the gate early, so you can board as soon as possible, before the overhead bins fill up.

Baggage allowances vary by carrier, destination, and ticket class. On international flights, you're usually allowed to check two bags weighing up to 70 pounds (32 kilograms) each, although a few airlines allow checked bags of up to 88 pounds (40 kilograms) in first class. Some international carriers don't allow more than 66 pounds (30 kilograms) per bag in business class and 44 pounds (20 kilograms) in economy. If you're flying to or through the United Kingdom, your luggage cannot exceed 70 pounds (32 kilograms) per bag. On domestic flights, the limit is usually 50 to 70 pounds (23 to 32 kilograms) per bag. In general, carry-on bags shouldn't exceed 40 pounds (18 kilograms). Most airlines won't accept bags that weigh more than 100 pounds (45 kilograms) on domestic or international flights. Expect to pay a fee for baggage that exceeds weight limits. Check baggage restrictions with your carrier before you pack.

Airline liability for baggage is limited to $2,500 per person on flights within the United States. On international flights it amounts to $9.07 per pound or $20 per kilogram for checked baggage (roughly $640 per 70-pound bag), with a maximum of $634.90 per piece, and $400 per passenger for unchecked baggage. You can buy additional coverage at check-in for about $10 per $1,000 of coverage, but it often excludes a rather extensive list of items, shown on your airline ticket.

Before departure, itemize your bags' contents and their worth, and label the bags with your name, address, and phone number. (If you use your home address, cover it so potential thieves can't see it readily.) Include a label inside each bag and **pack a copy of your itinerary.** At check-in, make sure each bag is correctly tagged with the destination airport's three-letter code. Because some checked bags will be opened for hand inspection, the U.S. Transportation Security Administration recommends that you leave luggage unlocked or use the plastic locks offered at check-in. TSA screeners place an inspection notice inside searched bags, which are re-sealed with a special lock.

If your bag has been searched and contents are missing or damaged, file a claim with the TSA Consumer Response Center as soon as possible. If your bags arrive damaged or fail to arrive at all, file a written report with the airline before leaving the airport.

⑦ Complaints U.S. Transportation Security Administration Contact Center ☎ 866/289–9673 ⊕ www.tsa.gov.

PASSPORTS & VISAS
When traveling internationally, carry your passport even if you don't need one (it's always the best form of ID) and **make two photocopies of the data page** (one for someone at home and another for you, to be carried separately from your passport). If you lose your passport, promptly call the nearest embassy or consulate and the local police.

U.S. passport applications for children under age 14 require consent from both parents or legal guardians; both parents must appear together to sign the application. If only one parent appears, he or she must submit a written statement from the other parent authorizing passport issuance for the child. A parent with sole authority must present evidence of it when applying; acceptable documentation includes the child's certified birth certificate listing only the applying parent, a court order specifically permitting this parent's travel with the child, or a death certificate for the nonapplying parent. Application forms and instructions are available on the Web site of the U.S. State Department's Bureau of Consular Affairs (⊕ travel.state.gov).

REST ROOMS
Major attractions and parks have public restrooms. In the downtown San Diego area, you can usually use the restrooms at major hotels and fast-food restaurants.

SAFETY
San Diego is generally a safe place for travelers who observe all normal precautions. Dress inconspicuously, remove badges when leaving convention areas, know the routes to your destination before you set out. At the beach check with lifeguards about any unsafe conditions such as dangerous rip tides or water pollution. The San Diego Convention & Visitors Bureau publishes a Visitor Safety Tips brochure listing normal precautions for many situations. It's available at the International Visitor Information Center.

SENIOR-CITIZEN TRAVEL
To qualify for age-related discounts, mention your senior-citizen status up front when booking hotel reservations (not when checking out) and before you're seated in restaurants (not when paying the bill). Be sure to have identification on hand. When renting a car, ask about pro-

motional car-rental discounts, which can be cheaper than senior-citizen rates.

⚏ Educational Programs Elderhostel ✉ 11 Ave. de Lafayette, Boston, MA 02111 ☎ 877/426-8056, 978/323-4141 international callers, 877/426-2167 TTY ⚎ 877/426-2166 ⊕ www.elderhostel.org.

SIGHTSEEING TOURS

BALLOON TOURS

Weather permitting, hot-air balloons lift off from various coastal locations in San Diego's North County and the Temecula wine country in adjoining Riverside County; the average cost is $155 to $208 per person. Flights float at sunrise in Temecula and at sunset in the Del Mar area.

⚏ California Dreamin' Balloon Adventure ✉ 33133 Vista Del Monte, Suite F35, Temecula ☎ 800/373-3359 ⊕ www.californiadreamin.com. **A Skysurfer Balloon Company** ✉ 2658 Del Mar Heights Rd. #198, Del Mar ☎ 858/481-6800 or 800/660-6809 ⊕ www.sandiegohotairballoons.com.

BOAT TOURS

San Diego Harbor Excursion and Hornblower Cruises & Events both operate one- and two-hour harbor cruises departing from the Broadway Pier. No reservations are necessary for the tours, which cost $15–$20; both companies also do dinner cruises ($55–$75) and brunch cruises. Classic Sailing Adventures, at Shelter Island Marina, has afternoon and evening cruises of the harbor and San Diego Bay aboard six-passenger sailing ships ($65 per person). These companies also operate during whale-watching season, from mid-December to mid-March. Other fishing boats that do whale watches in season include H&M Landing and Seaforth Sportfishing.

⚏ Classic Sailing Adventures ✉ 1220 Rosecrans St., No. 137 ☎ 800/659-0141 ⊕ www.classicsailingadventures.com. **Hornblower Cruises & Events** ✉ 1066 N. Harbor Dr. ☎ 619/234-8687 ⊕ www.hornblower.com. **San Diego Harbor Excursion** ✉ 1050 N. Harbor Dr. ☎ 619/234-4111 or 800/442-7847 ⊕ www.harborexcursion.com. **H&M Landing** ✉ 2803 Emerson St., Point Loma ☎ 619/222-1144 ⊕ www.hmlanding.com. **Seaforth Sportfishing** ✉ 1641 Quivira Rd. ☎ 619/223-1681 ⊕ www.seaforthboatrental.com.

BUS & TROLLEY TOURS

Free two-hour bus tours of the downtown redevelopment area, including the Gaslamp Quarter, are conducted by Centre City Development Corporation's Downtown Information Center. Tours take place on the first and third Saturday of the month at 10 AM and noon. Advance reservations are necessary. The tour may be canceled if there aren't enough passengers.

Contactours provides narrated sightseeing tours, picking up passengers at many hotels; tours include San Diego as well as Tijuana, the San Diego Zoo, Wild Animal Park, and SeaWorld. Old Town Trolley Tours take you to eight sites including Old Town, Seaport Village, Horton Plaza and the Gaslamp Quarter, Coronado, the San Diego Zoo, and El Prado in Balboa Park. The tour is narrated, and for the price of the ticket ($25 for adults and $13.50 for children 4–12; under 4, free) you can get on and off as you please at any stop. The trolley leaves every 30 minutes, operates daily, and takes two hours to make a full loop. The Old Town Trolley Tour is included in the price of the San Diego Passport, along with one Hornblower cruise, admission to the San Diego Zoo, the Maritime Museum, the San Diego Museum of Art, and other goodies for a total package price of $79. The passport is available at visitors centers and is good for one year.

⚏ Centre City Development Corporation Downtown Information Center ✉ 225 Broadway, Suite 160 ☎ 619/235-2222 ⊕ www.ccdc.com or www.sandiegodowntown.org. **Contactours** ✉ 1726 Wilson Ave., National City ☎ 619/477-8687 ⊕ www.contactours.com. **Old Town Trolley Tours** ✉ 4010 Twiggs St. ☎ 619/298-8687 ⊕ www.trolleytours.com.

WALKING TOURS

Several fine walking tours are available on weekdays or weekends; upcoming walks are usually listed in the Thursday Night and Day section of the *San Diego Union-Tribune*. Coronado Walking Tours offers an easy 90-minute stroll ($12, Tuesday, Thursday, Saturday at 11 AM) through Coronado's historic district with departures from the Glorietta Bay Inn. Make reservations. On Saturday at 10 AM and

11:30 AM, Offshoot Tours conducts free, hour-long walks through Balboa Park that focus on history, palm trees, and desert vegetation. Urban Safaris, led by long-time San Diego resident Patty Fares, are two-hour-long Saturday walks ($10) through interesting neighborhoods such as Hillcrest, Ocean Beach, and Point Loma. The tours, which always depart from a neighborhood coffee house, focus on art, history, and ethnic eateries. Reservations are required. The Gaslamp Quarter Historical Foundation leads two-hour historical walking tours of the downtown historic district on Saturday at 11 AM ($8).

7 Coronado Walking Tours ⊠ Glorietta Bay Inn Coronado ☎ 619/435–5993. **Offshoot Tours** ⊠ Balboa Park, Downtown ☎ 619/239–0512 ⊕ www.balboapark.org. **Urban Safaris** ☎ 619/944–9255 ⊕ www.walkingtoursofsandiego.com. **Gaslamp Quarter Historical Foundation** ⊠ 410 Island Ave. ☎ 619/233–4692 ⊕ www.gaslampquarter.org.

SMOKING

California has become distinctly hostile to smokers, even when they want to puff peacefully in the open air. The newest laws require those smoking outside office buildings to be at least 30 feet from the nearest entrance. Smoking is banned even in the seating area of outdoor stadiums, but there are designated areas (generally outside the main structure) where it's possible to smoke without breaking the law. Note that some restaurant patios do permit cigarettes. But smoking indoors, other than in private residences and designated hotel rooms, is illegal, even in bars. The luxurious Westgate Hotel now bans smoking anywhere indoors, including guest rooms.

STUDENTS IN SAN DIEGO

San Diego State University (SDSU) is just east of Mission Bay, not to be confused with the University of California at San Diego (UCSD) in northern La Jolla. Most museums and other attractions have a discounted rate for students with identification.

7 IDs & Services STA Travel ⊠ 10 Downing St., New York, NY 10014 ☎ 212/627–3111, 800/777–0112 24-hr service center ☎ 212/627–3387 ⊕ www.sta.com. **Travel Cuts** ⊠ 187 College St., Toronto, Ontario M5T 1P7, Canada ☎ 800/592–2887 in the U.S.,

416/979–2406 or 866/246–9762 in Canada ☎ 416/979–8167 ⊕ www.travelcuts.com.

TAXES
SALES TAX

In San Diego County a sales tax of 7.75% is added to the price of all goods, except food purchased at a grocery store or as take-out from a restaurant. Hotel taxes are 9%–13%.

TAXIS

Taxis departing from the airport are subject to regulated fares—all companies charge the same rate ($1.80 for the first mile, $1.20 for each additional mile). Fares on other routes, including the ride back to the airport, vary among companies. If you call ahead and ask for the flat rate ($8), you'll get it; otherwise you'll be charged by the mile (which works out to $9 or so). Taxi stands are located at shopping centers and hotels; otherwise you must call and reserve a cab. The companies listed below do not serve all areas of San Diego County. If you're going someplace other than downtown, **ask if the company serves that area.**

7 Taxi Companies Orange Cab ☎ 619/291–3333 ⊕ www.orangecabsandiego.com. **Silver Cabs** ☎ 619/280–5555. **Yellow Cab** ☎ 619/234–6161 ⊕ www.driveu.com.

TIME

San Diego is in the Pacific time zone. Pacific Daylight Time is in effect from early April through late October; Pacific Standard Time, the rest of the year. Clocks are set ahead one hour when Daylight Time begins, back one hour when it ends.

TIPPING

At restaurants, a 15%–20% tip is standard for waiters, depending on the level of service provided. The same goes for taxi drivers, bartenders, and hairdressers. Coat-check operators usually expect $1; bellhops and porters should get 50¢ to $1 per bag; hotel maids should get about $1 per day of your stay—$2 in upscale hotels. A concierge typically receives a tip of $5 to $10, with an additional gratuity for special services or favors. On package tours, conductors and drivers usually get $10 per day from the group as a whole; check whether this has already been figured into your cost. For local sightseeing tours, you may individually tip the driver-guide $1 if he or she has been helpful or informative. Ushers in theaters do not expect tips.

TOURS & PACKAGES

Because everything is prearranged on a packaged tour or independent vacation, you spend less time planning—and often get it all at a good price.

BOOKING WITH AN AGENT

Travel agents are excellent resources. But it's a good idea to collect brochures from several agencies, as some agents' suggestions may be influenced by relationships with tour and package firms that reward them for volume sales. If you have a special interest, find an agent with expertise in that area. The American Society of Travel Agents (ASTA) has a database of specialists worldwide; you can log on to the group's Web site to find one near you.

Make sure your travel agent knows the accommodations and other services of the place being recommended. Ask about the hotel's location, room size, beds, and whether it has a pool, room service, or programs for children, if you care about these. Has your agent been there in person or sent others whom you can contact?

Do some homework on your own, too: local tourism boards can provide information about lesser-known and small-niche operators, some of which may sell only direct to the consumer and not through a travel agency.

BUYER BEWARE

Each year consumers are stranded or lose their money when tour operators—even large ones with excellent reputations—go out of business. So check out any tour operator whose package you are considering using. Ask several travel agents about its reputation, and try to **book with a company that has a consumer-protection program.** (Look for information in the company's brochure.) In the United States, members of the United States Tour Operators Association are required to set aside funds (up to $1 million) to help compen-

sate eligible customers in the event a member company defaults. It's also a good idea to choose a company that participates in the American Society of Travel Agents' Tour Operator Program; ASTA will act as mediator in any disputes between you and your tour operator.

Remember that the more your package includes, the better you can predict the ultimate cost of your vacation. Make sure you know exactly what is covered, and beware of hidden costs. Are taxes, tips, and transfers included? Entertainment and excursions? These can add up.

🈺 Tour-Operator Recommendations American Society of Travel Agents (⇨ Travel Agencies). **National Tour Association** ✉ 546 E. Main St., Lexington, KY 40508 ☎ 859/226-4444 or 800/682-8886 🖷 859/226-4404 ⊕ www.ntaonline.com. **United States Tour Operators Association** (USTOA) ✉ 275 Madison Ave., Suite 2014, New York, NY 10016 ☎ 212/599-6599 🖷 212/599-6744 ⊕ www. ustoa.com.

TRAIN TRAVEL TO & FROM SAN DIEGO

Amtrak serves downtown San Diego's Santa Fe Depot with daily trains to and from Los Angeles, Santa Barbara, and San Luis Obispo. Connecting service to Oakland, Seattle, Chicago, Texas, Florida, and points beyond is available in Los Angeles. Amtrak trains stop in San Diego North County at Solana Beach and Oceanside.

Coaster commuter trains, which run between Oceanside and San Diego Monday–Saturday and northbound on some Friday nights, stop at the same stations as Amtrak plus others. The Oceanside, Carlsbad, and Solana Beach stations have beach access. You can pick up Coaster flyers or brochures with detailed itineraries for each stop, including walking directions and connections to local bus service. Trains are typically on time.

Metrolink operates high-speed rail service between the Oceanside Transit Center and Union Station in Los Angeles.

FARES & SCHEDULES

You can obtain Amtrak timetables at any Amtrak station, or by visiting the Amtrak Web site.

The Coaster runs between Oceanside and San Diego about every half hour during the rush hours on weekdays. There are four trains on Saturday, none on Sunday. The Coaster occasionally offers Friday evening northbound service from downtown. One-way fares are $3.75 to $5.25, depending on the distance traveled.

🚆 Train Information Amtrak ☎ 800/872-7245 ⊕ www.amtrak.com. Coaster ☎ 800/266-6883 ⊕ www.sdcommute.com. Metrolink ☎ 800/371-5465. Oceanside train station ☎ 760/722-4622. Santa Fe Depot ⊠ 1050 Kettner Blvd. ☎ 619/239-9021. Solana Beach Amtrak station ☎ 858/259-2697.

PAYING

Amtrak and the Coaster vending machines accept all major credit cards. Metrolink requires cash.

RESERVATIONS

Many Amtrak trains require advance reservations, especially for long-distance transcontinental routes. Reservations, which you can make online, are suggested for trains running on weekends between San Diego and Santa Barbara. For security reasons, Amtrak requires ticket purchasers to appear in person with photo ID.

TRANSPORTATION AROUND SAN DIEGO

Most of San Diego was laid out after the invention of the automobile, so a car is a necessity for most visitors. Though public transportation serves most of the major attractions, getting from one place to another—from downtown to the beaches north of La Jolla, for instance—can take a long time. Two exceptions are the San Diego Trolley, which can save you time if you're heading from downtown to Old Town or Qualcomm Stadium, or to the Mexican border, and the Coronado Ferry, the scenic route from the harbor to Coronado. Public transportation agencies have integrated their services in an effort to provide convenient connections between rail and bus travel throughout San Diego County. Information on getting from one place to another is available at the Web site of the Metropolitan Transit System,

⊕ www.sdcommute.com or calling ☎ 800/266-6883.

Smoking is prohibited on all forms of public transport in California.

TRAVEL AGENCIES

A good travel agent puts your needs first. Look for an agency that has been in business at least five years, emphasizes customer service, and has someone on staff who specializes in your destination. In addition, **make sure the agency belongs to a professional trade organization.** The American Society of Travel Agents (ASTA) has more than 10,000 members in some 140 countries, enforces a strict code of ethics, and will step in to mediate agent-client disputes involving ASTA members. A directory of ASTA agents can be found on its Web site; ASTA's TravelSense.org, a trip planning and travel advice site, can also help to locate a travel agent who caters to your needs. (If a travel agency is also acting as your tour operator, see Buyer Beware in Tours & Packages.)

🚆 Local Agent Referrals American Society of Travel Agents (ASTA) ⊠ 1101 King St., Suite 200, Alexandria, VA 22314 ☎ 703/739-2782 or 800/965-2782 24-hr hotline 🖶 703/684-8319 ⊕ www.astanet.com and www.travelsense.org. Association of British Travel Agents ⊠ 68-71 Newman St., London W1T 3AH ☎ 020/7637-2444 🖶 020/7637-0713 ⊕ www.abta.com. Association of Canadian Travel Agencies ⊠ 130 Albert St., Suite 1705, Ottawa, Ontario K1P 5G4 ☎ 613/237-3657 🖶 613/237-7052 ⊕ www.acta.ca. Australian Federation of Travel Agents ⊠ Level 3, 309 Pitt St., Sydney, NSW 2000 ☎ 02/9264-3299 or 1300/363-416 🖶 02/9264-1085 ⊕ www.afta.com.au. Travel Agents' Association of New Zealand ⊠ Level 5, Tourism and Travel House, 79 Boulcott St., Box 1888, Wellington 6001 ☎ 04/499-0104 🖶 04/499-0786 ⊕ www.taanz.org.nz.

TROLLEY TRAVEL

The bright-orange trolleys of the San Diego Trolley light rail system serve downtown San Diego, Mission Valley, Old Town, South Bay, the U.S. border, and East County. The trolleys operate seven days a week from about 5 AM to midnight, depending on the station, at intervals of about 15 minutes. The trolley system connects with San Diego Transit bus routes—bus connections are posted at each trolley station. Bicycle lockers are available at most. Trolleys can get crowded during morning and evening rush hours. On-time performance is excellent.

FARES & SCHEDULES

San Diego Trolley tickets are priced according to the number of stations traveled, beginning at $1.25 for travel within the downtown area and rising to $1.50 for one station, $1.75 for two stations, and up to $3 for 20 stations. Within the downtown area, tickets are good for two hours of unlimited travel in any direction from the time of purchase. Beyond the downtown area they are good for two hours, but for one-way travel only. Round-trip tickets are double the one-way fare. Tickets are dispensed from self-service ticket machines at each stop; exact fare in coins is recommended, although some machines accept bills in $1, $5, $10, and $20 denominations. Transfers between buses and/or the trolley are free or require an upgrade if the second fare is higher.

Day Tripper passes, available for one, two, three, or four days ($5, $9, $12, and $15, respectively), give unlimited rides on regional buses and the San Diego Trolley. They may be purchased from most trolley vending machines, at the Transit Store, and at some hotels.

🚹 Trolley Information **San Diego Transit** ☎ 619/233-3004, 619/234-5005 TTY, TDD ⊕ www.sdcommute.com for city transit and San Diego Trolley.

VISITOR INFORMATION

For general information and brochures before you go, contact the San Diego Convention & Visitors Bureau, which publishes the helpful *San Diego Official Visitors Planning Guide* and *San Diego Visitors Pocket Guide*. When you arrive, stop by one of the local visitors centers for general information. Any written correspondence should me mailed to the B Street address.

🚹 City-Wide **San Diego Convention & Visitors Bureau International Visitor Information Center** ☒ 1040 1/3 W. Broadway at the Cruise Ship termi-

nal, San Diego ☎ 619/236-1212 ⊕ www.sandiego.org ☒ **La Jolla Visitor Center** ☒ 7966 Herschel Ave. at Prospect St. ☎ 619/236-1212 ⊕ www.sandiego.org ☒ 401 B St., Suite 1400, San Diego 92101.

🚹 Local Information **Balboa Park Visitors Center** ☒ 1549 El Prado ☎ 619/239-0512 ⊕ www.balboapark.org, open daily 9–4. **San Diego Visitor Information Center** ☒ 2688 E. Mission Bay Dr., off I-5 at Clairemont Dr. exit ☎ 619/276-8200 for recorded information ⊕ www.infosandiego.com, open daily 9–dusk.

🚹 San Diego County **Borrego Springs Chamber of Commerce and Visitors Center** ☒ 786 Palm Canyon Dr., 92004 ☎ 760/767-5555 ⊕ www.borregosprings.org. **Carlsbad Convention & Visitors Bureau** ☒ 400 Carlsbad Village Dr., 92008 ☎ 800/227-5722 ⊕ www.visitcarlsbad.com. **Chula Vista Convention & Visitors Bureau** ☒ 750 E. St., 91910 ☎ 619/425-4444 ⊕ www.chulavistaconvis.com. **Coronado Visitor Center** ☒ 1100 Orange Ave., 92118 ☎ 619/437-8788 ⊕ www.coronadovisitorcenter.com. **Del Mar Regional Chamber of Commerce** ☒ 1104 Camino del Mar, 92014 ☎ 858/793-5292 ⊕ www.delmarchamber.org. **Encinitas Chamber of Commerce** ☒ 138 Encinitas Blvd., 92024 ☎ 760/753-6041 ⊕ www.encinitaschamber.com. **Julian Chamber of Commerce** ☒ 2129 Main St., 92036 ☎ 760/765-1857 ⊕ www.julianca.com. **Promote La Jolla, Inc.** ☒ 1150 Silverado St., No. 202, 92037 ☎ 858/454-5718 ⊕ www.lajollabythesea.com. **California Welcome Center Oceanside** ☒ 928 N. Coast Hwy., 92054 ☎ 760/721-1011 or 800/350-7873 ⊕ www.oceansidechamber.com. **San Diego East Visitors Bureau** ☒ 5005 Willows Rd., No. 208, Alpine 91901 ☎ 619/445-0180 or 800/463-0668 ⊕ www.visitsandiegoeast.com. **San Diego North Convention & Visitors Bureau** ☒ 360 N. Escondido Blvd., Escondido 92025 ☎ 760/745-4741 or 800/848-3336 ⊕ www.sandiegonorth.com.

🚹 Statewide **California Travel and Tourism Commission** ☒ 980 Ninth St., Suite 480, Sacramento, CA 95814 ☎ 916/444-4429 or 800/862-2543 ⊕ www.visitcalifornia.com.

🚹 In the U.K. **California Tourist Office** ⌖ ABC California, Box 35, Abingdon, Oxfordshire OX14 4TB ☎ 0891/200-278. Calls cost 50p per minute peak rate or 45p per minute cheap rate; send check for £3 for brochures.

🚹 Government Advisories **Consular Affairs Bureau of Canada** ☎ 800/267-6788 or 613/944-6788 ⊕ www.voyage.gc.ca. **U.K. Foreign and Common-**

wealth Office ✉ Travel Advice Unit, Consular Direc-torate, Old Admiralty Bldg., London SW1A 2PA ☎ 0870/606-0290 or 020/7008-1500 ⊕ www.fco.gov.uk/travel. **Australian Department of Foreign Affairs and Trade** ☎ 300/139-281 travel advisories, 02/6261-1299 Consular Travel Advice ⊕ www.smartraveller.gov.au or www.dfat.gov.au. **New Zealand Ministry of Foreign Affairs and Trade** ☎ 04/439-8000 ⊕ www.mft.govt.nz.

WEB SITES

Do check out the World Wide Web when planning your trip. You'll find everything from weather forecasts to virtual tours of famous cities. Be sure to visit Fodors.com (⊕ www.fodors.com), a complete travel-planning site. You can research prices and book plane tickets, hotel rooms, rental cars, vacation packages, and more. In addition, you can post your pressing questions in the Travel Talk section. Other planning tools include a currency converter and weather reports, and there are loads of links to travel resources.

The California Department of Parks & Recreation site, ⊕ www.parks.ca.gov, has information about state-run parks in the San Diego area. The National Park Service site, ⊕ www.nps.gov, has listings about all San Diego–area parks and other lands administered by the park service. The Web site ⊕ www.sandiegohistory.org is a wonderful site covering San Diego's history, buildings, and personalities with articles, archival photos, links, and more. The San Diego Zoo and the Wild Animal Park maintain ⊕ www.sandiegozoo.org, which has up-to-the-minute reports on new facilities, animal guests, and Webcams on the giant pandas.

Homeport San Diego's Web page, ⊕ www.homeport-sd.com, carries regional weather and other information. *San Diego Magazine's* ⊕ www.sandiegomag.com carries feature stories about the city and capsule dining reviews. The site of the *San Diego Reader,* ⊕ www.sdreader.com, isn't visually impressive, but it provides a thorough guide to dining, nightlife, and the arts. The *San Diego Union-Tribune* operates ⊕ www.signonsandiego.com, which does a good job covering local shopping and dining.

Exploring
San Diego

WORD OF MOUTH

"The Zoo (in my opinion) is a must! It was our favorite part of the trip. . . . We LOVED San Diego . . . everyone was so nice."

—travelmonkey

"San Diego is one of the most interesting places in the USA to visit. We loved to look at the incoming ships and drive the coast."

—JJ5

"Point Loma is a must-see. Terrific views, a neat old lighthouse, and some great tide pools."

—J_Correa

"Take film [to Point Loma]. You'll get some nice pics of your kids with all of SD as your back-drop."

—Kal

By Edie Jarolim

Updated by
Lenore Greiner

EXPLORING SAN DIEGO MAY BE AN ENDLESS ADVENTURE, but there are limitations, especially if you don't have a car. San Diego is more a chain of separate communities than a cohesive city, and many of the major attractions are separated by some distance. Walking is good for getting an up-close look at how San Diegans live, but true Southern Californians use the freeways that crisscross the county. Interstate 5 runs a direct north–south route through the coastal communities from Orange County in the north to the Mexican border. Interstates 805 and 15 do much the same inland. Interstate 8 is the main east–west route. Routes 163, 52, and 94 serve as connectors.

If you're going to drive around San Diego, study the map before you hit the road. The freeways are convenient and fast most of the time, but if you miss your turnoff or get caught in commuter traffic, you'll experience a none-too-pleasurable hallmark of Southern California living—freeway madness. Drivers rush around on a complex freeway system with the same fervor they use for jogging scores of marathons each year. They particularly enjoy speeding up at interchanges and entrance and exit ramps. Be sure you know where you're going before you join the chase.

Public transportation has improved a great deal in the past decade: the San Diego Trolley has expanded from Old Town to beyond Mission Valley, ending near Mission San Diego; a commuter line called the *Coaster* runs from Oceanside into downtown; and the bus system covers almost all of the county. However, it's time-consuming to make the connections necessary to see the various sights. Fashion Valley shopping center in Mission Valley is one of the three major bus transfer points—downtown and Old Town are the others—but because many of the city's major attractions are along the coast, and because the coast is itself a major attraction, you'll be best off staying there if you're carless. The bike-path system is extensive and well marked, the weather is almost always bicycle-friendly, and lots of buses have bike racks, so two-wheeling is a good option for the athletic. The large distances between sights render taxis prohibitively expensive for general transportation, although cabs are useful for getting around once you're in a given area. Old Town Trolley Historic Tours has a hop-on, hop-off route of eight popular spots around the city, but it takes so long to cover the route that you're unlikely to see more than two areas in one day (fortunately, a two-day trolley pass is available).

San Diego County's warm climate nurtures some amazing flora. Golden stalks of pampas grass grow in wild patches near SeaWorld. Bougainvilleas cover roofs and hillsides in La Jolla, spreading magenta blankets over whitewashed adobe walls. Towering palms and twisted junipers are far more common than maples or oaks, and fields of wild daisies and chamomile cover dry, dusty lots. Red-and-white poinsettias proliferate at Christmas, and candy-colored pink- and yellow-flowered ice plants edge the roads year-round. Jasmine blooms on bushes and vines in front yards and parking lots; birds-of-paradise poke up straight and tall, tropical testimonials to San Diego's temperate ways. Citrus groves pop up in unlikely places, along the freeways and back roads. When the orange, lemon, and lime trees bloom in spring, the fragrance of their tiny white

blossoms is nearly overpowering. Be sure to drive with your windows down—you'll be amazed at the sweet, hypnotic scent.

Unless you're on the freeway, it's hard *not* to find a scenic drive in San Diego, but an officially designated 52-mi Scenic Drive over much of central San Diego begins at the foot of Broadway. Road signs with a white sea gull on a yellow-and-blue background direct the way through the Embarcadero to Harbor and Shelter islands, Point Loma and Cabrillo Monument, Mission Bay, Old Town, Balboa Park, Mount Soledad, and La Jolla. It's best to take this three-hour drive, outlined on some local maps, on the weekend, when the commuters are off the road.

BALBOA PARK

Overlooking downtown and the Pacific Ocean, 1,200-acre Balboa Park is the cultural heart of San Diego. Ranked as one of the world's best parks by the Project for Public Spaces in 2004, it's the place where you can find most of the city's museums and its world-famous zoo. Most first-time visitors see only these attractions, but Balboa Park is really a series of botanical gardens. Thanks to the "Mother of Balboa Park," Kate Sessions, who first suggested hiring a landscape architect in 1889, gardens both cultivated and wild are an integral part of Balboa Park. Sessions—a bronze statue of her stands at Sefton Plaza at the park's west entrance—made sure both the park's developed and undeveloped acreage bloomed with the purple blossoms of the jacaranda tree, and she planted thousands of palms and other trees throughout. What Balboa Park would have looked like had she left it alone can be seen at Florida Canyon (between the main park and Morley Field, along Park Boulevard)—an arid landscape of sagebrush, cactus, and a few small trees.

Land for what was then known as City Park was set aside by the city's founders in 1868. Rechristened in 1910, the park hosted the Panama–California International Exposition, celebrating the opening of the Panama Canal in 1915, and gained some Spanish colonial revival buildings meant to be temporary exhibit halls. City leaders realized the buildings' value, however, and instead of tearing them down afterward, incorporated them into their plans for a second exposition in Balboa Park, the California–Pacific International Exposition of 1935–36. The Spanish theme instituted in the early 1900s was in part carried through in new buildings designed for the later exposition, although architectural details from the temples of the Maya and other indigenous peoples of the Americas were added.

The historic buildings dating from San Diego's 1915 expo are strung along the park's main east–west thoroughfare, El Prado, which leads from 6th Avenue eastward over the Laurel Street Bridge (also known as the Cabrillo Bridge), the park's official gateway. In recent years, many of the buildings on El Prado have undergone major restoration or complete historic reconstruction. The 100-bell carillon in the California Tower, El Prado's highest structure, tolls the hour; figures of California's historic personages decorate the base of the 200-foot spire, and a magnificent blue-tile dome shines in the sun.

The parkland across the Cabrillo Bridge, at the west end of El Prado, has been set aside for picnics and athletics. Rollerbladers zip along Balboa Drive, which leads to the highest spot in the park, Marston Point, overlooking downtown. At the green beside the bridge, ladies and gents in all-white outfits meet regularly on summer afternoons for lawn-bowling tournaments—a throwback to an earlier era. Dirt trails lead into pine groves with secluded picnic areas.

East of Plaza de Panama, El Prado becomes a pedestrian mall and ends at a footbridge that crosses over Park Boulevard, the park's main north–south thoroughfare, to the perfectly tended Rose Garden, which has more than 2,000 rosebushes. In the adjacent Cactus Garden, trails wind around prickly cacti and soft green succulents from around the world. Palm Canyon, north of the Spreckels Organ Pavilion, has more than 50 varieties of palms along a shady bridge. Pepper Grove, along Park Boulevard south of the museums, has lots of picnic tables as well as play equipment.

The size, scope, and diversity of Balboa Park's attractions make it necessary to spend a few days' time to adequately explore everything. For an in-depth look at the park's history and hidden treasures, consult *Discover Balboa Park: A Complete Guide to America's Greatest Urban Park*, by Pamela Crooks, available at the visitor center in the House of Hospitality.

Parking near Balboa Park's museums is no small accomplishment, especially on sunny summer days, when the lots, which are all free, fill up quickly. If you're driving in via the Laurel Street Bridge, the first parking area you come to is off El Prado to the right, going toward Pan American Plaza. Don't despair if there are no spaces here; you'll see more lots as you continue along the same road. If you end up parking a bit far from your destination, consider the stroll back through the greenery part of the day's recreation. Alternatively, you can just park at Inspiration Point on the east side of the park, off Presidents Way. Free trams run from there to the museums every 8–10 minutes, 9:30–5:30 daily.

Numbers in the text correspond to numbers in the margin and on the Balboa Park map.

Two Good Walks

It's impossible to cover all the park's museums in one day, so choose your focus before you head out. If your interests run to the aesthetic, the Museum of Photographic Arts, the San Diego Museum of Art, the Mingei International Museum of Folk Art, and the Timken Museum of Art should be on your list; architecture buffs will want to add the Marston House. Those with a penchant for natural and cultural history shouldn't miss the San Diego Natural History Museum and the Museum of Man; folks oriented toward space and technology should see the Reuben H. Fleet Science Center, the San Diego Aerospace Museum, and the San Diego Automotive Museum. If you're traveling with kids, the Mingei and Reuben H. Fleet are musts, as is catching a show at the Marie Hitchcock Puppet Theater.

On a nice day, you might just want to stroll outside and enjoy the architecture of the museum complex, with its wonderful Spanish and Mexican designs. A walk along El Prado is about 1 mi round-trip.

Enter via Cabrillo Bridge through the West Gate, which depicts the Panama Canal's linkage of the Atlantic and Pacific oceans. Park south of the **Alcazar Garden ❶** ☞. It's a short stretch north across El Prado to the landmark California Building, modeled on a cathedral in Mexico and now home to the **San Diego Museum of Man ❷**. Look up to see busts and statues of heroes of the early days of the state carved on the facade. Next door are the **Globe Theatres ❸**, which adjoin the sculpture garden of the **San Diego Museum of Art ❹**, an ornate Plateresque-style structure built to resemble the 17th-century University of Salamanca in Spain.

Continuing east you'll come to the **Timken Museum of Art ❺**, the **Botanical Building ❻**, and the Spanish colonial revival–style Casa del Prado, where the San Diego Floral Association has its offices and a gift shop. At the end of the row is the **San Diego Natural History Museum ❼**; you'll have to detour a block north to visit the **Spanish Village Art Center ❽**. If you were to continue north, you would come to the **carousel ❾**, the **miniature railroad ❿**, and, finally, the entrance to the **San Diego Zoo ⓫**.

Return to the Natural History Museum and cross the Plaza de Balboa—its large central fountain is a popular meeting spot—to reach the **Reuben H. Fleet Science Center ⓬**. (Beyond the parking lot to the south lies the **Centro Cultural de la Raza ⓭**.) You're now on the opposite side of the Prado and heading west. You'll next pass **Casa de Balboa ⓮**; inside are the model-railroad and photography museums and the historical society. Next door in the **House of Hospitality ⓯** is the Balboa Park Visitors Center, where you can buy a reduced-price pass to the museums, and the Prado restaurant. Across the Plaza de Panama, the Franciscan mission–style **House of Charm ⓰** houses a folk art museum and a gallery for San Diego artists. Your starting point, the Alcazar Garden, is west of the House of Charm.

A second walk leads south from the Plaza de Panama, which doubles as a parking lot. The majority of the buildings along this route date from the 1935 fair, when the architecture of the Maya and native peoples of the Southwest was highlighted. The first sight you'll pass is the **Japanese Friendship Garden ⓱**. Next comes the ornate, crownlike **Spreckels Organ Pavilion ⓲**, with the round seating area forming the base and the stage as its diadem. The road forks here; veer to the left to reach the **House of Pacific Relations ⓳**, a Spanish mission–style cluster of cottages and one of the few structures on this route built for the earlier exposition. Another is the Balboa Park Club, which you'll pass next. Now used for park receptions and banquets, the building resembles a mission church; you might want to step inside to see the huge mural. Continue on beyond the Palisades Building, which hosts the **Marie Hitchcock Puppet Theater ⓴**, to reach the **San Diego Automotive Museum ㉑**, which, appropriately, is in the building that served as the Palace of Transportation in the 1935–36 exposition.

The road loops back at the spaceshiplike **San Diego Aerospace Museum and International Aerospace Hall of Fame** ㉒. As you head north again you'll notice the Starlight Bowl, an amphitheater on your right. Next comes perhaps the most impressive structure on this tour, the Federal Building, the home of the **San Diego Hall of Champions** ㉓. Its main entrance was modeled after the Palace of Governors in the ancient Mayan city of Uxmal, Mexico. You'll be back at the Spreckels Organ Pavilion after this, having walked a little less than a mile.

TIMING Unless you're pressed for time, you'll want to devote an entire day to the perpetually expanding zoo; there are more than enough exhibits to keep you occupied for five or more hours, and you're likely to be too tired for museum-hopping when you're through.

Although some of the park's museums are open on Monday, most are open Tuesday–Sunday 10–4; in summer a number have extended hours—phone ahead to ask. On Tuesday the museums have free admission to their permanent exhibits on a rotating basis; ⇨ *see* What's Free When box. Free architectural, historical, or nature tours depart from the visitor center every Saturday at 10, while park ranger–led tours start out from the visitor center at 1 PM every Wednesday and Sunday. Free concerts take place Sunday afternoons at 2 PM year-round at the Spreckels Organ Pavilion, and the House of Pacific Relations hosts Sunday-afternoon folk-dance performances.

Sights to See

▶ ❶ **Alcazar Garden.** The gardens surrounding the Alcazar Castle in Seville, Spain, inspired the landscaping here; you'll feel like royalty resting on the benches by the tiled fountains. The flower beds are ever-changing horticultural exhibits featuring more than 6,000 annuals for a nearly perpetual bloom. Bright orange-and-yellow poppies appear in spring and deep rust and crimson chrysanthemums arrive in fall. ⊠ *Off El Prado, Balboa Park.*

❻ **Botanical Building.** The graceful redwood-lathed structure, built for the 1915 Panama-California International Exposition, now houses more than 2,000 types of tropical and subtropical plants plus changing seasonal flower displays. Ceiling-high tree ferns shade fragile orchids and feathery bamboo. There are benches beside miniature waterfalls for resting in the shade. The rectangular pond outside, filled with lotuses and water lilies that bloom in spring and fall, is popular with photographers. ⊠ *1550 El Prado, Balboa Park* ☎ *619/239–0512* ▣ *Free* ☉ *Fri.–Wed. 10–4.*

❾ **Carousel.** Suspended an arm's-length away on this antique merry-go-round is the brass ring that could earn you an extra free ride (it's one of the few carousels in the world that continue this bonus tradition). Hand-carved in 1910, the bobbing animals include zebras, giraffes, and dragons; real horsehair was used for the tails. ⊠ *1889 Zoo Pl., behind zoo parking lot, Balboa Park* ☎ *619/460–9000* ▣ *$1.75* ☉ *Mid-June–Labor Day, daily 11–6 during school year; school holidays and weekends 11–5:30.*

Balboa Park

⑭ Casa de Balboa. This building on El Prado's southeast corner houses three museums: the Museum of Photographic Arts, the San Diego Historical Society, and the San Diego Model Railroad Museum. ✉ *1649 El Prado, Balboa Park.*

⑬ Centro Cultural de la Raza. An old water tower was converted into this center for Mexican, Native American, and Chicano arts and culture. Attractions include a gallery with rotating exhibits and a theater, as well as a collection of mural art, a fine example of which may be seen on the tower's exterior. ✉ *2004 Park Blvd., Balboa Park* ☎ *619/235–6135* ⊕ *www.centroraza.com* ✉ *Donation suggested* ☉ *Thurs.–Sun. noon–5.*

need a break? **HILLCREST –** Northwest of Balboa Park, Hillcrest is San Diego's center for the gay community and artists of all types. University, 4th, and 5th Avenues are filled with cafés and interesting boutiques, including several indie bookstores selling new and used books along 5th below University; chain stores and eateries have been making strong inroads, however. The self-contained residential-commercial Uptown District, on University Avenue at 8th Avenue, was built to resemble an inner-city neighborhood, with shops and restaurants within easy walking distance of high-price town houses. To the northeast, Adams Avenue, reached via Park Boulevard heading north off Washington Street, has many antiques stores. Adams Avenue leads east into Kensington, a handsome old neighborhood that overlooks Mission Valley.

❸ Globe Theatres. Even if you're not attending a play, this complex, comprising the Cassius Carter Centre Stage, the Lowell Davies Festival Theatre, and the Old Globe Theatre, is a pleasant place to relax between museum visits. The theaters, done in a California version of Tudor style, sit between the sculpture garden of the San Diego Museum of Art and the California Tower. A gift shop (open Tuesday–Sunday noon–9:30 when there are performances, noon–5 other days) sells theater-related wares, including posters, cards, and brightly colored puppets. ✉ *1363 Old Globe Way, Balboa Park* ☎ *619/239–2255* ⊕ *www.theglobetheatres.org.*

⑯ House of Charm. This structure was rebuilt from the ground up in the mid-1990s to replicate the Franciscan mission style of the original expo building. Inside are the main branch of the Mingei International Museum of Folk Art and the San Diego Art Institute. ✉ *1439 El Prado, Balboa Park.*

⑮ House of Hospitality. At the Balboa Park Visitors Center in this building, you can pick up schedules and route maps for the free trams that operate around the park. You can also purchase the Best of Balboa Park Combo Pass, which affords entry to 13 museums and the zoo for $55; it's worthwhile if you want to visit more than a few museums and aren't entitled to the discounts that most give to children, senior citizens, and military personnel. In addition, you can pick up a flyer that details the excellent free park tours that depart from here (or phone for a schedule). Also note the beautiful structure itself. A late 1990s rebuilding of the 1915 original, it has won myriad awards for its painstaking attention to historical detail; 2,000 paint scrapes were taken, for example, to get the art deco colors exactly right. ✉ *1549 El Prado, Balboa Park* ☎ *619/239–0512* ⊕ *www.balboapark.org* ⊗ *Daily 9–4.*

⑲ House of Pacific Relations. This is not really a house but a cluster of red-tile–roof, stucco cottages representing some 30 foreign countries. And the word "pacific" refers not to the ocean—most of the nations represented are European, not Asian—but to the goal of maintaining peace. The cottages, decorated with crafts and pictures, are the scene of Sunday afternoon open houses, during which you can chat with transplanted natives and try out different ethnic foods. From the first Sunday in March through the last Sunday in October folk song and dance performances take place on the outdoor stage around 2 PM—check the schedule at the park visitor center. Across the road from the cottages but not affiliated with them is the Spanish colonial–style **United Nations Building.** Inside, the United Nations Association's International Gift Shop, open daily, has reasonably priced crafts, cards, and books. ✉ *2160 Pan American Rd. W, Balboa Park* ☎ *619/234–0739* ⊕ *www.sdhpr.org* ✉ *Free, donations accepted* ⊗ *Early Sept.–late May, Sun. noon–4; Memorial Day–Labor Day, Sun. noon–5.*

⑰ Japanese Friendship Garden. A koi pond with a cascading water wall, a 60-foot-long wisteria arbor, a large activity center, and a sushi bar are highlights of the park's authentic Japanese garden, designed to inspire contemplation. You can wander the various peaceful paths, meditate in the traditional stone-and-sand garden, or, at times, learn such arts as origami and flower arranging at the exhibit hall. Long-term plans are to develop an additional 9 acres with more attractions, including a teahouse, tea garden, and cherry orchard. ✉ *2215 Pan American Rd., Balboa Park* ☎ *619/232–2721* ✉ *$3* ⊗ *Tues.–Sun. 10–4.*

☾ ⑳ Marie Hitchcock Puppet Theater. One of the last of its kind, the theater has been presenting shows for more than 50 years. Performances incorporate marionettes, hand puppets, rod puppets, shadow puppets, and ventriloquism, while the stories range from traditional fairy tales to folk legends and contemporary puppet plays. Pantomime, comedy, and music round out the program. Kids will be wide-eyed at the short, energy-filled productions. Adults will be overcome with nostalgia. ✉ *2130 Pan American Plaza, Balboa Park* ☎ *619/685–5990* ⊕ *www.balboaparkpuppets. com* ✉ *$5* ⊗ *Showtimes mid-June–Labor Day, Wed.–Sun. 11, 1, 2:30; Sept.–mid-June, Wed.–Fri. 10 and 11:30, Sat.–Sun. 11, 1, 2:30.*

Marston House. George W. Marston (1850–1946), a San Diego pioneer and philanthropist who financed the architectural landscaping of Balboa Park—among his myriad other San Diego civic projects—was visited by such prominent people as President Teddy Roosevelt and Booker T. Washington. His 16-room home at the northwest edge of the park, now maintained by the San Diego Historical Society, was designed in 1905 by San Diego architects Irving Gill and William Hebbard. It's a classic example of the American Arts and Crafts style, which emphasizes simplicity and functionality of form, as are the furnishings, which include pieces by Tiffany, Roycroft, and Gustav Stickley. On the 5-acre grounds is a lovely English Romantic garden, as interpreted in California. Hour-long docent tours—the only way to see the house—illuminate many aspects of San Diego history in which the Marstons played a part. ⊠ *3525 7th Ave., Balboa Park* ☎ *619/298–3142* 🖅 *$5* ☉ *Fri.–Sun. 10–4:30, last tour at 3:15.*

⟲ **⑯ Mingei International Museum of Folk Art.** All ages will enjoy the Mingei's col-
Fodor'sChoice orful and creative exhibits of toys, pottery, textiles, costumes, and gadgets
★ from around the globe. Traveling and permanent exhibits in the high-ceiling, light-filled museum include everything from antique American carousel horses to the latest in Japanese ceramics. The name Mingei comes from the Japanese words *min,* meaning "all people," and *gei,* meaning "art." Thus, the museum's name describes what you'll find under its roof: "art of all people." It's hard to predict what you'll see, but you can depend on its being delightful. The gift shop has a great selection of Navajo, Hopi, and Huichol Indian artwork. ⊠ *House of Charm, 1439 El Prado, Balboa Park* ☎ *619/239–0003* ⊕ *www.mingei.org* 🖅 *$6* ☉ *Tues.–Sun. 10–4.*

⟲ **⑩ Miniature Railroad.** Adjacent to the zoo parking lot and across from the carousel, a pint-size, 48-passenger train runs a ½-mi loop through 4 tree-filled acres of the park. The engine of this rare 1948 model train is a ⅕ scale version of a General Motors F-3 locomotive and is one of only 50 left in the world. ⊠ *2885 Zoo Pl., Balboa Park* ☎ *619/231–1515 Ext. 4219* 🖅 *$1.25* ☉ *June–Aug., daily 11–6:30; Sept.–May, weekends and school holidays 11–4:30.*

⟲ **Morley Field Sports Complex.** In addition to the 2-mi fitness course and ball diamonds, the park's athletic center has a flying-disc golf course, where players toss their Frisbees over canyons and treetops to reach the challenging "holes"—wire baskets hung from metal poles. Morley Field also has a public pool, a velodrome, an archery range, playgrounds, and boccie, badminton, and tennis courts. The complex is at the northeast corner of Balboa Park, across Park Boulevard and Florida Canyon. ⊠ *2221 Morley Field Dr., Balboa Park* ☎ *619/692–4919* ⊕ *www. morleyfield.com.*

★ **⑭ Museum of Photographic Arts.** World-renowned photographers such as Ansel Adams, Imogen Cunningham, Henri Cartier-Bresson, and Edward Weston are represented in the permanent collection, which includes everything from 19th-century daguerreotypes to contemporary photojournalism prints and Russian Constructivist images (many by Alexander Rodchenko). The 28,000-square-foot facility has a state-of-the-art theater for screening cinema classics as well as a learning center. On Thursday nights, the museum is open late for movie presentations and the occasional jazz recital. ⊠ *Casa de Balboa, 1649 El Prado, Balboa Park* ☎ *619/238–7559* ⊕ *www.mopa.org* 🖅 *$6 museum, $7 theater* ☉ *Daily 10–5, 10–9 on Thurs.*

⟲ **⑫ Reuben H. Fleet Science Center.** The Fleet Center's clever interactive ex-
Fodor'sChoice hibits are artfully educational. You can reconfigure your face to have
★ two left sides, or, by replaying an instant video clip, watch yourself com-

ing and going at different speeds. The IMAX Dome Theater, the world's first, screens exhilarating nature and science films. The SciTours simulator is designed to take you on virtual voyages—stomach lurches and all. The Meteor Storm lets up to six players at a time have an interactive virtual-reality experience, this one sans motion-sickness potential. A big hit is the Nierman Challenger Learning Center—a realistic mock mission-control and futuristic space station. ✉ *1875 El Prado, Balboa Park* ☎ *619/238–1233* ⊕ *www.rhfleet.org* 🎟 *Gallery exhibits $6.75, gallery exhibits and 1 IMAX film $11.75* ☉ *Mon.–Thurs. 9:30–5, Fri. and Sat. 9:30–8, Sun. 9:30–6; closing hrs vary, call ahead.*

★ ☾ ㉒ **San Diego Aerospace Museum and International Aerospace Hall of Fame.** By day, the streamlined edifice commissioned by the Ford Motor Company for the 1935–36 exposition looks unlike any other structure in the park; at night, outlined in blue neon, the round building appears—appropriately enough—to be a landed UFO. Every available inch of space in the rotunda is filled with exhibits about aviation and aerospace pioneers, including examples of enemy planes during the world wars. All in all, there are 68 full-size aircraft on the floor and literally hanging from the rafters, and interactive exhibits that kids love (such as the DC-3 cockpit display where they can pretend to fly). In addition to exhibits from the dawn of flight to the jet age, the museum also displays a growing number of space-age exhibits, including the actual Apollo 9 space capsule. A collection of real and replicated aircraft fills the central courtyard. ✉ *2001 Pan American Plaza, Balboa Park* ☎ *619/234–8291* ⊕ *www.aerospacemuseum.org* 🎟 *$9, behind-the-scenes restorations $3 extra* ☉ *Daily 10–4:30, 5:30 in summer.*

⑯ **San Diego Art Institute.** Outside juries decide which works created by members of the Art Institute will be displayed in rotating shows, which change every four to six weeks. Painting, sculpture, mixed media, digital art, and photography are represented—everything except crafts, reserved for the excellent small gift shop. The David Fleet Young Artists Gallery shows art executed by students at area schools. ✉ *House of Charm, 1439 El Prado, Balboa Park* ☎ *619/236–0011* ⊕ *www.sandiego-art.org* 🎟 *$3* ☉ *Tues.–Sat. 10–4, Sun. noon–4.*

㉑ **San Diego Automotive Museum.** Even if you don't know a choke from a chassis, you're bound to admire the sleek designs of the autos in this impressive museum. The core collection comprises vintage motorcycles and cars, ranging from an 1886 Benz to a De Lorean, as well as a series of rotating exhibits from collections around the world. There's an ongoing automobile restoration program, and the museum sponsors many outdoor automotive events; call to find out about any rallies, races, or shows that might be scheduled. ✉ *2080 Pan American Plaza, Balboa Park* ☎ *619/231–2886* ⊕ *www.sdautomuseum.org* 🎟 *$7* ☉ *Daily 10–5, last admission at 4:30.*

☾ ㉓ **San Diego Hall of Champions.** In a 70,000-square-foot building, this museum celebrates local jock heroes—such as baseball great Ted Williams and basketball star Bill Walton—via a vast collection of memorabilia, uniforms, paintings, photographs, and computer and video displays. An amusing bloopers film is screened at the Sports Theater. The Center Court activity area hosts changing programs—everything from a Chargers minitraining camp to interactive bobsled races. In keeping with the progressive nature of the San Diego sports community, there are also exhibits of such extreme sports as skateboarding, surfing, and street luge. ⊠ *Federal Bldg., 2131 Pan American Rd., Balboa Park* ☎ *619/234–2544* ⊕ *www.sdhoc.com* ▨ *$6* ⊗ *Daily 10–4.*

⑭ San Diego Historical Society Museum. The San Diego Historical Society maintains its research library in the basement of the Casa de Balboa and organizes shows on the first floor. Permanent and rotating exhibits, which are often more lively than you might expect, survey local urban history after 1850, when California entered the Union. A 100-seat theater hosts public lectures, workshops, and educational programs, and a gift shop carries a good selection of books on local history as well as reproductions of old posters and other historical collectibles. ⊠ *Casa de Balboa, 1649 El Prado, Balboa Park* ☎ *619/232–6203* ⊕ *www.sandiegohistory. org* ▨ *$6* ⊗ *Daily 10–5.*

☾ ⑭ San Diego Model Railroad Museum. At 28,000 square feet, this is the largest indoor operating railroad museum in the world. The four main displays, built and maintained by local model railroad clubs, represent California railroads in "miniature," with the track laid on scale models of actual San Diego County terrain. The Cabrillo & Southwestern layout is in O scale, ¼₈ actual size; two others are in HO scale, ¹⁄₈₇ actual size; and the fourth, Pacific Desert Lines, is in N scale, actual size. When these impressive exhibits are in operation, you can hear the sounds of chugging engines, screeching brakes, and shrill whistles. A Toy Train Gallery contains an interactive Lionel exhibit that includes a camera car hooked up to a TV set showing an engineer's eye view of the layout. Children under 15 get in free with an adult. ⊠ *Casa de Balboa, 1649 El Prado, Balboa Park* ☎ *619/696–0199* ⊕ *www.sdmodelrailroadm.com* ▨ *$5* ⊗ *Tues.–Fri. 11–4, weekends 11–5.*

★ ❹ San Diego Museum of Art. Known primarily for its Spanish baroque and Renaissance paintings, including works by El Greco, Goya, Rubens, and van Ruisdael, San Diego's most comprehensive art museum also has strong holdings of South Asian art, Indian miniatures, and contemporary California paintings. The Baldwin M. Baldwin collection includes more than 100 pieces by Toulouse-Lautrec. An outdoor Sculpture Court and Garden exhibits both traditional and modern pieces. The IMAGE (Interactive Multimedia Art Gallery Explorer) system allows you to call up the highlights of the museum's collection on a computer screen and custom-design a tour, call up historical information on the works and artists, and print color reproductions. The museum's goal is to "connect people to art and art to people," so its exhibits tend to have broad appeal, and if traveling shows from other cities come to town, you can expect to see them here. A good mix of American and international treasures and shows featuring recognized masters is rounded out by lectures, concerts, and film events. Free docent tours are offered throughout the day. ⊠ *Casa de Balboa, 1450 El Prado, Balboa Park* ☎ *619/232–7931*

⊕ *www.sdmart.org* ✉ *$9, $10–$12 for special exhibits* ⊙ *Tues.–Sun. 10–6, to 9 on Thurs.*

need a break? | Take a respite from museum-hopping with a cup of coffee or a glass of California chardonnay in the San Diego Museum of Art's **Waters Café** (☎ 619/237–0675), in the outdoor sanctuary of the Museum's Sculpture Court and Garden. The café serves a small selection of tasty sandwiches and salads Tuesday–Sunday 8:30–4 (it's often open for dinner, too, in summer). You can also get coffee and various noshes from a food cart outside the café.

🕒 ❷ **San Diego Museum of Man.** Exhibits at this highly respected anthropological museum focus on Southwestern, Mexican, and South American cultures. Carved monuments from the Mayan city of Quirigua in Guatemala, cast from the originals in 1914, are particularly impressive. Rotating shows might include examples of intricate beadwork from across the Americas, and demonstrations of such skills as weaving and tortilla-making are held regularly. Other great exhibits show the lifestyles of the Kumeyaay peoples who inhabited San Diego before Europeans arrived. Among the museum's more recent additions is the hands-on Children's Discovery Center. ⊠ *California Bldg., 1350 El Prado, Balboa Park* ☎ *619/239– 2001* ⊕ *www.museumofman.org* ✉ *$6* ⊙ *Daily 10–4:30.*

★ 🕒 ❼ **San Diego Natural History Museum.** There are 7.5 million fossils, dinosaur models, and even live reptiles and other specimens under this roof. Favorite exhibits include the Foucault pendulum, suspended on a 43-foot cable and designed to demonstrate the Earth's rotation; a full-size grey-whale skeleton; and *Ocean Oasis,* the world's first large-format film about Baja California and the Sea of Cortéz. Traveling exhibits make a stop here, and the museum also sponsors community events. Call ahead for information on films, lectures, and free guided nature walks. ⊠ *1788 El Prado, Balboa Park* ☎ *619/232–3821* ⊕ *www.sdnhm.org* ✉ *$9* ⊙ *Daily 10–5.*

🕒 ⓫ **San Diego Zoo.** Balboa Park's—and perhaps the city's—most famous attraction is its 100-acre zoo, and it deserves all the press it gets. Nearly 4,000 animals of some 800 diverse species roam in hospitable, expertly crafted habitats that replicate natural environments as closely as possible. The flora in the zoo, including many rare species, is even more costly than the fauna. Walkways wind over bridges and past waterfalls ringed with tropical ferns; elephants in a sandy plateau roam so close you're tempted to pet them.

Fodor's Choice ★

Exploring the zoo fully requires the stamina of a healthy hiker, but open-air double-decker buses that run throughout the day let you zip through three-quarters of the exhibits on a guided 35- to 40-minute, 3-mi tour. There are also express buses, used for quick transportation, that make five stops around the grounds and include some narration. The Skyfari Aerial Tram, which soars 170 feet above the ground, gives a good overview of the zoo's layout and, on clear days, a panorama of the park, downtown San Diego, the bay, and the ocean, far past the San Diego–Coronado Bridge. Unless you come early, however, expect to wait to be moved around. The line for the regular bus, and especially for the top tier, can take more than 45 minutes; if you come at midday on a weekend or school holiday, you'll be doing the in-line shuffle for a while.

In any case, the zoo is at its best when you wander its paths, such as the one that climbs through the huge, enclosed **Scripps Aviary,** where brightly colored tropical birds swoop between branches just inches from your face, and into the neighboring **Gorilla Tropics,** among the zoo's latest ventures into bioclimatic zone exhibits. Here animals live in enclosed environments modeled on their native habitats. These zones may look natural, but they're helped a lot by modern technology: the sounds of the tropical rain forest emerge from a 144-speaker sound system that plays CDs recorded in Africa.

The zoo's simulated Asian rain forest, **Tiger River,** has 10 exhibits with more than 35 species of animals. The mist-shrouded trails winding down a canyon into Tiger River pass by fragrant jasmine, ginger lilies, and orchids, giving you the feeling of descending into an Asian jungle. Tigers, Malayan tapirs, and Argus pheasants wander among the exotic trees and plants. **Ituri Forest**—a 4-acre African rain forest at the base of Tiger River—lets you glimpse huge but surprisingly graceful hippos frolicking underwater, and buffalo cavorting with monkeys on dry land. In **Sun Bear Forest** playful beasts constantly claw apart the trees and shrubs that serve as a natural playground for climbing, jumping, and general merrymaking. At the popular **Polar Bear Plunge,** where you can watch the featured animals take a chilly dive, Siberian reindeer, white foxes, and other Arctic creatures are separated from their predatory neighbors by a series of camouflaged moats. The lush, tropical environment at **Absolutely Apes,** where orangutans and siamangs climb, swing, and generally live almost as they would in the wild, is lined with 110-foot-long and 12-foot-high viewing windows that offer a unique opportunity to view these endangered apes close up.

The San Diego Zoo houses the largest number of koalas outside Australia, and they remain major crowd pleasers, but these and other zoo locals are always overshadowed by the pandas and especially the baby pandas that result from the work being done by the zoo's department of Conservation and Research for Endangered Species. Following its success with Hua Mei, born at the zoo in 1999 and the first giant panda cub born in the United States to survive past four days, the zoo was able to successfully impregnate Hua Mei's mother, Bai Yun, a second time. A male panda cub, Mei Sheng, was born to Bai Yun and Gao Gao, her mate, in August 2003. Hua Mei now lives in China (all pandas born at the zoo are transferred to China after their third birthday) but Mei Sheng and his mother and father are generally available for viewing from 9:00 to 4:15 each day at the SBC Giant Panda Research Station. Call the panda hotline for up-to-date information.

For a hands-on experience there's the **Children's Zoo,** where goats, sheep, bunnies, and guinea pigs beg to be petted. There are two viewer-friendly nurseries where you may see various baby animals bottle-feed and sleep peacefully in large-size baby cribs. Children can see entertaining creatures of all sorts nearby at the Wegeforth National Park Sea Lion Show in Wegeforth Bowl and at the Wild Ones Show in Hunte Amphitheater, both put on daily.

The zoo's newest exhibit, opened in mid-2005, is **Monkey Trails and Forest Tales.** Spanning three acres, this multilevel exhibit represents African and Asian forests and is the largest and most elaborate animal habitat in the zoo's history. You can follow an elevated trail at treetop level and trek paths on the forest floor, observing some of nature's most unusual and threatened animals and birds, including African mandrills, Asia's clouded leopard, the rare pygmy hippopotamus, Visayan warty pigs from the Philippines, weaver birds that build the most elaborate nests of any species, not to mention flora such as endangered mahogany trees, rare, exotic orchids, and insect-eating plants.

The zoo rents strollers, wheelchairs, and cameras; it also has a first-aid office, a lost and found, and an ATM. It's best to avert your eyes from the two main gift shops until the end of your visit; you can spend a half day just poking through the wonderful animal-related posters, crafts, dishes, clothing, and toys. There is one guilt-alleviating fact if you buy too much: some of the profits of your purchases go to zoo programs. Audio tours, behind-the-scenes tours, walking tours, tours in Spanish, and tours for people with hearing or vision impairments are available; inquire at the entrance. Lastly, when you've finished here, you haven't seen it all until you've seen the San Diego Wild Animal Park, the zoo's 1,800-acre extension to the north at Escondido. ⊠ *2920 Zoo Dr., Balboa Park* ☎ *619/234–3153, 888/697–2632 Giant panda hotline* ⊕ *www. sandiegozoo.org* ✏ *$21 includes zoo, Children's Zoo, and animal shows; $32 includes above, plus guided bus tour, unlimited express bus rides, and round-trip Skyfari Aerial Tram rides; zoo free for children under 12 in Oct.; $54.45 pass good for admission to zoo and San Diego Wild Animal Park within 5 days* ⊟ *AE, D, MC, V* ⊙ *July–Sept., daily 9–9; Sept.–May, daily 9–4; Children's Zoo and Skyfari ride generally close 1 hr earlier.*

need a break?
Plenty of **food stands** at the zoo sell popcorn, pizza, and enormous ice-cream cones. Their menus can be pricey for families, however, so it doesn't hurt to pack a picnic and dine among the locals. If you want to eat among strolling peacocks—who will try to cadge your food—consider the **Flamingo Café,** inside the main entrance, serving sandwiches, salads, and light meals. Of the zoo's indoor restaurants, the best is **Albert's,** part of a three-tier dining complex near Gorilla Tropics. Grilled fish, homemade pizza, and fresh pasta are among the offerings, and this is the only place where wine and beer are sold.

❽ Spanish Village Art Center. Glassblowers, enamel workers, wood-carvers, sculptors, painters, jewelers, photographers, and other artists rent space in these 35 red-tile–roof studio-galleries that were set up for the 1935–36 exposition in the style of an old Spanish village. The artists give demonstrations of their work on a rotating basis, aware, no doubt, that it's fun to buy wares that you've watched being created. ⊠ *1770 Village*

WHAT'S FREE WHEN

WHILE BEACHCOMBING, sunbathing, or simply strolling along the beach and bay will always be San Diego's most popular free activities, there are many other options for those days when you want to shake the sand out of your shoes and see another side of the city. The downtown location of the Museum of Contemporary Art is free every day except Wednesday, when it's closed. The La Jolla location is free the first Sunday and second Tuesday of each month. Old Town State Historic Park is free at all times, as are many of the museums within its boundaries. The most options for freebies can be found in Balboa Park, both on a weekly basis and at special times of the year. You can pick up a free garden tour map at the visitor's center and use that to explore the dozens of gardens covering the park's 1,200 acres, but you aren't limited to just that. The San Diego Zoo is free for kids under 13 the whole month of October, and everyone gets in free on Founder's Day, October 1. The December Nights festival on the first Friday and Saturday of that month includes free admission and later hours to most of the Balboa Park museums. The outdoor events during the festival make it something not to miss. The free concerts at the Spreckels Organ Pavilion take place Sunday afternoons at 2 PM year-round and on summer Monday evenings. The Timken Museum of Art is always free. The Centro Cultural de la Raza and Veterans Memorial Center are free, but a donation is requested at each. The best deal is the Free Tuesdays in the Park, a rotating schedule of free admission to most all of Balboa Park's museums.

First Tuesday:

San Diego Model Railroad Museum

San Diego Natural History Museum

Reuben H. Fleet Science Center

Second Tuesday:

Museum of Photographic Arts

Museum of San Diego History

Third Tuesday:

San Diego Art Institute

San Diego Museum of Art

San Diego Museum of Man

Japanese Friendship Garden

Mingei International Museum

Fourth Tuesday:

San Diego Aerospace Museum

San Diego Automotive Museum

San Diego Hall of Champions

House of Pacific Relations International Cottages

Fifth Tuesday:

Normal museum prices are in effect.

Pl., Balboa Park ☎ 619/233–9050 ⊕ *www.spanishvillageart.com* ✆ *Free* ☉ *Daily 11–4.*

⓲ Spreckels Organ Pavilion. The 2,000-seat pavilion, dedicated in 1915 by sugar magnates John D. and Adolph B. Spreckels, holds the 4,445-pipe Spreckels Organ, the largest outdoor pipe organ in the world. You can hear this impressive instrument at one of the year-round, 2 PM Sunday concerts, regularly performed by civic organist Carol Williams. On Monday evenings in summer, military bands, gospel groups, and barbershop quartets also perform. At Christmastime the park's Christmas tree and life-size Nativity display turn the pavilion into a seasonal wonderland. ⊠ *2211 Pan American Rd., Balboa Park* ☎ 619/702–8138 ⊕ *www.sosorgan.com.*

❺ Timken Museum of Art. Somewhat out of place in the architectural scheme of the park, this modern structure is made of travertine imported from Italy. The small museum houses works by major European and American artists as well as a superb collection of Russian icons. ⊠ *1500 El Prado, Balboa Park* ☎ 619/239–5548 ⊕ *www.timkenmuseum.org* ✆ *Free* ☉ *Tues.–Sat. 10–4:30, Sun. 1:30–4:30.*

DOWNTOWN

Downtown is San Diego's Lazarus. Written off as moribund by the 1970s, when few people willingly stayed in the area after dark, downtown is now one of the city's prime draws. The turnaround began in the late 1970s with the revitalization of the Gaslamp Quarter Historic District and massive redevelopment that gave rise to the Horton Plaza shopping center and the San Diego Convention Center, as well as to elegant hotels, upscale condominium complexes, and swank, trendy restaurants and cafés. Now people linger downtown well into the night—and also wake up there the next morning.

Downtown's natural attributes were easily evident to its original booster, Alonzo Horton (1813–1909), who arrived in San Diego in 1867. Horton looked at the bay and the acres of flatland surrounded by hills and canyons and knew he had found San Diego's heart. Although Old Town, under the Spanish fort at the Presidio, had been settled for years, Horton understood that it was too far away from the water to take hold as the commercial center of San Diego. He therefore bought 960 acres along the bay at 27½¢ per acre and gave away the land to those who would develop it or build houses. Within months he had sold or given away 226 city blocks.

The transcontinental railroad arrived in 1885, and the land boom was on. San Diego's population soared from 5,000 to 35,000 in less than a decade—a foreshadowing of its future. In 1887 the Santa Fe Depot was constructed at the foot of Broadway, two blocks from the water. Freighters chugged in and out of the harbor, and by the early 1900s the U.S. Navy had moved in.

As downtown grew into San Diego's transportation and commercial hub, residential neighborhoods blossomed along the beaches and inland valleys. The business district gradually moved farther away from the original heart of downtown, at 5th Avenue and Market Street, past Broadway, up toward Balboa Park. Downtown's waterfront fell into bad times during World War I, when sailors, gamblers, and prostitutes were drawn to one another at the waterfront bars.

But Alonzo Horton's modern-day followers, city leaders intent on prospering while preserving San Diego's natural beauty, reclaimed the downtown area. The Centre City Development Corporation (CCDC), a public, nonprofit organization, spearheaded development of the Gaslamp Quarter Historic District, and that attracted a groundswell of investment after the adjacent Horton Plaza shopping complex opened to huge success in 1985. This in turn led the way for the hotels, restaurants, and housing developments that are now rising on every square inch of available space. Waterfront transformation also proceeded apace, as old shipyards and canneries were replaced by hotel towers and waterfront parks. The Martin Luther King Jr. Promenade project put 14 acres of greenery, a pedestrian walkway, and lots of artwork along Harbor Drive from Seaport Village to the convention center, and landscaped the railroad right-of-way from the Santa Fe Depot to 8th Avenue. The San Diego Convention Center, which hosted its first events in 1990, proved so successful with events like the 1996 Republican National Convention that it has doubled in size to about 1.7 million square feet.

Of the newest downtown projects—there are more than 100 in the works—the most ambitious is the 26-block Ballpark District, which occupies the East Village area that extends between the railroad tracks up to J Street, and from 6th Avenue east to around 10th Street. It includes Petco Park, a new 42,000-seat baseball stadium for the San Diego Padres, opened in 2004; a distinctively San Diego–style, 8-acre "Park at the Park" from which fans watch games while picnicking; a sports-related retail complex; at least 850 hotel rooms; and several apartment and condominium complexes. On downtown's waterfront sits the USS *Midway,* the home of the San Diego Aircraft Carrier Museum, which also opened in 2004.

Downtown's main thoroughfares are Harbor Drive, running along the waterfront; Broadway, through the center of downtown; and 6th Avenue, between Harbor Drive and Balboa Park. The numbered streets run roughly north–south; the lettered and named streets—Broadway, Market, Island, and Ash—run east–west. Only Broadway, Market Street, Harbor Drive, and Island Avenue have two-way traffic. The rest alternate one-way directions.

There are reasonably priced ($4–$7 per day) parking lots along Harbor Drive, Pacific Highway, and lower Broadway and Market Street. The price of many downtown parking meters is $1 per hour, with a maximum stay of two hours (meters are in effect Monday–Saturday [except holidays], 8–6); unless you know for sure that your stay in the area will be short, you're better off in a lot.

Numbers in the text correspond to numbers in the margin and on the Central San Diego map.

Central San Diego

Mission Bay

Morena Blvd.

Linda Vista Rd.

W. Mission Bay Dr.

◆ **Sea World**

Friars Rd.

Hotel Circle

Presidio Hills Park

OCEAN BEACH W. Point Loma Blvd.

Sports Arena Blvd.

Midway Dr.

Sports ◆ **Arena**

Juan St.

OLD TOWN

B St. Pier

San Diego Ave.

Bacon

Sunset Cliffs Blvd.

Voltaire

Narragansett Ave.

Nimitz Blvd.

Barnett Ave.

Pacific Hwy.

Broadway Pier

◆ **Coron Ferry**

Point Loma Ave.

Chatsworth

Blvd.

OLD U.S. NAVAL TRAINING CENTER

✈ **San Diego International Airport Lindbergh Field**

N. Harbor Dr.

Tuna Harbor

Hill St.

Canon St.

Rosecrans St.

Scott St.

Harbor Island 23

Canon Blvd.

Canon St.

Shelter Is. Dr.

21

San Diego Bay

Catalina Blvd.

22

Shelter Island

POINT LOMA

Naval Reservation

NAVAL AIR STATION, NORTH ISLAND

North Island

3rd St.

CORONADO

Orange Ave.

13

Cabrillo Memorial Dr.

19

14

Pom

15 16

Coronado Beach

18

N. Harbor Dr.

1
2
3
4
5
8
209
20
E
F

Two Good Walks

Most people do a lot of parking-lot hopping when visiting downtown, but for the energetic, two distinct areas may be explored on foot.

To stay near the water, start a walk of the **Embarcadero ❶** ▸ at the foot of Ash Street on Harbor Drive, where the *Berkeley,* headquarters of the **Maritime Museum ❷**, is moored. A cement pathway runs south from the *Star of India,* one of the museum's sailing ships, along the waterfront to the pastel B Street Pier, but if you're traveling with firehouse fans, detour inland four blocks on Ash and north two blocks to the **Firehouse Museum ❺**, at the corner of Cedar and Columbia in Little Italy. Otherwise, another two blocks south on Harbor Drive brings you to the foot of Broadway and the Broadway Pier, where you can catch harbor excursion boats and the ferry to Coronado. Approximately one block south of Broadway is the Navy Pier, home of the **San Diego Aircraft Carrier Museum ❹**. Take Broadway inland two long blocks to Kettner Boulevard to reach the **Transit Center ❻**—you'll see the mosaic-domed Santa Fe Depot and the tracks for the trolley to Tijuana out front—and, right next door, the downtown branch of the **Museum of Contemporary Art, San Diego ❼**. (If you've detoured to the Firehouse Museum, take Kettner Boulevard south to the Transit Center.) Return to Harbor Drive and continue south past Tuna Harbor to **Seaport Village ❽**.

A tour of the working heart of downtown can begin at the corner of 1st Avenue and Broadway, near Spreckels Theater, a grand old stage that presents pop concerts and touring plays. Two blocks east and across the street sits the historic **U. S. Grant Hotel ❾**. If you cross Broadway, you'll be able to enter **Horton Plaza ❿**, San Diego's favorite retail playland. Fourth Avenue, the eastern boundary of Horton Plaza, doubles as the western boundary of the 16-block **Gaslamp Quarter Historic District ⓫**. Head south to Island Avenue and 4th Avenue to the William Heath Davis House, where you can get a touring map of the district.

TIMING   The above walks take about an hour each, although there's enough to do in downtown San Diego to keep you busy for at least two days. Weather is a determining factor in any Embarcadero stroll, which is pretty much an outdoors endeavor, but San Diego rarely presents any problems along that line. Most of downtown's attractions are open daily, but the Museum of Contemporary Art is closed on Monday, and the Firehouse Museum is only open from Wednesday through Sunday. If you want to take a guided tour of the Gaslamp Quarter Historic District, plan to visit on a Saturday. A boat trip on the harbor, or at least a hop over to Coronado on the ferry, is a must at any time of year, but from December through March, when the gray whales migrate between the Pacific Northwest and southern Baja, you should definitely consider booking a whale-watching excursion from the Broadway Pier.

Sights to See

▸ ❶ **Embarcadero.** The bustle comes less these days from the activities of fishing folk than from the throngs of tourists, but this waterfront walkway along San Diego Bay remains the nautical soul of the city. People here still make a living from the sea. Seafood restaurants line the piers, as do sea vessels of every variety—cruise ships, ferries, tour boats, houseboats, and naval destroyers.

On the north end of the Embarcadero, at Ash Street, you'll find the Maritime Museum. South of it, the **B Street Pier** is used by ships from major cruise lines as both a port of call and a departure point. The cavernous pier building has a cruise-information center as well as a small bar—nice for cooling off on a hot day—and gift shop. Walk another block south and you can't miss the massive USS *Midway,* home of the San Diego Aircraft Carrier Museum.

Day-trippers getting ready to set sail gather at the **Broadway Pier,** also known as the excursion pier. Tickets for the harbor tours and whale-watching trips are sold here. The terminal for the Coronado Ferry lies just beyond the Broadway pier.

The U.S. Navy has control of the next few waterfront blocks to the south—**aircraft carriers, submarines, destroyers** cruise in and out, some staying for weeks at a time. It used to be possible to tour these floating cities, but for security reasons they are no longer open to the public (although the Navy does do tours for pre-arranged groups, usually local ones (☎619/553–8643 for submarines, 619/545–1133 for aircraft carriers, 619/437–5260 for other types). **Tuna Harbor,** at the foot of G Street, was once the hub of one of San Diego's earliest and most successful industries, commercial tuna fishing. The tuna-fishing industry has gone south to Mexico, so these days there are more pleasure boats than tuna boats tied up at the G Street Pier, but the United States Tuna Foundation still has offices here. The pleasant Tuna Harbor Park offers a great view of boating on the bay and across to any aircraft carriers docked at the North Island naval base.

The next bit of seafront greenery is a few blocks south at **Embarcadero Marina Park North,** an 8-acre extension into the harbor from the center of Seaport Village. It's usually full of kite fliers, in-line skaters, and picnickers. Seasonal celebrations are held here and at the similar **Embarcadero Marina Park South.**

The **San Diego Convention Center,** on Harbor Drive between 1st and 5th avenues, is a waterfront landmark designed by Canadian architect Arthur Erickson. The backdrop of blue sky and sea complements the building's nautical lines. The center often holds trade shows that are open to the public, and tours of the building are available.

need a break? Those waiting for their boats at the Broadway Pier can enjoy a fresh seafood salad or some New England–style clam chowder in an edible sourdough bowl at the **Bay Café** (✉ 1050 N. Harbor Dr., Embarcadero ☎ 619/595–1083).

⑤ Firehouse Museum. Fire-fighting artifacts of all sorts fill this converted fire station, which at one time also served as the repair shop for all of San Diego's fire-fighting equipment. Three large rooms contain everything from 19th-century horse- and hand-drawn fire engines to 20th-century motorized trucks, the latest dating from 1942. Extinguishers, helmets, and other memorabilia from all over the world are also on display. Ages 12 and under are free. ⊠ *1572 Columbia St., Little Italy* ☎ *619/232–3473* ⊠ *$3* ⊙ *Wed.–Fri. 10–2, weekends 10–4.*

⓫ Gaslamp Quarter Historic District. The 16½-block national historic district contains most of the Victorian-style buildings that rose in San Diego after Alonzo Horton arrived in 1867 bent on supplanting San Diego's Old Town with a new downtown closer to the waterfront. Business boomed in New Town in the late 1800s, when Market Street was the center of the downtown commercial district, but at the turn of the 20th century commerce moved west toward Broadway, and many of San Diego's first buildings fell into disrepair. During the early 1900s, prostitutes picked up sailors in lively area taverns and dance halls, and crime flourished; the blocks between Market Street and the waterfront were best avoided. The quarter became known as the Stingaree district, possibly because, it was said, you could be stung as easily here as by a stingray in San Diego Bay.

When the move for downtown redevelopment gained momentum in the 1970s, there was talk of bulldozing the buildings and starting from scratch. History buffs, developers, architects, and artists formed the Gaslamp Quarter Council, however, and gathered funds from the government and private benefactors to clean up and preserve the quarter, restoring the finest old buildings, and attracting businesses and the public back to its heart. Their efforts have paid off. Former flophouses have become choice office buildings, and the area is filled with trendy shops, restaurants and nightclubs that draw crowds. During baseball season, the streets flood with Padres fans, and festivals, such as Mardi Gras in the Gaslamp in February, bring in the partygoers. At lunchtime, the eateries are crowded with conventioneers who stroll over in the sunshine from the nearby convention center. ⊠ *Between 4th and 5th Aves., from Broadway to Market St.*

William Heath Davis House (⊠ 410 Island Ave., at 4th Ave., Gaslamp Quarter ☎ 619/233–4692), one of the first residences in town, houses the Gaslamp Quarter Historical Foundation, the district's curator. Before Alonzo Horton came to town, Davis, a prominent San Franciscan—born in Honolulu to a Boston shipping family—had made an unsuccessful attempt to develop the waterfront area. In 1850 he had this prefab saltbox-style house shipped around Cape Horn and assembled in San Diego (it was originally located at State and Market streets). Docents give tours ($3) of the house during museum hours, which are Tuesday–Saturday 10–6, Sunday 9–3. Regularly scheduled two-hour walking tours of the historic district leave from the house on Saturday at 11 and cost $8. The museum also sells detailed self-guided tour maps of the district for $2.

The Victorian **Horton Grand Hotel** (⊠ 311 Island Ave., Gaslamp Quarter ☎ 619/544–1886) was created in the mid-1980s by joining together two historic hotels, the Kahle Saddlery and the Grand Hotel, built in the boom days of the 1880s; Wyatt Earp stayed at the Kahle Saddlery—then called the Brooklyn Hotel—while he was in town speculating on real estate ventures and opening gambling halls. The two hotels were not originally located at this address; they were once about four blocks away, but were dismantled and reconstructed to make way for Horton Plaza. A small Chinese Museum behind the lobby serves as a tribute to the surrounding Chinatown district, a collection of modest structures that once housed Chinese laborers and their families.

The majority of the quarter's landmark buildings are on 4th and 5th avenues, between Island Avenue and Broadway. If you don't have much time, stroll down 5th Avenue, where highlights include the Backesto Building (No. 614), the Mercantile Building (No. 822), the Louis Bank of Commerce (No. 835), and the Watts-Robinson Building (No. 903). The Romanesque-revival **Keating Building** (⊠ 432 F St., at 5th Ave., Gaslamp Quarter) was designed by the same firm that created the famous Hotel Del Coronado. At the corner of 4th Avenue and F Street, peer into the Hard Rock Cafe, which occupies a restored turn-of-the-20th-century tavern with a 12-foot mahogany bar and a spectacular stained-glass domed ceiling.

The section of G Street between 6th and 9th avenues has become a haven for galleries; stop in one of them to pick up a map of the downtown arts district. Just to the north, on E and F streets from 6th to 12th avenues, the evolving Urban Art Trail has added pizzazz to drab city thoroughfares by transforming such things as trash cans and traffic controller boxes into canvases. For additional information about the historic area, call the **Gaslamp Quarter Association** (☎ 619/233–5227) or log on to their Web site www.gaslamp.org.

need a break? Fifth Avenue between F and G streets is lined with restaurants, many with outdoor patios. Hip coffeehouses have also sprung up. You can nurse a double espresso or imported beer at **Café LuLu** (⊠ 419 F St., Gaslamp Quarter ☎ 619/238–0114).

★ ❿ **Horton Plaza.** Downtown's centerpiece is the shopping, dining, and entertainment mall that fronts Broadway and G Street from 1st to 4th avenues and covers more than six city blocks. Designed by Jon Jerde and completed in 1985, Horton Plaza is far from what one would imagine a shopping center—or city center—to be. A collage of pastels with elaborate, colorful tile work on benches and stairways, banners waving in the air, and modern sculptures marking the entrances, Horton Plaza rises in uneven, staggered levels to six floors; great views of downtown from the harbor to Balboa Park and beyond can be had here. The complex's architecture has strongly affected the rest of downtown's development—new apartment and condominium complexes along G and Market streets mimic its brightly colored towers and cupolas.

Horton Plaza has a multilevel parking garage; even so, lines to find a space can be long. The first three hours of parking are free with validation; after that it's $1 for every 20 minutes. If you use this notoriously confusing fruit-and-vegetable–themed garage, be sure to remember at which produce level you've left your car. If you're staying downtown, inquire at your hotel about the complimentary Horton Plaza shopping shuttle, which stops at the cruise ship terminal and the convention center in addition to several downtown lodgings.

Macy's, Nordstrom, and Mervyn's department stores anchor the plaza, and an eclectic assortment of more than 140 clothing, sporting-goods, jewelry, book, and gift shops flank them. Other attractions include the country's largest Sam Goody music store and a Planet Hollywood. A movie complex, restaurants, and a long row of take-out ethnic food shops and dining patios line the uppermost tier. The respected San Diego Repertory Theatre has two stages below ground level. Most stores are open 10–9 weekdays, 10–6 Saturday, and 11–7 Sunday, but during the winter holidays and in summer many places stay open longer. ☎ 619/238–1596 ⊕ www.hortonplaza.shoppingtown.com.

3 International Visitor Information Center. One of the two visitor information centers operated by the San Diego Convention and Visitors Bureau (the other is in La Jolla), this is the best resource for information on the city. The staff members and volunteers who run the center speak many languages and are acquainted with the myriad needs and requests of tourists. They dispense information on hotels, restaurants, and tourist attractions, including those in Tijuana, and provide discount coupons for many. ⊠ 1040 1/3 W. Broadway, at Harbor Dr. ☎ 619/236–1212 ⊕ www.sandiego.org ⊙ June–Aug., daily 9–5; Sept.–May, Thurs.–Tues. 9–4.

need a break? Hungry shoppers sit at the counters and tables outside the informal eateries on Horton Plaza's top level, where you can get everything from fresh hot cinnamon rolls to pizza and sushi. Just want a caffeine recharge? Coffee carts include the **Expresso Bar,** outside Nordstrom on level 1. **Starbucks** fans can get their fix inside stores on level 1 and on the street level, off Broadway Circle.

2 Maritime Museum. A must for anyone with an interest in nautical history, **Fodor'sChoice** this collection of six restored and replica ships affords a fascinating ★ glimpse of San Diego during its heyday as a commercial seaport. The museum's headquarters are the *Berkeley,* an 1898 ferryboat moored at the foot of Ash Street. The steam-driven ship, which served the Southern Pacific Railroad in San Francisco until 1958, played its most important role during the great earthquake of 1906, when it saved thousands of people from the fires that had engulfed San Francisco by carrying them across San Francisco Bay to Oakland. Its ornate carved-wood paneling, stained-glass windows, and plate-glass mirrors have been restored, and its main deck serves as a floating museum, with permanent exhibits on West Coast maritime history and complementary rotating exhibits. Anchored to the north of the *Berkeley* is the small Scottish steam yacht *Medea,* launched in 1904, which may be boarded but has no interpretive displays.

A large number of visitors are drawn to the museum's sailing ships. The newest is a replica of an 18th-century British Royal Navy frigate, HMS *Surprise,* used in the Academy Award-winning *Master and Commander: The Far Side of the World,* starring Russell Crowe. Before the museum purchased the *Surprise* and put it on permanent exhibit in 2004, the best known ship in its collection was the *Star of India,* often considered a symbol of the city. An iron windjammer built in 1863, the *Star of India* made 21 trips around the world in the late 1800s, when it traveled the East Indian trade route, shuttled immigrants from England to New Zealand, and served the Alaskan salmon trade. Once sailing ships became obsolete, the *Star* was spared demolition by a group of San Diegans who bought it and retired it to San Diego in 1927. It has been a harbor landmark since then, although it had to wait until 1959 before volunteers could begin the laborious task of stripping its wooden decks, mending its sails, polishing its figurehead, and carrying out other restoration work. The oldest active iron sailing ship in the world, it makes rare short excursions but for the most part stays moored at the pier to receive visitors. If you crave more than a dockside experience, you can take to the water in the museum's other sailing ship, the *Californian,* a replica of a 19th-century revenue cutter that patrolled the shores of California. Designated the official tall ship of the State of California, it can be boarded for a variety of half- and full-day sails (weather permitting) on weekends. (Typically, weekday cruises are reserved for schoolchildren.) Tickets may only be purchased at the museum on day of sail. Full-day sails leave at 10 AM and half-day sails leave at 1 PM. The sails are most popular on sunny days, when it's recommended to show up at least one hour ahead of desired departure. Another ship in the museum's collection is the *Pilot,* which guided ships into and out of San Diego Bay for 82 years. Removed from service in 1996, it was refurbished and retrofitted for use as a floating classroom. ⊠ *1492 N. Harbor Dr., Embarcadero* ☎ *619/234–9153* ⊕ *www.sdmaritime.org* ▨ *$8 includes entry to all ships* ☉ *Daily 9–8, until 9 PM in summer.*

➐ Museum of Contemporary Art, San Diego. The downtown branch of the city's modern art museum has taken on its own personality. Its postmodern, cutting-edge exhibitions are perfectly complemented by the steel-and-glass transportation complex of which it's a part. Four small galleries in the two-story building host rotating shows, some from the permanent collection in the older La Jolla branch, others loaned from far-flung international museums. If you get the chance, stop by TNT (Thursday Night Thing), an eclectic series of free events held at 7 PM the first Thursday of each month. Happenings include live bands, DJ lessons, films, or interpretive artists. ⊠ *1001 Kettner Blvd., Downtown* ☎ *619/234–1001* ▨ *Free* ☉ *Daily 11–5* ☉ *Closed Wed.*

➍ San Diego Aircraft Carrier Museum. After 47 years of worldwide service, the retired USS *Midway* began a new tour of duty on the south side of the Navy pier in 2004. Launched just after the end of World War II, the 1,001-foot-long ship was the largest in the world for the first 10 years of its existence. Now it serves as the most visible landmark on the north Embarcadero and as a floating interactive museum—an appropriate addition to the town that is the home of one-third of the Pacific fleet and the birthplace of naval aviation. Start on the hangar deck, where an F-14 Tomcat jet fighter is just one of several aircraft displayed onboard. Through passageways and up and down ladderwells, you'll get to see how the *Midway's* 4,500 crew members lived and worked on this "city at sea." While the entire tour is impressive, you'll find yourself saying "wow" when you step out onto the 4-acre flight deck—not only the best place to get an idea of the ship's scale, but also one of the most interesting vantage points for a view of the bay and the city skyline. The museum also includes changing displays of aircraft, a flight simulator, and interactive exhibits focusing on naval aviation. There is a café and a gift shop. ⊠ *Navy Pier, 11A, Downtown* ☎ *619/544–9600* ⊕ *www.midway. org* ⊠ *$13* ☉ *Daily 10–5.*

★ ♺ **8** **Seaport Village.** On a prime stretch of waterfront that spreads out across 14 acres connecting the harbor with hotel towers and the convention center, the village's three bustling shopping plazas are designed to reflect the architectural styles of early California, especially New England clapboard and Spanish mission. A ¼-mi wooden boardwalk that runs along the bay and 4 mi of paths lead to specialty shops—everything from a kite store and rubber-stamp emporium to a shop devoted to left-handed people—as well as snack bars and restaurants, many with harbor views; there are about 75 in all. Seaport Village's shops are open daily 10 to 9 (10 to 10 in summer); a few eateries open early for breakfast, and many have extended nighttime hours, especially in summer.

The **Seaport Village Carousel** has 54 animals—lots of horses plus a giraffe, dragon, elephant, dog, and others—hand-carved and hand-painted by Charles Looff in 1895. (This is a replacement for Seaport Village's previous historic carousel, also a Looff, which was sold to a private collector in 2004.) Tickets are $2. Strolling clowns, balloon sculptors, mimes, musicians, and magicians are also on hand throughout the village to entertain kids; those not impressed by such pretechnological displays can duck into the Time Out entertainment center near the carousel and play video games. ⊠ *Downtown* ☎ *619/235–4014, 619/235–4013 events hotline, 888/387–3879 carousel information,* ⊕ *www. seaportvillage.com.*

need a break?

The food court near the carousel serves up fast Greek, Mexican, Italian, deli, and all-American fare—pretty much anything you can think of. You can sit at a table in a shaded courtyard, on a harborside patio, or on the nearby seawall. **Upstart Crow & Co.** (⊠ Seaport Village, Central Plaza, Embarcadero ☎ 619/232–4855), a combination bookstore and coffeehouse, serves good cappuccino and espresso with pastries and cakes.

6 **Transit Center.** The Mission revival–style **Santa Fe Depot,** which replaced the original 1887 station on this site when it opened in 1915 for the Panama–California International Exposition, serves Amtrak and Coaster passengers. A booth here has bus schedules, maps, and tourist brochures. Formerly an easily spotted area landmark, the graceful, tile-domed depot is now overshadowed by **1 America Plaza,** the 34-story office tower across the street. At the base of this skyscraper, designed by architect Helmut Jahn, is a center linking the city's train, trolley, and bus systems. The building's signature crescent-shaped, glass-and-steel canopy arches out over the trolley tracks. The Greyhound bus station (120 West Broadway) is a few blocks away. ⊠ *Broadway and Kettner Blvd., Downtown.*

9 U. S. Grant Hotel. Far more formal than most other hotels in San Diego, the doyenne of downtown lodgings has a marble lobby, gleaming chandeliers, attentive doormen, and other touches that hark back to the more gracious era when it was built (1910). Funded in part by the son of the president for whom it was named, the hotel was extremely opulent from the beginning; 350 of its 437 rooms had private baths, highly unusual for that time. Through the years it became noted for its famous guests—U.S. presidents from Woodrow Wilson to George Bush (the elder) have stayed here. Taking up a city block—it's bounded by 3rd and 4th avenues, C Street, and Broadway—the hotel occupies the site of San Diego's first hotel, constructed by Alonzo Horton in 1870. ⊠ 326 Broadway, Gaslamp Quarter ☎ 619/232–3121.

off the beaten path

VILLA MONTEZUMA – Built as the residence of Jesse Shepard, an English-born pianist, spiritualist, and novelist prominent on the San Diego social scene briefly in the 1880s, this "Painted Lady" of 1887 adapts the elements of high Queen Anne style to its original owner's unique aesthetic interests. It's filled with fascinating period and personal details: stained-glass windows depicting Shakespeare, Beethoven, Mozart, Sappho, and Goethe; redwood panels; tiled fireplaces; family portraits; and tributes from Shepard's famous admirers. The villa, which is in a not-yet-gentrified area east of I–5, was restored by the San Diego Historical Society, whose docents give continuous tours. Architecture buffs will enjoy combining a visit to this house with one to the Marston House in Balboa Park, 10 minutes to the north and also operated by the Historical Society. ⊠ 1925 K St., Downtown ☎ 619/239–2211 ☜ $5 ☽ Fri.–Sun. 10–4:30, Dec. also open Thurs. 10–4:30; last tour at 3:45.

CORONADO

Although it's actually an isthmus, easily reached from the mainland if you head north from Imperial Beach, Coronado has always seemed like an island—and is often referred to as such. The Spaniards called it Los Coronados, or "the Crowned Ones," in the late 1500s and the name stuck. Today's residents, many of whom live in grand Victorian homes handed down for generations, tend to consider their community a sort of royal encampment, safe from the hassles and hustle of San Diego proper.

North Island Naval Air Station was established in 1911 on Coronado's north end, across from Point Loma, and was the site of Charles Lindbergh's departure on the transcontinental flight that preceded his famous solo flight across the Atlantic (a San Diego–area company manufactured the *Spirit of St. Louis*). Today high-tech aircraft and seacraft arrive and depart from North Island, providing a real-life education in military armament. Coronado's long relationship with the U.S. Navy and its desirable real estate have made it an enclave for wealthy military personnel; it's said to have more retired admirals per capita than anywhere else in the United States.

The streets of Coronado are wide, quiet, and friendly, with lots of neighborhood parks where young families mingle with the area's many senior citizens. Grand old homes face the waterfront and the Coronado Municipal Golf Course, under the bridge at the north end of Glorietta Bay; it's the site of the annual July 4 fireworks display. Community celebrations and concerts take place in Spreckels Park on Orange Avenue.

Coronado is visible from downtown and Point Loma and accessible via the arching blue 2$\frac{9}{10}$-mi-long San Diego–Coronado Bridge. The bridge handles some 68,000 cars each day, and rush hour tends to be slow, which is fine, because the view of the harbor, downtown, and the island is breathtaking, day and night.

Until the bridge was completed in 1969, visitors and residents relied on the Coronado Ferry, which ran across the harbor from downtown San Diego but shut down when the bridge opened, much to the dismay of those who were fond of traveling at a leisurely pace. In 1987 the ferry returned. Residents and commuting workers have quickly adapted to this traditional mode of transportation, and the ferry has become quite popular with bicyclists, who shuttle their bikes across the harbor and ride Coronado's wide, flat boulevards for hours.

San Diego's Metropolitan Transit System runs a shuttle bus, No. 904, around the island; you can pick it up where you disembark the ferry and ride it out as far as Silver Strand State Beach. Buses start leaving from the ferry landing at 10:30 AM and run once an hour on the half hour until 6:30 PM.

You can board the ferry, operated by **San Diego Harbor Excursion** (☎ 619/ 234–4111, 800/442–7847 in CA ⊕ www.sdhe.com), at the Broadway Pier on the Embarcadero in downtown San Diego; you'll arrive at the Ferry Landing Marketplace in Coronado. Boats depart every hour on the hour from the Embarcadero and every hour on the half hour from Coronado, daily 9–9 from San Diego, 9:30 to 9:30 from Coronado; the fare is $2.25 each way, 50¢ extra for bicycles. Buy tickets at the Broadway Pier or the Ferry Landing Marketplace. San Diego Harbor Excursion also offers water-taxi service weekdays 2 PM–10 PM, and weekends 11 AM–11 PM, later hours can be arranged. The taxi can run between any two points in San Diego Bay. The fare is $6 per person. Call ☎ 619/ 235–8294 to book.

Numbers in the text correspond to numbers in the margin and on the Central San Diego map.

a good tour

Coronado is easy to navigate without a car. When you depart the ferry, you can explore the shops at the **Ferry Landing Marketplace** ⑫ ☛ and from there rent a bicycle or catch the shuttle bus that runs down **Orange Avenue** ⑬, Coronado's main street. You might disembark the bus at 10th Street and Orange to pick up a map at the Coronado Visitor Center, in the lobby of the **Coronado Museum of History and Art** ⑭ building, and then keep strolling along the boutiques-filled promenade until you reach the **Hotel Del Coronado** ⑮ at the end of Orange Avenue. Right across the street from the Del is the **Glorietta Bay Inn** ⑯, another of the island's outstanding early structures. If you've brought your swimsuit, you might continue on to **Silver Strand State Beach ⑰**—just past the Hotel Del, Orange Avenue turns into Silver Strand Boulevard, which soon resumes its original across-the-bridge role as Route 75.

TIMING A leisurely stroll through Coronado takes an hour or so, more if you shop or walk along the beach. If you're a history buff, you might want to visit on Tuesday, Thursday, or Saturday, when you can combine the tour of Coronado's historic homes that departs from the Glorietta Bay Inn at 11 AM with a visit to the Coronado Museum of History and Art, open Tuesday through Saturday. Whenever you come, if you're not staying overnight, remember to get back to the dock in time to catch the final ferry out, at 9:30 (10:30 on weekends).

Sights to See

⑭ **Coronado Museum of History and Art.** The neoclassical First Bank of Commerce building, constructed in 1910, holds the headquarters and archives of the Coronado Historical Association and a museum. The collection celebrates Coronado's history with photographs and displays of its formative events and major sights. Three galleries have permanent displays while a fourth hosts traveling exhibits; all offer interactive activities for children and adults. To check out the town's historic houses, pick up a copy of the inexpensive *Coronado California Centennial History & Tour Guide* at the gift shop. There's also a café and lecture hall. The museum also sponsors a 60-minute walking tour of the architecturally and historically significant buildings that surround it. The tour departs from the museum lobby on Wednesday at 2 PM and Friday at 10:30 AM and costs $8. ⊠ *1100 Orange Ave., Coronado* ☎ *619/435-7242* ☞ *Donations accepted* ⊙ *Weekdays 9–5, Sat. 10–5, Sun. 11–4.*

★ ☾ ► ⑫ **Ferry Landing Marketplace.** This collection of shops at the point of disembarkation for the ferry is on a smaller—and generally less interesting—scale than Seaport Village, but you do get a great view of the downtown San Diego skyline from here. The little shops and restaurants resemble the gingerbread domes of the Hotel Del Coronado. If you want to rent a bike or in-line skates, stop in at **Bikes and Beyond** (⊠ No. 122 ☎ 619/435-7180). ⊠ *1201 1st St., at B Ave., Coronado* ☎ *619/435-8895.*

⑯ **Glorietta Bay Inn.** The former residence of John Spreckels, the original owner of North Island and the property on which the Hotel Del Coronado stands, is now a popular hotel. On Tuesday, Thursday, and Saturday mornings at 11 it's the departure point for a fun and informative 1½-hour walking tour of a few of the area's 86 officially designated historic homes. Sponsored by the Coronado Historical Association, the tour focuses on the Glorietta Bay Inn and the Hotel Del Coronado across the street. In addition, it includes—from the outside only—some spectacular mansions and the Meade House, where L. Frank Baum, author of *The Wizard of Oz,* wrote additional Oz stories. ⊠ *1630 Glorietta Blvd., Coronado* ☎ *619/435-3101, 619/435-5892 tour information* ☞ *$8 for historical tour.*

⑮ Hotel Del Coronado. One of San Diego's best-known sites, the hotel has
Fodor'sChoice been a national historic landmark since 1977. It has a colorful history,
★ integrally connected with that of Coronado itself. The Hotel Del, as natives call it, was the brainchild of financiers Elisha Spurr Babcock Jr.
and H. L. Story, who saw the potential of Coronado's virgin beaches
and its view of San Diego's emerging harbor. They purchased a 4,100-
acre parcel of land in 1885 for $110,000 and threw a lavish July 4 bash
for prospective investors in their hunting and fishing resort. By the end
of the year they had roused public interest—and had an ample return
on their investment. The hotel opened in 1888, although it wasn't actually completed for another six years.

The Del's distinctive red-tile peaks and Victorian gingerbread architecture has served as a set for many movies, political meetings, and extravagant social happenings. It's said that the Duke of Windsor first met
Wallis Simpson here. Fourteen presidents have been guests of the Del,
and the film *Some Like It Hot*—starring Marilyn Monroe, Jack Lemmon, and Tony Curtis—was filmed here.

Broad steps lead up to the main, balconied lobby, which is adorned with
grand oak pillars and ceiling and opens out onto a central courtyard
and gazebo. To the right is the cavernous **Crown Room,** whose arched
ceiling of notched sugar pine was constructed without nails. You can
tell by looking at this space that the hotel's architect, James Reed, had
previously designed railroad stations. A lavish Sunday brunch is served
here 9–2. To the left past the reception desk is the hotel's Signature Shop,
as well as a stairwell descending to the 22-shop Galleria level. Also on
this level is the History Gallery, which displays photos from the Del's
early days.

The patio surrounding the swimming pool is a great place to sit back
and imagine what the bathers looked like during the 1920s, when the
hotel rocked with the good times. To its right, the new Windsor Lawn
provides a green oasis between the hotel and the beach. To the pool's
left are the two seven-story Ocean Tower accommodations. The gift shop
sells books that elaborate on the hotel's history and Kate Morgan, the
Del's resident ghost. Guided tours are available for registered hotel
guests. ⊠ *1500 Orange Ave., Coronado* ☎ *619/435–6611* ⊕ *www.
hoteldel.com.*

⑬ Orange Avenue. It's easy to imagine you're on a street in Cape Cod when
you stroll along this thoroughfare, Coronado's version of a downtown:
the clapboard houses, small restaurants, and boutiques—selling everything from upscale clothing to surfboards—are in some ways more
characteristic of New England than they are of California. But the East
Coast illusion dissipates as quickly as a winter fog when you catch sight
of one of the avenue's many citrus trees—or realize it's February and
the sun is warming your face. The **Coronado Visitor Center** (⊠ 1100
Orange Ave., Coronado ☎619/437–8788 ⊕www.coronadovisitors.com)
is open weekdays 9–5, Saturday 10–5, and Sunday 11–4 year-round.

need a break?   There's an abundance of places to find a caffeine fix on Orange Avenue between 8th Street and the Hotel Del. At the hip **Cafe 1134** (⊠ 1134 Orange Ave., Coronado ☎ 619/437–1134) you can get a good curried tuna sandwich on French bread to accompany your espresso. Peruse the latest art magazine while sipping a latte at the sidewalk café of **Bay Books** (⊠ 1029 Orange Ave., Coronado ☎ 619/435–0070), San Diego's largest independent bookstore. For a deliciously sweet pick-me-up, check out the rich ice cream, frozen yogurt, and sorbet made fresh daily on the premises of **Mootime Creamery** (⊠ 1025 Orange Ave., Coronado ☎ 619/435–2422).

Fodor'sChoice
★

 ⓚ ⑰ **Silver Strand State Beach.** The stretch of sand that runs along Silver Strand Boulevard from the Hotel Del Coronado to Imperial Beach is a perfect family gathering spot, with restrooms and lifeguards. Don't be surprised if you see groups exercising in military style along the beach; this is a training area for the U.S. Navy's SEAL teams. Across from the beach are the Coronado Cays, an exclusive community popular with yacht owners and celebrities, and the Loews Coronado Bay Resort.

en route   San Diego's Mexican-American community is centered in Barrio Logan, under the San Diego–Coronado Bridge on the downtown side. **Chicano Park**, spread along National Avenue from Dewey to Crosby streets, is the barrio's recreational hub. It's worth taking a short detour to see the huge murals of Mexican history painted on the bridge supports at National Avenue and Dewey Street; they're among the best examples of folk art in the city.

HARBOR & SHELTER ISLANDS & POINT LOMA

The populated outcroppings that jut into the bay just west of downtown and the airport demonstrate the potential of human collaboration with nature. Point Loma, Mother Nature's contribution to San Diego's attractions, has always protected the center city from the Pacific's tides and waves. It's shared by military installations, funky motels and fast-food shacks, stately family homes, huge estates, and private marinas packed with sailboats and yachts. Newer to the scene, Harbor and Shelter islands are poster children for landfill. Created out of sand dredged from the San Diego Bay in the second half of the past century, they've become tourist hubs, their high-rise hotels, seafood restaurants, and boat-rental centers looking as solid as those anywhere else in the city.

Numbers in the text correspond to numbers in the margin and on the Central San Diego map.

a good tour   Catalina Boulevard all the way south to the tip of Point Loma to reach **Cabrillo National Monument** ⑱ ▶; you'll be retracing the steps of the earliest European explorers if you use this as a jumping-off point for a tour. North of the monument, as you head back into the neighborhoods of Point Loma, you'll see the white headstones of **Fort Rosecrans National Cemetery** ⑲. Continue north on Catalina Boulevard to Hill Street and turn left to reach the dramatic **Sunset**

Cliffs ⑳, at the western side of Point Loma near Ocean Beach. Return to Catalina Boulevard and backtrack south for a few blocks to find Canon Street, which leads toward the peninsula's eastern (bay) side. Almost at the shore you'll see **Scott Street ㉑**, Point Loma's main commercial drag. Scott Street is bisected by Shelter Island Drive, which leads to **Shelter Island ㉒**. For another example of what can be done with tons of material dredged from a bay, go back up Shelter Island Drive, turn right on Rosecrans Street, and make another right on North Harbor Drive to reach **Harbor Island ㉓**.

TIMING   If you're interested in seeing the tide pools at Cabrillo National Monument, call ahead or check the weather page of the *Union-Tribune* to find out when low tide will occur. Scott Street, with its Point Loma Seafoods, is a good place to find yourself at lunchtime, and Sunset Cliffs Park is where you might want to be when the daylight starts to wane. This drive takes about an hour if you stop briefly at each sight, but you'll want to devote at least an hour to Cabrillo National Monument.

Sights to See

★ ☺ � ⑱ **Cabrillo National Monument.** This 144-acre preserve marks the site of the first European visit to San Diego, made by 16th-century explorer Juan Rodríguez Cabrillo (circa 1498–1543)—historians have never conclusively determined whether he was Spanish or Portuguese. Cabrillo, who had earlier gone on voyages with Hernán Cortés, landed at this spot, which he called San Miguel, in 1542. Government grounds were set aside to commemorate his discovery in 1913, and today the site, with its rugged cliffs and shores and outstanding overlooks, is one of the most frequently visited of all the national monuments.

The **visitor center** presents films and lectures about Cabrillo's voyage, the sea-level tide pools, and migrating gray whales. The center has an excellent shop with books about nature, San Diego, and the sea. Maps of the region, whale posters, flowers, shells, and the requisite postcards, slides, and film are also for sale. Restrooms and water fountains are plentiful along the paths that climb to the monument's various viewing points, but, except for a few vending machines at the visitor center, there's no food. Exploring the grounds consumes time and calories; bring a picnic and rest on a bench overlooking the sailboats.

Interpretive stations with recorded information in six languages—including, appropriately enough, Portuguese—have been installed along the walkways that edge the cliffs. Signs explain the views and wayside exhibits depict the various naval, fishing, and pleasure craft that sail into and fly over the bay. Directly south across the bay from the visitor center is the North Island Naval Air Station at the west end of Coronado. To the left on the shores of Point Loma is the Space and Naval Warfare Systems Center; nuclear-powered submarines are now docked where Cabrillo's small ships anchored in 1542.

A **statue of Cabrillo** overlooks downtown from the next windy promontory, where people gather to admire the stunning panorama over the bay, from the snowcapped San Bernardino Mountains, 130 mi north, to the hills surrounding Tijuana to the south. The stone figure standing on the bluff looks rugged and dashing, but he is a creation of an artist's imagination—no portraits of Cabrillo are known to exist. The statue was donated by the Portuguese navy in 1957.

The moderately steep **Bayside Trail** (☉ Daily 9–4), 2½ mi round-trip, winds through coastal sage scrub, curving under the cliff-top lookouts and taking you ever closer to the bay-front scenery. You cannot reach the beach from this trail and must stick to the path to protect the cliffs from erosion and yourself from thorny plants and snakes—including rattlers. You'll see prickly pear cactus and yucca, black-eyed Susans, fragrant sage, and maybe a lizard or a hummingbird. The climb back is long but gradual, leading up to the old lighthouse. (Note that a mudslide brought on by severe rains in early 2005 caused the lower half of the trail to be closed, awaiting reconstruction. Call park headquarters or check the Web site for news of its reopening.)

The oil lamp of the **Old Point Loma Lighthouse** (☉ Daily 9–5) was first lit in 1855. The light, sitting in a brass-and-iron housing above a white wooden house, shone through a state-of-the-art, French-made lens and was visible from the sea for 25 mi. Unfortunately, it was too high above the cliffs to guide navigators trapped in Southern California's thick offshore fog and low clouds. In 1891 a new lighthouse was built 400 feet below. The old lighthouse, restored to its 1880s appearance, is open to visitors. The U.S. Coast Guard still uses the newer lighthouse and a mighty foghorn to guide boaters through the narrow channel leading into the bay. On the edge of the hill near the old lighthouse sits a refurbished radio room from World War I. It contains displays of U.S. harbor defenses at Point Loma used during World War II.

The western and southern cliffs of Cabrillo National Monument are prime whale-watching territory. A sheltered **viewing station** has a tape-recorded lecture describing the great gray whales' yearly migration from the Bering and Chukchi seas near Alaska to Baja California, and high-powered telescopes help you focus on the whales' water spouts. Whales are visible on clear days from mid-January through March, with the highest concentration in January and February. Park rangers can help you spot them during the annual Whale Watch Weekend, held in the latter part of January, when interpretive programs and entertainment are provided. Note that when the whales return north in the spring, they are too far out in the ocean to be seen from the monument.

More accessible sea creatures can be seen in the **tide pools** (☉ Daily 9–4:30) at the foot of the monument's western cliffs. Drive north from the visitor center to the first road on the left, which winds down to the coast guard station and the shore. When the tide is low you can walk on the rocks around saltwater pools filled with starfish, crabs, anemones, octopuses, and hundreds of other sea creatures and plants. ⊠ *1800 Cabrillo Memorial Dr., Point Loma* ☎ *619/557–5450* ⊕ *www.nps. gov/cabr* ⊠ *$5 per car, $3 per person entering on foot or by bicycle, entrance pass allows unlimited admissions for 1 wk from date of purchase; free for Golden Age and Golden Access passport and National Parks Pass holders* ☉ *Park daily 9–5:15; call for summer hrs.*

19 **Fort Rosecrans National Cemetery.** In 1934, 8 acres of the 1,000 set aside for a military reserve in 1852 were designated as a burial site. About 79,000 people are now interred here; it's impressive to see the rows upon rows of white headstones that overlook both sides of Point Loma just north of the Cabrillo National Monument. Some of those laid to rest at this place were killed in battles that predate California's statehood; the graves of the 17 soldiers and one civilian who died in the 1874 Battle of San Pasqual between troops from Mexico and the United States are marked by a large bronze plaque. Perhaps the most impressive structure in the cemetery is the 75-foot granite obelisk called the Bennington Monument, which commemorates the 66 crew members who died in a boiler explosion and fire on board the USS *Bennington* in 1905. The cemetery, visited by many veterans, is still used for burials. ✉ *Rte. 209, Point Loma* ☎ *619/553–2084* ☉ *Daily 9–5:30.*

23 **Harbor Island.** Following the success of nearby Shelter Island—created in 1950 out of material left behind from dredging a channel in San Diego Bay during the 1930s—the U.S. Navy decided to use the residue that resulted from digging berths deep enough to accommodate aircraft carriers to build another recreational island. Thus in 1961 some 12 million cubic yards of sand and mud dredged from the bay were deposited adjacent to San Diego International Airport and became the 1½-mi-long peninsula known as Harbor Island. Restaurants and high-rise hotels now line its inner shore. The bay shore has pathways, gardens, and picnic spots for sightseeing or working off the calories from the various indoor or outdoor food fests held here. On the west point, Tom Ham's Lighthouse restaurant has a U.S. Coast Guard–approved beacon shining from its tower.

Across from the western end of Harbor Island, at the mainland's **Spanish Landing Park,** a bronze plaque marks the arrival in 1769 of a party from Spain that headed north from San Diego to conquer California. The group was a merger of the crews of two ships, the *San Carlos* and the *San Antonio,* and a contingent that came overland from Baja California. No one knows exactly where the men landed and camped; we can only be certain it wasn't Harbor Island.

21 **Scott Street.** Running along Point Loma's waterfront from Shelter Island to the old Naval Training Center on Harbor Drive, this thoroughfare is lined with deep-sea fishing charters and whale-watching boats. It's a good spot from which to watch fishermen (and women) haul marlin, tuna, and puny mackerel off their boats.

need a break? The freshest and tastiest fish to be found along Point Loma's shores—some would say anywhere in San Diego—comes from **Point Loma Seafoods** (✉ 2805 Emerson St., Point Loma ☎ 619/223–1109), off Scott Street behind the Vagabond Inn. There's a fish market selling raw catch of the day for customers to take home and prepare themselves, but there's also an adjacent take-out counter selling prepared hot or cold foods—seafood cocktails and salads, ceviche, crab and shrimp sandwiches made with freshly baked sourdough bread—for takeout and to be consumed on the premises.

There's outdoor and indoor seating (no waiter service), and you can expect crowds throughout the year. Park a few blocks away if you're coming on the weekend; the adjoining lot suffers from extreme gridlock.

㉒ Shelter Island. In 1950 San Diego's port director thought there should be some use for the sand and mud the Works Project Administration dredged up during the course of deepening a ship channel in the 1930s and '40s. He decided it might be a good idea to raise the shoal that lay off the eastern shore of Point Loma above sea level, landscape it, and add a 2,000-foot causeway to make it accessible.

His hunch paid off. Shelter Island—actually a peninsula—now supports towering mature palms, a cluster of resorts, restaurants, and side-by-side marinas. It's the center of San Diego's yacht-building industry, and boats in every stage of construction are visible in the yacht yards. A long sidewalk runs from the landscaped lawns of the **San Diego Yacht Club** (tucked down Anchorage Street off Shelter Island Drive), past boat brokerages to the hotels and marinas that line the inner shore, facing Point Loma. On the bay side, fishermen launch their boats or simply stand on shore and cast. Families relax at picnic tables along the grass, where there are fire rings and permanent barbecue grills. Within walking distance is the huge Friendship Bell, given to San Diegans by the people of Yokohama, Japan, in 1960.

⑳ Sunset Cliffs. As the name suggests, the 60-foot-high bluffs on the western side of Point Loma south of Ocean Beach are a perfect place to watch the sun descend over the sea. To view the tide pools along the shore, use the staircase off Sunset Cliffs Boulevard at the foot of Ladera Street.

The dramatic coastline here seems to have been carved out of ancient rock. The impact of the waves is very clear: each year more sections of the cliffs sport caution signs. Don't ignore these warnings—it's easy to lose your footing and slip in the crumbling sandstone, and the surf can be extremely rough. Small coves and beaches dot the coastline and are popular with surfers drawn to the pounding waves and locals from the neighborhood who name and claim their special spots. Needle's Eye is considered especially challenging. The homes along the boulevard—pink stucco mansions beside shingled Cape Cod–style cottages—are fine examples of Southern California luxury. ⊠ *Sunset Cliffs Blvd., Point Loma.*

LA JOLLA

La Jollans have long considered their village to be the Monte Carlo of California, and with good cause. Its coastline curves into natural coves backed by verdant hillsides covered with homes worth millions. Although La Jolla is considered part of San Diego, it has its own postal zone and a coveted sense of class; it's gotten far more plebeian these days, but old-monied residents still mingle here with visiting film stars and royalty who frequent established hotels and private clubs. Development and construction have radically altered the once serene and private character of the village, but it has gained a cosmopolitan air that makes it a popular vacation resort.

The Native Americans called the site La Hoya, meaning "the cave," referring to the grottoes that dot the shoreline. The Spaniards changed the name to La Jolla (same pronunciation as La Hoya), "the jewel," and its residents have cherished the name and its allusions ever since.

To reach La Jolla from I–5, if you're traveling north, take the Ardath Road exit, which veers into Torrey Pines Road, and turn right onto Prospect Street. If you're heading south, get off at La Jolla Village Drive exit, which also leads into Torrey Pines Road. Traffic is virtually always congested in this popular area, which is dotted with four-way stop signs and clogged with drivers dropping off passengers and/or trolling for a parking spot. Drive carefully and be prepared to stop frequently when you get into the village.

For those who enjoy meandering, the best way to approach La Jolla from the south is to drive on Mission Boulevard through Mission and Pacific beaches, past the crowds of in-line skaters, bicyclists, and sunbathers. The clutter and congestion ease up as the street becomes La Jolla Boulevard. Road signs along La Jolla Boulevard and Camino de la Costa direct drivers and bicyclists past homes designed by such respected architects as Frank Lloyd Wright and Irving Gill. As you approach the village, La Jolla Boulevard turns into Prospect Street.

Prospect Street and Girard Avenue, the village's main drags, are lined with expensive shops and office buildings. Girard holds the village's only movie house, which tends to show indie films. Through the years the shopping and dining district has spread to Pearl and other side streets. Wall Street, a quiet tree-lined boulevard off Girard Avenue, was once the financial heart of La Jolla, but banks and investment houses can now be found throughout the village. La Jolla's nightlife scene is an active one, with jazz clubs, piano bars, and watering holes for the well-heeled younger set.

Numbers in the text correspond to numbers in the margin and on La Jolla map.

a good tour

At the intersection of La Jolla Boulevard and Nautilus Street, turn toward the sea to reach **Windansea Beach** ❶ ⌐, one of the best surfing spots in town. **Mount Soledad** ❷, about 1½-mi east on Nautilus Street, is La Jolla's highest spot. In the village itself you'll find the town's cultural center, the **Museum of Contemporary Art, San Diego** ❸, on the less trafficked southern end of Prospect. A bit farther north, at the intersection of Prospect Street and Girard Avenue, sits the pretty-in-pink **La Valencia** ❹ hotel, looking out onto the village's great natural attraction, **La Jolla Cove** ❺, which can be accessed from Coast Boulevard, one block to the west. Past the far northern point of the cove, a trail leads down to **La Jolla Caves** ❻.

The beaches along La Jolla Shores Drive north of the caves are some of the finest in the San Diego area, with long stretches allotted to surfers or swimmers. Nearby is the campus of the Scripps Institution of Oceanog-

La Jolla

PACIFIC OCEAN

Torrey Pines State Beach and Reserve

N. Torrey Pines Rd.

S21

Genesee Ave.

Torrey Pines Rd.

La Jolla Village Dr.

TO GOLDEN TRIANGLE

La Jolla Scenic Dr. N.

Gilman Dr.

I-5

Scripps Pier

La Jolla Shores

La Jolla Shores Dr.

Point La Jolla

Shell Beach

Children's Pool

Marine St. Beach

Prospect St.

Torrey Pines

Girard Ave.

Virginia Way

Pearl St.

La Jolla Country Club

La Jolla Blvd.

Nautilus St.

Torrey Pines Rd.

La Jolla Pkwy.

52

0   1 mile
0   1 km

KEY
⚑ Start of tour

raphy. The institution's **Birch Aquarium at Scripps ❼** is inland a bit, off Torrey Pines Road.

La Jolla Shores Drive eventually curves onto Torrey Pines Road, off which you'll soon glimpse the world-famous **Salk Institute ❽**, designed by Louis I. Kahn. The road that leads to the institute ends at the cliffs used as the **Torrey Pines Glider Port ❾**. The hard-to-reach stretch of sand at the foot of the cliffs is officially named **Torrey Pines City Park Beach ❿**, but locals call it Black's Beach. At the intersection of Torrey Pines Road and Genesee Avenue you'll come to the northern entrance of the huge campus of the **University of California at San Diego ⓫** and, a bit farther north, to the stretch of wilderness that marks the end of what most locals consider San Diego proper, **Torrey Pines State Beach and Reserve ⓬**.

TIMING   This tour makes for a leisurely day, although it can be driven in a couple of hours, including stops to take in the views and explore the village of La Jolla (though not to hit any of the beaches—or even a fraction of all the pricey boutiques). The Museum of Contemporary Art is closed Monday, and guided tours of the Salk Institute are given on weekdays only.

Sights to See

☺ ❼ **Birch Aquarium at Scripps.** The largest oceanographic exhibit in the United States, maintained by the Scripps Institution of Oceanography, this sits at the end of a signposted drive leading off North Torrey Pines Road just north of La Jolla Village Drive. More than 60 tanks are filled with colorful saltwater fish, and a 70,000-gallon tank simulates a La Jolla kelp forest. Besides the fish themselves, attractions include a gallery with exhibits based on the institution's ocean-related research, other interactive educational exhibits, a simulated submarine ride, and supermarket shelves stocked with products derived from the sea (including some surprisingly common ones). A concession sells food, and there are outdoor picnic tables. ⊠ *2300 Expedition Way, La Jolla* ☎ *858/534–3474* ⊕ *www.aquarium.ucsd.edu* ⊠ *$10, parking free for 3 hrs* ☉ *Daily 9–5 last ticket sold at 4:30*.

Golden Triangle. La Jolla's newest enclave, spreading through the Sorrento Valley east of I–5, is a far cry from the beach communities with which the name La Jolla has long been associated. High-tech research-and-development companies, attracted to the Golden Triangle area in part by the facilities of the University of California at San Diego, the Scripps Institution of Oceanography, and the Salk Institute, have developed huge state-of-the-art compounds in places that were populated solely by coyotes and jays not so long ago. The area along La Jolla Village Drive and Genesee Avenue has become an architectural proving ground for futuristic buildings. The most striking are those in the Michael Graves–designed Aventine complex, visible from I–5 at La Jolla Village Drive exit. A bit south, near the Nobel exit, and eye-catching in another way, is the huge, white Mormon Temple. Completed in 1993, it looks like a psychedelic medieval castle and still startles drivers heading up the freeway. ⊠ *La Jolla*.

☺ ❻ **La Jolla Caves.** It's a walk of 145 sometimes slippery steps down a tunnel to Sunny Jim, the largest of the caves in La Jolla Cove and the only one reachable by land. The tunnel, man-made, took two years to dig, beginning in 1902; later, a shop was built at its entrance. La Jolla Cave Store, a throwback to that early shop, is still the entrance to the cave, which was named Sunny Jim after a 1920s cartoon character. The shop sells postcards, T-shirts, some stuffed animals and other toys, and watercolors by local artists; it also displays historic photos of La Jolla and collects cave admission fees. There's a coffee bar in the shop. ⊠ *1325 Cave St., La Jolla* ☎ *858/459–0746* 🗐 *$4* ⊙ *Daily 9–5.*

★ ⟳ ❺ **La Jolla Cove.** The wooded spread that looks out over a shimmering blue inlet is what first attracted everyone to La Jolla, from Native Americans to the glitterati; it's the village's enduring cachet. You'll find the cove—as locals always refer to it, as though it were the only one in San Diego—beyond where Girard Avenue dead-ends into Coast Boulevard, marked by towering palms that line a promenade where people strolling in drop-dead designer clothes are as common as Frisbee throwers.

Smaller beaches appear and disappear with the tides, which carve small private coves in cliffs covered with ice plants. Pathways lead down to the beaches. Keep an eye on the tide to avoid getting trapped once the waves come in. A long layer of sandstone stretching out above the waves provides a perfect sunset-watching spot, with plenty of tiny tide pools formed in eroded pockets in the rocks; starfish, sea anemones, and hermit crabs cluster here when the tide is in. Be careful, because these rocks can get slippery.

An underwater preserve at the north end of La Jolla Cove makes the adjoining beach the most popular one in the area. On summer days, when the water visibility reaches 20-feet deep or so, the sea seems to disappear under the mass of bodies floating face down, snorkels poking up out of the water. The small beach is covered with blankets, towels, and umbrellas, and the lawns at the top of the stairs leading down to the cove are staked out by groups of scuba divers, complete with wet suits and tanks. The **Children's Pool,** at the south end of the park, has a curving beach protected by a seawall from strong currents and waves. Since the pool and its beach have become home to an ever-growing colony of Harbor seals, it's no longer open to swimmers; however it's the best place on the coast to view these engaging creatures. If you're not here by noon, forget about finding a parking spot or a small square of sand for your towel. But no matter what time you arrive, walk through **Ellen Browning Scripps Park,** past the groves of twisted junipers to the cliff's edge. Perhaps one of the open-air shelters overlooking the sea will be free, and you can spread your picnic out on a table and enjoy the scenery.

❹ **La Valencia.** The art deco–style La Valencia, which has operated as a luxury hotel since 1928, has long been a gathering spot for Hollywood celebrities; in the 1940s Gregory Peck would invite friends to La Valencia's Whaling Bar to try to persuade them to participate in one of his favorite projects, La Jolla Theater. Today the hotel's grand lobby, with floor-to-ceiling windows overlooking La Jolla Cove, is a popular wedding spot, and the Whaling Bar is still a favorite meeting place for power brokers. ⊠ *1132 Prospect St., La Jolla* ☎ *858/454–0771* ⊕ *www.lavalencia.com.*

2 Mount Soledad. La Jolla's highest spot can be reached by taking Nautilus Street all the way east. The top of the mountain is an excellent vantage point from which to get a sense of San Diego's geography: looking down from here you can see the coast from the county's northern border to the south far beyond downtown—barring smog and haze. A half-acre on the summit is used to honor those killed in wars. The steel-and-concrete cross memorializes veterans, and services are held here on Memorial Day. ⊠ *La Jolla.*

★ 3 Museum of Contemporary Art, San Diego. The oldest section of La Jolla's branch of San Diego's modern art museum was originally a residence, designed by Irving Gill for philanthropist Ellen Browning Scripps in 1916. In the mid-1990s, the compound was updated and expanded by architect Robert Venturi and his colleagues at Venturi, Scott Brown and Associates, who respected Gill's original geometric structure and clean, mission-style lines while adding their own distinctive touches. The result is a striking contemporary building that looks as though it's always been here.

The light-filled Axline Court serves as the museum's entrance. From here, a patterned terrazzo floor leads to galleries where the museum's permanent collection and rotating exhibits are on display. The artwork inside gets major competition from the setting: you can look out from the top of a grand stairway onto a landscaped sculpture garden that contains rare 100-year-old California plant specimens and, beyond that, to the Pacific Ocean. The bookstore and the refurbished Sherwood Auditorium have separate outside entrances, so you don't have to enter the museum to browse the modern-art volumes and stylish design gifts or attend the auditorium's programs.

California artists figure prominently in the museum's permanent collection of post-1950s art, but the museum also includes examples of every major art movement since that time—works by Andy Warhol, Robert Rauschenberg, Frank Stella, Joseph Cornell, and Jenny Holzer, to name a few. Important pieces by artists from San Diego and Tijuana were acquired in the 1990s. The museum also gets major visiting shows. The Museum Café serves soups, salads, and sandwiches as well as drinks. ⊠ *700 Prospect St., La Jolla* ☎ *858/454–3541* ⊕ *www.mcasandiego. org* ⊑ *$6, free 1st Sun. and 3rd Tues. of month* ☉ *Thurs. 11–7, Fri.–Tues. 11–5.*

8 Salk Institute. The world-famous biological-research facility founded by polio vaccine developer Jonas Salk sits on 26 cliff-top acres. The twin structures that modernist architect Louis I. Kahn designed in the 1960s in consultation with Dr. Salk used poured concrete and other low-maintenance materials to clever effect. The thrust of the laboratory–office complex is outward toward the Pacific Ocean, an orientation that is accentuated by a foot-wide "Stream of Life" that flows through the center of a travertine marble courtyard between the buildings. The courtyard and stream of water were inspired by architect Louis Barragán. Architects-to-be and building buffs enjoy the free tours of the property; call ahead to book, because the tours take place only when enough people express interest. ⊠ *10010 N. Torrey Pines Rd., La Jolla* ☎ *858/453–4100 Ext. 1200* ⊕ *www.salk.edu* ⊡ *Free* ⊙ *Grounds weekdays 9–5; architectural tours Mon., Wed., and Fri. at noon, Thurs. at 12:30 and every other Tues. at 11. Reservations required, so call ahead.*

⑩ Torrey Pines City Park Beach. Black's Beach—as locals call it—is one of the most beautiful and secluded stretches of sand in San Diego, backed by cliffs whose colors change with the angle of the sun. There are no restrooms, showers, or snack shops, although some hardy (and law-breaking) entrepreneurs lug ice chests filled with sodas and beer down the cliffs to sell to the unprepared. The paths leading down to the beach are steep, and the cliffs are unstable—pay attention to the safety signs and stick to the well-traveled trails. Black's Beach was clothing-optional for many years; although nudity is now prohibited by law, many people still shed their suits whenever the authorities are out of sight. ⊠ *La Jolla.*

⑨ Torrey Pines Glider Port. On days when the winds are just right, gliders line the cliffs, waiting for the perfect gust to carry them into the sky. Seasoned hang gliders with a good command of the current can soar over the sea for hours, then ride the winds back to the cliffs. Less-experienced fliers sometimes land on the beach below, to the cheers and applause of the sunbathers who scoot out of the way. If you're coming via the freeway, take the Genesee Avenue exit west from I–5 and follow the signs when you approach the coast. ⊠ *La Jolla.*

⑫ Torrey Pines State Beach and Reserve. *Pinus torreyana*, the rarest native pine tree in the United States, enjoys a 1,750-acre sanctuary at the northern edge of La Jolla. About 6,000 of these unusual trees, some as tall as 60 feet, grow on the cliffs here. The park is one of only two places in the world (the other is Santa Rosa Island, off Santa Barbara) where the Torrey pine grows naturally. The reserve has several hiking trails leading to the cliffs, 300 feet above the ocean; trail maps are available at the park station. Wildflowers grow profusely in spring, and the ocean panoramas are always spectacular. When in this upper part of the park, respect the various restrictions. Not permitted: picnicking, smoking, leaving the trails, or collecting plant specimens.

You can unwrap your sandwiches, however, at Torrey Pines State Beach, just below the reserve. When the tide is out, it's possible to walk south all the way past the lifeguard towers to Black's Beach over rocky promontories carved by the waves (avoid the bluffs, however; they're unstable). **Los Peñasquitos Lagoon** at the north end of the reserve is one of the many natural estuaries that flow inland between Del Mar and Oceanside. It's a good place to watch shorebirds. Volunteers lead guided nature walks at 11:30 and 1:30 on most weekends. ⊠ *N. Torrey Pines Rd., Old Hwy. 101, La Jolla, Exit I–5 onto Carmel Valley Rd. going west, then turn left (south) on Old Hwy. 101* ☎ *858/755–2063* ⊡ *Parking $6* ⊙ *Daily 8–dusk.*

⑪ University of California at San Diego. The campus of San Diego's most prestigious research university spreads over 1,200 acres of coastal canyons and eucalyptus groves, where students and faculty jog, bike, and Rollerblade to class. If you're interested in contemporary art, ask at one of the two information booths for a map showing the location of the Stuart Collection of Sculpture—15 thought-provoking, site-specific works of art by artists such as Nam June Paik, William Wegman, Niki de St. Phalle, Jenny Holzer, and others arrayed around the campus. UCSD's Price Center has a well-stocked, two-level bookstore—the largest in San Diego—and a good coffeehouse, Espresso Roma. Look for the postmodern Geisel Library (named for longtime La Jolla residents "Dr. Seuss" and his wife), which resembles a large spaceship. ⊠ *Exit I–5 onto La Jolla Village Dr. going west; take Gilman Dr. off-ramp to right and continue on to information kiosk at campus entrance on Gilman Dr., La Jolla* ☎ *858/534–4414 campus tour information* ☼ *90-min campus tours Sun. at 2 from South Gilman Information Pavilion; reserve before 3 Fri.*

▶ ❶ **Windansea Beach.** Fans of pop satirist Tom Wolfe may recall *The Pump House Gang,* which pokes fun at the Southern California surfing culture. Wolfe drew many of his barbs from observations he made at Windansea, the surfing beach west of La Jolla Boulevard near Nautilus Street. The wave action here is said to be as good as that in Hawai'i. ⊠ *La Jolla.*

> **need a break?** A breakfast of the excellent buttery croissants or brioches at the **French Pastry Shop** (⊠ 5550 La Jolla Blvd., La Jolla ☎ 858/454–9094) is good preparation for time at Windansea Beach.

MISSION BAY & SEAWORLD

Mission Bay Park is San Diego's monument to sports and fitness. This 4,600-acre aquatic park has 27 mi of bay-shore beaches and 17 mi of ocean frontage. Admission is free. All you need for a perfect day is a bathing suit, shorts, and the right selection of playthings.

When explorer Juan Rodríguez Cabrillo first spotted the bay in 1542, he called it Bahía Falsa (False Bay) because the ocean-facing inlet led to acres of swampland that was inhospitable to boats and inhabitants. In the 1960s the city planners decided to dredge the swamp and build a bay with acres of beaches and lawns. Only 25% of the land was permitted to be commercially developed, and only a handful of resort hotels break up the striking natural landscape.

You don't have to go far from the freeway to experience the beach-party atmosphere of Mission Bay. A 5-mi-long pathway runs parallel to I–5 through the eastern section of the bay from a trailer park and miniature golf course, south past the high-rise Hilton Hotel to Sea World Drive. The sky above the lawns facing I–5 is flooded with the bright colors of huge, intricately made kites: the San Diego Kite Club meets on East Mission Bay Drive south of the Hilton, and on the weekends club members set loose their amazing creations.

Playgrounds and picnic areas abound on the beach and low grassy hills of the park. Group gatherings, company picnics, and birthday parties are common sights; huge parking lots accommodate swelling crowds on sunny days. On weekday evenings, joggers, bikers, and skaters take over. In the daytime, swimmers, water-skiers, anglers, and boaters—some in single-person kayaks, others in crowded powerboats—vie for space in the water. The San Diego Crew Classic, which takes place in late March or April, fills this area of the bay with teams from all over the country. College reunions, complete with flying school colors and keg beer, are popular at the event.

North of Belmont Park to Pacific Beach, Mission Boulevard runs along a narrow strip embraced by the Pacific Ocean on the west, called Mission Beach, and the bay on the east. The pathways in this area are lined with vacation homes, many of which can be rented by the week or month. Those who are fortunate enough to live here year-round have the bay as their front yard, with wide sandy beaches, volleyball courts, and—less of an advantage—an endless stream of sightseers on the sidewalk.

One Mission Bay caveat: swimmers should note signs warning about water pollution; certain areas of the bay are chronically polluted, and bathing is strongly discouraged.

Numbers in the text correspond to numbers in the margin and on the Mission Bay map.

a good tour

If you're coming from I–5, the **San Diego Visitor Information Center ❶** ⌐ is just about at the end of the Clairemont Drive–East Mission Bay Drive exit (you'll see the prominent sign). At the point where East Mission Bay Drive turns into Sea World Drive you can detour left to **Fiesta Island ❷**, popular with jet skiers and speedboat racers. Continue around the curve to the west to reach **SeaWorld San Diego ❸**, the area's best-known attraction.

You'll next come to Ingraham Street, the central north–south drag through the bay. If you take it north, you'll shortly spot Vacation Road, which leads into the focal point of this part of the bay, the waterskiing hub of **Vacation Isle ❹**. At Ingraham, Sea World Drive turns into Sunset Cliffs Boulevard and intersects with West Mission Bay Drive. Past this intersection, Quivira Way leads west toward **Hospitality Point ❺**, where there are nice, quiet places to have a picnic.

If you continue west on West Mission Bay Drive, just before it meets Mission Boulevard, you'll come to the Bahia Resort Hotel, where you can catch the *Bahia Belle* ❻ for a cruise around the bay. Ventura Cove, opposite the Bahia Hotel, is another good spot to unpack your cooler. Almost immediately south of where West Mission Bay Drive turns into Mission Boulevard is the resurrected **Belmont Park ❼**.

TIMING It would take less than an hour to drive this tour. You may not find a visit to SeaWorld fulfilling unless you spend at least a half day; a full day is recommended. Belmont Park is open daily, but not all its attractions are open year-round.

Sights to See

❻ *Bahia Belle.* At the dock of the Bahia Resort Hotel, on the eastern shores of West Mission Bay Drive, you can board a restored stern-wheeler for a sunset cruise of the bay and party until the wee hours. There's always music, mostly jazz, rock, and blues, and on Friday and Saturday nights the music is live. You can imbibe at the Belle's full bar, which opens at 9:30 PM, but many revelers like to disembark at the Bahia's sister hotel, the Catamaran Resort, and have a few rounds at the Cannibal Bar there before reboarding (the boat cruises between the two hotels, which co-own it, stopping to pick up passengers every half hour). The first cruise on Sunday is devoted to kids, but most cruises get a mixed crowd of families, couples, and singles. ⊠ *998 W. Mission Bay Dr., Mission Bay* ☎ *858/539–7779* 🖅 *$6 for unlimited cruising; 9:30 PM or later, cruisers must be at least 21; free for guests of Bahia and Catamaran hotels* ⊘ *Sept.–Nov. and Jan.–June, Fri. and Sat. 6:30 PM–1 AM, departures every hr on the ½ hr; June, Wed.–Sun. 6:30 PM–1 AM; July and Aug., daily 6:30 PM–1 AM; closed in Dec.*

🐾 **❼** **Belmont Park.** The once-abandoned amusement park between the bay and Mission Beach boardwalk is now a shopping, dining, and recreation complex. Twinkling lights outline the **Giant Dipper,** an antique wooden roller coaster on which screaming thrill-seekers ride more than 2,600 feet of track and 13 hills (riders must be at least 4′2″). Created in 1925 and listed on the National Register of Historic Places, this is one of the few old-time roller coasters left in the United States. The **Plunge,** an indoor swimming pool, also opened in 1925, and was the largest—60 feet by 125 feet—saltwater pool in the world at the time (it's had fresh water since 1951). Johnny Weismuller and Esther Williams are among the stars who were captured on celluloid swimming here. Other Belmont Park attractions, nonvintage, include **Pirate's Cove,** a fantastic maze of brightly colored tunnels, slides, an obstacle course, and more, all with a pirate theme; a video arcade; a submarine ride; bumper cars; a tilt-a-whirl; an antique carousel; and a trampoline. Belmont Park also has the most consistent wave in the county at the **Wave House,** where the FlowRider provides surfers and bodyboarders a near perfect simulated wave on which to practice their skills. Plans to incorporate a skatepark are in place, as well. ⊠ *3146 Mission Blvd., Mission Bay* ☎ *858/488–1549, 858/488–3110 for pool* ⊕ *www.belmontpark.com* ✉ *$4 for roller coaster, $3 for bumper cars, vertical plunge, and tilt-a-whirl, all other rides $2; full-day unlimited ride package $16.95 for 50″ and over, $11.95 for under 50″; all rides 75¢ June–Aug., Tues. 4 PM to closing; pool $5 for one-time entry* ⊙ *Park opens at 11 daily, ride hrs vary seasonally; pool open weekdays 5:30–8 AM, noon–1 PM, and 2:30–8 PM and weekends 8–4.*

② **Fiesta Island.** The most undeveloped area of Mission Bay Park, this is popular with bird-watchers (there's a large protected nesting site for the California tern at the northern tip of the island) as well as with dog owners—it's the only place in the park where pets can run free. Jet skiers and speedboat racers come here, too. At Christmas the island provides an excellent vantage point for viewing the bay's Parade of Lights. In July the annual Over-the-Line Tournament, a competition involving a local version of softball, attracts thousands of players and oglers, drawn by the teams' raunchy names and outrageous behavior. When you drive onto Fiesta Island you can't immediately turn back, as the road leads one way around the perimeter.

⑤ **Hospitality Point.** Enjoy lunch in this pretty, secluded spot, which has a view of sailboats and yachts entering the open sea. At the entrance to Hospitality Point, the City of San Diego Park and Recreation Department office supplies area maps and other recreational information. ⊠ *2581 Quivira Ct., Mission Bay* ☎ *619/221–8901* ⊙ *Weekdays 9–5; closed city holidays.*

> **need a break?**

Sportsmen's Sea Foods (⊠ 1617 Quivira Rd., Mission Bay ☎ 619/224–3551) serves good fish-and-chips to eat on the inelegant but scenic patio—by the marina, where sportfishing boats depart daily—or to take out to your chosen picnic spot.

▶ **①** **San Diego Visitor Information Center.** In addition to being an excellent resource for tourists—it makes hotel and motel reservations, sells tickets to several attractions at a discount, offers various maps and guides, and has a small gift shop—this privately owned information center also a gathering spot for runners, walkers, and exercisers. For boaters it's the place to pick up a map detailing Mission Bay Park launch depths and speeds. ⊠ *2688 E. Mission Bay Dr., Mission Bay* ☎ *619/276–8200* ⊕ *www.infosandiego.com* ⊙ *Mon.–Sat. 9–5, until 6 in summer; Sun. 9:30–4:30, until 5:30 in summer.*

⟲ ❸ **SeaWorld San Diego.** One of the world's largest marine-life amusement
Fodor's Choice parks, SeaWorld is spread over 100 tropically landscaped bay-front
★ acres—and it seems to be expanding into every available square inch of
space with new exhibits, shows, and activities. The biggest attraction
in its 40 years of existence opened on Memorial Day 2004: **Journey to
Atlantis** involves a cruise on an eight-passenger "Greek fishing boat"
down a heart-stopping 60-foot plunge to explore a lost, sunken city. On
this journey serenaded by dolphins calls, you view a 130,000 gallon tank,
home to exotic Commerson's dolphins, a small black-and-white South
American species known for speed and agility.

The majority of SeaWorld's exhibits are walk-through marine environments. In a perpetual favorite, the **Penguin Encounter,** a moving sidewalk
passes through a glass-enclosed Arctic area where hundreds of emperor
penguins slide over glaciers into icy waters. (The penguins like it cold, so
consider bringing a light sweater along for this one.) Kids get a particular kick out of the **Shark Encounter,** where they come face-to-face with
sandtiger, nurse, bonnethead, black-tipped, and white-tipped reef sharks
by walking through a 57-foot clear acrylic tube that passes through the
280,000-gallon shark habitat. The hands-on **California Tide Pool** exhibit
gives you a chance to get to know San Diego's indigenous marine life. At
Forbidden Reef you can feed bat rays and go nose-to-nose with creepy
moray eels. At **Rocky Point Preserve** you can view bottlenose dolphins,
as well as Alaskan sea otters. At **Wild Arctic,** which starts out with a simulated helicopter ride to a research post at the North Pole, beluga whales,
walruses, and polar bears can be viewed in areas decked out like the wrecked
hulls of two 19th-century sailing ships. **Manatee Rescue** lets you watch
the gentle-giant marine mammals cavorting in a 215,000-gallon tank. Various **freshwater and saltwater aquariums** hold underwater creatures from
around the world. And for younger kids who need to release lots of energy, **Shamu's Happy Harbor** is a hands-on fun zone that features, among
other attractions, a two-story ship, where pretend pirates aim water cannons at one another (be prepared with a change of dry clothes).

SeaWorld's highlights are its large-arena entertainments. You can get front-
row seats if you arrive 10 or 15 minutes in advance, and the stadiums
are large enough for everyone to get a seat even at the busiest times. The
traditional favorite is the **Shamu Adventure,** with synchronized killer
whales bringing down the house. Another favorite is the 3-D movie
R. L. Stine's Haunted Lighthouse, a spine-tingling tale of a quest to find
the secret of a lighthouse's haunting. The movie, starring Christopher
Lloyd as Cap'n Jack, introduces a "fourth dimension," namely special
effects like sprays of water, blasts of air, and other wild surprises designed to bring you into the scene. A new sea lion and otter production,
Clyde and Seamore in Deep, Deep Trouble, debuted in 2005.

Not all the shows are water-oriented. **Pets Rule!** showcases the antics
of more-common animals like dogs, cats, birds, and even a pig, all set
to prove the supremacy of our four-legged (or feathered) friends. One
segment of the show actually has regular house cats climbing ladders
and hanging upside down as they cross a high-wire. The majority of the
animals used in the show were adopted from shelters.

Trainer For A Day gives you a first-hand look at how Sea World's trainers spend a work day and allows you to help them with everything from food preparation to training techniques. The $495 fee may seem hefty, but it buys a once-in-a-lifetime opportunity. A less expensive treat ($32 adults, $18 children) is the **Dine with Shamu** package, which includes a buffet lunch in an area restricted to trainers and allows you the thrill of eating while the whales swim up to you or happily play nearby.

Shipwreck Rapids, SeaWorld of California's first adventure ride, offers plenty of excitement—but you may end up getting soaked. For five minutes, nine "shipwrecked" passengers career down a river in a raftlike inner tube, encountering a series of obstacles, including several waterfalls. There's no extra charge, making this one of SeaWorld's great bargains—which means that you should expect long lines. Those who want to head to higher ground might consider the **Southwest Airlines Skytower,** a glass elevator that ascends 320 feet; the views of San Diego County from the ocean to the mountains are especially spectacular in early morning and late evening. The **Bayside Skyride,** a five-minute aerial tram ride that leaves from the same spot, travels across Mission Bay. Admission for the Skytower and the tram is $3 apiece. The fact that Anheuser-Busch is the park's parent company is evident in the presence of the beer company's signature Clydesdales, huge horses that you can visit in their "hamlet" when they're not putting on shows.

SeaWorld is chockablock with souvenir shops and refreshment stands (the only picnic grounds are outside the park entrance), so it's hard to come away from here without spending a lot of money on top of the hefty entrance fee (the children's single-day admission is $40.95) and $8 parking tab. You can get a 10% discount on the single-day admission by buying your ticket online, but an even better deal is the 2 Days of Fun eticket, which allows you to come back for a second day (within seven days of the first) all for the price of the single-day ticket. This is a good idea, because if you try to get your money's worth by fitting everything in on a single day, you're likely to end up tired and cranky. Many hotels, especially those in the Mission Bay area, also offer SeaWorld specials that may include rate reductions or two days' entry for the price of one. It's also a good idea to take a change of clothes along, especially when the weather is on the cool side and you sit in the first 10 rows at one of the marine shows, or ride Shipwreck Rapids; you can rent a locker to stow belongings. And remember that SeaWorld concessions won't provide drink lids or straws, which endanger the animals—so bring that sippy cup if you need it. ✉ *1720 South Shores Rd., near west end of I–8, Mission Bay* ☎ *619/226–3815, 619/226–3901 recorded information* ⊕ *www.seaworld.com* ✆ *$50.95; parking $8 cars, $4 motorcycles, $9 RVs and campers; 1-hr behind-the-scenes walking tours $11 extra* ▭ *AE, D, MC, V* ☺ *Daily 10–dusk; extended hrs in summer.*

need a break?

One of the perks of visiting a theme park owned by a beer distributor is free samples of suds, a good way to wash down the corned-beef sandwiches and the like served at **The Deli,** in the Anheuser-Busch Hospitality Center near the park entrance. Healthier fare—grilled fish, vegetables, and salads, along with cheeseburgers and fries—are the order of the day at the huge **Shipwreck Reef Cafe,** where you're likely to be entertained by park animals and juggling castaways.

❹ Vacation Isle. Ingraham Street bisects this island, providing two distinct experiences for visitors. The west side is taken up by the San Diego Paradise Point Resort, but you don't have to be a guest to enjoy the hotel's lushly landscaped grounds and bay-front restaurants. The water-ski clubs congregate at **Ski Beach** on the east side of the island, where there's a parking lot as well as picnic areas and restrooms. Ski Beach is the site of the annual Thunderboat Regatta, held in September. At a pond on the south side of the island, children and young-at-heart adults take part year-round in motorized miniature boat races. ⊠ *Mission Bay.*

OLD TOWN

San Diego's Spanish and Mexican roots are most evident in Old Town, the area north of downtown at Juan Street, near the intersection of Interstates 5 and 8, that was the first European settlement in Southern California. Old Town San Diego's first houses, of sun-dried adobe bricks arranged around a central plaza, began to appear in the 1820s; by the 1850s, after the discovery of gold drew prospectors to California from around the globe, they began to be replaced with wood-frame structures. In the 1860s, however, the advent of Alonzo Horton's New Town to the southeast stole thunder from Old Town, which began to wither. Efforts to preserve it began early in the 20th century, and when it became a state historic park in 1968, the process of restoration gained momentum.

Although Old Town was largely a 19th-century phenomemon, the pueblo's true beginnings took place much earlier and on a hill overlooking it, where soldiers from New Spain established a military outpost in May 1769 and two months later Father Junípero Serra established the first of California's missions, San Diego de Alcalá. The missionaries forced San Diego's original inhabitants, the Kumeyaay Indians—called the Diegueños by the Spaniards—to abandon their seminomadic lifestyle and live at the mission; they also expected the Indians to adopt Spanish customs and Christianity as their religion, although the Indians resisted fiercely. The mission suffered other problems: for security reasons it had been built on a hill, but it lacked an adequate water supply, and food became scarce as the number of Kumeyaays and Spanish soldiers occupying the site increased.

In 1774 the hilltop was declared a Royal Presidio, or fortress, and the mission was moved 6 mi west to a new site along the San Diego River. The Kumeyaays, responding to the loss of more of their land, attacked and burned it in 1775. Their revolt was short-lived, however. A later assault on the presidio was less successful, and by 1800 about 1,500 Kumeyaays were living on the mission's grounds, receiving religious instruction and adapting to Spanish ways.

The pioneers living within the presidio's walls were mostly Spanish soldiers, poor Mexicans, and mestizos of Spanish and Native American an-

CALIFORNIA'S PADRE PRESIDENT

SAN DIEGO, the first European settlement in Southern California, was founded by Father Junípero Serra in July 1769. A member of the Franciscan order, Father Serra was part of a larger expedition that was headed by explorer Don Gaspar de Portola. King Charles III of Spain, responding to pressure from English and Russian explorers and traders moving down the West Coast, chartered the party to travel from outposts in Baja California north to explore and occupy the territory known then as Alta California.

When they arrived in San Diego, the Spaniards found about 20,000 Kumeyaay Indians living in a hundred or so villages along the coast and inland. To establish the foothold for the king, the missionaries attempted to convert the Kumeyaays to Christianity, and taught them agricultural and other skills so they could work what would become the missions' vast holdings.

Mission San Diego Alcalá, established on a hillside above what is now Mission Valley in San Diego, was the first of the 21 that the Franciscans ultimately built along the coast of California. After establishing the mission and presidio in San Diego, Serra and Portola moved on, founding the Mission San Carlos Borromeo and presidio at Monterey. Mission San Carlos was later moved to Carmel, where Father Serra settled and maintained his headquarters until his death in 1784.

Father Serra, the padre president of California, established nine missions. Besides those at San Diego and Monterey, these were: San Antonio de Padua, 1771; San Gabriel, 1771; San Luis Obispo, 1772; Mission Dolores, 1776; San Juan Capistrano, 1776; Santa Clara, 1777; and San Buenaventura, 1782. He personally oversaw the planning, construction, and staffing of each of these, and conferred the sacraments. His work took him from Carmel to locations the length of California. It's estimated that during this period he walked more than 24,000 mi in California visiting missions.

The missions, which became known as Serra's Beads, comprised millions of acres and were in fact small self-sufficient cities with the church as the centerpiece. In addition to converting the Indians to Christianity and teaching them European ways, the padres managed farming, education, and industries such as candle making and tanning. San Diego is the southernmost mission, while the mission at Sonoma, San Francisco Solano, the last to be founded, in 1823, is the northernmost; each was established about 30 mi—or a day's walk—from the previous one and was linked to the El Camino Highway. The missions were also the earliest form of lodging in the Golden State, known far and wide for the hospitality they afforded visitors.

Father Serra spent barely a year in San Diego before embarking on his journey to establish missions across California, but his presence left a lasting imprint on the city. You can see some of the history at the Junípero Serra Museum and at Mission San Diego Alcalá. And you can trace his footsteps along El Camino Real by driving U.S. 101, the historic route that traverses coastal California from south to north.

—Bobbi Zane

cestry, many of whom were unaccustomed to farming San Diego's arid land. When Mexico gained independence from Spain in 1821, the new nation claimed Spanish lands in California and flew the Mexican flag over the presidio. The Mexican government, centered some 2,000 mi away in Monterrey, stripped the missions of their lands, and an aristocracy of landholders began to emerge. At the same time, settlers began to move down from the presidio to what is now Old Town.

A rectangular plaza was laid out along today's San Diego Avenue to serve as the settlement's center. In 1846, during the war between Mexico and the United States, a detachment of U.S. Marines raised the Stars and Stripes over the plaza for the first time. The flag was removed once or twice, but by early 1848 Mexico had surrendered California, and the U.S. flag remained. San Diego became an incorporated city in 1850, with Old Town as its center.

Access to Old Town is easy thanks to the nearby Transit Center. Ten bus lines stop here, as do the San Diego Trolley and the Coaster commuter rail line. Two large parking lots linked to the park by an underground pedestrian walkway ease some of the parking congestion, and signage leading from I–8 to the Transit Center is easy to follow. If you're not familiar with the area, however, avoid the "Old Town" exit from I–5, which leaves you floundering near Mission Bay without further directions.

Numbers in the text correspond to numbers in the margin and on the Old Town San Diego map.

a good tour

Because of the steep hills leading up to Heritage Park and Presidio Park, it's best to use a car to see all of Old Town's sights.

Visit the information center at Robinson-Rose House on Wallace Street, facing Old Town Plaza, to orient yourself to the various sights in **Old Town San Diego State Historic Park ❶ ↱**. When you've had enough history, cross north on the west side of the plaza to **Plaza del Pasado ❷**, where you can shop or stop for a bite to eat. Walk down San Diego Avenue, which flanks the south side of Old Town's historic plaza, east to Harney Street and the **Thomas Whaley Museum ❸**. It's best to hop in a car at this point for the next sights. Continue east 2½ blocks on San Diego Avenue beyond Arista Street to **El Campo Santo ❹** cemetery. **Heritage Park ❺** is perched on a hill above Juan Street, north of the museum and cemetery. Drive west on Juan Street and north on Taylor Street, which leads to Presidio Drive. This takes you up the hill on which **Presidio Park ❻** and the **Junípero Serra Museum ❼** sit.

TIMING   It takes about two hours to walk through Old Town. Try to time your visit to coincide with the free daily tours given by costumed park staff. They depart daily at 11 AM from the Robinson-Rose House Visitor Center and take about one hour. If you go to Presidio Park, definitely drive instead of walk, and allot another hour to explore the grounds and museum.

Sights to See

❷ **Plaza del Pasado.** North of San Diego's Old Town Plaza lies the area's unofficial center, built to represent a colonial Mexican square and until recently known as Bazaar del Mundo. In mid-2005, this collection of shops and restaurants around a central courtyard always in blossom with magenta bougainvillea, scarlet hibiscus, and other flowers in season, had just been transferred to new management, and changes were afoot. Plans included remodelling the area to what it might have looked like in the early California days, from 1821 to 1872, complete with shops stocked with items reminiscent of that era. At presstime, some of the planned 11 stores were already open (although scheduled to close briefly for renovations one by one), as was a restaurant, Casa de Reyes, serving Mexican food. The whole project was due to be completed at the end of 2006. ⊠ *2754 Calhoun St., Old Town* ☎ *619/297–3100* ⊕ *www. plazadelpasado.com* ⊙ *Shops daily 9–10.*

❹ **El Campo Santo.** The old adobe-walled cemetery established in 1849 was the burial place for many members of Old Town's founding families—as well as for some gamblers and bandits who passed through town—until 1880. Antonio Garra, a chief who led an uprising of the San Luis Rey Indians, was executed at El Campo Santo in front of the open grave he had been forced to dig for himself. These days the small cemetery is a peaceful stop for visitors to Old Town. Most of the markers give only approximations of where the people named on them are buried; some of the early settlers laid to rest at El Campo Santo really reside under San Diego Avenue. ✉ *North side of San Diego Ave. S, between Arista and Ampudia Sts., Old Town.*

❺ Heritage Park. A number of San Diego's important Victorian buildings are the focus of this 7⁸⁄₁₀-acre park, up the Juan Street hill near Harney Street. The buildings, moved here and restored by Save Our Heritage Organization, include Southern California's first synagogue, a one-room classic revival–style structure built in 1889 for Congregation Beth Israel. The most interesting of the park's six former residences might be the Sherman Gilbert House, which has a widow's walk and intricate carving on its decorative trim. It was built for real estate dealer John Sherman in 1887 at the then-exorbitant cost of $20,000—indicating just how profitable the booming housing market could be. Bronze plaques detail the history of all the houses, some of which may seem surprisingly colorful, but in fact accurately represent the bright tones of the era. The homes are now used as offices and shops, except for two of them, the 1887 Bushyhead House and the adjacent 1889 Christian House, which together are doing business as the Heritage Park Inn. The climb up to the park is a little steep, but the view of the harbor is great. Only the synagogue is open to visitors. ✉ *County parks office: 2455 Heritage Park Row, Old Town* ☎ *858/694–3049.*

☺ ❼ Junípero Serra Museum. The hill on which San Diego's original Spanish presidio (fortress) and California's first mission were perched is now the domain of a Spanish mission–style museum established, along with Presidio Park, by department store magnate and philanthropist George Marston in 1929 to commemorate the history of the site from the time it was occupied by the Kumeyaay Indians through its Spanish, Mexican, and American periods. Artifacts include Kumeyaay baskets, Spanish riding gear, and a painting that Father Serra would have viewed in Mission San Diego de Alcalá. The education room has hands-on stations where kids can grind acorns in *metates* (stones used for grinding grain), dig for buried artifacts with archaeology tools, or dress up in period costumes—one represents San Diego founding father Alonzo Horton. Ascend the tower to compare the view you'd have gotten before 1929 with the one you have today. The museum, now operated by the San Diego Historical Society, is at the north end of Presidio Park, near Taylor Street. ✉ *2727 Presidio Dr., Old Town* ☎ *619/297–3258* ⊕ *www.sandiegohistory.org* ✑ *$5* ☉ *Daily 10–5.*

> **off the beaten path**
>
> **MISSION SAN DIEGO DE ALCALÁ –** It's hard to imagine how remote California's earliest mission once must have been; these days, it's accessible by a major freeway (I–15) and by the San Diego Trolley. Mission San Diego de Alcalá, the first of a chain of 21 missions stretching northward along the coast, was established by Father Junípero Serra on Presidio Hill in 1769 and moved to this location in 1774. There was no greater security from enemy attack here: Padre Luis Jayme, California's first Christian martyr, was clubbed to death by Kumeyaay Indians, whom he was trying to convert, in 1775. The present church is the fifth built on the site; it was reconstructed in

1931 following the outlines of the 1813 church. It measures 150 feet long but only 35 feet wide because, without easy means of joining beams, the mission buildings were only as wide as the trees that served as their ceiling supports were tall. Father Jayme is buried in the sanctuary; a small museum named for him documents the history of the mission and exhibits tools and artifacts from the early days. From the peaceful palm-bedecked gardens out back you can gaze at the 46-foot-high *campanario* (bell tower), the mission's most distinctive feature; one of its five bells was cast in 1822. ✉ *10818 San Diego Mission Rd., Mission Valley, from I–15, take Friars Rd. east and Rancho Mission Rd. south* ☎ *619/281–8449* ⊕ *www. missionsandiego.com* 🎟 *$3* ⊙ *Daily 9–4:45.*

★ ▶ ❶ **Old Town San Diego State Historic Park.** The six square blocks on the site of San Diego's original pueblo are the heart of Old Town. Most of the 20 historic buildings preserved or re-created by the park cluster around **Old Town Plaza,** bounded by Wallace Street on the west, Calhoun Street on the north, Mason Street on the east, and San Diego Avenue on the south. The plaza is a pleasant place for resting and regrouping as you plan your tour of the park and watch passers-by. San Diego Avenue is closed to vehicle traffic here.

Some of Old Town's buildings were destroyed in a fire in 1872, but after the site became a state historic park in 1968, efforts were begun to re-construct or restore the structures that remained. Seven of the original adobes are still intact. The tour pamphlet available at Robinson-Rose House gives details about all of the historic houses on the plaza and in its vicinity; a few of the more interesting ones are noted below. Several reconstructed buildings serve as restaurants or as shops purveying wares reminiscent of those that might have been available in the original Old Town; Racine & Laramie, a painstakingly reproduced version of San Diego's first (1868) cigar store, is especially interesting. The noncommercial houses are open daily 10–5; none charge admission, though donations are appreciated.

The **Robinson-Rose House** (☎ 619/220–5422), on Wallace Street facing Old Town Plaza, was the original commercial center of old San Diego, housing railroad offices, law offices, and the first newspaper press. Built in 1853 but in ruins at the end of the 19th century, it has been reconstructed and now serves as the park's visitor center and administrative headquarters. It contains a model of Old Town as it looked in 1872, as well as various historic exhibits. Just behind the Robinson-Rose house is a replica of the Victorian-era Silvas-McCoy house, originally built in 1869.

On Mason Street, at the corner of Calhoun Street, is the **Cosmpolitan Hotel/Casa de Bandini,** once one of the prettiest haciendas in San Diego. Built in 1829 by a Peruvian, Juan Bandini, the house served as Old Town's social center during Mexican rule. Albert Seeley, a stagecoach entrepreneur, purchased the home in 1869, built a second story, and turned it into the Cosmopolitan Hotel, a way station for travelers on the daylong trip south from Los Angeles. It later served as a store and a factory and, in recent decades, as the popular Casa de Bandini restaurant. In mid-2005, the building once again became the Cosmopolitan Restaurant and Hotel. Under the same management as the Plaza del Pasado, the property will ultimately be restored to its mid-19th century appearance. It consists of a ground-floor restaurant serving Mexican and American food (scheduled to close for renovations for two months in mid-2006) and, upstairs, nine bed-and-breakfast rooms due to open at the end of 2006.

Seeley Stable (✉ 2630 Calhoun St., Old Town 🕾 619/220–5427), next door to the Cosmopolitan building, became San Diego's stagecoach stop in 1867 and was the transportation hub of Old Town until near the turn of the century, when trains became the favored mode of travel. The stable houses a collection of horse-drawn vehicles, some so elaborate that you can see where the term "carriage trade" came from. Also inside are western memorabilia, including an exhibit on the California *vaquero*, the original American cowboy, and a collection of Native American artifacts.

The **Casa de Estudillo** (✉ 4001 Mason St., Old Town) was built on Mason Street in 1827 by the commander of the San Diego Presidio, Jose Maria Estudillo. The largest and most elaborate of the original adobe homes, it was occupied by members of the Estudillo family until 1887. It was purchased and restored in 1910 by sugar magnate and developer John D. Spreckels, who advertised it in bold lettering on the side as "Ramona's Marriage Place." Despite the meticulous attention to historical detail of the restoration, Spreckels' claim that the small chapel in the house was the site of the wedding in Helen Hunt Jackson's popular novel *Ramona* had no basis in fact; that didn't stop people from coming to see it, however.

The **San Diego Union Museum** (✉ Twigg St. and San Diego Ave., Old Town 🕾 No phone) is in a New England–style, wood-frame house prefabricated in the eastern United States and shipped around Cape Horn in 1851. The building has been restored to replicate the newspaper's offices of 1868, when the first edition of the *San Diego Union* was printed.

Also worth exploring in the plaza area are the free **Dental Museum, Mason Street School, Wells Fargo History Museum, First San Diego Courthouse, Casa de Machado y Silvas Commercial Restaurant Museum, Sheriff's Museum** and the **Casa de Machado Y Stewart.** Ask at the visitor center for locations.

❻ **Presidio Park.** The hillsides of the 40-acre green space overlooking Old Town from the north end of Taylor Street are popular with picnickers, and many couples have taken their wedding vows on the park's long stretches of lawn, some of the greenest in San Diego. You may encounter enthusiasts of the sport of grass skiing gliding over the grass and down the hills on their wheeled-model skis. It's a nice walk from Old Town to the summit if you're in good shape and wearing the right shoes—it should take about half an hour. You can also drive to the top of the park via Presidio Drive, off Taylor Street.

If you do decide to walk, look in at the Presidio Hills Golf Course on Mason Street. It has an unusual clubhouse that incorporates the ruins of Casa de Carrillo, the town's oldest adobe, constructed in 1820. At the end of Mason Street, veer left on Jackson Street to reach the **Pre-**

sidio Ruins, where adobe walls and a bastion have been built above the foundations of the original fortress and chapel. Archaeology students from San Diego State University who excavated the area have marked off the early chapel outlines, although they reburied the artifacts they uncovered in order to protect them. Also on-site are the 28-foot-high Serra Cross, built in 1913 out of brick tiles found in the ruins, and a bronze statue of Father Serra. Before you do much poking around here, however, it's a good idea to get some historical perspective at the Junípero Serra Museum, just to the east. Take Presidio Drive southeast of the museum and you'll come to the site of Fort Stockton, built to protect Old Town and abandoned by the United States in 1848. Plaques and statues also commemorate the Mormon Battalion, which enlisted here to fight in the battle against Mexico. ✉ *1 block north of Old Town.*

❸ Thomas Whaley Museum. Thomas Whaley was a New York entrepreneur who came to California during the gold rush. He wanted to provide his East Coast wife all the comforts of home, so in 1856 he had Southern California's first two-story brick structure built. The house, which served as the county courthouse and government seat during the 1870s, stands in strong contrast to the Spanish-style adobe residences that surround the nearby historic plaza and marks an early stage of San Diego's "Americanization."

Period furnishings in the living quarters include a miniature dress dummy designed to look like Mary Todd Lincoln, a sofa from Andrew Jackson's White House, and a piano that belonged to singer Jenny Lind. Among the historical artifacts in the reconstructed courtroom is one of the six life masks of Abraham Lincoln. A garden out back includes many varieties of Old Garden roses from before 1867, when roses were first hybridized. The place is perhaps most famed, however, for the ghosts that are said to inhabit it; this is one of the few houses authenticated by the U.S. Department of Commerce as being haunted. ✉ *2482 San Diego Ave., Old Town* ☎ *619/297–7511* ⊕ *www.whaleyhouse.org* 💲 *$5* ◎ *Daily 10–4:30* ◎ *Closed Wed.*

Where to Eat

"We were told that the Sunday brunch at the Del Coronado is San Diego's best. It is certainly the city's most scenic. . . . To dine so sumptuously while overlooking the hotel's beautiful gardens giving way to a wide Pacific Ocean beach was to spend a few hours in sublime comfort."

—Neal Sanders

"When I go home to San Diego, I always head straight for any taqueria ending in -bertos: Robertos, Albertos, Johnbertos—they've got a million of them, and they are almost all incomparably good!"

—vorona

By David
Nelson

SAN DIEGO'S STATUS AS A VACATIONER'S PARADISE and its growth into the seventh-largest city in the United States have made it a magnet for restaurateurs and chefs from around the globe. A good deal of the new talent also is homegrown, and it's not unusual for local youths to attend leading culinary academies and return home fired by the desire to remake San Diego cuisine. The city's growing corps of innovative and cutting-edge chefs includes Bernard Guillas at the Marine Room, Jesse Frost at Prince of Wales, Stephen Window at Roppongi, and Jean-Michel Diot at Tapenade. The new point of view is that a region this blessed with gorgeous vegetables, fruits, herbs, and seafood should make a culinary statement. An intriguing new restaurant in Hillcrest took the name Region to emphasize the delicious uses to which local products can be put.

Few other American cities yield so many dining options, indoors and out. Although the town as yet fails to offer a Tibetan eatery, it now takes for granted cuisines such as Cambodian, Ethiopian, Afghan, and Laotian. Many of these far-flung cuisines are served outside the center in the city's ever more diverse neighborhoods. Downtown, the dramatically restored Gaslamp Quarter offers vigorous nightlife and some 100 restaurants and can feel like the corner of Broadway and 42nd Street at times. The eateries range from down-at-the-heels holdouts from the days when this historic area had declined to Skid Row status, to stylish establishments priced for those doing business at the nearby San Diego Convention Center. In truth, Gaslamp is something of a victim of its own success, with difficult parking (valet parking is quite expensive) and more and more national chain feederies. But both locals and visitors identify it as San Diego's "party central," and the crowds come for lively fun. Definitely a family-friendly district, it has options for every group, and the sizeable number of nightclubs attract a clientele that steadily grows younger as the night wears on.

A stroll down the 5th Avenue restaurant row (which now extends to both 4th and 6th avenues) reveals San Diego's preference for Italian cuisine above all others, but the choice nonetheless is cosmopolitan and embraces casual, burgers-and-fries fare, Spanish tapas and paellas, traditional and nuevo Mexican cuisine, and all-American steaks cut thick enough to choke a horse. At the time of this writing, fine, expensive steak houses remain the hot San Diego trend, thanks partly to prosperity in the local high-tech industries and perhaps partly to boredom with the warnings of health mavens. Seafood abounds, and there's a whole lot of "fusion" going on, which is to say that many menus now present their chef's own rendition of contemporary cuisine, which borrows idiosyncratically from a mixture of culinary traditions. Sad to say, there's not a single fine Chinese restaurant downtown, but good Japanese cuisine is readily available.

Near the waterfront on the upper western edge of downtown, the rapidly gentrifying Little Italy district has become a center for excellent, affordable Italian dining, both traditional and more contemporary. The area has a few surprises to offer, too, such as an authentic English pub frequented by Commonwealth loyalists from around the globe, a charming Cajun café, and a Southwestern-style grill that is the ultimate in trendiness.

In addition to downtown, other areas of San Diego share in the keen sense of energy, fueled by a collective caffeine high acquired in the coffeehouses (some of which are listed in Chapter 4) springing up everywhere from the Gaslamp Quarter to the gas station on the corner. The uptown neighborhoods centered by Hillcrest—an urbane district with a hip San Francisco flavor—are marked by increasing culinary sophistication. Mission Valley, the city's commercial heart, abounds in big restaurants of varying quality, interspersed by a few establishments devoted to superior fare. Just to the north, Convoy Street—the commercial spine of the busy Kearny Mesa area—is the unofficial Asian Restaurant Row of San Diego, and presents a comprehensive selection of Chinese, Korean, and Vietnamese restaurants, a number of which qualify as "best in class." And rich, elegant La Jolla, with many of San Diego's most expensive restaurants, offers some of the best dining in the city. To be sure, great cooking blossoms beyond the city's official borders. In nearby Chula Vista, look for authentic, palate-pleasing Mexican fare, while Coronado—the peninsula city across San Diego Bay—has both casual, neighborhood-style eateries and grand hotel dining rooms with dramatic water views. And to the north in the plush suburbs of Del Mar, Solana Beach, and Rancho Santa Fe, elegant surroundings seem to demand good fare.

Coronado & South Bay

American

¢–$$ ✕ **McP's Irish Pub & Grill.** The mood always tends to St. Paddy's Day, but the cuisine takes a stance as all-American as the United States Navy Seals who make this their off-duty headquarters, and the gargantuan portions reflect the appetites of men who train hard on the beaches south of town. On the casual side, the menu lists a "good old-fashioned hamburger" that fully lives up to the description and continues in a beefy mood with hefty steaks, a mulligan stew served in a hollowed sourdough loaf, and corned beef and cabbage. Chicken teriyaki, sandwiches, and several elaborate salads create options for a crowd that often includes both seniors and small children. The nightly live entertainment commences at 8 PM. ⊠ *1107 Orange Ave., Coronado* ☎ *619/435–5280* ▤ *MC, V.*

¢ ✕ **Aunt Emma's Pancakes.** The quintessential breakfast place, this decades-old Chula Vista landmark is 10 minutes south of downtown San Diego, and two blocks east of the E Street exit from I–5. Despite the motto "It's Always Pancake Time," Aunt Emma's serves from 6 AM to 3 PM only, when it bustles with people from every walk of life. The first menu item—fluffy, butter-drenched buttermilk pancakes—is as far as many guests read. Besides 20 pancake varieties, including mango crêpes, Aunt Emma's offers waffles, egg dishes, and Mexican specialties. The lunch menu includes burgers and sandwiches. ⊠ *700 E St., Chula Vista* ☎ *619/427–2722* ⌂ *Reservations not accepted* ▤ *MC, V* ⊙ *No dinner.*

¢ ✕ **Miracle Mile Delicatessen.** Nightly entrée specials that top out at $8.95 explains why Navy personnel, seniors, and guests of Coronado's many hotels arrive for hand-carved roast turkey, chicken noodle casserole, corned

A fair number of San Diego restaurants offer "early-bird specials" before peak dining hours. There's no rule about the time for the specials, but they're generally offered between 5 PM and 6:30 PM on weekdays. Finer restaurants rarely offer such deals, yet there are some. La Jolla's oh-so-French Tapenade serves a set-price early-bird menu on weeknights before 6:30 PM.

With the boom of new apartments and condominiums in Little Italy, parking near many of its restaurants has become a problem. However, the local San Diego Trolley stop is less than two blocks from Little Italy's India Street restaurant row. A plus, especially for those who lunch here, is the proximity of San Diego Bay, which is just a few streets to the west. It offers a superb promenade that both leads to interesting places and helps with the digestion of vast plates of pasta. If you use the trolley to get to downtown and Gaslamp Quarter restaurants, you can avoid parking fees that may exceed $15 and valets who expect healthy tips.

2

Children

San Diego rolls out the red carpet for everyone, including children, although some of the more formal establishments and large, expense account-oriented steak houses probably are inappropriate venues for junior citizens. Children's menus are neither unknown nor particularly common, but most establishments will cheerfully offer a few suggestions for the younger set if asked. Fast food is readily available in all quarters of the city, and you'll rarely be more than a pepperoni's toss from a pizza parlor. Hillcrest, while decidedly adult in nature, has the most popular "kid magnet" in town, the Corvette Diner Bar & Grill, where birthday parties are a standard feature thanks to a 1950s menu and decor, and to servers who entertain with song and dance. Children are well received at the Convoy Street Chinese restaurants that specialize at lunch time in dim sum (myriad tiny pastries and dumplings). Youngsters who have never before seen such items sometimes develop quite a taste for egg rolls, fried pork dumplings, barbecued pork buns, and fried shrimp rolls. California-style Mexican cuisine that's usually a hit with kids for its messiness is not hard to find, especially in the bustling Old Town area. Fish tacos are all the rage, but if you're not sure what your kids will like, try a cheese quesadilla (melted cheese in a flour tortilla), chips, and guacamole, or rolled tacos with guacamole. Always sample the salsa before offering it to your little ones, as it will be spicy more often than not.

Dress

San Diego restaurants have largely abandoned the battle to require stylish attire of their patrons, and while "Appropriate Dress Required" signs are sometimes displayed in the entrance, this generally means nothing more than clean and reasonably neat clothing. Some "dress-up" places remain, notably the Fontainebleau Room at the Westgate Hotel, Bertrand at Mister A's, and La Jolla institutions like Top of the Cove and George's at the Cove. Otherwise, a "come-as-you-are" attitude generally prevails.

Mealtimes

Unless otherwise noted, the restaurants listed in this guide are open daily for lunch and dinner. Lunch is typically served 11:30–2:30, and dinner service in most restaurants begins at 5:30 and ends at 10. A number of establishments serve until 11 or later on Friday and Sunday nights, and one top-quality downtown restaurant, Rainwater's on Kettner, always seats until at least 11 PM without exception.

Prices

Meals still cost somewhat less in San Diego than in other major metropolitan areas. However, greatly increasing real estate prices and rents are reflected by more expensive entrées, especially in choice districts like La Jolla, the Gaslamp Quarter, and Little Italy. Some locals take advantage of the city's traditionally large portions by splitting any course they like, from appetizer to dessert. Most restaurants tolerate this, while several charge a few dollars extra for a shared plate. Choosing restaurants in less-expensive neighborhoods is one way to economize, and without question, diners can find reasonably priced meals along the Convoy Street Asian restaurant row, in Ocean Beach, and in other neighborhoods away from downtown. Even in the Gaslamp district, outposts of national chains (i.e., TGI Friday's) offer relatively affordable menus, although these do not feature the San Diego cuisine that the town's better chefs are currently inventing. As a rule, Mexican restaurants offer extremely good value, and in most cases will fill you up. The old-line pizza and spaghetti houses, such as the Filippi's chain, perform a similar service, although they are not the culinary equals of the new wave of Italian restaurants. These are operated by entrepreneurs who have come to San Diego as international businesspeople rather than immigrants.

WHAT IT COSTS					
	$$$$	**$$$**	**$$**	**$**	**¢**
AT DINNER	over $30	$23–$30	$16–$22	$10–$15	under $10

Prices are for a main course at dinner, excluding 7.75% tax.

Some restaurants listed are marked with a price range ($$–$$$, for example). This indicates one of two things: either the average cost straddles two categories, or if you order strategically, you can get out for less than most diners spend.

Reservations

Reservations are always a good idea; we mention them only when they're essential or not accepted. Book as far ahead as you can, and reconfirm as soon as you arrive. (Large parties should always call ahead to check the reservations policy.)

Smoking

Smoking is banned in restaurants but some permit cigarette smoking on their terraces.

Specialties

Because of its multiethnic population, you can find cuisine from nearly every part of the world in San Diego. A local specialty is the fish taco, filled with any sort of fish the restaurant chooses. These are sold at restaurants in the Rubio's chain as well as at beach-side taco stands and in a few other eateries. During the local spiny lobster season, which runs roughly from late October to early March, restaurants serve these tasty beasts simply grilled, or lightly fried Baja California–style, or elaborately sauced and presented in the shell in good—and not so good—interpretations of lobster thermidor. In addition to Mexican fare, San Diego has three Chinese restaurants that specialize in the luxurious Hong Kong–style of cooking. Emerald Chinese Seafood, Jas-

2

mine, and China Max are on Convoy Street in the heavily commercial Kearny Mesa neighborhood, and the menus at all three balance reasonably priced, generally delicious dishes with fresh-from-the-tank seafood that is priced according to the market and can be quite extravagant (i.e., a giant Australian king crab for $200). Beyond these, the city's better chefs are busy building a local cuisine, and the way to sample it is to seek out locally owned, stand-alone establishments, such as Region, Marine Room, George's at the Cove, and Po Pazzo.

Tipping Most locals tip a standard 15% to 18%. But beware: many restaurants note on the menu that they automatically add an 18% tip to the check for parties of six or more. Guests who don't pay attention when signing the credit card slip often add a standard tip themselves, and realize too late that they have inadvertently and wildly over-tipped. A diner who feels the service was inadequate can decline to tip, and can decline the automatic tip added to checks for large parties.

Wine, Beer & Spirits Alcohol may be served between the hours of 6 AM and 2 AM. The legal age to buy alcoholic beverages in California is 21. Alcoholic beverages can be purchased in liquor stores, supermarkets, and virtually all convenience stores. As one of the wine capitals of the world, California produces an extraordinary selection of fine vintages in all price categories. San Diego restaurants generally present well-selected, reasonably priced lists, and a few attract national attention with their collections. Servers can often—but by no means always—assist in selecting a good accompaniment to dinner. In general, Asian and Mexican restaurants are weak in the wine category, but even here there are some shining stars. Note that several Mexican restaurants offer 100 or more kinds of tequila, many of them intriguingly flavored, and sometimes rather pricey. One notable tequila destination is Baja Betty's in Hillcrest.

---

beef and cabbage, and similar stick-to-the-ribs standards. The drawback is a somewhat sterile decor and a semi-self-service approach: order from the cooks at the steam table, and a runner delivers your food on a tray. Made-to-order sandwiches rise high with hot pastrami, rare roast beef, and other quality fillings. Cakes and other desserts easily serve two. ⊠ *980 Orange Ave., Coronado* ☎ *619/435–6655* ▤ *MC, V.*

Contemporary

$–$$ ✕ **Coronado Brewing Company.** The carefully crafted beers are good by themselves, but they also make a good accompaniment to beer-steamed bratwurst and beer-battered onion rings, served in mountainous portions. There's indoor seating, a pair of sidewalk terraces and, best of all, a walled garden that provides a quiet haven from the bustle of Orange Avenue. Simple choices are the wisest, from the Philadelphia-style steak sandwich to wood-fired pizzas to baby back ribs basted with spicy, ginger-flavor barbecue sauce. It's a brewery, but popular with families with children. ✉ *170 Orange Ave., Coronado* ☎ *619/437–4452* ▤ *MC, V.*

¢–$$ ✕ **Tent City.** In the historic First Bank of Commerce building along with the Coronado Museum of History and Art, this restaurant in the heart of downtown Coronado serves an eclectic cuisine that emphasizes strong flavors and light effects, as in starters such as minced chicken with *ponzu* sauce and lettuce "wraps," and a "stacked" salad of crab, shrimp, and sliced yellow tomatoes. Main events include a grilled portobello mushroom sandwich and, on the formal side, salmon baked in parchment. The restaurant's name memorializes the waterside summer camp that San Diego residents frequented from 1900 to 1939. The dining room is pleasant, but the sidewalk terrace beckons in fine weather. ✉ *1100 Orange Ave., Coronado* ☎ *619/435–4611* ▤ *MC, V.*

French

$$–$$$$ ✕ **Chez Loma.** This is widely considered one of the most romantic restaurants in Southern California, and it's a favorite with guests at nearby Hotel Del Coronado. Lots of windows, soft lighting, and an upstairs Victorian parlor for coffee and dessert are some of the charms. The more elaborate dishes among the carefully prepared meals are boeuf bourguignon, pan-roasted lamb loin with vanilla-merlot sauce, and New York steak au poivre. There's sidewalk dining and Sunday brunch, and chef–proprietor Ken Irvine is a whiz at locating choice, small-grower California vintages for his wine list. ✉ *1132 Loma Ave., Coronado* ☎ *619/435–0661* ▤ *AE, DC, MC, V* ☻ *No lunch.*

¢–$ ✕ **Tartine.** There's always a dish of water for canine pals on the terrace of this oh-so-French café a block from San Diego Bay. In France, a "tartine" is a toasted length of baguette, sometimes simply buttered, sometimes turned into a sandwich. At Tartine, these can be as hearty as a ham-and-Brie combo slathered with grain mustard, or as pinky-in-the-air as a layering of Gorgonzola cheese, walnuts, watercress, and sliced pears. Other sandwiches, along with clever salads, an oft-beguiling soup of the day, and a pâté plate round out the day-and-night menu. Continental breakfast commences at 6 AM, when just-baked, costly pastries silently command "Eat me!" ✉ *1106 1st St., Coronado* ☎ *619/435–4323* ▤ *MC, V.*

Seafood

$$$–$$$$ ✕ **Azzura Point.** Decorated in a romantic, 1930s style, Azzura Point is ideal for a leisurely and memorable meal. The view up San Diego Bay to the Coronado Bridge and the downtown skyline is unbeatable. Expect thoroughly contemporary preparations of first-class seasonal produce, such as seared duck breast with citrus glaze, an elaborately garnished veal porterhouse, and grilled escolar with a Portuguese-style seafood sauce. Five-course tasting menus change with the season. The herbs often come from the restaurant's extensive garden. Several choice, artisan cheeses are an alternative to the deftly executed desserts, and the wine list is written and served with particular skill. ✉ *Loews Coronado Bay Resort, 4000 Coronado Bay Rd., Coronado* ☎ *619/424–4477* ▤ *AE, DC, MC, V* ☻ *Closed Mon. No lunch.*

Where to Eat in
Downtown & Little Italy

$$$-$$$$ ✕ **Prince of Wales.** The 1930s live on in the Hotel Del Coronado's re-
Fodor'sChoice stored Prince of Wales restaurant, which affords sweeping ocean views
★ from an elegant indoor room and a breezy terrace. The inventive menu changes seasonally and may offer such creations as a "Napoleon" of Hudson Valley foie gras with Port wine–fig mousse, a pan-crisped filet of Hawaiian red snapper with cauliflower mousse, and or roasted duck breast with Port-braised short ribs and a toothsome "hash" of root vegetables. After all this, the "trilogy" of a molten-centered cake, a mousse, and a soup of white chocolate and walnuts concludes the affair convincingly. ⊠ *Hotel Del Coronado, 1500 Orange Ave., Coronado* ☎ *619/435–6611* ▤ *AE, D, DC, MC, V* ☽ *No lunch.*

¢-$$$$ ✕ **Baja Lobster.** To experience something akin to dining in Puerto Nuevo,
Fodor'sChoice Baja California—the famed lobstering village south of the border—
★ head to this excellent but quite informal eatery, easily reached from I–5. Local lobsters are split and lightly fried, served with family-style portions of fresh flour tortillas, creamy beans crammed with flavor, and well-seasoned rice. While lobsters are the big catch, steak and chicken options are on the menu, too, and there's full bar service. A pair of high-quality shrimp tacos costs just $5.95. Note that a similarly named chain, Rockin' Baja Lobster, is not related to Baja Lobster. ⊠ *1060 Broadway, Chula Vista* ☎ *619/425–2512* ▤ *MC, V.*

Downtown

American

¢-$$ ✕ **Hard Rock Cafe.** If you've been to one Hard Rock, you've been to them all, but there's no denying that the mix of rock-and-roll memorabilia, ear-splitting music, vivacious young staff, and generally satisfying, all-American fare can be fun. A juicy, half-pound burger or high-rising, bacon-rich chicken club will curb your appetite for a while. Best of all perhaps are the "famous" grilled beef fajitas served with tortillas that let you roll your own. As over-the-top as it may sound, a thick malted milk shake goes well with any of these gut-busters. The bar hops at night. ⊠ *801 4th Ave., Gaslamp Quarter* ☎ *619/615–7625* ▤ *AE, DC, MC, V.*

$ ✕ **Sluggers.** Take a break from a trolley tour of the new San Diego at this ballpark-district hot dog emporium next to the major 12th Avenue–Market Street trolley stop. The name honors the players at nearby Petco Park, and the menu recalls Chicago appetites with a variety of hot dog specialties, as well as Italian sausage and roast beef sandwiches, half-pound and full-pound burgers, and the "Ted Williams" clam roll. The red chili is blanketed with cheese and onions. ⊠ *1219 Market St., Downtown* ☎ *619/546–5973* ⚄ *Reservations not accepted* ▤ *MC, V.*

¢ ✕ **Ghirardelli Soda Fountain & Chocolate Shop.** This outpost of San Francisco's famed Ghirardelli chocolatier specializes in ice cream, served in every size and form from a single scoop in a freshly baked waffle cone, to elaborate sundaes and banana splits. Ambitious types can attempt the Earthquake, a well of eight different ice creams, eight toppings, bananas, nuts, embarrassing quantities of whipped cream, and heaps of glistening red cherries. This is the perfect "time out" place for families with children, but in truth, adults usually are in the majority. It's an oasis of calm in the explosive Gaslamp Quarter. ✉ *643 5th Ave., Gaslamp Quarter* ☎ *619/234–2449* ▭ *AE, MC, V.*

Brazilian

$$–$$$$ ✕ **Rei do Gado.** Bearing skewers of 14 different kinds of grilled meat, servers at this classic "churrascaria" will encourage you to truly eat all you can. Choices include filet mignon, skirt steak, linguica (a popular Portuguese sausage), pork loin, lamb leg, and even chicken hearts. The all-inclusive option extends to the salad, side dish, and dessert buffets and costs $29.95 weeknights, $34.95 on weekends and holidays. ✉ *939 4th Ave., Gaslamp Quarter* ☎ *619/702–8464* ▭ *AE, DC, MC, V.*

Contemporary

$$–$$$ ✕ **Dobson's Bar & Restaurant.** As innovative today as when it opened in 1983, this "power" dining spot for downtown movers and shakers, socialites, and operagoers has never changed the recipe for its famous mussel bisque, baked in a deep crock covered with tender pastry. Owner Paul Dobson generally keeps a close eye on tables in both the downstairs room, where the bar frequently is packed, and in the upstairs mezzanine, which has a choice view of all the action. Specialties include porcini mushroom ravioli, a salad of rare, house-smoked filet mignon, and maple-roasted chicken breast. ✉ *956 Broadway Circle, Downtown* ☎ *619/231–6771* ☉ *Closed Sun. No lunch Sat.*

$$–$$$ ✕ **Rice.** The W Hotel hit San Diego like a storm in 2003, and its trio of bars (including the roof-top Beach, with a sandy floor) became the top destinations for on-the-town singles. Amidst all the nightlife, the Rice dining room is a calm haven for serious contemporary dining, much of it in the "fusion" style that marries two or more cuisines. The menu changes, but expect satisfying appetizers such as quail tempura with mango sauce, prosciutto-wrapped salmon with a spicy barbecue sauce, and five-spice-crusted pork tenderloin. Servers and decor are as hip as the crowd. ✉ *421 W. B St., Downtown* ☎ *619/231–8220* ▭ *AE, D, MC, V.*

★ ¢ ✕ **Bread on Market.** The baguettes at this artisan bakery near the Petco Park baseball stadium are every bit as good as the ones you'd buy in Paris. Baguettes, focaccia, and other superior loaves are the building blocks for solid, sometimes creative sandwiches, which range from the simple goodness of Genoa salami and sweet butter, to a vegan sandwich that includes locally grown avocado. The menu extends to a daily soup, a fruit-garnished cheese plate, and an appetizing Mediterranean salad. Snackers gravitate here for fudge-textured brownies, orange-almond biscotti, and other irresistible sweets. ✉ *730 Market St., Downtown* ☎ *619/795–2730* ▭ *MC, V* ☉ *Closed Sun. No dinner.*

French

★ $$$–$$$$ ✕ **Le Fontainebleau.** On the second floor of the elegant Westgate Hotel, this is worthy of the famous chateau for which it is named. Normandy-born chef Fabrice Hardel writes seasonal menus, but usually offers classics like French pepper steak (dramatically flambéed at your table), along with contemporary creations like baked John Dory in a bouillon scented with star anise. Pairing the multicourse tasting menu with specially selected wines costs in excess of $100 per person, a price that seems not unreasonable when read to the accompaniment of the harp or piano music that is a Le Fontainebleau staple. ✉ *1055 2nd Ave., Downtown* ☎ *619/557–3655* 🏛 *Jacket required* 🖃 *AE, D, DC, MC, V.*

★ **$$–$$$$** ✕ **Bertrand at Mister A's.** Restaurateur Bertrand Hug's sumptuous 12th-floor dining room has vanilla walls, contemporary paintings, and a view that stretches from the mountains to Mexico and San Diego Bay. You can watch the aerial ballet of jets descending upon nearby Lindbergh Field. Ideal for a special occasion, Bertrand at Mister A's serves luxurious seasonal dishes such as sautéed foie gras with caramelized fruit and Dover sole in lemon butter. The dessert list encompasses a galaxy of sweets every bit as memorable as the view. ✉ *2550 5th Ave., Middletown* ☎ *619/239–1377* 🍽 *Reservations essential* 🏛 *Jacket required* 🖃 *AE, DC, MC, V* ☟ *No lunch weekends.*

$–$$ ✕ **Cafe Chloe.** What a difference a ballpark makes. Until the opening of nearby Petco Park in 2004, the intersection of 9th and G was far from everywhere. Now it's the center of a district of new luxury high-rises and hotels, and the area's new residents make Cafe Chloe their headquarters. Pretty and Parisian, it charms as a quiet spot for afternoon coffee and bustles at breakfast, lunch, and dinner, when the kitchen turns out such creative fare as chive French toast topped with cured salmon, a casserole of macaroni, pancetta, and Gorgonzola, and a chicken and mushroom vol-au-vent. ✉ *721 9th Ave., Downtown* ☎ *619/232–3242* 🖃 *AE, D, DC, MC, V.*

Greek

$$–$$$ ✕ **Athens Market.** This cheerful eatery with an outdoor patio bustles with office workers and members of San Diego's small but active Greek community. Appetizers such as *taramosalata* (fish roe dip), hummus, and stuffed grape leaves are particularly tasty. Entrées include *arni psito* (roast leg of lamb), a very convincing rendition of moussaka, and the house Greek pasta, with garlic, onion, and cheese. The *galaktobouriko* (a layering of crisp phyllo pastry, eggy custard, and clove-scented syrup) makes an excellent dessert. Athens Market seems as timeless as Greece itself. ✉ *109 W. F St., Downtown* ☎ *619/234–1955* 🖃 *AE, D, DC, MC, V* ☟ *No lunch weekends.*

Indian

★ **$–$$** ✕ **Monsoon.** An exceptionally attractive restaurant, Monsoon delights with features such as a room-centering waterfall that splashes like a cloudburst from a bower of hanging plants. Folding doors allow some tables to share the outdoor atmosphere of the terrace, but at a distance from the sidewalk. The menu offers many dishes not easily found at local Indian eateries, including a sweetly spiced mango soup, and "balti"-style pan-sautéed lamb. The dozens of curries and similar dishes are spiced to taste. ✉ *729–733 4th Ave., Gaslamp Quarter* ☎ *619/234–5555* 🖃 *AE, MC, V.*

Irish

$–$$ ✕ **The Field.** A family-run pub decorated with artifacts from an Irish farm, the Field has character to spare. Both on the outdoor terrace and indoors, diners enjoy solid meals of Irish stew, corned beef and cabbage, or, best of all, a *boxty*, a lacy but substantial potato pancake served crisp and hot with such fillings as sage-flavored chicken or Irish bacon and cheese. As the evening wears on, the crowd grows younger, livelier, louder, and sometimes rowdier. A traditional Irish breakfast is served Saturday and Sunday. ⊠ *544 5th Ave., Gaslamp Quarter* ☎ *619/232–9840* ⊟ *MC, V.*

Italian

$$–$$$$ ✕ **Trattoria Mare & Monti.** The sea and mountains that contribute their special products to Italian cuisine are paid tribute in the name of this comfortable restaurant. The menu attempts to differentiate itself from those of other restaurants in the neighborhood and is notable for a "Martini" of shellfish and tart *limoncello* liqueur, a stylish lobster salad, and *pappardelle* (wide ribbons of pasta) in a red wine–rich lamb sauce. On the more affordable side, the kitchen turns out excellent pizzas baked in a wood-fired oven. Choose between a table on the narrow sidewalk terrace or in the spacious dining room. ⊠ *644 5th Ave., Gaslamp Quarter* ☎ *619/235–8144* ⊟ *AE, DC, MC, V.*

¢–$ ✕ **Assaggio.** Assaggio coaxes diners away from the pricier 5th Avenue drag with old-world flavors at unbeatable prices. The small sidewalk terrace usually fills before the well-lighted dining room, but both are pleasant settings in which to enjoy a savory soup of homemade *maltagliati* pasta and cannellini beans, a *caprese* salad of buffalo mozzarella and tomatoes, or a richly stuffed lasagna. The oven is the source of both excellent, thinly crusted pizzas and delicious cakes and cookies. ⊠ *835 4th Ave., Gaslamp Quarter* ☎ *619/234–6538* ⊟ *MC, V.*

Japanese

$–$$$ ✕ **Kiyo's.** On quiet F Street, this restaurant and sushi bar seems an island of tranquillity buffered from the business of 5th Avenue. The menu is comprehensive, and the sushi chefs are renowned for their creativity. Sushi rolls delight or challenge: the "caterpillar" roll pairs local avocado with freshwater eel. Hot meals include *gyoza* (small dumplings), beef drenched in *shoga* (ginger) sauce, a tasty pork *tonkatsu* (breaded cutlet), excellent shrimp tempura, or, perhaps, *una ju*, which is broiled eel basted with a sweet sauce. This is a favorite with Japanese visitors. ⊠ *531 F St., Gaslamp Quarter* ☎ *619/238–1726* ⊟ *AE, MC, V.*

¢–$$ ✕ **RA Sushi Bar Restaurant.** Servers in semi-sensational T-shirts (mottos include "Practice Safe Sushi") challenge a young clientele to strive for "attitude" in this small, intimate space carved out of a former department store. Two ultrahip bars—one for cocktails, one for sushi—fuel the popularity, bolstered by a dining room menu from which you can make a meal out of the many appetizers, such as coconut shrimp tempura and scallops in spicy "dynamite" sauce. Otherwise, choose sushi combination plates, spare ribs in smoked plum sauce, savory meat and seafood teriyaki specialties, and hearty noodle dishes. ⊠ *1014 5th Ave., entrance on Broadway, Downtown* ☎ *619/321–0021* ⊟ *AE, DC, MC, V.*

Mexican

$$$–$$$$ ✕ **Candelas.** The scents and flavors of imaginative Mexican cuisine permeate this handsome, romantic little hideaway in the shadow of San Diego's tallest residential towers. Candles glow everywhere around the small, comfortable dining room. There isn't a burrito or taco in sight. Fine openers such as cream of black bean and beer soup, and salad of watercress with bacon and pistachios warm diners up for local lobster stuffed with mushrooms, jalapeño peppers, and aged tequila; or tequila-flamed jumbo prawns over creamy, seasoned goat cheese. The new, adjacent bar pours many elegant tequilas. ⊠ *416 3rd Ave., Gaslamp Quarter* ☎ *619/702–4455* ⊟ *MC, V* ☺ *Closed Sun. No lunch weekends.*

¢–$ ✕ **Chuey's Numero Uno.** You'll never come up one taco shy of a combination plate at this vintage-1956 eatery in a blue-collar neighborhood near downtown. Cops love it, Navy brass love it, guys who wear hard hats love it—in fact, just about everyone is enamored of the huge, Quonset hut setting, the cheerful servers, and the keep-you-going-all day meals. The only disappointment: Chuey's closes at 6 PM, so fill up on steak ranchero, *chile verde* (pork stewed in a very spicy green sauce), and chicken enchiladas before this hour, or return in the morning for huevos rancheros and other zesty egg dishes. ⊠ *1894 Main St., Barrio Logan* ☎ *619/234–6937* ⊟ *MC, V* ☺ *No dinner.*

Seafood

$$$$ ✕ **Osetra the Fishhouse.** Aimed squarely at conventioneers and expense-account types, Osetra is named for one of the kinds of caviar served, caviar you can consume with some of the companionable champagne that is stocked aplenty in the soaring wine tower that dominates the two-story dining room. In this Las Vegas–style extravaganza, your bottle is retrieved for you by a "wine angel" who takes flight via a cable hoist to reach it. The restaurant's handling of luxury seafood is very good, particularly specialties like lobster salad with chive rémoulade sauce, and an impressively presented bouillabaisse, but those scared by the luxury prices can still enjoy the scene by sipping a drink at the ice-topped bar. ⊠ *904 5th Ave., Gaslamp Quarter* ☎ *619/239–1800* ⊟ *AE, D, DC, MC, V* ☺ *No lunch.*

$$$–$$$$ **Star of the Sea.** This is the flagship of the Anthony's chain of seafood restaurants, its most formal dining room (although dress is quite casual) and long an all-around favorite for location, cuisine, and design. The menu changes seasonally, but frankly, the food and service seem to have suffered declines of late, and while this remains an exceptional setting, the best bet when ordering is probably to take a conservative approach. To be sure, have one of the baked-to-order soufflés, which are puffy, fragrant, and lovely on the palate. The outdoor patio takes full advantage of the choice waterfront location. ⊠ *1360 N. Harbor Dr., Downtown* ☎ *619/232–7408* ⊟ *AE, D, DC, MC, V* ☺ *No lunch.*

$$–$$$$ ✕ **Blue Point Coastal Cuisine.** If there's a convention in town, Blue Point gets jammed with diverse diners who share a taste for sophisticated seafood. The menu swims with international accents, so that the spicy calamari appetizer is served with Thai red chili sauce, and a ginger-soy butter sauce suavely finishes grilled ahi. Among choices from the land, Moroccan-spice couscous cakes add a certain zing to grilled rack of lamb, and green peppercorn sauce livens a prime New York strip. The wine list is serious, and the service efficient and friendly. The airy dining room has gleaming woodwork and walls of windows looking onto 5th Avenue and Market Street, a prime corner for people-watching. ⊠ *565 5th Ave., Gaslamp Quarter* ☎ *619/233–6623* ⊟ *AE, D, DC, MC, V* ☺ *No lunch.*

$–$$$$ ✕ **Fish Market.** Fresh mesquite-grilled, steamed, and skewered fish and shellfish are the specialty at this informal restaurant. There's also an excellent little sushi bar and good steamed clams and mussels. The view is stunning: enormous plate-glass windows look directly out onto the harbor. A more formal restaurant upstairs, the Top of the Market ($$$–$$$$), is expensive but worth the splurge, and is the place to find such rarities as true Dover sole, which the kitchen delicately browns in butter and finishes with a lemon-caper sauce. The Dungeness crab cocktail is well worth the cost. ⊠ *750 N. Harbor Dr., Downtown* ☎ *619/ 232–3474 Fish Market, 619/234–4867 Top of the Market* ⌣ *Reservations not accepted* ▭ *AE, D, DC, MC, V.*

★ $$–$$$$ ✕ **Oceanaire Seafood Room.** Engineered to recall the bold, sprawling America of the 1940s—there are tubes of Brylcreem in the men's room, for goodness sake—Oceanaire is a bit put-on, but nonetheless admirable for a carefully prepared menu that offers up to 25 daily "fresh catches," as well as a host of specialties ranging from convincing Maryland crab cakes and steaming oysters Rockefeller to richly stuffed California sole, a luxurious one-pound pork chop, and irresistible hash brown potatoes. Service is a sometime thing in San Diego, which makes the professional staff here all the more notable. ⊠ *400 J St., Gaslamp Quarter* ☎ *619/ 858–2277* ▭ *AE, D, DC, MC, V* ⊘ *No lunch.*

★ ¢–$ ✕ **The Tin Fish.** On the rare rainy day, the staff takes it easy at this eatery less than 100 yards from the Petco Park baseball stadium (its 100-odd seats are all outdoors). Musicians entertain some evenings, making this a lively spot for dinners of grilled and fried fish and shellfish, as well as Mexican-style seafood burritos and tacos. The quality here routinely surpasses that at grander establishments—for instance, the bread used for sandwiches stuffed with fried oysters and the like is baked on the premises. For kids (or unadventurous grown-ups) there's an inexpensive peanut butter and jelly sandwich. Service hours vary with the day of the week and the weather, but generally, Tin Fish closes at 3 PM weekdays and 8 PM weekends. ⊠ *170 6th Ave., Gaslamp Quarter* ☎ *619/ 238–8100* ⌣ *Reservations not accepted* ▭ *MC, V.*

Spanish

$$–$$$ ✕ **Sevilla.** Increasingly a nightclub, Sevilla fills Thursday through Sunday evenings with youthful throngs who crowd the ground-floor bar for drinks, tapas, and professional flamenco dancing. Others head to the downstairs club for classics from the Spanish kitchen and live music. There isn't a quiet corner to be found. The kitchen does a respectable job with the traditional shellfish and chicken paella (there are also strictly meat and seafood versions). It also makes highly flavorful baked rabbit and roasted pork tenderloin. Dinner shows take place Friday through Sunday, when a three-course meal is priced at $15.95. ⊠ *555 4th Ave., Gaslamp Quarter* ☎ *619/233–5979* ▭ *AE, MC, V* ⊘ *No lunch.*

Steak Houses

★ $$$–$$$$ ✕ **Rainwater's on Kettner.** San Diego's premier homegrown steak house also ranks as the longest running of the pack, not least because it has the luxurious look and mood of an old-fashioned Eastern men's club. The cuisine is excellent: open with the signature black bean soup with

Madeira. Continue with the tender, expertly roasted prime rib, the superb calves' liver with onions and bacon, broiled free-range chicken, fresh seafood, or the amazingly succulent pork chops, all served in vast portions with plenty of hot-from-the-oven cornsticks on the side. The well-chosen wine list has pricey but superior selections. ⊠ *1202 Kettner Blvd., Downtown* ☎ *619/233–5757* ▭ *AE, D, MC, V* ⊗ *No lunch weekends.*

★ **$$–$$$$** ✕ **Morton's of Chicago.** Housed in the soaring Harbor Club towers near both the San Diego Convention Center and the Gaslamp Quarter, Morton's often teems with conventioneers out for a night on the town. Servers present the menu by wheeling up a cart laden with crimson prime steaks, behemoth veal and lamb chops, thick cuts of swordfish, and huge Maine lobsters that may wave their claws in alarm when they hear the prices (based on the market, but always astronomical) quoted. Expect a treat, since this restaurant knows how to put on a superb spread that takes the concept of indulgence to new heights. ⊠ *Harbor Club, 285 J St., Downtown* ☎ *619/696–3369* ▭ *AE, D, MC, V* ⊗ *No lunch.*

$–$$$$ ✕ **Lou & Mickey's.** The restaurant nearest the San Diego Convention Center, this handsome, 1940s-style establishment (it opened in 2002) lures with thick steaks and chops, equally meaty seafood cuts such as the unusual T-bone of Alaskan halibut, richly sauced pastas, and chicken dishes of surprising flavor and sophistication. Be extravagant by opening with top-quality oysters and moving on to the $45-per-serving Alaskan king crab legs. Budgets can be met by investing in a filling and rather tasty garlic meat loaf po' boy sandwich, which costs just $8.95. Either way, plan on finishing with an impressive wedge of key lime pie. ⊠ *224 5th Ave., Gaslamp Quarter* ☎ *619/237–4900* ▭ *AE, DC, MC, V* ⊗ *No lunch.*

Thai

$–$$ ✕ **Rama.** Gauzy draperies and a rock wall flowing with water create a
Fodor's Choice dreamy rain-forest effect in the back room of this excellent newcomer
★ to the Gaslamp Quarter's booming restaurant row. Without question the best Thai restaurant in San Diego, Rama combines memorable decor and professional service with a kitchen that understands the subtle demands of spicing the myriad dishes. The tart, pungent, spiced-to-order (as everything can be) *talay* (seafood soup—it literally means "ocean") pairs well with a crispy duck salad as a light meal for two. Dozens of curries and stir-fries take the tastebuds on exciting adventures in flavor. ⊠ *327 4th Ave., Gaslamp Quarter* ☎ *619/501–8424* ▭ *AE, D, DC, MC, V.*

Little Italy

American

¢ ✕ **The Waterfront.** Not a destination for children, this historic bar and eatery, which opened in the 1930s and claims to be San Diego's oldest watering hole, is an attraction for anyone in search of genuine atmosphere. The bar has supported the elbows of tuna fishermen and aviation workers in earlier eras and now attracts lawyers, construction workers, and other souls hungry for a $5.25 bowl of really good chili, burgers that can't be beat, smoking-hot onion rings and french fries, and other great-tasting grub, including fish tacos. The Waterfront serves from early morning until midnight or later. ✉ *2044 Kettner Blvd., Little Italy* ☎ *619/232–9656* ▭ *MC, V.*

British

$ ✕ **Princess Pub & Grille.** Packed to the rafters during any televised British football (soccer) championship, this cheerful neighborhood place is the unofficial headquarters of transplanted Brits, Australians, and New Zealanders. The selection of imported beers and ales, most of them from Merrie Olde, is quite impressive, and the menu complements them well with such offerings as sausage rolls, fish-and-chips, spicy chicken curry, and an elaborate Cheshire mixed grill of meats, sausage, egg, and mushrooms. The oversize buffalo burgers have a loyal following. The patrons seem equally fond of conversation and darts. ✉ *1665 India St., Little Italy* ☎ *619/702–3021* ▭ *MC, V.*

Cajun–Creole

$ ✕ **Bud's Louisiana Food Shoppe.** Tiny, informal, intimate, and often crowded, this alternative to the virtual buffet of Italian restaurants in Little Italy is the creation of a well-experienced, Louisiana-born restaurateur who previously operated a larger, quite successful (and now closed) eatery in the Gaslamp Quarter. There's a tiny terrace on which to enjoy steaming seafood gumbo, po' boy sandwiches filled with fried shrimp or oysters, and main courses like shrimp creole, crayfish étouffée, and jambalaya. The rich creole pecan pie starts with a layer of cheesecake and gets better from there. ✉ *2034 Kettner Blvd., Little Italy* ☎ *619/239–4210* ⟁ *Reservations not accepted* ▭ *AE, D, DC, MC, V* ◷ *Closed weekends.*

Italian

$$–$$$$ ✕ **Po Pazzo.** An eye-catching new creation from leading Little Italy
Fodor's Choice restaurateurs Joe and Lisa Busalacchi, Po Pazzo earns its name, which
★ means "a little crazy," by featuring silverware and glasses that seem to curve away from the hand. A steak house with an accent, this stylish eatery offers attractive salads and thick cuts of prime beef, as well as a top-notch presentation of veal saltimbocca, and pasta in an osso buco "sauce" that defines richness. It's pricey but fun, although at lunch, the Kobe beef burger with fresh-from-the-fat fries is an affordable way to enjoy the experience. ✉ *1917 India St., Little Italy* ☎ *619/238–1917* ▭ *AE, D, DC, MC, V* ◷ *No lunch weekends.*

★ $–$$$ ✕ **Buon Appetito.** Little Italy is booming again, and one charming arrival is Buon Appetito, which serves old-world–style cooking in a casual but decidedly sophisticated environment. The young Italian waiters' good humor makes the experience fun. Choose a table on the breezy sidewalk or in an indoor room jammed with art and fellow diners. Baked eggplant *all'amalfitana*, in a mozzarella-topped tomato sauce, is a dream of a dish, and in San Diego, tomato sauce doesn't get better than this. Consider also veal with tuna sauce, a hot chicken liver salad, fusilli pasta in savory duck ragout, and hearty seafood cioppino. ✉ *1609 India St., Little Italy* ☎ *619/238–9880* ▭ *MC, V.*

$–$$ ✕ **Zagarella.** Take a seat in the small dining room or in the vast courtyard and relax to recorded opera music while studying a menu that suggests such appetizers as sautéed herbed shrimp on a bed of shoestring potatoes, or a plate of tender roasted peppers crowned with a whole school of anchovies. The Italian menu avoids clichés in favor of specialties like warm duck salad accented with pine nuts and golden raisins, baked eggplant timbale, ravioli tossed with radicchio braised in cream, and veal scallopini with artichokes and lemon sauce. The shady courtyard is a quiet haven. ☒ *1655 India St., Little Italy* ☎ *619/236–8764* 🖷 *MC, V.*

$ ✕ **Trattoria Fantastica.** Sicilian flavors abound on the menu, which is highlighted by such offerings as a salad of tomatoes, red onions, olive oil, and oregano; and the pasta *palermitana*—rigatoni with spicy sausage, olives, capers, and marinara sauce. Many pastas come with cargoes of fresh seafood, and the pizzas baked in the wood-burning oven are robust and beautifully seasoned. Reserve ahead if you want to score a table in the shady courtyard, and also keep this in mind as a snack break for beautiful pastries, remarkable gelato, and freshly brewed Italian coffees. ☒ *1735 India St., Little Italy* ☎ *619/234–1735* 🖷 *AE, DC, MC, V.*

¢-$ ✕ **Cefalu's.** A welcome budget addition to an increasingly expensive, trendy neighborhood, Cefalu's serves excellent pizza by the slice until 4 PM daily, and one wedge is big enough to make a satisfying lunch. Spaghetti with meatballs or made-in–Little Italy sausage makes a good alternative to a strong list of torpedo sandwiches (sliced sirloin with onions and peppers, anyone?), and the pizza list encompasses familiar favorites and house specialties like the "Fantasia," which is highlighted with sun-dried tomatoes and Gorgonzola cheese. ☒ *1655B India St., Little Italy* ☎ *619/236–9622* 🚫 *Reservations not accepted* 🖷 *MC, V.*

Southwestern

$$-$$$ ✕ **Indigo Grill.** Chef–partner Deborah Scott uses inspirations from Mexico to Alaska to infuse her contemporary Southwestern cuisine. Indigo Grill has both a stone interior and a broad terrace whose cool breezes do nothing to moderate the chilies that heat such one-of-a-kind offerings as stacked beet salad, pecan-crusted trout, salmon roasted on a well-seasoned wooden plank, and beautifully flavored venison chops. Creative desserts are often so generous in size that they can satisfy two with ease. Despite increasing competition in the neighborhood, this remains the hottest spot. ☒ *1536 India St., Little Italy* ☎ *619/234–6802* 🖷 *AE, D, DC, MC, V* 🕑 *No lunch weekends.*

Uptown

American

$-$$$ ✕ **Hash House A Go Go.** Expect to wait an hour for weekend breakfast
Fodor's Choice at this trendy Hillcrest eatery, whose walls display photos of farm ma-
★ chinery and other icons of middle America, but whose menu takes an up-to-the-minute look at national favorites. At breakfast, huge platters carpeted with fluffy pancakes sail out of the kitchen and return empty in a matter of moments, while at noon, customers favor the overflowing chicken potpies crowned with flaky pastry. The parade of old-fashioned good eats continues at dinner with hearty meat and seafood dishes, including the grand sage-flavored fried chicken, bacon-flavored waffle, and hot maple syrup combination. ☒ *3628 5th Ave., Hillcrest* ☎ *619/298–4646* 🖷 *MC, V.*

★ ¢–$$ ✕ **Hob Nob Hill.** That Hob Nob never seems to change suits San Diego just fine; this is the type of place where regulars delight in ordering the same meal they've been ordering for 20 years. With its dark-wood booths and patterned carpets, the restaurant seems suspended in the 1950s, but you don't need to be a nostalgia buff to appreciate the bargain-price American home cooking—dishes such as oat-raisin French toast, fried chicken, and corned beef like your mother never really made. The crowds line up morning, noon, and night. Reservations are suggested for Sunday breakfast. ✉ *2271 1st Ave., Middletown* ☎ *619/239–8176* ▭ *AE, D, MC, V.*

☾ ¢–$ ✕ **Corvette Diner Bar & Grill.** The absolute San Diego County favorite for children's parties and other family occasions, Corvette Diner showcases a real Corvette (changed every two or three months) in a kitschy, 1950s-style dining room dominated by vintage movie posters and singing servers. The menu has what you'd expect—macaroni and cheddar, plump burgers, piled-high deli sandwiches, spaghetti and meatballs, greasy chili-cheese fries, and thick milk shakes. The daily "Blue Plate Specials" are well-priced classics like grilled pork chops and "picnic basket" fried chicken. ✉ *3946 5th Ave., Hillcrest* ☎ *619/542–1001* ▭ *AE, D, MC, V.*

Chinese

¢ ✕ **Chef Lau's Asian Tapas Cafe.** Change "tapas" to "appetizers" and the concept is more familiar, if less trendy, and everybody knows that Hillcrest eateries like to ride the crest of the highest wave. The clever menu, which primarily features noodles, dumplings, and other small dishes, makes a varied meal quite affordable, as well as a genuine pleasure. The many dumpling fillings (choices include shrimp, chicken, beef, and vegetables) run to toothsome items like minced pork flavored with garlic chives; the scallion flatbreads, turnip cakes, curry-filled pastries, and pickled kim chi salad are also delicious. ✉ *3739B 6th Ave., Hillcrest* ☎ *619/692–4189* ▭ *MC, V.*

Contemporary

$$–$$$$ ✕ **Laurel.** This top destination had changed hands at time of writing, and it's not known in what direction the new owners will take the long-running favorite. However, it seems likely that they will retain the polished service, smart, contemporary design, and notable wine list. The new chef is well-versed in French Mediterranean cuisine, and Laurel should remain a favorite with guests attending theatrical events in nearby Balboa Park. ✉ *505 Laurel St., Middletown* ☎ *619/239–2222* ▭ *AE, D, DC, MC, V* ☾ *No lunch.*

$–$$$ ✕ **The Prado.** This beautiful restaurant in the House of Hospitality on Balboa Park's museum row brings an inventive, contemporary menu to an area where picnic lunches are the only other option. The striking interior has elegantly painted ceilings and elaborate glass sculptures, and the bar is a fashionable pre- and post-theater destination for such light nibbles as crab cakes and steamed Manila clams. In the dining room, well-trained servers offer dishes that range from a dressy "farmer's salad" to saffron linguine with shellfish of the day, marinated baby lamb rack, and steamed sea bass with mango-jalapeño salsa. ✉ *1549 El Prado, Balboa Park* ☎ *619/557–9441* ▭ *AE, D, MC, V.*

Where to Eat
in San Diego

$–$$$ ✕ **Region.** Rich in talented owner-chefs who use the finest local produce
Fodor's Choice to create traditional recipes, Region is one of the most intriguing restau-
★ rants in San Diego. The kitchen's approach nears perfection with dishes
like veal osso buco, roast pork with sweet potatoes, and pan-gilded skate
(a type of ray) that flakes at the touch of a fork. The menu changes daily,
but count on fine sweets like cooked-to-order donuts with olive oil gelato.
A chalkboard not only lists the evening's special fruits and vegetables and
their provenance but also illustrates some of them. The food and prices
at this purposely informal place (the waiters wear jeans) mean value for
the money, making it competitive with more formal establishments. Reser-
vations are strongly advised. ⊠ *3671 5th Ave., Hillcrest* ☎ *619/299–6499*
🖃 *AE, D, DC, MC, V* ⊘ *No lunch. No dinner Sun. and Mon.*

$–$$$ ✕ **Terra.** Catching the wave of special diets, this restaurant offers menus
that have been a hit with diabetics and followers of the Atkins Diet. The
grilled meats and seafood with light but savory, vegetable-based sauces
are very good indeed. On the seasonal standing menu, chef–proprietor
Jeff Rossman offers options like sage-roasted chicken with pumpkin purée
and forest mushroom risotto, and grilled filet mignon in a racy, Argen-
tine-style *chimichurri* sauce (oil and vinegar flavored with more than a
dozen herbs). Filling the terrace in summer are the weekly barbecues
accompanied by live jazz. ⊠ *3900 Vermont St., Hillcrest* ☎ *619/293–
7088* 🖃 *AE, D, MC, V* ⊘ *No lunch weekends.*

Eclectic

$$–$$$ ✕ **Parallel 33.** True to its name, Parallel 33 traces this imaginary line around
the globe, serving dishes based on American, Moroccan, Middle East-
ern, Chinese, and Japanese cuisines. Chef-proprietor Amiko Gubbins
has a sure handle on everything she cooks. Her Moroccan-style chicken-
and-egg pie hides a deliciously savory filling inside a flaky phyllo crust,
and the spiced vegetarian samosas are joined by contrasting, excitingly
flavorful chutneys. Among other favorites are pan-seared, Goa-style
shrimp curry, Moroccan lamb *tajine,* or stew, and grilled duck breast
with sweet potato gnocchi. A newly constructed second dining room is
one of the hippest spots in town. ⊠ *741 W. Washington St., Mission
Hills* ☎ *619/260–0033* 🖃 *AE, D, MC, V* ⊘ *Closed Sun. No lunch.*

Indian

★ **$–$$$** ✕ **Bombay Exotic Cuisine of India.** Notable for its elegant dining room, Bom-
bay employs a chef whose generous hand with raw and cooked vegeta-
bles gives each course a colorful freshness reminiscent of California
cuisine, though the flavors definitely hail from India. Try the tandoori
lettuce wrap appetizer and any of the stuffed *nan* (a delectably chewy
tandoori bread). The unusually large selection of curries may be ordered
with meat, chicken, fish, or tofu. The curious should try the *dizzy noo
shakk,* a sweet and spicy banana curry. Try a *thali,* a plate that includes
an entrée, traditional sides, nan, dessert, and tea. ⊠ *Hillcrest Center, 3975
5th Ave., Suite 100, Hillcrest* ☎ *619/298–3155* 🖃 *AE, D, DC, MC, V.*

Italian

$–$$$ ✕ **Busalacchi's Ristorante.** This long-running hit on the fringe of Hillcrest
offers a romantic, low-key dining room and a stylish, sheltered patio
that overlooks busy 5th Avenue. The lengthy menu zeroes in on elegant,

fully flavored Sicilian specialties—it may be the only place in San Diego offering an *insalata di cetrioli*, a salad of cucumbers, beets, roasted pearl onions, and Gorgonzola. The pasta dishes include familiar favorites, but classically Sicilian is the rigatoni in an aromatic sausage-caper sauce; the stuffed, breaded veal *spiedini* (on skewers) also is superb. ⊠ *3683 5th Ave., Hillcrest* ☎ *619/298–0119* ☰ *AE, DC, MC, V* ☽ *No lunch weekends.*

$–$$ ✕ **La Pizzeria Arrivederci.** The wood-burning oven roars on what pass for cold nights in San Diego, sending the shadows of dancing flames across the cozy dining room. Out come pizzas topped with forest mushrooms and smoky *scamorza* cheese, or perhaps *alla messicana*, a Mexican-style pie whose topping includes pork sausage, cilantro, and crushed red peppers. The list of imaginative pizzas is long (yes, you can get a pepperoni pizza, too), but there are also expertly made pastas such as penne in creamy vodka sauce with smoked salmon, and penne in pungent puttanesca sauce. Young waiters from Italy treat guests well. ⊠ *3789 4th Ave., Hillcrest* ☎ *619/542–0293* ☰ *MC, V* ☽ *No lunch weekends.*

★ **$–$$** ✕ **Sambuca Italian Bistro.** It's a wonder the streets of central Hillcrest don't collapse beneath the weight of all the restaurants, but the district has become such a dining and entertainment center that new eateries continue to open. A particularly fine addition is this cozy, candlelighted place with reasonable prices and a well-prepared menu that differs more than a bit from the competition. Dishes marked "signature" are particularly noteworthy, like the signature Sambuca shrimp appetizer with a unique lime-garlic sauce. Creamy flavors make the four-cheese fusilli pasta with lobster an extravagant treat, while there is delicious subtlety to the roasted chicken with brandied Gorgonzola sauce. ⊠ *3888 4th Ave., Hillcrest* ☎ *619/298–8700* ☰ *AE, DC, MC, V.*

Mexican

¢–$ ✕ **Baja Betty's.** A margarita and a combination plate speak to the soul of many a San Diegan. Pair this duo with a sizzling scene and smoking music and you come up with a hot spot like Baja Betty's, which offers dozens of tequilas—some quite spectacular—and a long list of cocktails built upon them. The salsa similarly sizzles, and can dress everything from the excellent *carnitas* quesadilla, filled with shredded pork, to the "flamenco" flautas, filled with a choice of shredded beef or chicken. Large portions, good cooking, friendly servers, and low prices make this a find. ⊠ *1421 University Ave., Hillcrest* ☎ *619/269-8510* ☰ *AE, D, DC, MC, V.*

Thai

★ **¢–$$** ✕ **Celadon Fine Thai Cuisine.** Talk to young proprietor Alex Thao if you want to try some of the specialties not listed on the menu, like the spicy, stir-fried cashew appetizer or the tart, invigorating stir-fry of shredded dried beef and citrus sauce. These dishes are superb, but the everyday menu is good enough to keep the small, well-furnished dining room jumping, even on Monday nights. Start with "Celadon squares," small toasts covered with a paste of shrimp and pork, and move along to refreshing, if spicy, papaya salad, the excellent *tom kha* (chicken soup), and such entrées as deep-fried whole striped bass with green mangoes. ⊠ *540 University Ave., Hillcrest* ☎ *619/297–8424* ☰ *MC, V.*

Kearny Mesa

Argentinian

$–$$$ ✕ **Pampas Argentine Grill.** Meats, mostly cut in hefty portions, grilled and served with zesty, herb-rich chimichurri sauce, are the main thrust of the menu at this comfy steakery a few blocks east of the Convoy Street restaurant row. Choices include rib eye, filet mignon, and strip steaks, along with marinated boneless chicken and the seafood of the day. The spacious restaurant is gently lighted and hung with paintings that strive for the romance of the tango. Live music is offered several evenings each week. ⊠ *8690 Aero Dr., Kearny Mesa* ☎ *858/278–5971* ▤ *AE, MC, V* ⊘ *Closed Mon. No lunch.*

Chinese

★ **$–$$$$** ✕ **Emerald Chinese Seafood Restaurant.** Emerald holds pride of place among fanciers of elaborate, carefully prepared, and sometimes costly seafood dishes. Even when the restaurant is full to capacity with 300 diners, the noise level is moderate and conversation flows easily between bites of the best Chinese cuisine in the area. The shrimp, prawns, lobsters, clams, and fish reside in tanks until the moment of cooking. Simple preparations flavored with scallions, black beans, and ginger are among the most worthy. Other recommended dishes include beef with Singapore-style satay sauce, honey-walnut shrimp, baked chicken in five spices, Peking duck served in two savory courses, and, at lunch, the dim sum. ⊠ *3709 Convoy St., Kearny Mesa* ☎ *858/565–6888* ▤ *AE, MC, V.*

¢–$$$$ ✕ **Jasmine.** This cavernous, Hong Kong–style establishment seats no fewer than 800 people; even so, there frequently are lines outside during lunchtime on weekends, when groups arrive en masse to enjoy fragrant soups, steaming noodles, and dim sum pastries from carts that constantly circle the room. At dinner it's a hard choice between the seafood from the wall-mounted tanks and "Peking duck two ways"—the crisp skin sandwiched in tasty buns as a first course, the meat deliciously stir-fried for a savory follow-up. A supplementary menu of "special-priced dishes" offers bargains like one-half of a roasted chicken for $7.50. ⊠ *4609 Convoy St., Kearny Mesa* ☎ *858/268–0888* ▤ *AE, MC, V.*

¢–$$ ✕ **China Max.** This new addition to Convoy Street took the neighborood by storm, not only because of the quality, variety, and authenticity of the cooking, but because a value-priced late-supper menu is offered nightly from 9 PM until midnight. Dishes not to be missed include the stir-fried shrimp with lettuce "taco," fish and beef meatball soup with *mei fun* noodles, the one-of-a-kind sautéed cruller with pungent Chinese chives, and pan-fried lamb chops in black-pepper sauce. Tanks team with seafood, all priced according to the market. ⊠ *4698 Convoy St., Kearny Mesa* ☎ *858/650–3333* ▤ *AE, DC, MC, V.*

★ **¢–$** ✕ **Dumpling Inn.** Modest, family-style, and absolutely wonderful, this is in some ways the best of Convoy Street's Asian eateries. The tiny establishment loads its tables with bottles of aromatic and spicy condiments for the boiled, steamed, and fried dumplings that are the house specialty. These delicately flavored, hefty mouthfuls preface a meal that may continue simply, with hearty pork and pickled cabbage soup, or elaborately, with Shanghai-style braised pork shank. Ask about daily

WHERE TO REFUEL AROUND TOWN

SAN DIEGO HAS A FEW HOME-GROWN CHAINS as well as many stand-alone eateries that will amiably fill you up without demanding too much in return.

The Mission, a local minichain open only for breakfast and lunch, has three locations: Mission Beach, North Park, and the Petco Park district. The latter, the newest, occupies a vintage-1870 building originally known as Rosario Hall. Called the Mission SoMa (short for "South of Market Street"), it fulfills its mission as a breakfast-and-lunch destination (as at the other two, there's no service after 3 PM) with a menu that runs the gamut from banana-blackberry pancakes to a Zen breakfast complete with tofu and brown rice, to creative black bean burritos and a smoked turkey sandwich.

If there's something for everyone at the Mission, the statement is equally true of San Diego's enormously popular Sammy's Woodfired Pizza chain. With convenient outlets in La Jolla, Mission Valley, and the Gaslamp Quarter, Sammy's makes friends with oversize salads, a vast selection of pizzas, entrées, and pastas, and the fun "messy sundae," which lives up to its name.

Filippi's Pizza Grotto locations (the best are on India Street in Little Italy and in Pacific Beach) please crowds with vast platters of spaghetti and meatballs, as well as very good pizzas.

Also home-grown and from the same post-World War II era as Filippi's, Anthony's Fish Grotto enjoys considerable renown for batter-fried fish filets and shellfish, as well as chowders, char-broiled fish, and other simple, well-prepared offerings. Anthony's on the Embarcadero, downtown (next door to Star of the Sea, the flagship of the chain), is built over the water and often has a line at the door; the Chula

Vista branch is at freeway Exit 10, minutes south of downtown.

If you can't leave San Diego without downing a fish taco, be advised that the nation-spanning Rubio's chain was founded here and has multiple locations.

Besides chains, keep these streets or neighborhoods in mind for refueling: funky Ocean Beach, famed for its easy-going breakfast places; Little Italy (India Street), with endless Italian options; and Hillcrest in the vicinity of the 5th Avenue–University Avenue intersection, a buffet of international cuisines. If you want Asian, Convoy Street is the place to go.

–David Nelson

specials, such as shredded pork in plum sauce served on a sea of crispy noodles. You may bring your own wine or beer; the house serves only tea and soft drinks. ⊠ *4619 Convoy St., #F, Kearny Mesa* ☎ *858/268–9638* ⚇ *Reservations not accepted* ⊟ *MC, V* ⊗ *Closed Mon.*

Korean

$–$$$ ✕ **Buga Korean B.B.Q. Restaurant.** The cook-it-yourself fun of Korean barbecue and Japanese-style shabu-shabu focuses attention on your table's built-in cooking unit, not on the modest decor. Suspended exhaust fan hoods create something of a draft when the restaurant is full of guests barbecuing sharply marinated cuts of meat and seafood. Shabu-shabu, a multicourse meal of paper-thin meats, vegetables, and noodles, is cooked in iron pots of boiling liquid that provides a final course of tasty broth. Pleasant servers explain the cooking procedures. The restaurant is a few blocks west of the Convoy Street corridor. ⊠ *5580 Clairemont Mesa Blvd., Clairemont* ☎ *858/560–1010* ⊟ *MC, V.*

Vietnamese

¢–$$ ✕ **Phuong Trang.** Widely considered the leading Vietnamese restaurant in San Diego, Phuong Trang cooks up no fewer than 248 appetizers, soups, noodle dishes, and main courses, which can make choosing a meal a bewildering process. Waiters tend to steer you to tasty offerings like fried egg rolls, char-grilled shrimp paste wrapped around sugarcane, beef in grape leaves, and fresh spring rolls filled with pork and shrimp. Noodles topped with a grilled pork chop makes a satisfying meal. The large, relatively spare dining room gets packed to the rafters, but service is speedy, if sometimes curt. ⊠ *4170 Convoy St., Kearny Mesa* ☎ *858/565–6750* ⊟ *MC, V.*

Beaches

American

★ **¢–$** ✕ **Hodad's.** No, it's not a flashback. The 1960s live on at this fabulously funky burger joint founded in that era: an unrepentant hippy crowd sees to it. Walls are covered with license plates, and the amiable servers with tattoos. Still, this is very much a family place, and Hodad's clientele often includes toddlers and octogenarians. Burgers are the thing, loaded with onions, pickles, tomatoes, lettuce, and condiments, and so gloriously messy that you might wear a swimsuit so you can stroll to the beach for a bath afterwards. The mini-hamburger is good, the double bacon cheeseburger absolutely awesome. ⊠ *5010 Newport Ave., Ocean Beach* ☎ *619/224–4623* ⊟ *AE, MC, V.*

Cajun-Creole

¢–$ ✕ **Mardi Gras Cafe & Market Place.** The taste of New Orleans comes packed into weighty muffuletta sandwiches (round loaves piled with cold cuts, cheeses, and olive salad), po' boy sandwiches filled with batter-fried shellfish, seafood gumbo, crawfish étouffée, and a steaming bowl of red beans and rice fleshed out with chunks of smoked sausage. Not far from Ocean Beach, this market-cum-eatery sets its tables next to shelves crammed with canned goods, a remarkable selection of hot sauces, and a range of New Orleans culinary necessities. Portions are vast, and the prices low. ⊠ *3185 Midway Dr.* ☎ *619/223–5501* ⊟ *AE, MC, V.*

Contemporary

$$–$$$$ ✕ **Thee Bungalow.** Two generations of San Diegans have developed a taste for roast duck with a variety of sauces (orange, black cherry, green peppercorn, pepper-rum) at this old-style continental restaurant that's as comfortable as an old shoe. Decorated with flowers, eye-pleasing paintings, and tables set with crisp linens, Thee Bungalow amiably purveys garlic-herb-crusted lamb rack with sauce béarnaise, pepper steak in brandy-rich bordelaise sauce, crab-stuffed salmon baked in puff pastry, and a classic bouillabaisse. The cooking gets more adventurous at periodic wine dinners, when startlingly superior vintages flow. The wine list is always remarkable. ⊠ *4996 W. Point Loma Blvd., Ocean Beach* ☎ *619/224–2884* ▤ *AE, D, DC, MC, V* ⊗ *No lunch.*

Cuban

¢–$ ✕ **Andre's Restaurant.** For more than two decades, Andre's was San Diego's sole outpost for solid, savory Cuban cuisine. In a nondescript building in the Morena Boulevard home furnishings district near Pacific Beach, Andre's is not much to look at, although the enclosed-patio dining room is comfortable and servers smile as they place heaped-high plates of breaded steak, roast pork, and grilled marinated fish in front of impressed diners. For Cuban home cooking at its best, order the *picadillo*, a meat hash with bold and piquant flavors. Like all entrées, it's accompanied by oceans of delicious black beans and mountains of rice. ⊠ *1235 Morena Blvd., Morena District* ☎ *619/274–4114* ▤ *MC, V* ⊗ *Closed Sun.*

German

★ **$$–$$$** ✕ **Kaiserhof.** Without question this is the best German restaurant in San Diego County, and the lively bar and beer garden work to inspire a sense of *Gemutlichkeit* (happy well-being). Tourist board–style posters of Germany's romantic destinations hang on the wall, Warsteiner and St. Pauli Girl flow from the tap. Gigantic portions are accompanied by such side dishes as potato pancakes, bread dumplings, red cabbage, and spaetzle noodles. Entrées include sauerbraten, Wiener schnitzel, goulash, and smoked pork chops, plus excellent daily specials such as venison medallions in green peppercorn sauce. Reservations are a good idea. ⊠ *2253 Sunset Cliffs Blvd., Ocean Beach* ☎ *619/224–0606* ▤ *MC, V* ⊗ *Closed Mon. No lunch Tues.–Thurs.*

Italian

$$ ✕ **The Venetian.** The spacious back room of this neighborhood eatery is actually a sheltered garden that you can enjoy in all weather. The menu takes a personal view of Italian cuisine, with house specialties like seafood pasta in tangy marinara sauce, and bow-tie pasta tossed with prosciutto, peas, mushrooms, and a rose-tinted cream sauce. The well-priced selection of veal, chicken, and seafood dishes is excellent, but many regulars settle for the lavishly garnished antipasto salad and one of the tender-crusted pizzas. ⊠ *3663 Voltaire St., Ocean Beach* ☎ *619/223–8197* ▤ *MC, V.*

$–$$ ✕ **Old Venice.** This long-running favorite near Shelter Island is treasured for its casual, welcoming atmosphere and for a menu that has both well-made pizzas and familiar Italian dishes like cannelloni baked in a rich meat sauce, generously stuffed lasagna, and eggplant parmigiana. A creamy pesto sauce adds glamour and a pungent flavor to the baked, spinach-stuffed chicken breast Florentine. Request a table on the semi-enclosed terrace behind the restaurant. ⊠ *2910 Canon St., Point Loma* ☎ *619/222–5888* ▤ *MC, V* ⊘ *No lunch Sun.*

¢–$$$ ✕ **Caffe Bella Italia.** Contemporary Italian cooking as prepared in Italy—an important point in fusion-mad San Diego—is the rule at this simple restaurant near one of the principle intersections in Pacific Beach. The menu presents Neapolitan-style macaroni with sausage and artichoke hearts in spicy tomato sauce, pappardelle with a creamy Gorgonzola and walnut sauce, plus formal entrées like chicken breast sautéed with balsamic vinegar, and slices of rare filet mignon tossed with herbs and topped with arugula and Parmesan shavings. Impressive daily specials include beet-stuffed ravioli in creamy saffron sauce. ⊠ *1525 Garnet Ave., Pacific Beach* ☎ *858/273–1224* ▤ *MC, V* ⊘ *Closed Mon.*

Japanese

★ ¢–$$ ✕ **Sushi Ota.** Wedged into a minimall between a convenience store and a looming medical building, Sushi Ota initially seems less than prepossessing. Still, San Diego–bound Japanese business people frequently call for reservations before boarding their trans-Pacific flights. Look closely at the expressions on customers' faces as they stream in and out of the doors, and you can see eager anticipation and satisfied glows due to San Diego's best sushi. Besides the usual California roll and tuna and shrimp sushi, sample the sea urchin or surf clam sushi, and the soft-shell crab roll. Sushi Ota offers the cooked as well as the raw. There's additional parking behind the mall. ⊠ *4529 Mission Bay Dr., Pacific Beach* ☎ *858/270–5670* ⌕ *Reservations essential* ▤ *AE, D, MC, V* ⊘ *No lunch Sat.–Mon.*

Mexican

$–$$ ✕ **Gringo's.** About a stone's throw from the ocean in the heart of lively Pacific Beach, this sizeable restaurant often seems to be having a party. A good variety of margaritas help fuel the atmosphere, but so does a menu cleverly divided between "Cali-Mex" favorites like quesadillas, enchiladas, burritos, and fajitas, and authentic regional specialties from the Mexican heartland. The latter includes dishes like *chiles en nogada* (meat-stuffed chilies in a walnut-cream sauce) and oven-roasted pork chops in Oaxacan-style mole sauce. Make reservations, because this joint jumps. ⊠ *4474 Mission Blvd., Pacific Beach* ☎ *858/490–2877* ▤ *AE, D, DC, MC, V.*

¢–$$ ✕ **Cantina Panaderia.** You can find Asian accents on the menu at this family destination a few blocks from the blue Pacific, but South-of-the-Border flavors prevail at the " Bakery Cantina," so named because the premises housed a neighborhood bakery for decades. Appetizers like steak-filled lettuce wraps and plantains dressed with sour cream and caviar are fun; expect to be filled up by such entrées as the wood-fired rotisserie chicken with black beans, rice, and crisp plantains, or green chile tamales with tofu. The coconut flan finishes the meal nicely. A small selection of Mexican artworks reinforce the theme of the cuisine. ⊠ *966 Felspar St., Pacific Beach* ☎ *858/272–8400* ▤ *AE, DC, MC, V.*

Seafood

★ ¢–$ ✕ **Hudson Bay Seafood.** Part of the pleasure in this small, friendly, waterside fish house is watching the day-charter boats arrive at the adjacent dock and discharge their passengers, some seasoned fishermen and some first-timers grateful to be back on dry land. More than a few march up the wooden walkway to Hudson Bay, which bakes the sourdough rolls in which it places delicately fried fish fillets or shellfish. The french fries are freshly cut, the fish tacos taste of Mexico, and even the tartar sauce is homemade. There are salads and excellent breakfasts, too, and even the burgers are exceptional. ⊠ *1403 Scott St., Shelter Island* ☎ *619/222–8787* ▭ *MC, V.*

La Jolla

American

¢ ✕ **Chicago On A Bun.** Hot dog! Fans of Chicago-style hot dogs know where to go when they get a craving for Windy City sidewalk cuisine. The decor—mostly built around Chicago Cubs memorabilia—is imported from the City of the Broad Shoulders, as are the Vienna-brand beef hot dogs, and even the steamed poppy seed buns. Garnish a dog your way, or take it Chicago-style, which means piled with mustard, onion, relish, chopped tomatoes, tiny hot peppers, celery salt, and dill pickles. A basket of fried-to-order potato chips is almost obligatory with hot dogs, juicy Italian beef sandwiches, or chili cheeseburgers. A great budget choice. ⊠ *8935 Towne Centre Dr., Golden Triangle–La Jolla* ☎ *858/622–0222* ▭ *MC, V.*

Contemporary

★ $$$–$$$$ ✕ **Marine Room.** Gaze at the ocean from this venerable La Jolla Shores mainstay and, if you're lucky, watch the grunion run or the waves race across the sand and beat against the glass. Long-running chef Bernard Guillas, now an internationally known celebrity, takes a bold approach to combining ingredients. Creative seasonal menus score with "trilogy" plates that combine three meats, sometimes including game, in distinct preparations. Disparate elements like candied chestnuts, apple curry sauce, and green beans contribute to the success of such entrées as gooseberry-glazed chicken breast. Watercress salad and a limoncello liqueur–chervil emulsion add sparkle to the taste of butter-basted lobster tail. Sunday brunch is lavish; in winter call for information about the high-tide breakfasts. ⊠ *2000 Spindrift Dr., La Jolla* ☎ *858/459–7222* ▭ *AE, D, DC, MC, V.*

$$$–$$$$ ✕ **Top of the Cove.** Although flashier newcomers rival this once peerless La Jolla institution, the elegant but comfortable Top of the Cove still receives high marks from San Diegans for the romantic ocean view from its cottage windows and its fine European-American cuisine. The menu provides plenty for the thoughtful diner to consider, such as roasted Cornish game hen with chestnut gnocchi, and a thick, succulent prime New York steak with cream cheese–rich mashed potatoes. Subtle flavors pervade these simple-sounding preparations. The service is attentive but not overbearing, and the wine list leaves nothing to be desired. ⊠ *1216 Prospect St., La Jolla* ☎ *858/454–7779* ▭ *AE, DC, MC, V.*

\$\$–\$\$\$\$ ✕ **Cafe Japengo.** Framed by marbled walls and accented with bamboo trees and unusual black-iron sculptures, this Pacific Rim restaurant serves Asian-inspired cuisine with many North and South American touches. The curry-fried calamari and the pot sticker appetizers are guaranteed to wake up your mouth. There's also a selection of grilled, wood-roasted, and wok-fried entrées; try the 10-ingredient fried rice, or the crispy whole striped bass. The sushi is always very fresh, and many regard it as the best in town. Service can be slow, but the pace in the bar, crowded with young locals, is fast and lively. If you savor quiet, avoid weekend evenings. ⊠ *Aventine Center, 8960 University Center La., Golden Triangle, La Jolla* ☎ *858/450–3355* ▭ *AE, D, DC, MC, V* ⊘ *No lunch weekends.*

★ **\$\$–\$\$\$\$**   ✕ **Roppongi.** A hit from the moment it opened, Roppongi serves global cuisine with strong Asian notes. The contemporary dining room done in wood tones and accented with Asian statuary has a row of comfortable booths along one wall. It can get noisy when crowded; tables near the bar are generally quieter. Order the imaginative Euro-Asian tapas as appetizers or combine them for a full meal. Try the barbecued mini lamb chops, seafood pot stickers with caviar sauce, and the high-rising Polynesian crab stack. Good entrées are boneless beef shortribs with honey-mustard glaze, and fresh seafood. The restaurant added a creative sushi bar in late 2004. ⊠ *875 Prospect St., La Jolla* ☎ *858/551–5252* ▭ *AE, D, DC, MC, V.*

Deli

¢–\$ ✕ **Elijah's.** Formerly known as Blumberg's, this large, somewhat sterile-looking, brightly-lighted delicatessen is in the La Jolla Village area near Interstate 5. Prominent are towering sandwiches, blintzes, smoked fish plates, and specialties like "mish-mosh" soup, which combines noodles, matzo balls, and shredded crépes in a big bowl of steaming chicken broth. Count on reliable chopped liver, hearty breakfasts, and dinners like chicken-in-the-pot and savory beef brisket. The restaurant prides itself on Reuben sandwiches, which do impress. Friendly servers keep their arms in shape with the over-laden plates. ⊠ *8861 Villa La Jolla Dr., La Jolla* ☎ *858/455–1462* ▭ *AE, D, MC, V.*

French

\$\$\$–\$\$\$\$
Fodor's Choice
★
   ✕ **Tapenade.** Named after the delicious Provençal black olive–and–anchovy paste that accompanies the bread here, Tapenade specializes in the cuisine of the south of France—although that cuisine has lost some of its weight in the trip across the Atlantic. It now matches the unpretentious, light, and airy room, lined with 1960s French movie posters, in which it is served. Very fresh ingredients, a delicate touch with sauces, and an emphasis on seafood characterize the menu, which changes frequently. If you're lucky, it may include pan-gilded sea scallops in fragrant curry sauce, veal with morel mushrooms, and desserts like crisp, pear-stuffed spring rolls with caramel sauce. The two-course "Riviera Menu" served at lunch for \$17.50 is a fabulous steal. ⊠ *7612 Fay Ave., La Jolla* ☎ *858/551–7500* ▭ *AE, D, DC, MC, V.*

★ **¢–\$\$\$**   ✕ **Michele Coulon Dessertier.** A "dessertier" confects desserts, a job that Michele Coulon does exceedingly well in the back of a small, charming shop in the heart of La Jolla. The colorful raspberry pinwheel *bombe* (a molded dessert of cake, jam, and creamy filling), the cherry torte, and a tricolor mousse of chocolate and coffee creams are a few treats. This is not just a place for dessert, however. Lunch (Monday-through-Saturday) and dinner (Thursday-through-Saturday) are also served, prepared by son Nathan Coulon, whose evening specialties include chicken breast in Normandy-style cream sauce, halibut with artichokes, and a meltingly tender pepper steak. ✉ *7556 Fay Ave., La Jolla* ☎ *858/456–5098* ⟐ *Reservations essential* ▱ *AE, D, MC, V* ✆ *Closed Sun. No dinner Mon.–Wed.*

Italian

$–$$$ ✕ **Aurora Trattoria.** La Jolla is defined by its views, and from this second-story eatery set back a few blocks above La Jolla Cove, the scenery stretches across blue water to the northward-marching coastline, with palm trees in the foreground seeming like decorative embroidery. The Italian cooking is self-assured, traditional, and rewarding; favorites include chicken Marsala, a combination of clams and mussels steamed in a garlic-scented white wine broth, filet of beef with porcini mushroom sauce, and—an uncommon entrée—snails in a fragrant saffron sauce. Live music is offered on weekends, and guests dance on the slate floor. ✉ *1025 Prospect St., La Jolla* ☎ *858/551–8554* ▱ *AE, D, DC, MC, V.*

$–$$$ ✕ **Trattoria Acqua.** Reservations are a good idea for this Mediterranean-inspired bistro above La Jolla Cove. On the lower level of Coast Walk center, this romantic eatery has dining rooms that are semi-open to the weather and the view, yet sufficiently sheltered for comfort. Choose from stuffed, deep-fried zucchini blossoms, lobster-filled ravioli in a lobster-scented *beurre blanc* (white-wine and butter sauce), and stuffed roasted quail flavored with bacon. The superb wine list earns kudos from aficionados. ✉ *1298 Prospect St., La Jolla* ☎ *858/454–0709* ▱ *AE, DC, MC, V.*

$–$$ ✕ **Osteria Romantica.** The name means "Romantic Inn," and with a sunny
Fodor'sChoice   location a few blocks from the beach in La Jolla Shores, the look does
★   suggest a trattoria in Positano. The kitchen's wonderfully light hand shows up in the tomato sauce that finishes the scampi La Jolla Shores and other dishes, and in the pleasing Romantica salad garnished with figs and walnuts. Savory pasta choices include lobster-filled *mezzelune* (half moons) in saffron sauce, and among main events are chicken with fennel and a nice plate of breaded veal scallops crowned with chopped arugula and tomatoes. The warm, informal service suits the neighborhood just fine. ✉ *2151 Avenida de la Playa, La Jolla* ☎ *858/551–1221* ▱ *AE, D, DC, MC, V.*

¢–$$$ ✕ **Barolo.** This cozy, candlelight restaurant in the Golden Triangle's Renaissance Towne Center uses its namesake to sauce the house specialty, Gorgonzola-topped beef filet in a Barolo reduction. This filling dish joins other specialties like veal scallops with pesto and goat cheese, and polenta-crusted salmon in horseradish sauce. The salad of chopped tomato and red onion with blue cheese dressing nicely kicks off a meal that may go on simply to a sausage pizza, or to the enjoyable pear-stuffed ravioli. Ask for a banquette table and enjoy the suave, eager-to-please service. ✉ *8953 Towne Center Dr., Golden Triangle–La Jolla* ☎ *858/ 622–1202* ▱ *AE, D, MC, V* ✆ *No lunch weekends.*

CloseUp

TALKING TACOS

ACITY OF TRANSPLANTS—FROM AROUND THE UNITED STATES, *from south of the border, from Asia, and from everywhere else—San Diego introduces newcomers to local topics such as surfing, sunblock, and how to beat rush hour on the freeways (you can't). Even though terms like tacos, burritos, enchiladas, and tostadas are as common as macaroni and cheese to San Diegans, don't count on widespread agreement among residents as to what they mean. Authentic cuisine brought from Mexico is quite at odds with Southern California's home-grown "Cal-Mex" style of cooking, although both can be delicious.*

An authentic taco never takes the form of a folded, fried-hard shell piled high with ground beef, sour cream, and chopped lettuce and tomatoes. Even so, this is the version many novices encounter the first time around, and as San Diegans say, finding one is "no problemo." If you meet a soft tortilla—more authentically made from corn flour dough (masa) than from white flour—rolled around a filling and served fresh, fragrant, and hot, it's the real thing. Fillings can be shredded beef or chicken, or slowly simmered tongue in green sauce, or grilled or deep-fried fish or seafood, or just about any savory tidbit. Garnishes usually include a drizzle of salsa and often a squeeze of tart Mexican lime (a citrus different from the one raised in the United States), along with cilantro sprigs, sliced radishes, chopped onion, and whatever else the cook is in the mood for. Some San Diego entrepreneurs identify the city as the fish taco capital of the planet, but that title really belongs to Ensenada, a port city about 60 mi south of the California border. There, arranged cheek-by-jowl with the sizeable, attractively stocked, and decidedly aromatic waterside fish market, are a good 100 stands offering a kaleidoscope

of tacos, each slightly different from the others and all accompanied by a slightly varied selection of condiments.

In San Diego, to be "one taco shy of a combination plate" is to be, shall we say, rather divorced from reality. A combination plate is anchored by such constants as delicately flavored rice and frijoles refritos, smooth, creamy, well-cooked beans that must be draped with melted shredded cheese and usually support a small raft of shredded lettuce dabbed with a bit of sour cream. Any empty spaces (you shouldn't see more of the plate than the rim) will be hidden by the preferred combination of tacos, tortillas, chiles rellenos, and burritos. What are those? Tortillas can be filled with cheese, chicken, or beef and topped with savory enchilada sauce. Chiles rellenos are mild, deep-fried peppers stuffed with cheese. Burritos are tortillas filled with beans and shredded meat. A platter might even include a mini-tostada, a sort of salad-buffet arranged on a crisply fried tortilla. It's good, filling food, and you'll enjoy it. And that's the whole enchilada.

–David Nelson

Mexican

¢–$$$ ✕ **Alfonso's of La Jolla.** Some things never change, and laid-back Alfonso's is one of them. From the sidewalk terrace on busy Prospect Street, you can review the passing parade while downing sizeable margaritas and plates laden with carne asada. This marinated, grilled steak is a house specialty and arrives both garnished *tampiquena*-style—with a cheese enchilada, rice, and beans—or chopped as a filling for tacos and quesadillas. The menu extends to typical enchiladas and burritos, as well as to a couple of piquant shrimp preparations. The continuity of quality cuisine guarantees this landmark's popularity. ⊠ *1251 Prospect St., La Jolla* ☎ *858/454–2232* ▭ *AE, MC, V.*

Seafood

$$$–$$$$ ✕ **George's at the Cove.** Hollywood types and other visiting celebrities **Fodor'sChoice** can be spotted in the elegant main dining room, where a wall-length window overlooks La Jolla Cove. Renowned for fresh seafood and fine preparations of beef and lamb, this also is the place to taste the wonders chef Trey Foshee works with seasonal produce from local specialty growers. Give special consideration to imaginatively garnished, wild California salmon, or choice cuts of beef and pork from the state's celebrated Niman Ranch. For more informal dining and a sweeping view of the coast try the rooftop Ocean Terrace ($–$$). The main dining room now serves dinner only (no lunch). ⊠ *1250 Prospect St., La Jolla* ☎ *858/454–4244* ⚑ *Reservations essential* ▭ *AE, D, DC, MC, V.*

$$–$$$ ✕ **Fresh.** By all means request a patio table when reserving at this hip, very popular eatery that doubles as a fashion show of some of La Jolla's ladies-who-lunch. The food can be very good indeed, from ultrafresh oysters on the half-shell with green apple-cucumber mignonette sauce to prosciutto-wrapped pork tenderloin and crisp roast chicken in red wine sauce. Seafood stars in all courses, starting with a Maine lobster "Napoleon" appetizer and continuing with a poached seafood salad, coriander-crusted mahimahi, and shellfish-stuffed rainbow trout. ⊠ *1044 Wall St., La Jolla* ☎ *858/551–7575* ▭ *AE, D, DC, MC, V.*

Mission Valley

American

☺ $–$$ ✕ **Cheesecake Factory.** This cavernous eatery in San Diego's leading shopping mall, Fashion Valley, can be relied on to have a line at the door at peak meal hours. Part of the patronage is drawn by the huge, creamy cheesecakes, and more by the multipage menu featuring innovative pizzas, gigantic salads, pastas, and such house specialties as chicken with biscuits, mashed potatoes, and country gravy. When the crowd is in full cry the noise can be deafening, but the friendly and eager-to-please servers handle the crush well. ⊠ *Fashion Valley Center, 7067 Friars Rd., Mission Valley* ☎ *619/683–2800* ▭ *AE, D, MC, V.*

★ ¢–$ ✕ **Mr. Peabody's.** Burgers and beer are an unbeatable combination anywhere, but especially within a stone's throw of the pricy Fashion Valley mall. Friendly and informal, this bustling eatery is fine for kids at the lunch hour, but perhaps not after that. The attractions range from juicy half-pound burgers that rank among the best in Southern California, to a variety of tacos and a convincing, gently priced rib-eye steak. Order a basket of excellent fries or onion rings for the table, but not both, because the portion is beyond huge. ⊠ *6110 Friars Rd., Mission Valley* ☏ *619/542–1786* ⌧ *Reservations not accepted* ▤ *MC, V.*

☾ ¢–$ ✕ **Ricky's Family Restaurant.** Chain feederies haven't driven out San Diego's old-line family restaurants, and this unpretentious place on the quiet fringe of Mission Valley remains dear to the city's heart. A traditional three-meals-daily restaurant, Ricky's serves big portions of unassuming, well-prepared, all-American cooking, but is famed for its breakfasts, when savory corned-beef hash and fluffy, strawberry-crowned Belgian waffles are the rule. The spectacular apple pancake, a soufflé-like creation that takes 20 minutes to bake, arrives burning hot and is irresistible to the last molecule of molten cinnamon sugar. Ricky's popularity never wanes. ⊠ *2181 Hotel Circle S, Mission Valley* ☏ *619/291–4498* ▤ *MC, V.*

Italian

$–$$$ ✕ **Prego Ristorante.** Since the late 1980s, this Tuscan-style villa in Hazard Center has drawn diners searching for good Italian fare in Mission Valley. Possessed of an unusually good service staff, Prego greets the budget-conscious with excellent pizzas, including an unusual pie topped with meaty portobello mushrooms and goat cheese. More formal meals might consist of linguine sauced with prawns and Manila clams, lobster-filled *agnolotti* pasta, plump mesquite-grilled pork chops, and the day's meats and poultry from the rotisserie. The restaurant also offers one of the most comfortable bars in the valley. ⊠ *1370 Frazee Rd., Mission Valley* ☏ *619/294–4700* ▤ *AE, D, DC, MC, V.*

Japanese

¢–$$ ✕ **Oki Ton Japanese Bistro.** The best Japanese fare in Mission Valley is found in Oki Ton, a good-looking but informal eatery in the imposing Fenton Marketplace center just off busy Friars Road. The sushi chefs acquit themselves well with specialty rolls like the "inside-out" dragon roll of eel, avocado, shrimp tempura, and crab. The heaped sushi combination plate satisfies you nicely, and the kitchen does equally well with an excellent chicken teriyaki, grilled salmon with ginger sauce, and a katsu platter of crisply breaded pork, chicken breast, and prawns. The filling meals include Japanese pickles, rice, salad, and the special house miso soup. ⊠ *2408 Northside Dr., Mission Valley* ☏ *619/284–8036* ▤ *AE, DC, MC, V.*

Seafood

¢–$$$$ ✕ **King's Fish House.** This warehouse-size restaurant remains wildly popular with shoppers at Mission Valley's many malls, owing to extremely friendly and efficient service, tanks filled with lively lobsters and Dungeness crabs, and a daily-changing menu with a fine selection of freshly shucked oysters. Specialties include New Orleans–style barbecued shrimp and a full-size New England clambake complete with red potatoes and sweet corn on the cob. Fish and shellfish are char-grilled, deep-fried, sautéed, steamed, and skewered, and the menu obliges meat-eaters with a convincing cheeseburger, roasted chicken, and grilled sirloin. When jammed, the scene recalls a train station. ✉ *825 Camino de la Reina N, Mission Valley* ☎ *619/574–1230* ▭ *AE, DC, MC, V.*

★ ¢–$$ ✕ **Little Fish Market.** This spin-off of downtown's Fish Market is custom-designed for the restaurant row at the Fenton Marketplace near Qualcomm Stadium. It's billed as a "quick service restaurant" because you order at the counter, but it still has table service. The menu includes shellfish cocktails, smoked fish plates, sushi, chowder served in a bread bowl, and more significant meals of deep-fried and char-broiled fish and shellfish. ✉ *1401 Fenton Pkwy., Mission Valley* ☎ *619/280–2277* ⌦ *Reservations not accepted* ▭ *MC, V.*

Old Town

Mexican

★ $–$$$ ✕ **Zocalo Grill.** Try for a table by the fireplace on the covered terrace, but the contemporary cuisine tastes just as good anywhere in the spacious and handsome eatery. Instead of cooking the carnitas (in this case, chunks of pork) the traditional way, simmering them in well-seasoned lard, Zocalo braises them in a mixture of honey and Porter beer and serves the dish with mango salsa and avocado salad. Recommended starters include artichoke fritters and crisp shrimp skewers with pineapple-mango relish. The Seattle surf and turf roasts wild salmon and forest mushrooms on a cedar plank. ✉ *2444 San Diego Ave., Old Town* ☎ *619/298–9840* ▭ *AE, D, DC, MC, V.*

★ ¢–$ ✕ **Rancho Corona Mexican Restaurant.** A vast veranda wraps around a smallish dining room, and heaters keep the outdoor space enjoyable in virtually all kinds of weather. A fine new addition to Old Town's restaurant row, Rancho Corona captures authentic Mexican flavors better than most and offers an education in the variety of tacos found in Mexico by serving a half-dozen, including crisp, Texcoco-style lamb tacos. Tortilla soup opens a meal well and can be followed by Oaxaca-style marinated chicken, Puebla chicken enchiladas in dark mole sauce, and deliciously flavored pork rib carnitas. ✉ *2543 Congress St., Old Town* ☎ *619/291–9478* ▭ *AE, D, DC, MC, V.*

Thai

¢–$ ✕ **Saffron Noodles and Saté.** Comfortable outdoor tables on a narrow sidewalk and inexpensive prices make this and the neighboring Saffron Thai Grilled Chicken takeout worth a short detour from Old Town. The simple menu has spicy and mild noodle soups; stir-fried noodles with chicken, beef, pork, or turkey; a couple of uncommon Vietnamese and Thai-Indian noodle dishes bathed with aromatic sauces; and the namesake skewers of grilled chicken. The latter are served with jasmine rice, tart-sweet cucumber salad, and savory peanut sauce. ✉ *3737 India St., Old Town* ☎ *619/574–7737* ▭ *MC, V.*

Where to Stay

3

By Lenore
Greiner

SAN DIEGO IS SPREAD OUT, so the first thing to consider when selecting lodging is location. If you choose a hotel with a waterfront setting and extensive outdoor sports facilities, you may find yourself choosing to shorten your sightseeing agenda. But if you plan to sightsee, take into account a hotel's proximity to attractions. There are plenty of hotel-resorts for families in Mission Valley and Mission Bay, which are convenient to the San Diego Zoo, SeaWorld, or a day at the beach.

The downtown center has hip boutique hotels and preserved Victorian-era hostelries in the Gaslamp Quarter. High-end hotels can be found anywhere from the downtown area up to La Jolla, which also has a landmark 1920s Spanish-style hotel. Staying on the water isn't only for wealthy leisure travelers: surfers make themselves at home at Banana Bungalow in Pacific Beach, and conventioneers pack themselves into towers on San Diego Bay.

Die-hard aficionados of California's Craftsman architectural tradition can book themselves into a 1,500-square-foot suite at the Lodge at Torrey Pines; there, they can cuddle in front of a fire in Stickley chairs and enjoy sweeping ocean and golf course views. Others, enamored of the downtown skyline, can settle into a window seat at the stylish WOW Presidential Suite at the W San Diego Hotel, decorated to reflect local beach culture.

The latest news in San Diego lodging are the medium-range hotels slated for revitalized East Village, where San Diego's new Petco Park baseball stadium stands alongside the bay.

Coronado

Quiet, out-of-the-way Coronado feels like something out of an earlier, more gracious era. With boutiques and restaurants lining Orange Avenue—the main street—and its fine beaches, Coronado is great for a getaway. But if you plan to see many of San Diego's attractions, you'll probably spend a lot of time commuting across the bridge or riding the ferry.

$$$$
Fodor'sChoice
★

🏨 **Hotel Del Coronado.** "The Del" stands as a social and historic landmark, its whimsical red turrets and balconied walkways taking you as far back as 1888, the year it was built. U.S. presidents, European royalty, and movie stars have stayed in the Victorian rooms and suites, all now renovated with the necessities of modern-day life. Public areas always bustle with activity; for quieter quarters, consider staying in the contemporary, seven-story Ocean Towers building or in one of the eight beachfront cottages. Rates are defined largely by room views. ⊠ *1500 Orange Ave., Coronado 92118* ☎ *619/435–6611 or 800/468–3533* 🖷 *619/522–8262* ⊕ *www.hoteldel.com* ↝ *676 rooms* ⌂ *2 restaurants, coffee shop, room service, cable TV with movies, in-room data ports, 3 tennis courts, 2 pools, gym, hair salon, outdoor hot tub, massage, sauna, spa, steam room, beach, bicycles, 4 bars, piano bar, shops, children's programs (ages 3–17), laundry service, concierge, business services, convention center, meeting rooms, parking (fee); no smoking* ▭ *AE, D, DC, MC, V.*

$$$$ 🏨 **Loews Coronado Bay Resort.** You can park your boat at the 80-slip marina of this elegant resort, set on a secluded 15-acre peninsula on the Silver Strand. Rooms are tastefully decorated, and all have furnished balconies with views of water—either bay, ocean, or marina. The resort's 10,000-square-foot Zen-like spa offers a garden with alfresco showers. The Azzura Point restaurant specializes in seafood. ✉ *4000 Coronado Bay Rd., Coronado 92118* 🕾 *619/424–4000 or 800/815–6397* 🖷 *619/424–4400* ⊕ *www.loewshotels.com/coronado.html* ↩ *403 rooms, 37 suites* ♦ *3 restaurants, room service, minibars, cable TV with movies, in-room data ports, 5 tennis courts, 3 pools, health club, hair salon, 3 hot tubs, spa, beach, windsurfing, boating, jet skiing, waterskiing, bicycles, 3 bars, shop, children's programs (ages 4–12), laundry service, concierge, business services, convention center, meeting rooms, parking (fee); no smoking* 🖹 *AE, D, DC, MC, V.*

$$$–$$$$ 🏨 **Coronado Island Marriott Resort.** Near San Diego Bay, this snazzy hotel has many rooms with great views of the downtown skyline. Large rooms and suites in low-slung buildings are done in a cheerful California–country French fashion, with colorful impressionist prints; all rooms have separate showers and tubs and come with plush robes. The spa facilities are top-notch, but the service can be somewhat uncouth. ✉ *2000 2nd St., Coronado 92118* 🕾 *619/435–3000 or 800/543–4300* 🖷 *619/435–3032* ⊕ *www.marriotthotels.com/sanci* ↩ *273 rooms, 27 suites* ♦ *4 restaurants, room service, cable TV with movies, in-room data ports, 6 tennis courts, 3 pools, fitness classes, health club, hair salon, 2 outdoor hot tubs, massage, sauna, spa, beach, snorkeling, windsurfing, boating, jet skiing, waterskiing, bicycles, bar, shops, laundry service, concierge, business services, convention center, meeting rooms, parking (fee); no smoking* 🖹 *AE, D, DC, MC, V.*

$$–$$$$ 🏨 **Glorietta Bay Inn.** The main building on this property is an Edwardian-style mansion built in 1908 for sugar baron John D. Spreckels, who once owned much of downtown San Diego. Rooms in the mansion and in the newer motel-style buildings are attractively furnished. Some rooms have patios or balconies. The inn is adjacent to the Coronado harbor and near many restaurants and shops, but is much smaller and quieter than the Hotel Del across the street. Tours ($8) of the island's historical buildings depart from the inn three mornings a week. Ginger snaps and lemonade are served daily from 3 to 5. ✉ *1630 Glorietta Blvd., Coronado 92118* 🕾 *619/435–3101 or 800/283–9383* 🖷 *619/435–6182* ⊕ *www.gloriettabayinn.com* ↩ *100 rooms* ♦ *Dining room, some kitchenettes, refrigerators, cable TV with movies, in-room data ports, pool, outdoor hot tub, bicycles, library, laundry service, concierge, business services, free parking; no smoking* 🖹 *AE, MC, V.*

$$–$$$$ 🏨 **La Avenida Inn.** An old-school motor lodge surrounding a pool landscaped with palms and tropical flowers, this inn caters to a budget crowd in a tony area. It's the most economical choice on this half of the island. The big plus here is the convenient location one-half block from historic Hotel Del Coronado and one block from the beach. Continental breakfast is served daily and double-pane windows with plantation shutters in the rooms reduce the street noise. ✉ *1315 Orange Ave., Coro-*

San Diego has hotels in abundance, and several on the drawing boards could add more than 3,000 rooms in the next few years. All this means lower prices for those who shop around. When you make reservations, ask about specials. Hotel packages are your best bet; deals range from arts and culture escapes to relaxing spa weekends and special event getaways. Check hotel Web sites for Internet specials and try to call a hotel directly; sometimes your effort will result in a lower rate. Several properties in the Hotel Circle area of Mission Valley offer reduced rates and even free tickets to the San Diego Zoo, Wild Animal Park, SeaWorld, Legoland, and other attractions. Many hotels also promote discounted weekend packages to fill rooms after convention and business customers leave town. Since the weather is great year-round, don't expect substantial discounts in winter. You can save on hotels and attractions by visiting the San Diego Convention & Visitors Bureau Web site (www.sandiego.org) for a free Vacation Planning Kit with a Travel Value Coupon booklet.

3

As for rates, expect to pay around $80 at the very least for a simple room in San Diego, more if it's in a central area near a freeway or two. After that, the sky's the limit in terms of prices, since San Diego, like her California counterparts Los Angeles and San Francisco, is not a bargain destination.

Children

San Diego is a great year-round family destination. Virtually all its tourist-oriented areas have hotels suited to a family's budget and/or recreational needs, and many allow kids under 18 to stay free with their parents. You'll find the most choices and diversity in and around Mission Bay, which is close to SeaWorld, beaches, parks, and Old Town. Many Mission Bay hotels offer SeaWorld packages or discounts. Another central choice is Mission Valley, which has San Diego Trolley stations and malls. Some resorts, such as the Hilton San Diego Resort, may offer full- or half-day programs for kids ages 5–17 that include swimming, arts and crafts, and, for those over 12, golf and tennis. The programs run during the major spring and summer holidays and the month of August. Look for "children's programs" within the italicized service information below each lodging review if these services are important to you.

Prices

The lodgings we list run from bare-bones basic to lavishly upscale. Note that even in the most expensive areas, you can find some more affordable rooms. High season is summer, and rates are lowest in the fall. If an ocean view is important, request it when booking, but be aware that it will cost significantly more than a nonocean view room.

We always list a property's facilities, but we don't specify whether you'll be charged extra to use them; when pricing accommodations, always ask what's included. Our price categories are based on the range between a hotel's least and most expensive standard double rooms (or suites, in all suites properties) in nonholiday high season. Assume that hotels operate on the **European Plan** (EP, with no meals) unless we specify otherwise.

WHAT IT COSTS				
$$$$	**$$$**	**$$**	**$**	**¢**
FOR 2 PEOPLE over $250	$176–$250	$121–$175	$90–$120	under $90

Prices are for a standard double room in high (summer) season, excluding 10.5% tax.

Reservations
Book well in advance, especially if you plan to visit in summer, which is the busy season for most hotels. In spring and fall, conventions can fill every downtown hotel room. Special sports events such as golf or tennis tournaments also mean that host resorts and nearby hotels are fully booked.

Services
You can assume that all rooms have private baths, phones, TVs, and air-conditioning unless otherwise noted. Downtown hotels cater primarily to business travelers, while those at Mission Bay, in coastal locations such as Carlsbad and Encinitas, and at inland resorts offer golf and other sports facilities, spa services, children's activities, and more.

nado 92118 ☎ 619/435–3191 or 800/437–0162 🖷 619/435–5024 ⊕ www.laavenidainn.com ➴ 27 rooms, 2 suites ⌂ Cable TV, pool, free parking ⬔ CP ⊟ AE, DC, MC, V.

$$–$$$$ 🖫 **Villa Capri By The Sea.** Look for the world-famous "Diving Lady" neon sign outside this hotel. The classic 1950s architecture of this place befits its frequent brushes with fame—ask innkeeper John Miller about the hotel's storied history. ⊠ 1417 Orange Ave., Coronado 92118 ☎ 619/435–4137 🖷 619/435–3383 ⊕ www.villacapribythesea.com ➴ 7 rooms, 7 suites ⌂ Microwaves, refrigerators, in-room VCRs, pool ⊟ AE, D, DC, MC, V.

$–$$$$ 🖫 **El Cordova Hotel.** Built as a countryside mansion in 1902, this two-story Spanish-style building was converted into a hotel in 1930. Its quaint Old Mexico courtyard is populated with shops and cafés. Most rooms are suites, and you can walk to the beach from here. ⊠ 1351 Orange Ave., Coronado 92118 ☎ 619/435–4131 🖷 619/435–0632 ⊕ www.elcordovahotel.com ➴ 8 rooms, 32 suites ⌂ Picnic area, BBQs, some kitchenettes, cable TV, pool, business services ⊟ AE, D, DC, MC, V.

$–$$$ 🖫 **Cherokee Lodge.** This small inn, brought across the bay more than a century ago by barge, exudes elegance and charm with armoires, embroidered couches, polished headboards, and beautiful woodwork. ⊠ 964 D Ave., Coronado 92118 ☎ 877/743–6213 or 619/437–1967 🖷 619/437–1012 ⊕ www.cherokeelodge.com ➴ 12 rooms ⌂ Refrigerators, cable TV with movies, in-room data ports, laundry facilities; no a/c, no smoking.

$–$$$ 🖫 **Crown City Inn & Bistro.** On Coronado's main drag, the Crown City Inn is close to shops, restaurants, and the beach. For the price, it's easily one of the best deals on the island. However, this two-story motor inn lacks the amenities and prestige of Coronado's bigger and better-known lodgings. A public park is across the street. ⊠ 520 Orange Ave., Coronado 92118 ☎ 619/435–3116 or 800/422–1173 🖷 619/435–

HOTEL DEL CORONADO

THIS STATELY WHITE CLAPBOARD BUILDING IS A MUST-SEE for anyone in the San Diego area. "The Hotel Del," as it's known, was made famous by its legions of celebrated guests, and by its role in the 1959 movie Some Like it Hot. When stars Jack Lemmon and Tony Curtis pose as women in an all-girl band—with Marilyn Monroe as the band's singer and ukulele player—and hop a train south to Florida, where they really end up is the Hotel Del Coronado. Set on 26 acres of Pacific Ocean beachfront, this Victorian jewel still charms and delights.

In the late 1800s, two businessmen from the Midwest, Elisha Babcock and H. L. Story, dreamed of opening a resort hotel that would become the "talk of the Western world." To build it, they imported lumber and labor from San Francisco and built an electrical powerplant and a kiln to fire bricks on the site. They even had a mahogany bar built in Pennsylvania, then

transported by ship (fully assembled) around the tip of South America. Even back then, the hotel cost the astronomical sum of $1 million to construct and furnish.

In 1891 Benjamin Harrison became the first of many U.S. Presidents to stay at the Del. Charles Lindbergh was honored at the Del after his legendary solo trans-Atlantic flight in 1927. L. Frank Baum, the author of The Wonderful Wizard of Oz, is said to have based his vision of the Emerald City on the hotel's turreted design. And many think that Edward (then Prince of Wales) first met Wallis Spencer Simpson, the divorcée for whom he gave up the English throne, at the Del when he visited in 1920.

6750 ⊕ www.crowncityinn.com ➦ 33 rooms ⌂ Restaurant, room service, minibars, microwaves, refrigerators, cable TV with movies, in-room data ports, pool, bicycles, laundry facilities, parking (fee); no smoking ⊟ AE, D, DC, MC, V.

Downtown

A lively, continuously revitalized downtown has helped make the city center the hotel hub of San Diego. Types of accommodations range from budget chains to boutique and business hotels to major high-rises. Much to see is within walking distance—Seaport Village, the Embarcadero, the Gaslamp Quarter, theaters and nightspots, galleries and coffee-houses, and the Horton Plaza shopping center. The zoo and Balboa Park are also nearby. Downtown has plenty of good restaurants, especially along 4th and 5th avenues south of Broadway in the Gaslamp Quarter.

$$$$ ▦ **Hilton San Diego Gaslamp Quarter.** Just stepping into the lobby, which is modern and sophisticated, but with cozy lounge spaces and wood accents, tells you this isn't your usual downtown hotel. Inspired by the Gaslamp, this Hilton has unique style. The loft rooms in the Enclave Tower are urban retreats with extra-high ceilings, light dimmers, and

Where to Stay Downtown

portable phones; some have whirlpool tubs. An outdoor terrace, furnished like a comfy living room, affords relaxation amidst the city hustle. And you can't beat the location; the San Diego Trolley whizzes by, the San Diego Convention Center is across the street, and the nightlife and eateries of the Gaslamp are just outside your door. ⊠ *401 K St., Gaslamp Quarter 92101* ☎ *619/231–4040 or 800/445–8667* 🖷 *619/231–6439* ⊕ *www.sandiegogaslampquarter.hilton.com* 🛏 *282 rooms, 3 suites, 8 lofts* ⚘ *2 restaurants, room service, in-room safe, minibars, cable TV with movies and video games, in-room data ports, pool, health club, hair salon, bar, shop, dry cleaning, laundry service, concierge, business services, meeting rooms, airport shuttle, car rental, parking (fee); no smoking* ▭ *AE, D, DC, MC, V.*

$$$$ 🖳 **Manchester Grand Hyatt San Diego.** The 34- and 40-story towers ad-
Fodor'sChoice jacent to Seaport Village make the Manchester the West Coast's tallest
★ waterfront building. The interior combines old-world opulence with California airiness; palm trees pose next to ornate tapestry couches in the light-filled lobby. All of the British Regency–style guest rooms have water views and windows open to catch fresh bay breezes. The hotel's proximity to the convention center attracts a large business trade. The Business Plan includes access to an area with desks and office supplies. A trolley station is one block away and the Gaslamp's clubs and restaurants are also within walking distance. ⊠ *1 Market Pl., Embarcadero 92101* ☎ *619/232–1234 or 800/233–1234* 🖷 *619/233–6464* ⊕ *www. manchestergrand.hyatt.com* 🛏 *1,625 rooms, 95 suites* ⚘ *3 restaurants, room service, minibars, cable TV, in-room data ports, 4 tennis courts, pool, health club, outdoor hot tub, sauna, steam room, boating, bicycles, 2 bars, shops, dry cleaning, laundry service, concierge, concierge floor, business services, meeting rooms, airport shuttle, car rental, parking (fee); no smoking* ▭ *AE, D, DC, MC, V.*

$$$$ 🖳 **San Diego Marriott Hotel and Marina.** This 25-story twin tower next to the convention center has everything a businessperson—or leisure traveler—could want. As a major site for conventions, the complex can be hectic and impersonal, and the hallways can be noisy. Lending some tranquillity are the lagoon-style pools nestled between cascading waterfalls. The standard rooms are smallish, but pay a bit extra for a room with a balcony overlooking the bay and you'll have a serene, sparkling world spread out before you. Seaport Village and a trolley station are nearby. ⊠ *333 W. Harbor Dr., Embarcadero 92101* ☎ *619/234–1500 or 800/ 228–9290* 🖷 *619/234–8678* ⊕ *www.marriotthotels.com/sandt* 🛏 *1,300 rooms, 54 suites* ⚘ *3 restaurants, room service, cable TV with movies, in-room data ports, 6 tennis courts, 2 pools, fitness classes, health club, hair salon, outdoor hot tub, massage, sauna, boating, bicycles, basketball, 3 bars, recreation room, video game room, shops, laundry facilities, concierge, concierge floor, business services, convention center, meeting rooms, airport shuttle, car rental, parking (fee); no smoking* ▭ *AE, D, DC, MC, V.*

$$$$ 🖳 **Westgate Hotel.** A nondescript, modern high-rise near Horton Plaza
Fodor'sChoice hides what must be the most opulent hotel in San Diego. The lobby, mod-
★ eled after the anteroom at Versailles, has hand-cut Baccarat chandeliers. Rooms are individually furnished with antiques, Italian marble coun-

ters, and bath fixtures with 24-karat-gold overlays. From the ninth floor up the views of the harbor and city are breathtaking. Afternoon tea is served in the lobby to the accompaniment of piano and harp music. The San Diego Trolley stops right outside the door. ⊠ *1055 2nd Ave., Gaslamp Quarter 92101* ☎ *619/238–1818 or 800/221–3802, 800/ 522–1564 in CA* 🖷 *619/557–3737* ⊕ *www.westgatehotel.com* ➷ *223 rooms* ⚭ *2 restaurants, room service, cable TV with movies, in-room data ports, health club, hair salon, spa, bicycles, bar, concierge, business services, meeting rooms, airport shuttle, parking (fee); no smoking* 🖃 *AE, D, DC, MC, V.*

$$$–$$$$ 🛏 **Embassy Suites–San Diego Bay.** The front door of each spacious, contemporary suite opens out onto a 12-story atrium, and rooms facing the harbor have spectacular views. A cooked-to-order breakfast and afternoon cocktails are complimentary, as are airport transfers and a daily newspaper. Room rates vary greatly depending upon occupancy. The convention center, the Embarcadero, Seaport Village, and a trolley station are nearby. ⊠ *601 Pacific Hwy., Embarcadero 92101* ☎ *619/239– 2400 or 800/362–2779* 🖷 *619/239–1520* ⊕ *www.embassy-suites.com* ➷ *337 suites* ⚭ *Restaurant, room service, microwaves, refrigerators, cable TV with movies and video games, in-room data ports, tennis court, pool, health club, hair salon, outdoor hot tub, sauna, bicycles, bar, shops, laundry facilities, laundry service, concierge, business services, meeting rooms, airport shuttle, car rental, parking (fee); no smoking* 🖃 *AE, D, DC, MC, V.*

$$$–$$$$ 🛏 **Holiday Inn San Diego on the Bay.** On the Embarcadero and overlooking San Diego Bay, this hotel made up of twin high-rises has unsurprising but spacious rooms and hard-to-beat views from the balconies. Although the hotel grounds are nice if fairly sterile, the bay is just across the street and offers boat rides, restaurants, and picturesque walking areas. The hotel is very close to the airport and Amtrak station. The English-style Elephant and Castle Pub is a great place for food, drink, and meeting people. ⊠ *1355 N. Harbor Dr., Embarcadero 92101* ☎ *619/ 232–3861 or 800/877–8920* 🖷 *619/232–4924* ⊕ *www.holiday-inn. com* ➷ *600 rooms, 17 suites* ⚭ *3 restaurants, cable TV, in-room data ports, 2 pools, gym, outdoor hot tub, sauna, bar, shops, laundry facilities, concierge, business services, meeting rooms, airport shuttle, car rental, parking (fee); no smoking* 🖃 *AE, D, DC, MC, V.*

★ $$$–$$$$ 🛏 **Omni San Diego Hotel.** The product of burgeoning downtown growth, this modern masterpiece occupies the first 21 floors of a building that rises 32 stories above the new Petco Park baseball stadium. The hotel is connected to the stadium by a skybridge, and each baseball season offers a Bed and Baseball package that bundles the room along with tickets to a game. Though marred by surrounding construction in the revitalizing East Village area, the hotel doesn't fail to amaze. The modern lobby is stunning; all rooms have windows that open to the breeze, and most have views of the ocean, bay, or the downtown skyline (some into the Petco outfield). Pleasantly decorated, rooms have DVD players and soothing sound machines. The pool terrace has a stone fireplace, outdoor dining, and a tanning area. ⊠ *675 L St., Gaslamp Quarter 92101* ☎ *619/231–6664 or 800/843–6664* 🖷 *619/645–6517* ⊕ *www.omnisandiegohotel.com* ➷ *478* *rooms, 33 suites △ 3 restaurants, room service, in-room safe, minibars, cable TV with movies, in-room data ports, Wi-Fi, pool, gym, hot tub, lounge, shop, dry cleaning, laundry service, concierge, business services, meeting rooms, airport shuttle, parking (fee), pets (fee); no smoking ☐ AE, D, DC, MC, V.*

$$$–$$$$ 🏨 **Residence Inn San Diego Downtown.** This all-suite hotel is near the harbor; it's a short, refreshing walk to the bayfront, where you can watch cruise ships set sail. The suites have full kitchens, but if you don't want to cook, the hotel serves a convenient, buffet-style breakfast accompanied by a morning paper. ✉ *1747 Pacific Hwy., Little Italy 92101* ☎ *619/338–8200 or 800/331–3131* 🖷 *619/338–8219* ⊕ *www.marriott. com* 🛏 *121 suites △ Dining room, kitchens, refrigerators, cable TV with movies, in-room data ports, pool, gym, outdoor hot tub, babysitting, laundry facilities, laundry service, concierge, Internet, business services, meeting room, car rental, travel services, parking (fee), some pets allowed (fee); no smoking* ☐ *AE, D, DC, MC, V.*

$$$–$$$$ 🏨 **San Diego Marriott Gaslamp Quarter.** Opened in December, 2004, this 22-story hotel is in the midst of all the Gaslamp's restaurants and boutiques, a short walk to the trolley station, convention center, and Petco Park. It has sweeping views of the downtown and waterfront as well as right into the ballpark; be sure to visit Altitude, the rooftop bar. Rooms offer luxury linens, 27-inch flat-screen TVs, and gourmet coffee. There's wireless Internet throughout. ✉ *660 K St., Gaslamp Quarter 92101* ☎ *619/696–0234 or 800/228–2800* 🖷 *619/231–8199* ⊕ *www.marriott. com* 🛏 *291 rooms, 15 suites △ Restaurant, room service, in-room fax, in-room safes, cable TV with movies, Wi-Fi, gym, lounge, concierge, concierge floor, business services, meeting rooms, parking (fee), no pets* ☐ *AE, D, DC, MC, V.*

$$$–$$$$ 🏨 **U. S. Grant Hotel.** Across the street from the Horton Plaza shopping center, this 1910 San Diego classic was built by President Ulysses S. Grant's grandson. Crystal chandeliers, polished marble floors, and mahogany furnishings in the stately rooms recall the days when President Franklin D. Roosevelt and Charles Lindbergh stayed here. High-power business types gather at the hotel's clubby Grant Grill, and afternoon tea is served in the lobby 1 PM–4 PM Thursday through Saturday. The hotel closed in early 2005 so that $48 million in renovations could be carried out to recreate its 1910 ambience; at presstime its reopening was set for late 2005. ✉ *326 Broadway, Gaslamp Quarter 92101* ☎ *619/232–3121* 🖷 *619/232–3626* ⊕ *www.usgrant.net* 🛏 *225 rooms, 60 suites △ 2 restaurants, café, room service, cable TV with movies, in-room data ports, gym, bar, shops, concierge, Internet, business services, meeting rooms, airport shuttle, parking (fee); no smoking* ☐ *AE, D, MC, V.*

★ **$$$–$$$$** 🏨 **W Hotel.** The W chain's urban finesse adapts to San Diego with nautical blue-and-white rooms with beach-ball pillows and goose-down comforters atop the beds. The Beach bar has a heated sand floor and fire pit, but the pool is tiny by San Diego standards. The lobby doubles as the futuristic Living Room lounge, a local hipster nightspot where non-hotel guests have to wait behind a velvet rope. Be sure to get a room on an upper floor—the leather- and black-clad crowd parties into the night. The hotel restaurant, Rice, serves stylish Asian and Latin cuisine, and the Anatomy Spa caters to both body and spirit. ⊠ *421 West B St., Downtown 92101* 🕾 *619/231–8220 or 877/946–8357* 🖷 *619/232–3626* ⊕ *www.whotels.com/sandiego* ⟡ *277 rooms, 16 suites* ⚭ *Restaurant, room service, cable TV with video games, in-room VCRs, in-room data ports, gym, spa, bars, concierge, business services, meeting rooms, airport shuttle, parking (fee); no smoking* ⊟ *AE, D, MC, V.*

$$$–$$$$ 🏨 **Westin Hotel San Diego–Horton Plaza.** You know you're there when you see the startling lighted blue obelisk fronting this high-rise hotel. Inside, it's all understated cream-color marble and curved staircases— and guest rooms freshly redecorated in a stylish urban design in 2004. The lobby lounge is packed every night with business travelers and weary shoppers back from the adjacent Horton Plaza. ⊠ *910 Broadway Circle, Gaslamp Quarter 92101* 🕾 *619/239–2200 or 888/625–5144* 🖷 *619/239–0509* ⊕ *www.westin.com* ⟡ *450 rooms, 14 suites* ⚭ *2 restaurants, room service, cable TV with movies, in-room data ports, 2 tennis courts, pool, health club, hot tub, basketball, lounge, sports bar, shops, dry cleaning, laundry service, concierge, business services, meeting rooms, airport shuttle, car rental, parking (fee); no smoking* ⊟ *AE, D, DC, MC, V.*

$$–$$$$ 🏨 **Horton Grand Hotel & Suites.** A Victorian confection, the Horton Grand comprises two 1880s hotels moved brick by brick from nearby locations and fit together. The delightfully retro rooms are furnished with period antiques, ceiling fans, and gas-burning fireplaces. The choicest rooms overlook a garden courtyard that twinkles with miniature lights. The hotel is a charmer, but service can be erratic. ⊠ *311 Island Ave., Gaslamp Quarter 92101* 🕾 *619/544–1886 or 800/542–1886* 🖷 *619/239–3823* ⊕ *www.hortongrand.com* ⟡ *132 rooms, 24 suites* ⚭ *Restaurant, kitchenettes, microwaves, refrigerators, piano bar, theater, business services, meeting rooms, airport shuttle, parking (fee); no smoking* ⊟ *AE, D, DC, MC, V.*

$$–$$$$ 🏨 **Radisson Hotel–Harbor View.** This 22-story hotel dwarfs the many two-story Victorian homes in the area, providing many rooms with unobstructed views of San Diego Bay and the downtown skyline. The art deco–inspired rooms are ordinary, but most have balconies. Although the hotel is practically adjacent to a freeway offramp, the noise level is tolerable. The airport and the eateries and coffeehouses of Little Italy are nearby. ⊠ *1646 Front St., Downtown 92101* 🕾 *619/239–6800 or 800/333–3333* 🖷 *619/238–9561* ⊕ *www.radisson.com* ⟡ *313 rooms, 20 suites* ⚭ *2 restaurants, cable TV with video games, in-room data ports, pool, gym, hot tub, sauna, bar, lounge, business services, airport shuttle* ⊟ *AE, D, DC, MC, V.*

$$–$$$$ 🏨 **Ramada Inn & Suites–Downtown.** Found on the northern end of the Gaslamp, this historic, 12-story building was San Diego's tallest when it opened in 1913. Now a boutique hotel, it's conveniently close to many restaurants, nightclubs, and shops but away from the hustle and bustle on 4th and 5th avenues. Good value and location make up for small rooms. The suites come with robes, coffeemakers, and in some cases hot tubs, big-screen TVs, and breakfast nooks. ⊠ *830 6th Ave., Gaslamp Quarter 92101* 🕾 *619/531–8877 or 800/664–4400* 🖷 *619/231–8307* ⊕ *www. ramada.com* ⟡ *87 rooms, 12 suites* ⚭ *Restaurant, room service, mini-*

LET YOUR HOST BE A GHOST

S AN DIEGO'S FOUNDING DATES TO 1769, and its rich history has given rise to a fair share of ghost stories. Two of these tales involve local hostelries.

One story concerns a woman named Kate Morgan, who checked into the Hotel Del Coronado in November 1892. She failed to check out—or rather, soon after she checked in she checked out for good. The story goes that Morgan, who was pregnant at the time, had been anticipating the arrival of her estranged husband, but he never showed up. Her body was found along the hotel beachfront, with a gunshot wound in the head. The coroner's inquest ruled her death a suicide, but rumors have long circulated to the contrary.

Kate's spirit is said to haunt Room 3312 of the hotel, but there have been reports of ghostly occurrences in Room 3502 as well. Hotel guests and employees report having heard strange, unexplained noises and observed curtains billowing when windows are closed.

The Horton Grand Hotel is also said to have its resident phantoms. Most famous of the hotel's spooks is an 1880s-vintage gambler named Roger Whitaker, who is said to occupy Room 309. A number of peculiar occurrences here have ensured the hotel's reputation as haunted, by Whitaker and maybe some other ghosts, too. According to legend, Roger was caught cheating at cards one night at the hotel. He tried to hide in Room 309 but was found and shot and killed.

To find out more about San Diego's best haunts, take the **Ghosts and Gravestones Tour of San Diego** (☎ 619/298–8687 or 800/868–7482 ⊕ www. ghostsandgravestones.com).

---

bars, cable TV with movies, in-room data ports, meeting rooms, parking (fee); no smoking ⊟ AE, D, DC, MC, V.

\$\$–\$\$\$ 🏨 **Super 8 Bayview.** This motel's location is less noisy than those of the chain's other low-cost establishments in the area. The accommodations are nondescript but clean. Continental breakfast is complimentary. ⊠ 1835 Columbia St., Little Italy 92101 ☎ 619/544–0164 or 800/800–8000 🖶 619/237–9940 ⊕ www.super8.com ➯ 101 rooms ⚘ Some refrigerators, cable TV with movies, pool, gym, hot tub, laundry facilities, laundry service, airport shuttle, car rental, free parking; no smoking ⊟ AE, D, DC, MC, V ⊠ CP.

\$\$–\$\$\$ 🏨 **Wyndham San Diego at Emerald Plaza.** This property's office and conference facilities draw many business travelers. Still, the Wyndham is also fine for vacationers who want to be near downtown shopping and restaurants. The beige-dominated standard rooms are rather bland and not large, but many of the upper-floor rooms have panoramic views. The health club is fully equipped and rarely crowded. ⊠ 400 W. Broadway, Gaslamp Quarter 92101 ☎ 619/239–4500 or 800/996–3426 🖶 619/239–4527 ⊕ www.wyndham.com ➯ 416 rooms, 20 suites ⚘ Restaurant, minibars, cable TV with movies, in-room data ports, pool, health club, outdoor *hot tub, sauna, steam room, bar, shops, laundry service, concierge, Internet, business services, meeting rooms, airport shuttle, parking (fee); no smoking* ☰ *AE, D, DC, MC, V.*

$–$$$ 🏨 **The Bristol.** Pop Art by Peter Max and Andy Warhol on the walls marks the style of this splashy boutique hotel. Rooms are decorated in fearless red, yellow, orange, and bright blue and come with bathrobes and CD players. A nice perk is complimentary high-speed Internet access and free wireless Internet in the lobby, bar, and restaurant. The San Diego Trolley stops right outside at First and Broadway. ☒ *1055 1st Ave., Downtown 92101* ☎ *619/232–6141 or 800/622–4477* 🖷 *619/232–0118* ⊕ *www.thebristolsandiego.com* 🖙 *102 rooms* ⟨ *Restaurant, in-room data ports, gym, bar, concierge, Internet, business services, meeting rooms, parking (fee)* ☰ *AE, D, DC, MC, V.*

$–$$$ 🏨 **Gaslamp Plaza Suites.** On the National Register of Historic Places,
Fodor'sChoice this 11-story structure a block from Horton Plaza was built in 1913 as
★ one of San Diego's first "skyscrapers." Appealing public areas have old marble, brass, and mosaics. Although most rooms are rather small, they are well decorated with dark-wood furnishings that give the hotel an elegant flair. You can enjoy the view and a complimentary continental breakfast on the rooftop terrace. Book ahead if you're visiting in summer. ☒ *520 E St., Gaslamp Quarter 92101* ☎ *619/232–9500 or 800/ 874–8770* 🖷 *619/238–9945* ⊕ *www.gaslampplaza.com* 🖙 *52 suites* ⟨ *Restaurant, microwaves, refrigerators, cable TV, in-room VCRs, hot tub, bar, nightclub, parking (fee); no a/c* ☰ *AE, D, DC, MC, V* ⧉ *CP.*

$–$$ 🏨 **Days Inn.** On one of downtown's quieter streets, this chain property in Cortez Hill is clean, comfortable, and pleasantly decorated. Continental breakfast is complimentary. The hotel is near Balboa Park, the zoo, and freeways. ☒ *833 Ash St., Downtown 92101* ☎ *619/239– 2285 or 800/424–6423, 800/522–1528 in CA* 🖷 *619/235–6951* ⊕ *www. daysinn.com* 🖙 *44 rooms* ⟨ *Refrigerators, cable TV with movies, in-room data ports, hot tub, sauna, laundry facilities, business services, meeting rooms, free parking; no smoking* ☰ *AE, D, DC, MC, V* ⧉ *CP.*

¢–$$$ 🏨 **Little Italy Hotel.** This old world–style bed-and-breakfast, in a renovated 1910 property, has 22 unique, well-appointed rooms and a secluded courtyard pool, unusual for area B&Bs. Wide hallways lead to rooms with luxury touches like wood floors, whirlpool tubs, and free bottles of water, not to mention bay views. And the cafés, boutiques, and bakeries of Little Italy are steps away. The lowest-price rooms have shared baths; VCRs, DVD players, irons, ironing boards, hairdryers, fridges, and microwave are available upon request. ☒ *505 W. Grape St., Little Italy 92101* ☎ *619/230–1600 or 800/518–9930* 🖷 *619/230–0322* ⊕ *www.littleitalyhotel.com* 🖙 *22 rooms* ⟨ *Cable TV with movies, in-room safes, in-room data ports, Wi-Fi, pool,* ☰ *AE, D, DC, MC, V* ⧉ *CP.*

¢–$$ 🏨 **Comfort Inn Downtown.** This three-story, stucco property surrounds
Fodor'sChoice a parking lot and courtyard. There's nothing fancy about the accom-
★ modations, but some rooms on the south side of the hotel have good views of the city skyline. It's close to downtown hot spots as well as the attractions of Balboa Park. ☒ *719 Ash St., Downtown 92101* ☎ *619/ 232–2525 or 800/404–6835* 🖷 *619/687–3024* ⊕ *www.comfortinn. com* 🖙 *45 rooms* ⟨ *Microwave, cable TV with movies, in-room data*

ports, hot tub, business services, airport shuttle, car rental, free parking; no smoking ☰ *AE, D, DC, MC, V.*

¢ ▦ **500 West.** An $8 million renovation in 2004 transformed San Diego's historic 1924 Armed Services YMCA Building into this hip, urban boutique hotel. Catering to the style-conscious, the hotel has very small rooms big on quality, with flat-screen TVs and a postmodern decor. Catering to the single traveler, it has shared bathrooms and a sleek communal kitchen. The Grand Central Café serves breakfast and lunch daily, and the whole hotel has wireless Internet. The YMCA is still downstairs and guests can use it for $5 a day or $15 a week. ⊠ *500 Broadway, Downtown 92101* ☎ *619/269–9172 or 866/500–7533* 🖷 *619/234–5272* ⊕ *www.500westhotel.com* ⌦ *260 rooms* ⚴ *Café, cable TV, in-room data port, Wi-Fi, pool, gym, hot tub, sauna, steam room, basketball, lounge, laundry facilities, concierge, meeting rooms, parking (fee)* ☰ *MC, V.*

¢ ▦ **HI–San Diego Downtown.** In the center of the Gaslamp, this two-story hostel has basic, modern furnishings and facilities, including a large common kitchen and a TV room. A special event—from pizza and movie parties to discussions on traveling in Mexico—is scheduled almost every evening. There are 4-, 6-, and 10-person sex-segregated bunk rooms, as well as a 10-person coed dorm (a six-person coed dorm is being added) and three-person and five-person family rooms. About 20 private (double) rooms are available, with or without bath. ⊠ *521 Market St., Gaslamp Quarter 92101* ☎ *619/525–1531 or 800/909–4776* 🖷 *619/ 338–0129* ⊕ *www.sandiegohostels.org* ⌦ *150 beds* ⚴ *Bicycles, billiards, laundry facilities; no a/c, no room phones, no room TVs, no smoking* ☰ *MC, V.*

¢ ▦ **USA Hostels.** This bright, clean hostel is friendly and communal, but strictly for the independent backpacker (any nationality, any age) with a valid passport showing international travel. It makes its home in an 1887 Victorian hotel in the heart of the Gaslamp Quarter. There are 60 beds and five private rooms (two doubles and a triple). A variety of tours and parties are hosted weekly including beach and Tijuana trips. Continental breakfast is complimentary and there's a kitchen for guest use, but you are asked to clean up after yourself. ⊠ *726 5th Ave., Gaslamp Quarter 92101* ☎ *619/232–3100 or 800/438–8622* 🖷 *619/232–3106* ⊕ *www.usahostels.com* ⚴ *Recreation room, laundry facilities, airport shuttle, travel services; no a/c, no room phones, no room TVs, no smoking* ☰ *MC, V* ⦿ *CP.*

Harbor Island, Shelter Island & Point Loma

Harbor Island and Shelter Island, two man-made peninsulas between downtown and the community of Point Loma, both have grassy parks, tree-lined paths, lavish hotels, and good restaurants. Harbor Island is closer to downtown and less than five minutes from the airport. Narrower Shelter Island is nearer to Point Loma. Both locations command views of the bay and the downtown skyline. Not all the lodgings listed here are on the islands themselves, but all are in the vicinity.

$$$$ ▦ **Sheraton San Diego Hotel & Marina.** Of this property's two high-rises, the smaller, more intimate West Tower has larger rooms, with separate

areas suitable for business entertaining. The East Tower has better sports facilities. Rooms throughout are decorated with plush, contemporary furnishings. Views from the upper floors of both sections are superb, but because the West Tower is closer to the water it has fine outlooks from the lower floors, too. ⊠ *1380 Harbor Island Dr., Harbor Island 92101* ☎ *619/291–2900 or 888/625–5144* 🖷 *619/692–2337* ⊕ *www.sheraton. com* ⟿ *1,044 rooms, 50 suites* ⟐ *3 restaurants, patisserie, room service, minibars, cable TV with movies, in-room data ports, 4 tennis courts, 3 pools, wading pool, health club, 2 outdoor hot tubs, massage, sauna, beach, boating, marina, bicycles, 2 bars, shop, dry cleaning, laundry service, concierge, business services, meeting rooms, airport shuttle, parking (fee); no smoking* ⊟ *AE, D, DC, MC, V.*

$$–$$$$ 🏨 **Humphrey's Half Moon Inn & Suites.** This sprawling South Seas–style resort has grassy open areas with palms and tiki torches. Rooms, some with kitchens and some with harbor or marine views, have modern furnishings. Locals throng to Humphrey's, the hotel's seafood restaurant, and to the jazz lounge; the hotel also hosts outdoor jazz and pop concerts from June through October. ⊠ *2303 Shelter Island Dr., Shelter Island 92106* ☎ *619/224–3411 or 800/542–7400* 🖷 *619/224–3478* ⊕ *www.halfmooninn.com* ⟿ *128 rooms, 54 suites* ⟐ *Restaurant, room service, kitchenettes, minibars, refrigerators, cable TV with movies and video games, in-room data ports, putting green, pool, pond, health club, hot tub, boating, bicycles, croquet, Ping-Pong, bar, concert hall, laundry facilities, business services, meeting rooms, airport shuttle, free parking; no smoking* ⊟ *AE, D, DC, MC, V.*

$$–$$$ 🏨 **Bay Club Hotel & Marina.** Rooms in this appealing low-rise Shelter Island property are large, light, and furnished with rattan tables and chairs and Polynesian tapestries; all have balconies with views of either the bay or the marina. A buffet breakfast and limo service to and from the airport or Amtrak station are included. ⊠ *2131 Shelter Island Dr., Shelter Island 92106* ☎ *619/224–8888 or 800/672–0800* 🖷 *619/225–1604* ⊕ *www.bayclubhotel.com* ⟿ *95 rooms, 10 suites* ⟐ *Restaurant, room service, refrigerators, cable TV with movies, in-room data ports, pool, gym, outdoor hot tub, bar, shop, concierge, business services, meeting rooms, airport shuttle, free parking; no smoking* ⊟ *AE, D, DC, MC, V* ⧈*BP.*

$$–$$$ 🏨 **Best Western Island Palms Hotel & Marina.** This waterfront inn, with an airy lobby brightened by skylights, is a good choice if you have a boat to dock: the adjacent marina has guest slips. Both harbor- and marina-view rooms are available. Standard accommodations are fairly small; if you're traveling with family or more than one friend, the two-bedroom suites with kitchens are a good deal. ⊠ *2051 Shelter Island Dr., Shelter Island 92106* ☎ *619/222–0561 or 800/345–9995* 🖷 *619/ 222–9760* ⊕ *www.islandpalms.com* ⟿ *68 rooms, 29 suites* ⟐ *Restaurant, fans, kitchenettes, refrigerator, cable TV with movies and video games, in-room data ports, pool, gym, outdoor hot tub, boating, bar, laundry service, business services, meeting rooms, free parking; no smoking* ⊟ *AE, D, DC, MC, V.*

$$–$$$ 🏨 **Shelter Pointe Hotel & Marina.** This 11-acre property blends Mexican and Mediterranean styles. The spacious and light-filled lobby, with its Mayan sculptures and terra-cotta tiles, opens onto a lush esplanade that

Barnes & Noble Bookseller
2080 Ford Parkway
St. Paul, MN 55116
(651) 690-9443
01-19-06 S02623 R006

BARNES & NOBLE MEMBER   EXP:08-31-06

Fodor's Santa Fe 2006   15.25
9781400015955
DISCOUNT   X   16.95   1.70
Pacific Northwest   17.05
9781569754016
DISCOUNT   18.95   1.90

SUB TOTAL   32.30
SALES TAX   2.26
TOTAL   34.56
AMOUNT TENDERED
VISA   34.56
CARD #:   ************5309
AMOUNT   34.56
AUTH CODE   276628.

MEMBER SAVINGS   3.60

TOTAL PAYMENT   34.56
       Thank you for Shopping at
       Barnes & Noble Booksellers
395128 01-19-06 05:04P MM

Valid photo ID required for all returns, exchanges and to receive and redeem store credit. With a receipt, a full refund in the original form of payment will be issued for new and unread books and unopened music within 30 days from any Barnes & Noble store. Without an original receipt, a store credit will be issued at the lowest selling price. With a receipt, returns of new and unread books and unopened music from bn.com can be made for store credit. A gift receipt or exchange receipt serves as proof of purchase only.

Valid photo ID required for all returns, exchanges and to receive and redeem store credit. With a receipt, a full refund in the original form of payment will be issued for new and unread books and unopened music within 30 days from any Barnes & Noble store. Without an original receipt, a store credit will be issued at the lowest selling price. With a receipt, returns of new and unread books and unopened music from bn.com can be made for store credit. A gift receipt or exchange receipt serves as proof of purchase only.

overlooks the hotel's marina. The rooms are well appointed, if a bit small, and most look out onto either the marina or San Diego Bay. The attractive hotel is popular for business meetings. ⊠ *1551 Shelter Island Dr., Shelter Island 92106* ☎ *619/221–8000 or 800/566–2524* 🖷 *619/221–5953* ⊕ *www.shelterpointe.com* ↪ *206 rooms, 31 suites* ⟷ *Restaurant, room service, kitchenettes, cable TV with movies and video games, 2 tennis courts, 2 pools, health club, 2 hot tubs, 2 saunas, beach, boating, marina, bicycles, volleyball, bar, meeting rooms, airport shuttle, free parking; no smoking* ⊟ *AE, D, DC, MC, V.*

★ $$ 🖽 **Holiday Inn Express–SeaWorld Area.** In Point Loma near the West Mission Bay exit off I–8, this is a surprisingly quiet lodging despite proximity to bustling traffic. The three-story building is only about a half mile from both SeaWorld and Mission Bay. Continental breakfast is included. ⊠ *3950 Jupiter St., Sports Arena 92110* ☎ *619/226–8000 or 800/320–0208* 🖷 *619/226–1409* ⊕ *www.hiexpress.com* ↪ *70 rooms, 2 suites* ⟷ *Refrigerator, cable TV with movies, in-room data ports, pool, hot tub, laundry service, concierge, business services, free parking; no smoking* ⊟ *AE, D, DC, MC, V* ⑩ *CP.*

$–$$ 🖽 **Best Western Posada Inn at the Yacht Harbor.** Many of the rooms at this comfortable if plain inn have harbor views. Some rooms have microwaves, mini-refrigerators, and video players. Point Loma's seafood restaurants are within walking distance. Weekly rates, package plans, and senior discounts are available. Continental breakfast is included. ⊠ *5005 N. Harbor Dr., Point Loma 92106* ☎ *619/224–3254 or 800/231–3811* 🖷 *619/224–2186* ⊕ *www.bestwestern.com* ↪ *112 rooms* ⟷ *Restaurant, cable TV with movies, in-room data ports, pool, gym, outdoor hot tub, bar, laundry service, meeting rooms, airport shuttle, free parking; no smoking* ⊟ *AE, D, DC, MC, V* ⑩ *CP.*

$–$$ 🖽 **Vagabond Inn–Point Loma.** This two-story budget motel is safe, clean, and comfortable, close to the airport, yacht clubs, and Cabrillo National Monument—and the popular and excellent Point Loma Seafoods is next door. A daily newspaper and continental breakfast are included. ⊠ *1325 Scott St., Point Loma 92106* ☎ *619/224–3371* 🖷 *619/223–0646* ⊕ *www.vagabondinn.com* ↪ *40 rooms* ⟷ *Restaurant, in-room safes, some kitchens, some refrigerators, cable TV with movies, pool, bar, airport shuttle, free parking; no smoking* ⊟ *AE, D, DC, MC, V* ⑩ *CP.*

$ 🖽 **Comfort Inn at the Harbor.** You'll get the same view here as at the higher-price hotels—for far less money. Of course, there are fewer amenities and the neighborhood isn't as serene, but the rooms—all with coffeemakers—are adequate and clean. ⊠ *5102 N. Harbor Dr., Point Loma 92106* ☎ *619/223–8171 or 800/578–7878* 🖷 *619/222–7330* ⊕ *www.comfortinn.com* ↪ *45 rooms* ⟷ *Refrigerators, cable TV, in-room data ports, pool, free parking; no smoking* ⊟ *AE, D, DC, MC, V.*

$ 🖽 **Ramada Limited San Diego Airport.** The location is convenient, although on a busy street, and the rooms with bay views are quite a deal. Continental breakfast, daily newspaper, and local calls are complimentary. There's a heated pool and a bay-view bar with billiards, and there's a free shuttle to area attractions. ⊠ *1403 Rosecrans St., Point Loma 92106* ☎ *619/225–9461 or 888/298–2054* 🖷 *619/225–1163* ⊕ *www.ramada.com* ↪ *83 rooms* ⟷ *Restaurant, dining room, cable TV, pool,* *bar, meeting rooms, airport shuttle, free parking, some pets allowed (fee); no smoking* ⊟ *AE, D, DC, MC, V* ⦿❘ *CP.*

¢ ⊞ **HI–San Diego Point Loma.** This hostel is in a large converted house, in a quiet area straddling the Ocean Beach and Point Loma neighborhoods. Though it's far from San Diego's attractions and nightlife, there's a bus stop nearby. Special events are scheduled weekly. The hostel has a large kitchen, a large patio, and a TV room. Rates include linens and a free pancake breakfast. There are dorm rooms (generally sex-segregated), family rooms, and private rooms (sleeping two, without private bath). ⊠ *3790 Udall St., Ocean Beach 92107* ☎ *619/223–4778 or 800/909–4779 Ext. 44* 🖷 *619/223–1883* ⊕ *www.sandiegohostels.org* ↔ *53 beds* ♺ *Bicycles, laundry service, free parking; no a/c, no room phones, no room TVs, no smoking* ⊟ *MC, V* ⦿❘ *BP.*

Old Town & Vicinity

Staying in Old Town affords easy access to SeaWorld and the beaches to the west, the downtown area and Mexico to the south, and Mission Valley and the zoo to the east. But most important, it puts you smack in the middle of the most popular park in the California state system, the Old Town San Diego State Historic Park. Old Town has a few picturesque lodgings and some modestly priced chain hotels near I–5; when you're making reservations, request a room that doesn't face the freeway. West of the freeway is the Midway District, with a few budget hotels near the San Diego Sports Arena.

$$–$$$ ⊞ **Courtyard San Diego Old Town.** This hotel has Spanish colonial–style fountains and courtyards, and painted tiles and Southwestern decor in the rooms. A breakfast buffet and transfers to the airport, bus, and Amtrak stations are complimentary. ⊠ *2435 Jefferson St., Old Town 92110* ☎ *619/260–8500 or 800/255–3544* 🖷 *619/297–2078* ⊕ *www.marriott.com* ↔ *174 rooms, 19 suites* ♺ *Restaurant, cable TV with movies and video games, in-room data ports, pool, gym, outdoor hot tub, bar, shop, laundry service, concierge, Internet, business services, meeting rooms, airport shuttle, free parking; no smoking* ⊟ *AE, D, DC, MC, V* ⦿❘ *BP.*

★ **$$–$$$** ⊞ **Holiday Inn Express–Old Town.** Already an excellent value for Old Town, this cheerful property throws in such perks as garage parking, continental breakfast, and afternoon snacks. Rooms have a European look. When you've had enough of the heated pool off the shaded courtyard, you can tackle the historic park's attractions and restaurants nearby. ⊠ *3900 Old Town Ave., Old Town 92110* ☎ *619/299–7400 or 800/272–6232* 🖷 *619/299–1619* ⊕ *www.hiexpress.com* ↔ *125 rooms, 4 suites* ♺ *Restaurant, room service, microwaves, refrigerators, cable TV, in-room data ports, pool, outdoor hot tub, shops, laundry service, concierge, business services, meeting rooms, airport shuttle, free parking; no smoking* ⊟ *AE, D, DC, MC, V* ⦿❘ *CP.*

$–$$$ ⊞ **Heritage Park Inn.** The beautifully restored mansions in Heritage Park
Fodor's Choice include the romantic 1889 Queen Anne–style house that is the main house
★ of this B&B as well as the Italianate but plainer house of 1887 that serves as its extension. Rooms range from smallish to ample, and most are bright and cheery. A two-bedroom suite is decorated with period antiques, and

3

Apartment Rentals

If you're planning an extended stay or need lodgings for four or more people, consider an apartment rental. Oakwood Apartments rents comfortable furnished apartments in the Mission Valley, La Jolla, and Coronado areas with maid service and linens; there's a one-week to 30-day minimum stay depending on locations. Several hotels also offer special weekly and monthly rates, especially in the beach communities. Rental apartments and condominiums are also available through realtors who specialize in Mission Beach, Pacific Beach, La Jolla's Golden Triangle–University City area, Carlsbad, and Escondido. In addition, there are three Residence Inns by Marriott in San Diego; these sometimes offer good value for families traveling on weekends.

▪ International Agents Hideaways International ✉ 767 Islington St., Portsmouth, NH 03801 ☎ 603/430-4433 or 800/843-4433 ⎗ 603/430-4444 ⊕ www.hideaways.com, annual membership $185. **Vacation Home Rentals Worldwide** ✉ 235 Kensington Ave., Norwood, NJ 07648 ☎ 201/767-9393 or 800/633-3284 ⎗ 201/767-5510 ⊕ www.vhrww.com.

▪ Local Agents Oakwood Apartments ☎ 800/888-0808 ⊕ www.oakwood.com. **Penny Realty** ☎ 800/748-6704 ⊕ www.missionbeach.com. **San Diego Vacation Rentals** ☎ 800/222-8281 ⊕ www.sdvr.com.

Bed & Breakfasts

San Diego is known more for its resorts and solid chain properties, but the city has several bed-and-breakfasts, most of which are in private homes and are very well maintained and accommodating. Historic Julian, in the mountains east of San Diego, has many. The Bed and Breakfast Guild of San Diego lists a number of high-quality member inns. The Bed & Breakfast Directory for San Diego covers San Diego County.

▪ Reservation Services Bed & Breakfast Directory for San Diego ☎ 619/297-3130 or 800/619-7666 ⊕ www.sandiegobandb.com. **Bed and Breakfast Guild of San Diego** ☎ 619/523-1300 ⊕ www.bandbguildsandiego.org. **Julian Bed and Breakfast Guild** ☎ 888/765-4333 ⊕ www.julianbnbguild.com.

Chains

▪ Toll-Free Numbers Best Western ☎ 800/528-1234 ⊕ www.bestwestern.com. **Choice** ☎ 800/424-6423 ⊕ www.choicehotels.com. **Clarion** ☎ 800/424-6423 ⊕ www.choicehotels.com. **Comfort Inn** ☎ 800/424-6423 ⊕ www.choicehotels.com. **Days Inn** ☎ 800/325-2525 ⊕ www.daysinn.com. **Doubletree Hotels** ☎ 800/222-8733 ⊕ www.doubletree.com. **Embassy Suites** ☎ 800/362-2779 ⊕ www.embassysuites.com. **Fairfield Inn** ☎ 800/228-2800 ⊕ www.marriott.com. **Four Seasons** ☎ 800/332-3442 ⊕ www.fourseasons.com. **Hilton** ☎ 800/445-8667 ⊕ www.hilton.com. **Holiday Inn** ☎ 800/465-4329 ⊕ www.ichotelsgroup.com. **Howard Johnson** ☎ 800/446-4656 ⊕ www.hojo.com. **Hyatt Hotels & Resorts** ☎ 800/233-1234 ⊕ www.hyatt.com. **La Quinta** ☎ 800/531-5900 ⊕ www.lq.com. **Marriott** ☎ 800/228-9290 ⊕ www.marriott.com. **Quality Inn** ☎ 800/424-6423 ⊕ www.choicehotels.com. **Radisson** ☎ 800/333-3333 ⊕ www.radisson.com. **Ramada** ☎ 800/228-2828, 800/854-7854 international reservations ⊕ www.ramada.com. **Red Lion and WestCoast Hotels and Inns** ☎ 800/733-5466 ⊕ www.redlion.com. **Sheraton** ☎ 800/325-3535

⊕ www.starwood.com/sheraton. **Sleep Inn** ☎ 800/424-6423 ⊕ www.choicehotels. com. **Westin Hotels & Resorts** ☎ 800/228-3000 ⊕ www.starwood.com/westin. **Wyndham Hotels & Resorts** ☎ 800/822-4200 ⊕ www.wyndham.com.

Home Exchanges

If you would like to exchange your home for someone else's, join a home-exchange organization, which will send you its listings of available exchanges, regularly updated, for a year and will include your own listing in at least one of them. It's up to you to make specific arrangements.

🏢 Exchange Clubs **HomeLink USA** ⊠ 2937 NW 9th Terrace, Wilton Manors, FL 33311 ☎ 954/566-2687 or 800/638-3841 🖷 954/566-2783 ⊕ www.homelink.org; $75 yearly for a listing and online access; $45 additional to receive directories. **Intervac U.S.** ⊠ 30 Corte San Fernando, Tiburon, CA 94920 ☎ 800/756-4663 🖷 415/435-7440 ⊕ www.intervacus.com; $128 yearly for a listing, online access, and a catalog; $68 without catalog.

Hostels

No matter what your age, you can save on lodging costs by staying at hostels. Throughout San Diego, Hostelling International (HI), the worldwide umbrella group of a number of national youth-hostel associations, offers sex-segregated, dorm-style beds. They cater to college students and budget backpackers, and most require an international passport to check in. Rooms usually have four to six bunks; however, some hostels have a few private or double rooms.

Membership in any HI national hostel association, open to travelers of all ages, allows you to stay in HI-affiliated hostels at member rates; one-year membership is about $28 for adults (C$35 for a two-year minimum membership in Canada, £14 in the U.K., A$52 in Australia, and NZ$40 in New Zealand); hostels charge about $10–$30 per night. Members have priority if the hostel is full; they're also eligible for discounts around the world, even on rail and bus travel in some countries.

🏢 Organizations **Hostelling International—USA** ⊠ 8401 Colesville Rd., Suite 600, Silver Spring, MD 20910 ☎ 301/495-1240 🖷 301/495-6697 ⊕ www.hiusa.org. **Hostelling International—Canada** ⊠ 205 Catherine St., Suite 400, Ottawa, Ontario K2P 1C3 ☎ 613/ 237-7884 or 800/663-5777 🖷 613/237-7868 ⊕ www.hihostels.ca. **YHA England and Wales** ⊠ Trevelyan House, Dimple Rd., Matlock, Derbyshire DE4 3YH, U.K. ☎ 0870/ 870-8808, 0870/770-8868, or 0162/959-2600 🖷 0870/770-6127 ⊕ www.yha.org.uk. **YHA Australia** ⊠ 422 Kent St., Sydney, NSW 2001 ☎ 02/9261-1111 🖷 02/9261-1969 ⊕ www.yha.com.au. **YHA New Zealand** ⊠ Level 1, Moorhouse City, 166 Moorhouse Ave., Box 436, Christchurch ☎ 03/379-9970 or 0800/278-299 🖷 03/365-4476 ⊕ www. yha.org.nz.

---

there are also two junior suites. A full breakfast and afternoon tea are included. There's a two-night minimum stay on weekends, and weekly and monthly rates are available. Some rooms share a bath. Classic vintage films are shown nightly in the parlor on a small film screen. ⊠ 2470 *Heritage Park Row, Old Town 92110* ☎ *619/299–6832 or 800/995– 2470* 🖷 *619/299–9465* ⊕ *www.heritageparkinn.com* ➳ *9 rooms, 3 suites* ♿ *Cable TV, in-room data ports, library, meeting rooms; no smoking* ▤ *AE, MC, V* ⏺ *BP.*

$$ ☷ **Best Western Hacienda Suites–Old Town.** Pretty and white, with balconies and Spanish-tile roofs, the Hacienda is in a quiet part of Old Town, away from the freeway and the main retail bustle. The layout is somewhat confusing, and accommodations are not large enough to earn the "suite" label the hotel gives them, but they're decorated in tasteful Southwestern style and are well-equipped. ⊠ *4041 Harney St., Old Town 92110* ☎ *619/298–4707 or 800/888–1991* ☐ *619/298–4771* ⊕ *www. bestwestern.com* ⇔ *169 rooms* ⌂ *Restaurant, room service, microwaves, refrigerators, cable TV, in-room VCRs, pool, gym, outdoor hot tub, bar, laundry service, concierge, business services, meeting rooms, airport shuttle, car rental, travel services, free parking; no a/c, no smoking* ⊟ *AE, D, DC, MC, V.*

★ **¢–$** ☷ **Western Inn–Old Town.** The three-story Western Inn is decorated in a Spanish motif and is close to shops and restaurants, but far enough away from the main tourist drag that you don't have to worry about noise and congestion. There's a free continental breakfast, and a barbecue area where you can cook for yourself. A bus, trolley, and Coaster station is a few blocks away. ⊠ *3889 Arista St., Old Town 92110* ☎ *619/298– 6888 or 888/475–2353* ☐ *619/692–4497* ⊕ *www.westerninn.com* ⇔ *29 rooms, 6 suites* ⌂ *Refrigerators, cable TV, in-room data ports, airport shuttle, free parking; no smoking* ⊟ *AE, D, DC, MC, V* ⦿ *CP.*

Mission Valley & Hotel Circle

Mission Valley once thrived as an area of dairy farms, a history you'd never guess from its appearance today. Beginning in the late 1950s, hotels started popping up along what is now called Hotel Circle, in the western end of the valley. Today the area is paved over with shopping centers, car lots, the Qualcomm Stadium, and hotels except for a narrow greenbelt lining the San Diego River. Most of the 20 hotels along Hotel Circle are reasonably priced, their quality ranging from a bit shopworn and dated to brand new. A little farther east you can find a selection of bigger and pricier properties, although this puts you farther from major attractions and the beaches.

$$$ ☷ **Doubletree Hotel San Diego Mission Valley.** Near the Fashion Valley shopping mall and adjacent to the Hazard Center—which has a seven-screen movie theater, four major restaurants, a food pavilion, and more than 20 shops—the Doubletree is also convenient to Route 163 and I–8. A San Diego Trolley station is within walking distance. Public areas are bright and comfortable, well suited to this hotel's large business clientele. Spacious rooms have ample desk space; complimentary coffee, irons, and ironing boards are also provided. ⊠ *7450 Hazard Center Dr., Mission Valley 92108* ☎ *619/297–5466 or 800/222–8733* ☐ *619/297– 5499* ⊕ *www.doubletree.com* ⇔ *294 rooms, 6 suites* ⌂ *Restaurant, room service, minibars, cable TV with movies, in-room data ports, 2 tennis courts, 2 pools, gym, outdoor hot tub, sauna, 2 bars, shops, laundry facilities, laundry service, concierge, business services, meeting rooms, airport shuttle, free parking; no smoking* ⊟ *AE, D, DC, MC, V.*

★ **$$–$$$** ☷ **San Diego Marriott Mission Valley.** This 17-floor high-rise is well equipped for business travelers—the front desk provides 24-hour fax and photocopy services, and rooms come with desks and private voice mail. The hotel is in the middle of the San Diego River valley near Qualcomm Stadium and the Rio Vista Plaza shopping center, minutes from the Mission Valley and Fashion Valley malls. There's free transportation to the malls, and the San Diego Trolley stops across the street. Rooms are comfortable (with individual balconies) and the staff is friendly. ✉ *8757 Rio San Diego Dr., Mission Valley 92108* ☎ *619/692–3800 or 800/228–9290* 🖷 *619/692–0769* 🌐 *www.marriott.com* 🛏 *350 rooms, 5 suites* ♨ *Restaurant, room service, minibars, cable TV with movies, in-room data ports, tennis court, pool, gym, health club, outdoor hot tub, sauna, sports bar, nightclub, shops, laundry service, concierge, concierge floor, Internet, business services, meeting rooms, airport shuttle, parking (fee); no smoking* 🚬 *AE, D, DC, MC, V.*

$–$$ 🏨 **Handlery Hotel & Resort.** Well-managed and pleasant, this moderate hotel within walking distance of the Fashion Valley shopping mall has free shuttle service to area attractions. The Riverwalk Golf Club next door offers guests reduced rates to tee off. There's a heated outdoor pool, and an on-site shop covers necessities as well as souvenirs. ✉ *950 Hotel Circle N, Mission Valley 92108* ☎ *619/298–0511 or 800/843–4343* 🖷 *619/298–9793* 🌐 *www.handlery.com* 🛏 *217 rooms, 3 suites* ♨ *Restaurant, room service, refrigerators, cable TV with movies, in-room data ports, 2 pools, gym, hair salon, outdoor hot tub, shop, laundry facilities, laundry service, concierge, business services, meeting rooms, airport shuttle, car rental, parking (fee); no smoking* 🚬 *AE, D, DC, MC, V.*

$–$$ 🏨 **Red Lion Hanalei Hotel.** As the name suggests, the theme of this friendly property is Hawaiian: palms, waterfalls, koi ponds, and tiki torches abound. Rooms are decorated in tropical prints. What used to be a golf course next door has been restored to a bird sanctuary. Free transportation is provided to local malls and Old Town. The hotel is virtually surrounded by heavy traffic, which can make for a noisy stay. ✉ *2270 Hotel Circle N, Hotel Circle 92108* ☎ *619/297–1101 or 800/882–0858* 🖷 *619/297–6049* 🌐 *www.hanaleihotel.com* 🛏 *402 rooms, 14 suites* ♨ *2 restaurants, room service, cable TV, in-room data ports, pool, gym, hot tub, bar, laundry service, business services, meeting rooms, car rental, travel services, parking (fee); no smoking* 🚬 *AE, D, DC, MC, V.*

¢–$$ 🏨 **Mission Valley Resort.** Next to Interstate 8 on 20 acres, this Southwestern-style hotel with clean, modern rooms and large grassy areas is a favorite with families. ✉ *875 Hotel Circle S, Mission Valley 92108* ☎ *619/298–8282* 🖷 *619/295–5610* 🌐 *www.missionvalleyresort.com* 🛏 *202 rooms* ♨ *Coffee shop, room service, in-room safes, cable TV with movies, in-room data ports, 2 pools, gym, hair salon, shuffleboard, sports bar, shop, dry cleaning, laundry facilities, laundry services, meeting rooms, free parking* 🚬 *AE, D, DC, MC, V.*

¢–$$ 🏨 **Super 8 Motel.** Simple, clean rooms are available here in the same area as Mission Valley's pricier hotels. ✉ *445 Hotel Circle S, Mission Valley 92108* ☎ *619/692–1288 or 800/800–8000* 🖷 *619/298–0668* 🌐 *www.super8.com* 🛏 *144 rooms* ♨ *Some refrigerators, cable TV with movies, in-room data ports, pool, gym, laundry facilities, free parking* 🚬 *AE, D, DC, MC, V.*

La Jolla

Million-dollar homes line the beaches and hillsides of beautiful and prestigious La Jolla. Its exclusiveness and seclusion make it easy to forget that La Jolla is part of the city of San Diego and not a separate town. The village—the heart of La Jolla—is chockablock with expensive boutiques, galleries, and restaurants. Don't despair, however, if you're not old money or nouveau riche; this popular vacation spot has sufficient lodging choices for every purse.

$$$$ **Estancia La Jolla Hotel & Spa.** La Jolla's newest resort was once the site of a famous equestrian ranch, Blackhorse Farms, where thoroughbreds were trained. This coastal hotel has a rustic elegance, rambling California rancho-style architecture, and courtyards with bubbling fountains. Rooms have marble baths and come with robes and slippers and 24-hour room service. The resort offers free high speed and wireless Internet, a pool with private cabanas, and a spa where guests can be pampered with an outdoor massage in a private garden of eucalyptus, citrus, and lavender. Besides spa packages, the resort offers golf getaways at the nearby Torrey Pines Golf Course. ✉ *9700 N. Torrey Pines Rd., La Jolla 92037* ☎ *858/550–1000 or 877/437–8262* 🖷 *858/550–1001* ⊕ *www.estancialajolla.com* ⬐ *200 rooms, 10 suites* ♨ *3 restaurants, room service, in-room safes, minibars, cable TV with movies, in-room data ports, Wi-Fi, pool, fitness classes, gym, hair salon, outdoor hot tub, massage, spa, steam rooms, hiking, sports bar, shop, babysitting, dry cleaning, laundry services, concierge, business services, meeting rooms, airport shuttle, car rental, parking (fee); no pets, no smoking* 🖃*AE, D, MC, V* ❖*CP.*

$$$$ 🏨 **Hilton La Jolla Torrey Pines.** The hotel blends discreetly into the Tor-
Fodor'sChoice rey Pines cliff top, overlooking the Pacific Ocean and the 18th hole of
★ the Torrey Pines Golf Course, site of the 2008 U.S. Open. Oversize accommodations are simple but elegant; most have balconies or terraces. The menu at the hotel's restaurant, the Torreyana Grille, changes with the seasons; caesar salad and filet mignon are regulars, but you're likely to find lobster pot stickers and coffee-lacquered duck breast as well. ✉ *10950 N. Torrey Pines Rd., La Jolla 92037* ☎ *858/558–1500 or 800/774–1500* 🖷 *858/450–4584* ⊕ *www.hilton.com* ⬐ *377 rooms, 17 suites* ♨ *3 restaurants, room service, in-room safes, minibars, cable TV with movies, in-room data ports, putting green, 3 tennis courts, pool, gym, outdoor hot tub, sauna, bicycles, 3 bars, babysitting, laundry service, concierge, business services, meeting rooms, airport shuttle, car rental, parking (fee); no smoking* 🖃 *AE, D, DC, MC, V.*

★ **$$$$** 🏨 **Hotel Parisi.** A Zen-like peace welcomes you in the lobby, which has a skylighted waterfall and is filled with Asian art. The suites are decorated according to the principles of feng shui; you can order a massage, a yoga session, or the on-staff psychologist from room service. Favored by celebrities, the hushed, earth-tone suites have granite bathrooms, fluffy robes, and ergonomic tubs. The rooms are set back enough from the street noise, but in the ocean-view suites you have to look over buildings across the street to view the Pacific. Continental breakfast is served daily in a breakfast room off the lobby. ✉ *1111 Prospect St., La Jolla 92037* ☎ *858/454–1511* 🖷 *858/454–1531* ⊕ *www.hotelparisi.com*

⇨ *20 suites ♿ Room service, in-room safes, minibars, cable TV with movies, in-room VCR, in-room data ports, massage, business services, meeting rooms, free parking; no smoking* ☰ *AE, D, MC, V* ⦿| *CP.*

$$$$
Fodor'sChoice
★
⊡ **La Valencia.** This pink Spanish-Mediterranean confection drew Hollywood film stars in the 1930s and '40s with its setting and views of La Jolla Cove. Many rooms have a genteel European look, with antique pieces and richly colored rugs. The personal attention provided by the staff, as well as the plush robes and grand bathrooms, make the stay even more pleasurable. The hotel is near the shops and restaurants of La Jolla village. Rates are lower if you're willing to look out on the village rather than the ocean. Be sure to stroll the tiered gardens in back. ⊠ *1132 Prospect St., La Jolla 92037* ☎ *858/454–0771 or 800/451–0772* ⎙ *858/456–3921* ⊕ *www.lavalencia.com* ⇨ *117 rooms, 15 villas ♿ 3 restaurants, room service, in-room safes, minibars, cable TV with movies and video games, in-room VCRs, pool, health club, outdoor hot tub, massage, sauna, beach, bicycles, Ping-Pong, shuffleboard, bar, lounge, laundry facilities, concierge, business services, meeting rooms, airport shuttle, parking (fee); no smoking* ☰ *AE, D, MC, V.*

$$$$
Fodor'sChoice
★
⊡ **Lodge at Torrey Pines.** This beautiful Craftsman-style lodge sits on a bluff between La Jolla and Del Mar and commands a view of miles of coastline. You know you're in for a different sort of experience when you see the Scottish kilted doorman. Rooms, though dim, are roomy and furnished with antiques and reproduction turn-of-the-20th-century pieces. The service is excellent and the restaurant, A. R. Valentin, serves fine California cuisine. Beyond the 6-acre grounds are the Torrey Pines Golf Course and scenic trails that lead to the Torrey Pines State Beach and Reserve. The village of La Jolla is a 10-minute drive away. ⊠ *11480 N. Torrey Pines Rd., La Jolla 92037* ☎ *858/453–4420 or 800/995–4507* ⎙ *858/453–7464* ⊕ *www.lodgetorreypines.com* ⇨ *175 rooms ♿ 2 restaurants, in-room safes, kitchenettes, cable TV, in-room data ports, 18-hole golf course, pool, gym, hot tub, massage, spa, 2 bars, Internet, meeting rooms, free parking; no smoking* ☰ *AE, D, DC, MC, V.*

$$$$
⊡ **Sea Lodge.** One of few San Diego hotels actually on the beach, the Sea Lodge is at La Jolla Shores Beach and Tennis Club. Palms, fountains, red-tile roofs, and Mexican tile work lend character to the low-lying compound. Rooms have rattan furniture, floral-print bedspreads, and wood balconies overlooking the ocean. Hair dryers, coffeemakers, and irons are included. Tennis lessons are available. ⊠ *8110 Camino del Oro, La Jolla 92037* ☎ *858/459–8271 or 800/237–5211* ⎙ *858/456–9346* ⊕ *www.sealodge.com* ⇨ *127 rooms, 1 suite ♿ Restaurant, room service, some kitchenettes, refrigerators, cable TV, in-room data ports, 2 tennis courts, pool, health club, outdoor hot tub, massage, sauna, beach, volleyball, bar, laundry service, business services, meeting rooms, free parking; no smoking* ☰ *AE, D, DC, MC, V.*

$$$–$$$$
Fodor'sChoice
★
⊡ **Grande Colonial.** This white wedding-cake–style hotel has ocean views and is in the heart of La Jolla village. Built in 1913 and expanded and redesigned in 1925–26, the Colonial is graced with charming European details: chandeliers, a marble hearth, mahogany railings, oak furnishings, and French doors. The hotel's restaurant, Nine-ten, run by chef Michael Stebner, is well liked by locals for its fresh, seasonal California

cuisine. ✉ *910 Prospect St., La Jolla 92037* ☎ *858/454–2181 or 800/ 826–1278* 🖷 *858/454–5679* ⊕ *www.thegrandecolonial.com* 🛏 *58 rooms, 17 suites* ♿ *Restaurant, room service, cable TV with movies and video games, in-room data ports, pool, bar, meeting rooms, parking (fee); no smoking* 🖃 *AE, D, DC, MC, V.*

$$$–$$$$ 🏨 **Scripps Inn.** You'd be wise to make reservations well in advance for this small, quiet inn tucked away on Coast Boulevard; its popularity with repeat visitors ensures that it's booked year-round. Lower weekly and monthly rates (not available in summer) make it attractive to long-term guests. Rooms are done in Mexican and Spanish style, with wood floors, and all have ocean views; some have fireplaces. Continental breakfast is served in the lobby each morning. ✉ *555 S. Coast Blvd., La Jolla 92037* ☎ *858/454–3391 or 800/439–7529* 🖷 *858/456–0389* ⊕ *www.jcresorts. com* 🛏 *14 rooms* ♿ *In-room safes, some kitchens, cable TV, free parking; no smoking* 🖃 *AE, D, MC, V* ⧖ *CP.*

★ **$$–$$$$** 🏨 **Hyatt Regency La Jolla.** The Hyatt is in the Golden Triangle area, about 10 minutes from the beach and the village of La Jolla. The postmodern design of architect Michael Graves' striking lobby continues in the spacious rooms, where warm cherrywood furnishings contrast with austere gray closets. Fluffy down comforters and cushy chairs and couches make you feel right at home, though, and business travelers will appreciate the endless array of office and in-room services. The hotel's four trendy restaurants include Cafe Japengo. Rates are lowest on weekends. ✉ *Aventine Center, 3777 La Jolla Village Dr., La Jolla 92122* ☎ *858/552–1234 or 800/233–1234* 🖷 *858/552–6066* ⊕ *www.hyatt.com* 🛏 *419 rooms, 20 suites* ♿ *4 restaurants, room service, minibars, cable TV with movies, 2 tennis courts, pool, health club, hair salon, outdoor hot tub, massage, basketball, bar, dry cleaning, laundry service, concierge, business services, meeting rooms, parking (fee); no smoking* 🖃 *AE, D, DC, MC, V.*

$$–$$$ 🏨 **La Jolla Cove Suites.** It may lack the charm of some of the older properties of this exclusive area, but this motel with studios and suites (some with spacious oceanfront balconies) gives its guests the same first-class views of La Jolla Cove at lower rates. The beach is across the street and down a short cliff, and snorkelers and divers can take advantage of lockers and outdoor showers. Continental breakfast is served in the sunroom. The free underground lot is also a bonus in a section of town where a parking spot is a prime commodity. ✉ *1155 S. Coast Blvd., La Jolla 92037* ☎ *858/459–2621 or 800/248–2683* 🖷 *858/454–3522* ⊕ *www. lajollacove.com* 🛏 *96 rooms* ♿ *In-room safes, kitchenettes, cable TV with movies, putting green, pool, hot tub, bicycles, laundry service, business services, meeting rooms, airport shuttle, free parking; no a/c, no smoking* 🖃 *AE, D, DC, MC, V* ⧖ *CP.*

$$–$$$ 🏨 **La Jolla Inn.** One block from the beach and near some of the best shops and restaurants, this European-style inn with a delightful staff sits in a prime spot in the village of La Jolla. Many rooms have sweeping ocean views from their balconies; one spectacular penthouse suite faces the ocean, the other the village. Enjoy the delicious complimentary continental breakfast on the upstairs sundeck. ✉ *1110 Prospect St., La Jolla 92037* ☎ *858/454–0133 or 800/433–1609* 🖷 *858/454–2056* ⊕ *www.lajollainn. com* 🛏 *21 rooms, 2 suites* ♿ *Room service, some kitchenettes, some*

CloseUp

KID-FRIENDLY HOTELS

GOT KIDS IN TOW? *San Diego is perfect for family fun; the year-round sunny, warm weather ensures lots of play days. And* many hotels cater to families. Some let kids under 18 stay free—just ask. And check into kids' activity programs, family-size suites, in-room Nintendo or kitchenettes. Shop around for hotel packages, which often include tickets to local attractions.

Some of the high-end properties have special children's programs; most occur in summer, some year-round. The famous **Hotel Del Coronado** has tons of activities, from surfing lessons, treasure hunts, and kayak tours to making sand candles on the resort's white-sand beach. They also offer a "kid's nite out" so Mom and Dad can enjoy a couple's night out. The **Loews Coronado Bay Resort** has welcome gifts for children, a kids-only pool, a game library, and special menus. Some recreational fun is offered seasonally, such

as sunset sails and gondola rides. And kids can bring their pets.

Across the bay, resorts on family-friendly Mission Bay cater to moppets. The **Hilton San Diego Resort** holds a summer Kid's Kamp (ages 5–12, $7 per child per hour) with koi fish feeding, sand-castle building, and scavenger hunts. There's a special children's wading pool, a lawn croquet course, and a sand volleyball court, and plenty of water-sport rentals. Teddy bears await the kids arriving at the **Catamaran Resort Hotel**; just let reservations know you have young ones in your party. At the resort's library, kids over age 12 can play pool or watch movies borrowed from the concierge; it's open from 8 AM until 11 PM. And kids will enjoy the macaws and Black Australian swans that live on the property. The **Hyatt Islandia** has kids' menus, free Disney Channel, and a game room open from 7 AM until midnight.

–Lenore Greiner

refrigerators, cable TV with movies, in-room data ports, library, shop, dry cleaning, laundry facilities, concierge, business services, free parking; no smoking ▭ AE, D, DC, MC, V ⑩ CP.

$–$$$ ▧ **Holiday Inn Express–La Jolla.** Many rooms at this modest property in the southern section of La Jolla are remarkably large, with huge closets. The decor is nothing to write home about, but this is a good value for families who want to stay in La Jolla and still have a few dollars left over for shopping and dining. Continental breakfast is included. ✉ *6705 La Jolla Blvd., La Jolla 92037* ☎ *858/454–7101 or 800/451–0358* 🖷 *858/454–6957* ⊕ *www.hiexpress.com* ◁ *61 rooms, 11 suites* ⚭ *Some kitchenettes, refrigerators, cable TV, in-room data ports, pool, gym, outdoor hot tub, sauna, laundry service, business services, meeting rooms, airport shuttle, free parking; no smoking* ▭ *AE, D, DC, MC, V* ⑩ *CP.*

Mission Bay & the Beaches

Mission Bay Park, with its beaches, bike trails, boat-launching ramps, golf course, and grassy parks—not to mention SeaWorld—is a hotel haven. Next to the Mission Bay area are Mission Beach and Pacific Beach, which have many small hotels, motels, and hostels. All these coastal areas have a casual atmosphere and busy thoroughfares that provide endless shopping, dining, and nightlife possibilities. You can't go wrong with any of these beachfront areas, as long as the frenzy of crowds at play doesn't bother you.

$$$$ ☒ Crystal Pier Hotel. Crystal Pier, a Pacific Beach landmark, had its grand opening in 1927; 10 years later, the first of these cottages were built. They are rustic little oases with a charm all their own. True, they lack some of the amenities of comparably priced hotels, but you're paying for character and proximity to the ocean—the blue-and-white cottages here are literally on the pier. The units sleep four but cost the same no matter what the occupancy; only one has air-conditioning. Call four to six weeks in advance for reservations. There's a minimum stay requirement of three nights from mid-June through September, two nights the rest of the year. The cottages are a bargain in off-season. ☒ *4500 Ocean Blvd., Pacific Beach, 92109* ☎ *858/483–6983 or 800/748–5894* 🖷 *858/483–6811* ⊕ *www.crystalpier.com* 🖘 *29 cottages* ⚥ *Kitchenettes, cable TV, beach, fishing, free parking; no a/c in some rooms, no smoking* ☱ *D, MC, V.*

$$$$ ☒ Pacific Terrace Hotel. This terrific beachfront hotel offers great ocean views from most rooms and is the perfect place for watching sunsets over the Pacific. Private balconies (or patios) and coffeemakers come with every room; eight of the suites have indoor hot tubs. Continental breakfast is complimentary, as is the daily delivery of the *San Diego Union-Tribune*. Even the smallest room is fairly large. The friendly, casual staff makes for a comfortable stay. ☒ *610 Diamond St., Pacific Beach 92109* ☎ *858/581–3500 or 800/344–3370* 🖷 *858/274–3341* ⊕ *www. pacificterrace.com* 🖘 *73 rooms, 12 suites* ⚥ *In-room safes, some kitchenettes, minibars, cable TV with movies and video games, in-room data ports, pool, outdoor hot tub, laundry service, Internet, meeting rooms, parking (fee); no smoking* ☱ *AE, D, DC, MC, V* ❧❘ *CP.*

$$$$ ☒ Paradise Point Resort & Spa. The beautiful landscape at this 44-acre resort on Vacation Isle has been the setting for a number of movies. The botanical gardens have ponds, waterfalls, footbridges, waterfowl, and more than 600 varieties of tropical plants, a convincing backdrop for the Balinese spa. Many recreation activities are offered and there's access to a marina. The room's bright fabrics and plush carpets are cheery; unfortunately, the walls here are motel-thin. ☒ *1404 W. Vacation Rd., Mission Bay 92109* ☎ *858/274–4630 or 800/344–2626* 🖷 *858/581–5929* ⊕ *www.paradisepoint.com* 🖘 *462 cottages* ⚥ *3 restaurants, room service, refrigerators, cable TV with movies, in-room data ports, putting green, 6 tennis courts, 6 pools, pond, fitness classes, gym, outdoor hot tub, massage, sauna, spa, beach, boating, jet skiing, bicycles, croquet, shuffleboard, volleyball, 2 bars, concierge, business services, meeting rooms, airport shuttle, free parking; no smoking* ☱ *AE, D, DC, MC, V.*

$$$–$$$$ ☒ Bahia Resort Hotel. This huge complex on a 14-acre peninsula in Mission Bay Park has studios and suites with kitchens; many have wood-beam ceilings and a tropical theme. The hotel's Victorian-style sternwheeler, the *Bahia Belle*, offers guests complimentary cruises on the bay at sunset. Room rates are reasonable for a place so well located—within walking distance of the ocean—and with so many amenities, including use of the facilities at its sister hotel, the nearby Catamaran. ✉ *998 W. Mission Bay Dr., Mission Bay 92109* ☎ *858/488–0551 or 800/ 576–4229* 🖷 *858/488–1387* ⊕ *www.bahiahotel.com* 🍽 *321 rooms* ♨ *Restaurant, room service, kitchenettes, cable TV with movies, in-room data ports, 2 tennis courts, pool, gym, outdoor hot tub, boating, bicycles, 2 bars, shops, business services, meeting rooms, free parking; no smoking* ▭ *AE, D, DC, MC, V.*

$$$–$$$$ 🏨 **Best Western Blue Sea Lodge.** All rooms in this low-rise have patios or balconies, and many have ocean views. Suites have kitchenettes, and many of them front the ocean. A shopping center with restaurants and boutiques is nearby. ✉ *707 Pacific Beach Dr., Pacific Beach 92109* ☎ *858/488–4700 or 800/258–3732* 🖷 *858/488–7276* ⊕ *www.bestwestern-bluesea.com* 🍽 *128 rooms, 10 suites* ♨ *Café, in-room safes, some kitchenettes, cable TV with movies, pool, outdoor hot tub, fishing, bicycles, laundry service, concierge, travel services, parking (fee); no smoking* ▭ *AE, D, DC, MC, V.*

$$$–$$$$ 🏨 **Catamaran Resort Hotel.** Exotic birds perch in the lush lobby of this ap-
Fodor's Choice pealing hotel on Mission Bay. Tiki torches light the way through grounds
★ thick with tropical foliage to the six two-story buildings and the 14-story high-rise. The room design continues the Hawaiian theme. The popular Cannibal Bar hosts rock bands; a classical or jazz pianist tickles the ivories nightly at the Moray Bar. The resort's many water-oriented activities include free cruises on Mission Bay aboard the *Bahia Belle* stern-wheeler. ✉ *3999 Mission Blvd., Mission Beach 92109* ☎ *858/488–1081 or 800/ 422–8386* 🖷 *858/488–1387* ⊕ *www.catamaranresort.com* 🍽 *313 rooms* ♨ *Restaurant, room service, kitchenettes, refrigerators, cable TV with movies, in-room data ports, pool, gym, outdoor hot tub, beach, boating, jet skiing, bicycles, volleyball, 2 bars, nightclub, shops, business services, meeting rooms, parking (fee); no smoking* ▭ *AE, D, DC, MC, V.*

$$$–$$$$ 🏨 **Hilton San Diego Resort.** Trees, Japanese bridges, and ponds surround the bungalows at this deluxe resort; rooms and suites in the high-rise have views of Mission Bay. Rooms are well-appointed, with wet bars, coffeemakers, and spacious bathrooms; all have patios or balconies. Children stay free, and there's complimentary day care for children over five (daily in summer, on weekends the rest of the year). The sports facilities are excellent and aquatic sports equipment is available for rent at the resort's own boat dock on the beach. The Bayside Terrace Grill serves California coastal cuisine. Villa di Lusso spa is a full-service spa specializing in sports and therapeutic massages. ✉ *1775 E. Mission Bay Dr., Mission Bay 92109* ☎ *619/276–4010 or 800/445–8667* 🖷 *619/275–8944* ⊕ *www.hilton.com* 🍽 *337 rooms, 20 suites* ♨ *2 restaurants, room service, minibars, refrigerators, cable TV with movies, in-room data ports, 4 putting greens, 5 tennis courts, pool, wading pool, gym, hair salon, 4 outdoor hot tubs, massage, spa, beach, boating, waterskiing, bicycles, basketball, Ping-Pong, 2 bars, children's programs (ages 5–12), playground, laundry service, concierge, business services, meeting rooms, car rental, travel services, free parking; no smoking* ▭ *AE, D, DC, MC, V.*

$$$–$$$$ 🏨 **Hyatt Islandia.** This property has rooms in several low-level, lanai-style units, as well as marina suites and rooms in a high-rise building, all in Mission Bay Park. Many rooms overlook the hotel's gardens and koi fish pond; others have dramatic views of the bay area. This hotel is famous for its lavish Sunday champagne brunch. Whale-watching expeditions depart from the Islandia's marina in winter. ✉ *1441 Quivira Rd., Mission Bay 92109* ☎ *619/224–1234 or 800/233–1234* 🖷 *858/224–0348* ⊕ *www.hyatt.com* ⮑ *346 rooms, 76 suites* ⚭ *2 restaurants, room service, some kitchenettes, cable TV with movies, in-room data ports, pool, gym, outdoor hot tub, boating, fishing, bar, shops, dry cleaning, laundry service, concierge, business services, meeting rooms, car rental, free parking; no smoking* ☰ *AE, D, DC, MC, V.*

\$\$–\$\$\$ 🏨 **Dana Inn & Marina.** This hotel with an adjoining marina has a fun aquarium in its lobby. Rooms are done in bright pastels and those on the second floor have high ceilings; some have a view of the inn's marina. SeaWorld and the beach are within walking distance. The Marina Village Conference Center next door offers meeting and banquet rooms with bay views. ✉ *1710 W. Mission Bay Dr., Mission Bay 92109* ☎ *619/222–6440 or 800/326–2466* 🖷 *619/222–5916* ⊕ *www.danainn.com* ⮑ *196 rooms* ⚭ *Restaurant, room service, cable TV with movies, 2 tennis courts, 2 pools, 2 outdoor hot tubs, boating, waterskiing, fishing, bicycles, Ping-Pong, shuffleboard, bar, laundry service, business services, meeting rooms, airport shuttle, car rental, free parking; no smoking* ☰ *AE, D, DC, MC, V.*

\$\$ 🏨 **Beach Haven Inn.** This pleasant little hotel resembles an apartment building—rooms have exterior entrances and are situated around the pool and courtyard. It's on Mission Boulevard, the main beach drag, but on a fairly quiet stretch. Within two minutes you can sink your feet into the sand of Pacific Beach, and grassy Palisades Park, famous for its sunsets, is approximately three blocks away. Continental breakfast and a daily newspaper are included. ✉ *4740 Mission Blvd., Pacific Beach 92109* ☎ *858/272–3812 or 800/831–6323* 🖷 *858/272–3532* ⊕ *www.beachhaveninn.com* ⮑ *23 rooms* ⚭ *Kitchenettes, refrigerators, cable TV with movies, pool, outdoor hot tub, laundry service, free parking; no smoking* ☰ *AE, D, DC, MC, V* ⏐◯⏐ *CP.*

\$\$ 🏨 **Diamond Head Inn.** Directly on the boardwalk facing Pacific Beach, it has many rooms overlooking the beach and classic California sunsets. It's also within three blocks of Garnet Avenue, Pacific Beach's main drag, and the Pacific Beach Pier. Continental breakfast is complimentary. ✉ *605 Diamond St., Pacific Beach 92109* ☎ *858/273–1900* 🖷 *858/274–3341* ⊕ *www.diamondheadinn.com* ⮑ *21 rooms* ⚭ *Kitchenettes, cable TV with movies, beach, free parking, some pets allowed (fee); no a/c, no smoking* ☰ *AE, D, MC, V* ⏐◯⏐ *CP.*

\$\$ 🏨 **Pacific Shores Inn.** This property is less than a half block from the beach. Rooms, some of them spacious, have a simple contemporary style. Kitchen units with multiple beds are available at reasonable rates. Continental breakfast is included. ✉ *4802 Mission Blvd., Pacific Beach 92109* ☎ *858/483–6300 or 800/826–0715* 🖷 *858/483–9276* ⊕ *www.pacificshoresinn.com* ⮑ *56 rooms, 3 suites* ⚭ *Kitchenettes, refrigerators, cable TV with movies, pool, laundry service, free parking, some pets allowed (fee); no smoking* ☰ *AE, D, DC, MC, V* ⏐◯⏐ *CP.*

\$–\$\$
Fodor's Choice
★ 🏨 **Surfer Motor Lodge.** This four-story building is right on the beach and directly behind a shopping center with restaurants and boutiques. Rooms are plain, but those on the upper floors have good views. ✉ *711 Pacific Beach Dr., Pacific Beach 92109* ☎ *858/483–7070 or 800/787–3373*

🏛 858/274–1670 ⊕ *www.surfermotorlodge.com* 🔊 *52 rooms* 🖒 *Restaurant, kitchenettes, pool, beach, bicycles, laundry service, free parking; no a/c, no smoking* ▭ *AE, DC, MC, V.*

¢–$ 🏨 **Days Inn Mission Bay.** This modest, three-story hotel is near freeways and Mission Bay, and the price is right for its simple but clean rooms. Continental breakfast is complimentary. There's no elevator. ✉ *4540 Mission Bay Dr., Mission Bay 92109* 🏛 *858/274–7888 or 800/329–7466* ⊕ *www.daysinn.com* 🔊 *116 rooms* 🖒 *In-room safes, cable TV, pool, laundry service, airport shuttle, free parking, some pets allowed (fee); no smoking* ▭ *AE, D, DC, MC, V* ⦿ *CP.*

¢   🏨 **Banana Bungalow San Diego.** Literally a few feet from the beach, this hostel's location is its greatest asset. However, dampness and sand take their toll, and some parts of the hostel are in need of repair. All dorm rooms are coed and there are a total of 70 beds. Keg and movie-night parties are held weekly, as are various organized events. Complimentary continental breakfast is served on the sundeck. There are lockers and a small TV room. ✉ *707 Reed Ave., Pacific Beach 92109* 🏛 *858/273–3060 or 800/546–7835* 🏛 *858/273–1440* ⊕ *www.bananabungalow.com* 🖒 *Beach, bicycles, volleyball, airport shuttle, travel services; no a/c, no room phones, no room TVs, no smoking* ▭ *MC, V.*

¢   🏨 **Ocean Beach International Backpackers Hostel.** This converted 1920s hotel is two blocks from the beach and offers free use of surfboards and boogie boards. There are 100 beds. Private rooms with private baths are available. Continental breakfast is complimentary, and dinner is free on Tuesday and Friday. The hostel, which is close to many Ocean Beach restaurants and nightspots, has kitchen facilities, a storage area, vending machines, a TV room, a recreation room, and a patio. Weekly rates are available. ✉ *4961 Newport Ave., Ocean Beach 92107* 🏛 *619/223–7873 or 800/339–7263* 🏛 *619/223–7881* ⊕ *members.aol.com/obihostel/hostel* 🖒 *Bicycles, recreation room, laundry service, Internet, airport shuttle; no a/c, no room TVs, no smoking* ▭ *MC, V* ⦿ *CP.*

North Park

San Diego's North Park area is close to the San Diego Zoo and Balboa Park and melds into the neighborhoods of Hillcrest, Mission Hills, and University Heights. There are not many hotels to choose from, but these neighborhoods offer pedestrian-friendly shopping districts and great restaurants.

$–$$$ 🏨 **Balboa Park Inn.** This all-suites B&B occupies four Spanish colonial–style 1915 residences connected by courtyards. Prices are reasonable for romantic one- and two-bedroom suites, done in either Italian, French, Spanish, or early-California style. Some rooms have fireplaces, whirlpool tubs, patios, and kitchens. A generous, complimentary continental breakfast is delivered to your room on Monday–Saturday mornings; you also get a newspaper. The lack of off-street parking is inconvenient, but the San Diego Zoo is a 10-minute walk away. ✉ *3402 Park Blvd., North Park 92103* 🏛 *619/298–0823 or 800/938–8181* 🏛 *619/294–8070* ⊕ *www.balboaparkinn.com* 🔊 *26 suites* 🖒 *Some kitchenettes, some microwaves, refrigerators, cable TV with movies; no a/c, no smoking* ▭ *AE, D, DC, MC, V* ⦿ *CP.*

Nightlife & the Arts

WORD OF MOUTH

"I enjoy Old Town in the evening. Go wander around and have dinner there. . . . The Gaslamp district at night is good if you want to just bar hop (many charge a cover fee)."

—ltt

NIGHTLIFE

Updated by
Andrew Collins

PEOPLE COME TO SAN DIEGO FOR THE BEACH, and during the week out-of-towners will find they're the only ones populating the clubs. Crowds come out on the weekend, siphoning off into the various nightlife districts of the city. Downtown is where the majority of cultural events—symphony, theater, and opera—happen. Just down the street is the Gaslamp Quarter, where dozens of dance clubs and martini bars, as well as the most expensive drinks and cover charges in the city can be found. The beach areas offer a more casual atmosphere. The dance clubs and bars of Pacific Beach and Mission Beach appeal to a casually dressed, college-age crowd. Ocean Beach has no dance clubs and is preferred by bikers, drinkers, and patchouli-scented fans of reggae and Grateful Dead–style jam bands.

The Uptown district around Hillcrest is the heart of San Diego's gay nightlife and home to a few coffeehouses where conversation is the entertainment. Coffeehouse culture is still prevalent throughout the county and there's usually someone playing an acoustic set any given night.

San Diego's music scene centers around rock. Hard rock, alternative rock, and indie rock dominate the music listings. Despite that fact, some of the county's best known musical artists play a softer style of music: Jewel got her start in the city's coffeehouses and Grammy-winning gospel group Nickel Creek calls San Diego home. Nevertheless, local boys Ratt, Blink-182, and hard rockers P.O.D give testament to the fact that rockers can make it out of San Diego.

Check the *Reader,* San Diego's free alternative newsweekly (it comes out every Thursday), for the lowdown on nightlife, and check *San Diego* magazine's "Restaurant & Nightlife Guide" for further ideas. Also, the *San Diego-Union Tribune* publishes a weekly (Thursday) entertainment insert, *Night and Day.*

State law prohibits the sale of alcoholic beverages after 2 AM; last call is usually at about 1:40. You must be 21 to purchase and consume alcohol—be prepared to show an ID. California also has some of the most stringent drunken-driving laws in the country; sobriety checkpoints are not an uncommon sight. Also, unless operated exclusively for private members, all bars, nightclubs, and restaurants are smoke-free—although many have patios or decks where smoking is permitted.

Casual Bars & Pubs

Aero Club (⊠ 3365 India St., Middletown ☎ 619/297–7211) is a square cinderblock building named for its proximity to the airport. Local aerospace workers have long used it as a hangout. Formerly a dive, it's now a beer, wine, and pool bar popular with hiply dressed indie rockers who stop in for the low-key atmosphere and extensive list of wines by the glass and beer on tap. The rather dominant mural showing a historical progression of fighting warplanes is true to the club's roots.

Barefoot Bar and Grill (⊠ San Diego Princess Resort, 1404 W. Vacation Rd., Mission Bay ☎ 858/274–4630), a beachfront watering hole and hotel bar with a tiki feel, attracts flocks of singles, especially on Sunday nights in spring and summer. Live music and happy-hour specials fill the joint up early, making for long latecomer lines.

Dick's Last Resort (✉ 345 4th Ave., Gaslamp Quarter ☎ 619/231–9100) is not for Emily Post adherents. The surly waitstaff and abrasive service are part of the gimmick. The rudeness notwithstanding, fun-loving party people pile into this barnlike restaurant and bar. Dick's has live music nightly and one of the most extensive beer lists in San Diego.

The Field (✉ 544 5th Ave., Gaslamp Quarter ☎ 619/232–9840) is San Diego's resident Irish pub. Showing its Celtic pride, the pub promotes local Irish folksingers throughout the week and has Irish folkdancing on Sunday evenings.

Jimmy Love's (✉ 672 5th Ave., Gaslamp Quarter ☎ 619/595–0123) combines a dance club, a sports bar, and a restaurant on two levels. Upstairs, rock, funk, R&B, and jazz bands alternate nightly. Downstairs, hang at the bar or play a game of pool. Expect lines, though—Jimmy's is loved by many.

Karl Strauss' Old Columbia Brewery & Grill (✉ 1157 Columbia St., Downtown ☎ 619/234–2739 ✉ 1044 Wall St., La Jolla ☎ 858/551–2739) was the first microbrewery in San Diego. The original locale draws an after-work downtown crowd and later fills with beer connoisseurs from all walks of life; the newer La Jolla version draws a mix of locals and tourists. Beer-to-go by the gallon is a very popular choice. The vaguely German-inspired pub food here is above average.

Live Wire (✉ 2103 El Cajon Blvd., North Park ☎ 619/291–7450) is an underground hole-in-the-wall popular with the twentysomething pierced and tattooed set. DJs spin during the week and on occasional weekends. A well-stocked jukebox is the only other entertainment in this hip dive.

Maloney's on 5th (✉ 777 5th Ave., Gaslamp Quarter ☎ 619/232–6000), part of a regional Southwestern chain, is down a flight of stairs. Inside, big-screen TVs broadcast ball games to Maloney's crowd of sports nuts, nine-to-fivers, and regular joes. Grab a seat in one of the comfy booths and make yourself at home.

Moose McGillycuddy's (✉ 535 5th Ave., Gaslamp Quarter ☎ 619/702–5595), a major pickup palace, is also a great place to go with friends or hang out with the locals. A DJ spins house and Top 40 dance music that powers the dance floor while the staff serves up drinks and Mexican food.

Nunu's (✉ 3537 5th Ave., Hillcrest ☎ 619/295–2878) might be the coolest mainstream bar in très gay Hillcrest, but don't expect a glitzy facade. This retro-cool hangout with intentionally dated decor sits within the tatty walls of a white-brick box that probably hasn't had a facelift since the LBJ administration.

O'Hungry's (✉ 2547 San Diego Ave., Old Town ☎ 619/298–0133) is famous for its yard-long beers and sing-alongs. The seafaring decor stands in juxtaposition to the Mexican-theme Old Town San Diego State Historic Park—just outside the doors. Be sure to drink up quickly, though—this landmark saloon closes at midnight.

Old Bonita Store & Bonita Beach Club (✉ 4014 Bonita Rd., Bonita ☎ 619/479–3537), a South Bay hangout, has a DJ spinning retro house music every weekend. The decor is a cross between a family restaurant and a roadhouse, but Bonita is so far removed from the city center that looks don't matter, because it's the only place to go in this part of town.

Pacific Shores (✉ 4927 Newport Ave., Ocean Beach ☎ 619/223–7549) feels a bit cramped, not to mention silly with its strange mermaid mural, but that's part of the fun. A laid-back but see-and-be-seen crowd congregates here for relatively inexpensive drinks and Sinatra-esque tunes on the juke box.

Patrick's II (✉ 428 F St., Gaslamp Quarter ☎ 619/233–3077) serves up live New Orleans–style jazz, blues, and rock in an Irish setting.

RT's Longboard Grill (✉ 1466 Garnet Ave., Pacific Beach ☎ 858/270–4030) appeals to the young, tanned beach crowd that comes by to schmooze and booze under the indoor palapas that give this lively bar a south-of-the-border feel.

Shakespeare Pub & Grille (✉ 3701 India St., Middletown ☎ 619/299–0230), despite its Little Italy locale, captures all the warmth and camaraderie of a traditional pub in England—except that here you can enjoy consistently sunny and warm weather on the sprawling patio. The bar hands pour from a long list of imported ales and stouts.

Tavern at the Beach (✉ 1200 Garnet Ave., Pacific Beach ☎ 858/272–6066), streaked with purple neon, draws fun-loving college students. Drink specials and socializing are the main attractions, although if you get bored you can always watch one of the 30 TVs.

Turf Supper Club (✉ 1116 25th St., Uptown ☎ 619/234–6363) attracts musicians and local music industry types who come here for its divey feel and the self-serve grill where you can cook or burn your steak or burger to your liking. The neighborhood may seem a little rough around the edges, but the scene inside is relaxed and friendly, with red vinyl booths and many lively conversations.

The Waterfront (✉ 2044 Kettner Blvd., Downtown ☎ 619/232–9656) is San Diego's oldest neighborhood bar. It's not actually on the waterfront, but has been the workingman's refuge in Little Italy since the days when the area was the Italian fishing community. Because the bar is considered a local landmark, developers actually constructed an apartment building around it rather than tear it down. It's also famous for its bar burgers and it's still the hangout for working-class heroes, even if most of the collars are now white.

Coffeehouses

Like the rest of California, San Diego bestows unabashed adulation on its cafés and coffeehouses. If you're in the mood for caffeine-hopping, go to the Hillcrest–North Park area on University Avenue, which is abuzz with options—all of them grinding a variety of elixirs and proffering everything from full meals to light pastries. Many offer live entertainment on weekends. Most open their doors by 7 AM and continue serving until midnight or later. The crowds are diverse, ranging from lesbian and gay fashion plates to bookish college students to yuppies.

★ **Brockton Villa Restaurant** (✉ 1235 Coast Blvd., La Jolla ☎ 858/454–7393), a palatial café overlooking La Jolla Cove, has indoor and outdoor seating, as well as scrumptious desserts and coffee drinks; the beans are roasted in San Diego. It closes at 9 most nights, earlier on Sunday and Monday.

Café Bassam (✉ 401 Market St., Gaslamp Quarter ☎ 619/557–0173) offers a Parisian-inspired coffee-sipping experience—there's also a selection of about 150 teas. This is a favorite hangout for cigar-aficionados—you can both purchase and smoke tobacco here. It's open until 2 AM most nights, 3 on Friday and Saturday.

Claire de Lune (✉ 2906 University Ave., North Park ☎ 619/688–9845), on a corner in artsy North Park, won an award for its redesign of the historic Oddfellows building. High ceilings and huge arched windows give this wooden-floored hangout a funky charm. There are sofas and armchairs for lounging as well as tables for studying. Local musicians and poets take the stage on various nights, and San Diego's most popular, and longest running, open-mike poetry night takes place every Tuesday.

★ **Extraordinary Desserts** (✉ 2929 5th Ave., Hillcrest ☎ 619/294–2132 ✉ 1430 Union St., Middletown ☎ 619/294–7001) lives up to its name, which explains why there's a line at this café, even though it has ample seating. Paris-trained Karen Krasne turns out award-winning cakes, tortes, and pastries of exceptional beauty (many are decorated with fresh flowers). The Japanese-theme patio invites you to linger over yet another coffee drink. A branch in Little Italy has a patio with teak chairs, a wine bar, and a wider selection of savory nibbles.

Gelato Vero Caffe (✉ 3753 India St., Middletown ☎ 619/295–9269) is where a mostly young crowd gathers for some fine desserts and a second-floor view of the downtown skyline. The place is usually occupied by regulars who stay for hours at a time.

Javanican (✉ 4338 Cass St., Pacific Beach ☎ 858/483–8035) serves the young beach-community set. Aside from a good cup of joe, live acoustic entertainment is a draw. Adventurous musicians can sign up to play at the open mike Monday nights. Other local musicians headline throughout the week.

Living Room (✉ 1018 Rosecrans St., Point Loma ☎ 619/222–6852) is in an old house not far from the water. The wooden floors creak and there are plenty of cubbyholes for the studious college students who are regulars here. It's a great place to catch a caffeine buzz before walking along Shelter Island. There are several other locations, including popular branches in Hillcrest and La Jolla.

Pannikin (✉ 7467 Girard Ave., La Jolla ☎ 858/454–5453) is a bright coffeehouse with indoor and outdoor seating. Amidst the regulars are folks who have been shopping and sightseeing in La Jolla's village. Several locations are scattered throughout the county.

Twiggs Bakery & Coffee House (⊠ 4590 Park Blvd., University Heights ☎ 619/296–0616) is full of the din of conversation when music isn't playing. Poetry readings and musicians playing their acoustic originals make this venue a true bohemian experience. Open mike night on Wednesday is always popular.

Upstart Crow (⊠ 835 West Harbor Dr., Seaport Village ☎ 619/232–4855) is a bookstore and coffeehouse in one. The secluded upstairs space contains the java joint and is ideal for chatting or perusing the book that you just bought. Irreverent gifts are sold, too.

Urban Grind (⊠ 3797 Park Blvd., Hillcrest ☎ 619/294–2920) ranks among the city's most gay-popular java joints. It's a great place to meet locals, read a book, work on your laptop, or simply people-watch. It's open until midnight, too.

Zanzibar Coffee Bar and Gallery (⊠ 976 Garnet Ave., Pacific Beach ☎ 858/272–4762), a cozy, dimly lighted spot along Pacific Beach's main strip, is a great place to mellow out and eavesdrop, or to just watch the club-hopping singles make their way down the street.

Comedy & Cabaret

Comedy Store La Jolla (⊠ 916 Pearl St., La Jolla ☎ 858/454–9176), like its sister establishment in Hollywood, hosts some of the best national touring and local talent. Cover charges range from nothing on open mike nights to $20 or more for national acts. A two-drink minimum applies for all shows. Seating is at bistro-style tables.

Lips (⊠ 2770 5th Ave., Hillcrest ☎ 619/295–7900) serves you dinner while female impersonators entertain. Their motto, "where the men are men and so are the girls," says it all.

Shout! House (⊠ 655 4th Ave., Gaslamp Quarter ☎ 619/231–6700), where dueling pianos and rock-and-roll sing-alongs make for a festive, even boisterous, ambience, is open only on Thursday, Friday, and Saturday—so make reservations or come early to get a good seat.

Country–Western

In Cahoots (⊠ 5373 Mission Center Rd., Mission Valley ☎ 619/291–1184), with its great sound system, large dance floor, and DJ, is the destination of choice for cowgirls, cowboys, and city slickers alike. Free dance lessons are given every day except Wednesday, when seasoned two-steppers strut their stuff. Happy hour seven days a week is one of this bar's many lures.

Mulvaney's (⊠ 8861 N. Magnolia Ave., Santee ☎ 619/448–8550) serves as East County's country-music headquarters. Line dancers kick up their heels when local bands play on Friday and Saturday nights.

Tio Leo's (⊠ 5302 Napa St., Bay Park ☎ 619/542–1462) is a throwback to the days when lounges were dark and vinyl-filled. The crowd is retro-attired as well. The lounge is in a Mexican restaurant, and an incredible variety of country, rockabilly, zydeco, and swing acts grace the small stage.

Dance Clubs

Blue Tattoo (⊠ 835 5th Ave., Gaslamp Quarter ☎ 619/231–7041) pulls in crowds of hip-hop-loving young professionals. The club is open Thursday through Sunday; entertainment is provided by a variety of DJs, and there is a nominal cover charge.

Deco's (⊠ 721 5th Ave., Gaslamp Quarter ☎ 619/696–3326) is another popular, pricey martini–dance bar in the Gaslamp Quarter. Fashionably dressed urbanites line up outside for a chance to dance in one of two main areas: the indoor room plays house while the packed open-air area in the back plays hip-hop mixes. Loungy seating, white drapes, and floor-to-ceiling windows give you the feeling you're in a friend's ritzy loft apartment for the best house party ever.

E Street Alley (⊠ 420 E. St., Gaslamp Quarter ☎ 619/231–9200), or "Club E," is one of the city's below-street-level hot spots. The smartly designed, spacious club is a treat for the senses, with a good light show on the dance floor and an exquisite restaurant and sushi bar, Chino's. DJs spin Top 40 and club tunes Thursday through Saturday.

Olé Madrid (⊠ 755 5th Ave., Gaslamp Quarter ☎ 619/557–0146) is not for the meek or mild. Leave the squares at street level and head straight to the basement for deep house grooves and tribal rhythms spun by celebrated DJs from near and far. Between songs, sip a tangy sangria. Friday and Saturday the groove goes on until 4 AM.

★ **On Broadway** (⊠ 615 Broadway, Gaslamp Quarter ☎ 619/231–0011), in a former bank building, is the most exclusive dance club in town. A long line of wannabe patrons points the way, and even the $15 cover charge does little to discourage San Diego's best-dressed young professionals from waiting hours to spend their hard-earned money inside. The club gets crowded early and stays that way until closing, making it hard to get a drink from the sometimes unfriendly staff. The huge club is only open Friday and Saturday. The marble floors, Greek columns, and original vault doors mix well with the modern decor, computerized light show, and Leviathan sound system.

Rox (⊠ 901 5th Ave., Gaslamp Quarter ☎ 619/234–4166), underneath the Dakota Grill restaurant, spins house and Top 40 dance tunes Friday and Saturday only. A state-of-the-art, 100-inch plasma screen provides eclectic visuals.

Sevilla (⊠ 555 4th Ave., Gaslamp Quarter ☎ 619/233–5979) brings a Latin flavor to the Gaslamp Quarter with its mix of contemporary and traditional Spanish and Latin American music. Get fueled up at the tapas bar before venturing downstairs for dancing. This is the best place in San Diego to take salsa lessons.

Gay & Lesbian

Men's

Baja Betty's (⊠ 1421 University Ave., Hillcrest ☎ 619/269–8510) was opened in 2004 by the same folks who operate Hamburger Mary's and Kickers. This South of the Border–theme lounge and restaurant draws plenty of gay customers. It's a low-key but rather elegant space with chandeliers and soft lighting, and it stocks some 75 brands of tequila and plenty of other fancy cocktails.

Bourbon Street (⊠ 4612 Park Blvd., University Heights ☎ 619/291–0173) is one of the popular places to meet old friends or make new ones. Several scenes exist in this one bar. The front bar is a popular karaoke spot. The outdoor courtyard draws crowds that gather to watch and comment on whatever is showing on the large-screen TV. Weekends, a back area known as the Stable Bar has DJs who turn the small room into a dance floor.

★ **Club Montage** (⊠ 2028 Hancock St., Middletown ☎ 619/294–9590) is one of the largest and best clubs in town. The three-level nightspot was originally oriented to the gay crowd, but now all types come for the high-tech lighting system and world-class DJs. For a breath of fresh air, step out to view the skyline and enjoy a drink from the rooftop bar. It's open only on Friday and Saturday, but it pulses until 4 AM.

Flicks (⊠ 1017 University Ave., Hillcrest ☎ 619/297–2056), a hip video bar that's popular with the see-and-be-seen crowd, plays music and comedy videos on four big screens. Drink specials vary each night.

Kickers (⊠ 308 University Ave., Hillcrest ☎ 619/491–0400) rounds up country-music cowboys to do the latest line dance on its wooden dance floor Thursday through Saturday. The rest of the time it offers up disco, karaoke, and pop dance tunes. Free lessons are given weeknights from 7 to 8:30. If you're hungry after all that dancing, Hamburger Mary's, on the premises, serves until 11 on weekends.

Numbers (⊠ 3811 Park Blvd., North Park ☎ 619/294–9005) has a giant-screen TV, six pool tables, darts, and daily drink specials. A casually dressed crowd comes to hang out and watch showings of *Queer as Folk* and other shows with a gay theme.

Rich's (⊠ 1051 University Ave., Hillcrest ☎ 619/295–2195), a popular dance club, has frequent male revues. Thursday night's Club Hedonism spotlights groove house and tribal rhythms and is frequented by both gay and straight revelers.

Re:Bar (⊠ 3404 30th St., North Park ☎ 619/291–3730) was a leather-and-Levi's bar called Wolf's for more than two decades before morphing in 2004 into an all-purpose gay men's club, with go-go dancers, drag performers, and dancing to standard club tunes.

Women's

Six Degrees (⊠ 3175 India St., Middletown ☎ 619/296–6789), formerly Club Bom Bay, is still a popular hangout. It occasionally has live entertainment and always attracts a dancing crowd. It also hosts weekend barbecues.

The Flame (⊠ 3780 Park Blvd., Hillcrest ☎ 619/295–4163) has a red neon sign resembling a torch with a flame on top. A San Diego institution, this friendly dance club was remodeled after new (male) owners took over in 2003; it's still extremely popular with lesbians, but now guys sometimes hang out here, too.

Hip Lounges & Trendy Singles Bars

Altitude Skybar (⊠ 660 K St., Gaslamp Quarter ☎ 619/696–0234), which opened early in 2005 inside the swank new Marriott Hotel Gaslamp Quarter, occupies the hotel's 22nd-story rooftop. It's a great spot not only to people-watch but to admire the city skyline.

Bitter End (⊠ 770 5th Ave., Gaslamp Quarter ☎ 619/338–9300) is a trilevel martini bar and dance club that draws a crowd any night of the week. With its dark, molded wood paneling and a few overstuffed armchairs, at times you get the feeling of being in your rich uncle's study. Except that your uncle probably wouldn't make you stand in the long lines that form here on weekends. The martinis are potent and a stylish, dressy crowd keeps the night interesting.

Cafe Japengo (⊠ 8960 University Center La., La Jolla ☎ 858/450–3355) is the post–work socializing spot for young La Jolla professionals. A sushi bar is one draw, but most come here for the singles scene that plays itself out nightly.

5ifth Quarter (⊠ 600 5th Ave., Gaslamp Quarter ☎ 619/236–1616) is popular with the happy-hour sports crowd because of its 32 flat-screen and two big-screen TVs. Later in the evening, bands play retro disco, R&B, and '80s music. This locale has long been a major stop on the bachelorette party circuit.

Jose's Court Room (⊠ 1037 Prospect St., La Jolla ☎ 858/454–7655) is a hit with yuppies from La Jolla and other neighboring beach communities. This small but clean hole-in-the-wall's lack of space gives suave singles an excuse to get up close and personal.

Martini Ranch (⊠ 528 F St., Gaslamp Quarter ☎ 619/235–6100) mixes more than 30 varieties of its namesake. Actually two clubs in one, the original Martini Ranch hosts jazz groups on weekdays and a DJ spinning an eclectic mix on Friday and Saturday. Next door in the larger Shaker Room, local and traveling DJs spin all-star dance beats. In either room, if you ask nicely, the bartenders might show you one of their tricks, like mixing a martini on the forehead or pouring five drinks at one time.

Moondoggies (⊠ 832 Garnet Ave., Pacific Beach ☎ 858/483–6550) is not just for Gidget anymore, but is home to a mixed, laid-back crowd of people who don't mind bumping into each other or minor beer spills. A large, airy sports bar feel is heightened by the dozens of TVs in every available spot. Many TVs show surf and skate videos that remind you the beach is only two blocks away. A large, heated outdoor patio draws smokers. Occasionally, local rock, funk, or reggae bands play here.

Onyx Room/Thin (✉ 852 5th Ave., Gaslamp Quarter ☎ 619/235–6699) is the hippest split-level in town. Although Onyx and Thin are separate clubs, the fact that they share the same owners and building makes for many options as you move back and forth between the two, sampling each bar's distinctive decor and ambience. Onyx is downstairs and feels like two bars in one. In front there's a mood-lighted cocktail lounge, and in the next room acid-jazz bands and DJs keep the crowds dancing on the tiny dance floor. Thin, the upstairs venue, has a stainless-steel–heavy interior that could be the inside of a UFO. Thin is more conducive to the conversation-minded, although a DJ spins down-tempo acid jazz and funk tunes on weekends. Weekend cover charges allow entrance to both clubs.

Pacific Beach Bar & Grill (✉ 860 Garnet Ave., Pacific Beach ☎ 858/272–1242) is a block away from the beach. The popular nightspot has a huge outdoor patio so you can enjoy star-filled skies as you party. The lines here on the weekends are generally the longest of any club in Pacific Beach. There's plenty to see and do, from billiards and satellite TV sports to an interactive trivia game. The grill takes orders until 1 AM, so it's a great place for a late-night snack.

Side Bar (✉ 536 Market St., Downtown ☎ 619/696–0946), opened in 2003, is one of a few new, ultraposh lounges that have helped restore glamour to downtown. This stylish space with low-slung sofas and lounge chairs and mod lighting also has a pleasant patio, perfect for a breath of fresh air when you're tired of posing inside. DJ's spin a mix of house, underground, and hip-hop, and the bartenders turn out the usual range of fancy, colorful cocktails.

Typhoon Saloon (✉ 1165 Garnet Ave., Pacific Beach ☎ 858/373–3444) is an obligatory stop for college-age singles club-hopping on weekend nights. There are several levels, four bars, and two small dance floors. DJs play a Top 40 mix.

Fodor'sChoice The **W Hotel** (✉ 421 West B St., Downtown ☎ 619/231–8220) has
★ three bars, and together they've become the trendiest places to be for the young bar-hopping set. Start at the ground floor Living Room, where cozy chairs and couches in alcoves give a true lounge feel. You can take your drink from bar to bar, so move next to Rice, a restaurant bar where you can grab a bite to eat before heading to the beach—or, more accurately, Beach, the W's open-air rooftop with private beach cabanas, firepits, and tons of heated sand covering the floor. Get here before 9 PM on weekends to avoid a line.

Jazz

★ **Elario's Sky Lounge** (✉ 7955 La Jolla Shores Dr., La Jolla ☎ 858/459–0541) is the reincarnation of one of San Diego's most famous jazz venues, which closed in the mid-1990s, then returned half a decade later in a slightly different format. Perched on the top floor of the Hotel La

Jolla, Elario's delivers an ocean view and a lineup of locally acclaimed jazz musicians Tuesday through Saturday.

Croce's (⊠ 802 5th Ave., Gaslamp Quarter ☎ 619/233–4355), the intimate jazz cave of restaurateur Ingrid Croce (widow of singer-songwriter Jim Croce), books superb acoustic-jazz musicians.

Croce's Top Hat (⊠ 818 5th Ave., Gaslamp Quarter ☎ 619/233–4355), next door to Croce's, puts on live R&B nightly from 9 to 2. Musician A. J. Croce, son of Jim and Ingrid, often headlines at both clubs.

Dizzy's (⊠ 344 7th Ave., Gaslamp Quarter ☎ 858/270–7467) is one of the few venues in town that's totally devoted to music and the arts. The late-night jazz jam is your best bet on Friday after midnight. During the week you can count on the best in jazz, visual and performance-art shows, and the occasional spoken-word event. Refreshments are sold, but no alcohol is served.

Galoka (⊠ 5662 La Jolla Blvd., La Jolla ☎ 858/551–8610) offers the strange yet pleasing mix of very hot improvisational jazz and hip-hop music paired with a restaurant serving first-rate vegetarian Indian food. Somehow it all works, as evidenced by the packed (and very happy) crowds. It's open only Thursday through Sunday.

Humphrey's by the Bay (⊠ 2241 Shelter Island Dr., Shelter Island ☎ 619/224–3577), surrounded by water, is the summer stomping grounds of musicians such as the Cowboy Junkies and Chris Isaak. From June through September this dining and drinking oasis hosts the city's best outdoor jazz, folk, and light-rock concert series. The rest of the year the music moves indoors for some first-rate jazz most Sunday, Monday, and Tuesday nights, with piano-bar music on other nights.

Live Music Clubs

Belly Up Tavern (⊠ 143 S. Cedros Ave., Solana Beach ☎ 858/481–9022), a fixture on local papers' "best of" lists, has been drawing crowds of all ages since it opened in the mid-'70s. The "BUT"s longevity attests to the quality of the eclectic entertainment on its stage. Within converted Quonset huts, critically acclaimed artists play everything from reggae and folk to—well, you name it.

Blind Melons (⊠ 710 Garnet Ave., Pacific Beach ☎ 858/483–7844), a small, dark space, hosts well-known local and, occasionally, national bands playing rock, reggae, and especially potent blues. This is a good place to enjoy a drink before or after a nice walk on the boardwalk or on Crystal Pier, literally just steps away.

Brick by Brick (⊠ 1130 Buenos Ave., Bay Park ☎ 619/275–5483), a recently spruced up space in an industrial neighborhood, is always cranking out punk, alternative, or hard rock. Occasionally blues or underground dance acts will make an appearance, making this a very eclectic club.

'Canes Bar and Grill (⊠ 3105 Ocean Front Walk, Mission Beach ☎ 858/488–1780) is closer to the ocean than any other music venue in town. Step outside for a walk on the beach where the sounds of the national rock, reggae, and hip-hop acts onstage create a cacophony with the crashing waves. Step back inside to enjoy some of the best cutting-edge tunes in town.

Cannibal Bar (✉ 3999 Mission Blvd., Pacific Beach ☏ 858/539–8651) offers an eclectic lineup of live music acts. Swing, jazz, rock, and reggae are possibilities, and some nights a DJ spins tunes—usually Top 40 or classic rock. Because of its beach location, in the Catamaran Resort Hotel, this nightclub with a tropical theme attracts patrons of all ages, both visitors and locals, especially when it presents high-profile bands.

Casbah (✉ 2501 Kettner Blvd., Middletown ☏ 619/232–4355), near the airport, is a small club with a national reputation for showcasing up-and-coming acts. Nirvana, Smashing Pumpkins, and Alanis Morissette all played the Casbah on their way to stardom. Within San Diego, it's widely recognized as the headquarters of the indie rock scene. You can hear every type of band here—except those that sound like Top 40.

Dream Street (✉ 2228 Bacon St., Ocean Beach ☏ 619/222–8131) is the place to see up-and-coming (or good enough to drink to) local rock bands. The music is on the heavy side and the biker and rocker crowd that hangs out here can have a scary look about them. This is not the place for a quiet evening out.

4th & B (✉ 345 B St., Downtown ☏ 619/231–4343) is a live-music venue housed in a former bank that is only open when a concert is booked. All styles of music and occasional comedy acts take the stage.

Over the Border (✉ 3008 Main St., Chula Vista ☏ 619/427-5889) is the home of *rock en español* in San Diego. Cover bands usually play the weekends, but some of the top Latin Rock bands make this unassuming cinderblock club a destination for concertgoers from both sides of the border.

Soma (✉ 3350 Sports Arena Blvd., Sports Arena ☏ 619/226–7662) is a name that has been associated with the San Diego music scene since the '80s. Now near the Sports Arena, this all-ages club occupies a former cinema mulitplex converted into two concert halls. A smaller room features local acts while the huge main hall hosts some of the top touring indie rock and punk bands. Regardless of the room, Soma crowds love their mosh pits. There's no seating, so the uninitiated are advised to stand on the sidelines.

Winston's (✉ 1921 Bacon St., Ocean Beach ☏ 619/222–6822) is a sure bet for quality music in Ocean Beach. In a bowling alley–turned–rock club, Winston's hosts local bands, reggae groups, and occasionally 1960s-style bands. The crowd, mostly locals, are typically mellow, but can get rowdy.

Night Bay Cruises

Bahia Belle (✉ 998 W. Mission Bay Dr., Mission Bay ☏ 858/539–7630) is a stern-wheeler offering relaxing evening cruises along Mission Bay that include cocktails, dancing, and live music. Board from the Bahia

Resort Hotel. Cruises run from Wednesday through Sunday in summer and Friday and Saturday in winter (but no cruises in December). The $6 fare is less than most nightclub covers.

Hornblower Cruises (⊠ 1066 N. Harbor Dr., Downtown ☎ 619/668–4322) makes nightly dinner-dance cruises aboard the *Lord Hornblower*—passengers are treated to fabulous views of the San Diego skyline.

San Diego Harbor Excursion (⊠ 1050 N. Harbor Dr., Downtown ☎ 619/234–4111 or 800/442–7847) welcomes guests aboard with a glass of champagne as a prelude to nightly dinner-dance cruises.

Piano Bars

Hotel Del Coronado (⊠ 1500 Orange Ave., Coronado ☎ 619/522–8490), the famous fairy-tale hostelry, has piano music in its Crown Room and Palm Court. The Ocean Terrace Lounge has bands nightly 9–1.

Inn at the Park (⊠ 3167 5th Ave., Hillcrest ☎ 619/296–0057) offers large booths to settle into as a piano player entertains nightly beginning at 7 PM. This gay-popular venue makes for a nice stop after a day in Balboa Park.

Old Venice (⊠ 2910 Canon St., Point Loma ☎ 619/222–5888), a small restaurant-bar, attracts a good crowd of locals on weekdays with its casual, artsy atmosphere. It's a good bar to go to if you prefer not to have to raise your voice just to have a conversation.

Palace Bar (⊠ 311 Island Ave., Gaslamp Quarter ☎ 619/544–1886), in the historic Horton Grand Hotel, is one of the mellowest lounges in the Gaslamp Quarter. Rest up in an overstuffed chair and cradle your drink while deciding what sights to see next.

Top of the Cove (⊠ 1216 Prospect St., La Jolla ☎ 858/454–7779), also a magnificent contemporary European-American restaurant, has pianists playing show tunes and standards from the 1940s to the present. A well-heeled set hobnobs and peruses the extensive wine list, which includes more than 1,000 selections. The candlelight, brick walls, and overstuffed booths make a great setting from which to enjoy the panoramic views of La Jolla Cove.

Fodor'sChoice **Top of the Hyatt** (⊠ 1 Market Pl., Embarcadero ☎ 619/232–1234) ★ crowns the tallest waterfront building in California, affording great views of San Diego Bay, including Coronado to the west, the San Diego–Coronado Bridge and Mexico to the south, and Point Loma and La Jolla to the north. The wood paneling and mood lighting affect one of the most romantic spots in town. Tables by the windows always seem to be occupied longer because of the view and the well-padded chairs.

U. S. Grant Hotel (⊠ 326 Broadway, Gaslamp Quarter ☎ 619/232–3121), a favorite of the over-thirty business set, is the classiest spot in town for meeting fellow travelers while relaxing with a Manhattan or a martini at the mahogany bar. The best local Latin, jazz, and blues bands alternate appearances. The entire hotel, including the bar, underwent a massive overhaul in spring 2005.

Westgate Hotel (⌧ 1055 2nd Ave., Gaslamp Quarter ☎ 619/238–1818) is one of the most elegant settings in San Diego. "Old Money" is evoked with leather upholstered seats, marble tabletops, and a grand piano.

THE ARTS

National touring companies perform regularly at the 3,000-seat Civic Theatre, and in Escondido at the California Center for the Arts. Programs at San Diego State University, the University of California at San Diego, private universities, and community colleges host a range of artists, from well-known professionals to students. The *San Diego Union-Tribune* lists attractions and complete movie schedules. The *Reader* weekly devotes an entire section to upcoming cultural events. *San Diego* magazine publishes monthly listings and reviews. It's also worth checking out San Diego's many community micromags, found in most coffeehouses. You can also scan arts listings and book tickets through the Web site of **San Diego Art + Sol** (⊕ www.sandiegoartandsol.com), which is produced by a partnership of organizations, including the City of San Diego Commission for Arts and Culture and the San Diego Convention & Visitors Bureau.

Book tickets well in advance, preferably at the same time you make hotel reservations. Outlets selling last-minute tickets do exist, but you risk paying top rates or getting less-than-choice seats—or both.

You can buy half-price tickets to most theater, music, and dance events on the day of performance at **Times Arts Tix** (⌧ Horton Plaza, Gaslamp Quarter ☎ 619/497–5000). Advance full-price tickets are also sold here. **Ticketmaster** (☎ 619/220–8497) sells tickets to many performances. Service charges vary according to the event, and most tickets are non-refundable.

Dance

California Ballet Company (☎ 858/560–6741) performs high-quality contemporary and traditional works, from story ballets to Balanchine, September–May. The *Nutcracker* is staged annually at the **Civic Theatre** (⌧ 202 C St., Downtown); other ballets are presented at the **Lyceum** (⌧ 79 Horton Plaza, Gaslamp Quarter) and at the **Poway Center for the Performing Arts** (⌧ 15498 Espola Rd., Poway ☎ 858/668–4798).

San Diego Ballet (⌧ 5304 Metro St., Downtown ☎ 619/294–7378) performs a vast repertory of classic and contemporary ballets at several venues countywide.

Eveoke Dance Theater (⌧ 644 7th Ave., Downtown ☎ 619/238–1153), San Diego's major avant–garde dance company, performs a regular season of dance theater works, produces several special events, and presents community-focused classes and exhibitions.

Malashock (☎ 619/260–1622), the city's esteemed modern dance company, presents edgy, intriguing works at venues throughout the city; Malashock has often collaborated on performances with the San Diego Opera, the San Diego Symphony, and other important cultural institutions.

Film

Landmark Theatres (☎ 619/819–0236), known for first-run foreign, art, American independent, and documentary offerings, operates the following three theaters in the San Diego area. **La Jolla Village Cinemas** (✉ 8879 Villa La Jolla Dr., La Jolla) is a modern multiplex set in a shopping center. **Hillcrest Cinemas** (✉ 3965 5th Ave., Hillcrest) is a posh multiplex right in the middle of uptown's action. **Ken Cinema** (✉ 4061 Adams Ave., Kensington) is considered by many to be the last bastion of true avant-garde film in San Diego. It plays a roster of art and revival films that changes almost every night (many programs are double bills). It publishes its listings in the *Ken,* a small newspaper distributed in nearly every coffeehouse and music store in the county.

In its 226-seat theater, the **Museum of Photographic Arts** (✉ 1649 El Prado, Balboa Park ☎ 619/238–7559) runs a regular film program that includes classic American and international cinema by prominent filmmakers, as well as the occasional cult film. Each screening is preceded by an informative introduction from the museum staff.

The 500-seat **Sherwood Auditorium** (✉ 700 Prospect St., La Jolla ☎ 858/ 454–3541), at the Museum of Contemporary Art, hosts foreign and classic film series and special cinema events, including the wildly popular Festival of Animation, from January through March.

Science, space-documentary, observation-of-motion, and sometimes psychedelic films are shown on the IMAX screen at the **Reuben H. Fleet Science Center** (✉ 1875 El Prado, Balboa Park ☎ 619/238–1233).

Music

Coors Amphitheatre (✉ 2050 Otay Valley Rd., Chula Vista ☎ 619/671– 3500), the largest concert venue in town, can accommodate 20,000 concertgoers with reserved seats and lawn seating. It presents top-selling national and international acts during its late-spring to late-summer season.

Copley Symphony Hall (✉ 750 B St., Downtown ☎ 619/235–0804) has great acoustics surpassed only by an incredible Spanish Baroque interior. Not just the home of the San Diego Symphony Orchestra, the renovated 2,200-seat 1920s-era theater has also presented such popular musicians as Elvis Costello and Sting.

Cox Arena (✉ San Diego State University, 5500 Canyon Crest Dr., College Area ☎ 619/594–6947) attracts top-name acts like Eric Clapton and Depeche Mode to its 12,500-person confines.

East County Performing Arts Center (✉ 210 E. Main St., El Cajon ☎ 619/ 440–2277) hosts a variety of performing arts events, but mostly music. Internationally touring jazz, classical, blues, and world-beat musicians have ensured its popularity among locals.

La Jolla Music Society (☎ 858/459–3728) presents internationally acclaimed chamber ensembles, orchestras, and soloists at Sherwood Auditorium and the Civic Theatre.

Open-Air Theatre (⊠ San Diego State University, 5500 Campanile Dr., College Area ☎ 619/594–6947) presents top-name rock, reggae, and popular artists in summer concerts under the stars.

San Diego Chamber Orchestra (☎ 858/350–0290), a 50-member ensemble, performs once a month, October–April, in a number of different venues, including St. Joseph's Cathedral downtown.

San Diego Opera (⊠ Civic Theatre, 3rd Ave. and B St., Downtown ☎ 619/533–7000) draws international artists. Its season runs January–May. Past performances have included *Die Fledermaus, Faust, Idomeneo,* and *La Bohème,* plus concerts by such talents as Luciano Pavarotti.

San Diego Sports Arena (⊠ 3500 Sports Arena Blvd., Sports Arena ☎ 619/224–4171) holds 13,000-plus fans for big-name concerts.

San Diego State University School of Music and Dance (☎ 619/594–1696) presents concerts in many genres, including jazz, classical, and world music in different venues on campus.

San Diego Symphony Orchestra (⊠ 750 B St., Downtown ☎ 619/235–0804) puts on special events year-round, including classical concerts and summer and winter pops. Concerts are held at Copley Symphony Hall, except the Summer Pops series, which is held on the Embarcadero, beyond the San Diego Convention Center on North Harbor Drive.

Sherwood Auditorium (⊠ 700 Prospect St., La Jolla ☎ 858/454–2594), a 500-seat venue in the Museum of Contemporary Art, hosts classical and jazz events.

Spreckels Organ Pavilion (⊠ Balboa Park ☎ 619/702–8138) holds a giant outdoor pipe organ donated to the city in 1914 by sugar magnates John and Adolph Spreckels. The beautiful Spanish Baroque pavilion hosts concerts by civic organist Carol Williams on most Sunday afternoons and on most Monday evenings in summer. Local military bands, gospel groups, and barbershop quartets also perform here. All shows are free.

Spreckels Theatre (⊠ 121 Broadway, Downtown ☎ 619/235–9500), a designated-landmark theater erected in 1912, hosts musical events—everything from mostly Mozart to small rock concerts. Ballets and theatrical productions are also held here. Its good acoustics and historical status make this a special venue.

Theater

California Center for the Arts, Escondido (⊠ 340 N. Escondido Blvd., Escondido ☎ 800/988–4253) presents mainstream theatrical productions such as *Grease* and *The Odd Couple.*

Coronado Playhouse (⊠ Ferry Landing, 1335 1st St., Coronado ☎ 619/435–4856), a cabaret-type theater near the Hotel Del Coronado, stages regular dramatic and musical performances. Friday and Saturday dinner packages are available.

Cygnet Theatre (✉ 6663 El Cajon Blvd., East San Diego ☎ 619/435–4856) shows a mix of contemporary hits, modern classics, and offbeat comedies and musicals.

Diversionary Theatre (✉ 4545 Park Blvd., University Heights ☎ 619/220–0097) is San Diego's premier gay and lesbian company. It presents a range of original works that focus on gay and lesbian themes.

Horton Grand Theatre (✉ Hahn Cosmopolitan Theatre, 444 4th Ave., Gaslamp Quarter ☎ 619/234–9583) stages the long-running comedy, *Triple Espresso,* in its 250-seat space.

La Jolla Playhouse (✉ Mandell Weiss Center for the Performing Arts, University of California at San Diego, 2910 La Jolla Village Dr., La Jolla ☎ 858/550–1010) crafts exciting and innovative productions under the artistic direction of Dess McAnuff, May–November. Many Broadway shows, such as *Tommy* and *How to Succeed in Business Without Really Trying,* have previewed here before heading for the East Coast.

La Jolla Stage Company (✉ The Firehouse, 7877 Herschel Ave., La Jolla ☎ 858/459–7773) presents lavish productions of Broadway favorites and popular comedies year-round.

Lamb's Players Theatre (✉ 1142 Orange Ave., Coronado ☎ 619/437–0600) has a regular season of five productions from February through November and stages a musical, "Festival of Christmas," in December. "An American Christmas" is the company's dinner-theater event at the Hotel Del Coronado.

Lyceum Theatre (✉ 79 Horton Plaza, Gaslamp Quarter ☎ 619/544–1000) is the home of the San Diego Repertory Theatre and also presents productions from visiting theater companies.

Lyric Opera San Diego (✉ North Park Theatre, 2895 University Ave., North Park ☎ 619/239–8836) presents a variety of operas, operettas, and other musical theater productions including several Gilbert and Sullivan works each season. The company moved into the new Stephen and Mary Birch North Park Theatre in fall 2005.

Marie Hitchcock Puppet Theatre (✉ 2130 Pan American Rd. W, Balboa Park ☎ 619/685–5990) entertains with amateur and professional puppeteers and ventriloquists five days a week. The cost is just a few dollars for adults and children alike. If you feel cramped in the small theater, don't worry; the shows rarely run longer than a half hour.

Old Globe Theatre (✉ Off El Prado, Balboa Park ☎ 619/234–5623) is the oldest professional theater in California, presenting classics, contemporary dramas, and experimental works. It produces the famous summer Shakespeare Festival at the Old Globe and its sister theaters, the Cassius Carter Centre Stage and the Lowell Davies Festival Theatre.

Poway Center for the Performing Arts (✉ 15498 Espola Rd., Poway ☎ 858/748–0505), an ambitious theater in suburban San Diego, presents musical comedy and other lighthearted fare.

San Diego Junior Theater (☎ 619/239–8355) is a highly regarded school where children ages 8–18 study acting, singing, and dancing. Their productions are held at the school's home base, the Casa del Prado Theatre in Balboa Park, as well as at the Theatre on Third in Chula Vista and the Firehouse in La Jolla.

San Diego Repertory Theatre (✉ Lyceum Theatre, 79 Horton Plaza, Gaslamp Quarter ☎ 619/544–1000), San Diego's first resident acting company, performs contemporary works year-round.

San Diego State University Drama Department (✉ Don Powell Theatre and elsewhere on campus, 5500 Campanile Dr., College Area ☎ 619/594–6947) presents contemporary and classic dramas.

Sixth at Penn Theatre (✉ 6th Ave. at Pennsylvania Ave., Hillcrest ☎ 619/688–9210) performs superbly rendered classics and cutting-edge, provocative plays, often with gay and lesbian themes.

Sledgehammer Theatre (✉ 1620 6th Ave., Uptown ☎ 619/544–1484), one of San Diego's cutting-edge theaters, stages avant-garde pieces in St. Cecilia's Playhouse, a former church.

Starlight Musical Theatre (✉ Starlight Bowl, 2005 Pan American Plaza, Balboa Park ☎ 619/544–7827), a summertime favorite, is a series of musicals performed in an outdoor amphitheater mid-June–early September. Because of the theater's proximity to the airport, actors often have to freeze mid-scene while a plane flies over.

Sushi Performance & Visual Art (☎ 619/235–8469), a nationally acclaimed group, provides an opportunity for well-known performance artists to do their thing at a variety of venues around town. As of this writing, they were looking for a permanent home downtown, so stay tuned.

Theatre in Old Town (✉ 4040 Twiggs St., Old Town ☎ 619/688–2494) presents punchy revues and occasional classics, usually one show for many months at a time. (As of this writing, it was *The Male Intellect: An Oxymoron.* Previous shows like *Forbidden Broadway, Ruthless, Gilligan's Island,* and *Forbidden Hollywood* have made this a popular place.)

UCSD Theatre (✉ Mandell Weiss Center for the Performing Arts, University of California at San Diego, 2910 La Jolla Village Dr. and Expedition Way, La Jolla ☎ 858/534–4574) presents productions by students in the university's theater department, September–May.

Welk Resort Theatre (✉ 8860 Lawrence Welk Dr., Escondido ☎ 760/749–3448 or 888/802–7469), a famed dinner theater about a 45-minute drive northeast of downtown on I–15, puts on polished Broadway-style productions.

Sports & the Outdoors

Updated by
Andrew Collins **SAN DIEGO HAS A REPUTATION** as an active, outdoors-oriented community. The reputation makes perfect sense given the near perfect weather and the wealth of places to play: ocean, bay, lakes, mountains, deserts, parks, and golf courses offer a chance to practice nearly any sport conceivable. The ocean especially is one of San Diego's most popular natural attractions. Surfers, swimmers, kayakers, divers, snorkelers, sailboarders, and even kiteboarders have 70 mi of shorefront to explore. You can rent equipment and take lessons in any one of these sports or simply enjoy a fishing or whale-watching excursion aboard a charter boat. Even if you're inclined to do no more than sightsee, you can take a low-impact sunset stroll on a wide, sandy beach or explore secluded coves at low tide and study the microcosm of a tide pool.

The north coastal section of the county has lured many resident professional triathletes, surfers, and bicyclists, who all take advantage of the climate, both meteorologic and social, which looks favorably upon them. There's excellent hiking, mountain biking, and horseback riding in the county's eastern foothills and mountains.

At the end of the day at any beach in the county, you'll see a daily ritual as locals cease all activity to silently observe the sunset over the water.

Ballooning

Enjoy views of the Pacific Ocean, the mountains, and the coastline south to Mexico and north to San Clemente from a hot-air balloon at sunrise or sunset; most excursions include beverages and snacks, too. The conditions are perfect: necessary winds and wide-open spaces. **California Dreamin'** (⊠ 33133 Vista del Monte Rd., Temecula ☎ 800/373–3359 ⊕ www.californiadreamin.com) specializes in Temecula wine country flights and Del Mar sunset coastal excursions. **Skysurfer Balloon Company** (⊠ 1221 Camino del Mar, Del Mar ☎ 858/481–6800 or 800/660–6809 ⊕ www.sandiegohotairballoons.com) lifts off from several locations and will take you on one-hour flights in North County or Temecula.

Baseball

Long a favorite spectator sport in San Diego, where games are rarely rained out, baseball gained even more popularity in 2004 with the opening of Petco Park, a stunning 42,000-seat facility right in the heart of downtown. The **San Diego Padres** (⊠ 100 Park Blvd., Downtown ☎ 619/795–5000 or 877/374–2784 ⊕ www.sandiegopadres.com) slug it out for bragging rights in the National League West from April into October. Tickets are usually available on game day, but games with such rivals as the Los Angeles Dodgers and the San Francisco Giants usually sell out more quickly.

Basketball

Although there have been a few attempts to bring pro and semi-pro basketball to San Diego, no team has endured. Diehard basketball fans instead rely on college teams to give them a basketball fix. Both San

Diego State University and the private University of San Diego have teams that regularly reach the playoffs of their conferences.

The **San Diego State University Aztecs** (✉ Cox Arena, College Ave. Exit off I–8, San Diego State University ☎ 619/283–7378 ⊕ www.goaztecs. com) compete from December through March in the Western Athletic Conference with such powers as the University of Utah and Brigham Young University.

The **University of San Diego Toreros** (✉ Jenny Craig Pavilion, 5998 Alcalá Park, Linda Vista ☎ 619/260–4803 ⊕ www.usdtoreros.com) take on West Coast Conference opponents Pepperdine University, the University of San Francisco, the University of California at Santa Barbara, and other teams.

Beaches

Water temperatures are generally chilly, ranging from 55°F to 65°F from October through June, and 65°F to 75°F from July through September. For a surf and weather report, call 619/221–8824. For a general beach and weather report, call 619/289–1212. Pollution, which has long been a problem near the Mexican border, is inching north and is generally worse near rivermouths and storm drain outlets. The weather page of the *San Diego Union-Tribune* includes pollution reports along with listings of surfing and diving conditions.

Overnight camping is not allowed on any San Diego city beach, but there are campgrounds at some state beaches throughout the county (☎ 800/444–7275 for reservations). Lifeguards are stationed at city beaches from Sunset Cliffs up to Black's Beach in the summertime, but coverage in winter is provided by roving patrols only. Leashed dogs are permitted on most San Diego beaches and adjacent parks from 6 PM to 9 AM; they can run unleashed anytime at Dog Beach at the north end of Ocean Beach and, from Memorial Day through Labor Day, at Rivermouth in Del Mar. It's rarely a problem, however, to take your pet to isolated beaches in winter.

Pay attention to signs listing illegal activities; undercover police often patrol the beaches, carrying their ticket books in coolers. Glass containers are prohibited on all San Diego beaches if their purpose is to carry drinks, and fires are allowed only in fire rings or elevated barbecue grills. Alcoholic beverages—including beer—are completely banned on some city beaches; on others you are allowed to partake from noon to 8 PM. Imbibing in beach parking lots, on boardwalks, and in landscaped areas is always illegal. Although it may be tempting to take a starfish or some other sea creature as a souvenir from a tide pool, it upsets the delicate ecological balance and is illegal, too.

Parking near the ocean can be hard to find in summer but is unmetered at all San Diego city beaches. Del Mar has a pay lot and metered street parking around the 15th Street Beach.

The beaches below are listed from south to north, starting near the Mexican border. County Highway S21 runs along the coast between Torrey

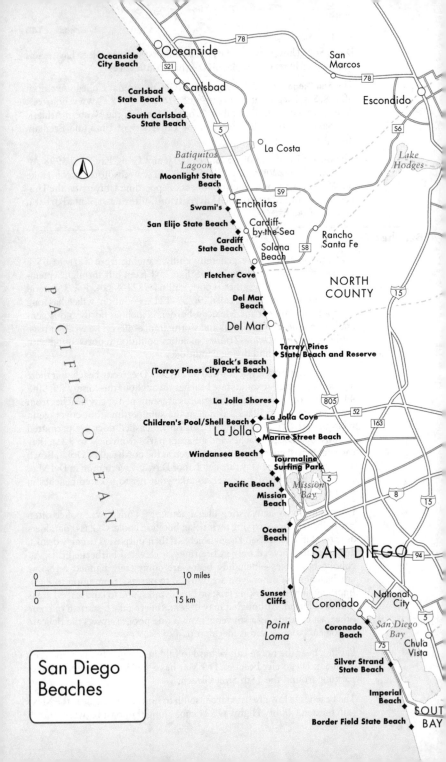

Pines State Beach and Reserve and Oceanside, although its local name, Old Highway 101 or Coast Highway 101, for example, varies by community. Most of the beaches north of Del Mar are plagued by erosion and bluff failure. It's always wise to stay clear of the bluffs, whether you're above or below them.

South Bay

Border Field State Beach. This southernmost San Diego beach is different from most California beaches; swimming is prohibited and the fence marking off the south end of the parking lot also marks the U.S.–Mexican border. On the other side of that fence is Tijuana's Bullring-by-the-Sea, one of the two bullrings in Tijuana. The beach is part of Border Field State Park, a marshy area with wide chaparral and wildflowers, a favorite among horseback riders and hikers. The park contains much of the Tijuana River Estuary, a haven for migrating birds. The beach is usually open 9–5. Beware that in winter the grounds are often posted with contamination signs because of sewer runoff from Tijuana. The beach has barbecue rings, plentiful parking, and restrooms. ⊠ *Exit I–5 at Dairy Mart Rd. and head west along Monument Rd., South San Diego.*

☾ **Imperial Beach.** In August this classic Southern California beach is the site of one of the nation's largest sand-castle competitions. The rest of the year, this laid-back town is a great place for long walks away from crowds. The surf here is often excellent, but sewage contamination can be a problem, especially in winter and after heavy rains. There are lifeguards in summer, restrooms, parking, and food vendors nearby. A walk on the pier, the southernmost in California, allows views of Mexico to the south and Point Loma to the north. A walk on the wide, sandy beaches south toward Border Field State Beach is a great way to experience a quiet, uncrowded shore—not always an easy thing to do. ⊠ *Take Palm Ave. west from I–5 until it hits water, Imperial Beach.*

Coronado

☾ **Silver Strand State Beach.** This quiet Coronado beach is ideal for families. The water is relatively calm, lifeguards and rangers are on duty year-round, and there are places to Rollerblade or ride bikes. Four parking lots provide room for more than 1,000 cars. Sites at a campground ($15–$26) for self-contained RVs are available on a first-come, first-served basis; stays are limited to seven nights. Foot tunnels under Route 75 lead to a bay-side beach, which affords great views of the San Diego skyline. ⊠ *From San Diego–Coronado Bridge, turn left onto Orange Ave., which becomes Rte. 75, and follow signs, Coronado* ☎ *619/435–5184.*

★ ☾ **Coronado Beach.** With the famous Hotel Del Coronado as a backdrop, this stretch of sandy beach is one of San Diego County's largest and most picturesque. It's perfect for sunbathing, people-watching, or Frisbee. Exercisers include Navy SEAL teams, as well as the occasional Marine Recon unit, who have training runs on the beaches in and around Coronado. Parking can be difficult on the busiest days. There are plenty of restrooms and service facilities, as well as fire rings. ⊠ *From the bridge, turn left on Orange Ave. and follow signs, Coronado.*

Point Loma

Sunset Cliffs. Beneath the jagged cliffs on the west side of the Point Loma peninsula is one of the more secluded beaches in the area. A few miles long, it's popular with surfers and locals. At the south end of the peninsula, near Cabrillo Point, tide pools teeming with small sea creatures are revealed at low tide. Farther north the waves lure surfers and the lonely coves attract sunbathers. Stairs at the foot of Bermuda and Santa Cruz avenues provide beach access, as do some (treacherous at points) cliff trails. There are no facilities. A visit here is more enjoyable at low tide; check the local newspaper for tide schedules. ☒ *Take I–8 west to Sunset Cliffs Blvd. and head west, Point Loma.*

San Diego

Ocean Beach. Much of this mile-long beach is a haven for volleyball players, sunbathers, and swimmers. The area around the municipal pier at the south end is a hangout for surfers and transients; the pier itself is open to the public 24 hours a day for fishing and walking and there's a restaurant at the middle. The beach is south of the channel entrance to Mission Bay. You'll find food vendors and fire rings; limited parking is available. Swimmers should beware of unusually vicious rip currents here. There's a dog beach at the north end. ☒ *Take I–8 west to Sunset Cliffs Blvd. and head west. Turn right on Santa Monica Ave., Ocean Beach.*

Mission Beach. San Diego's most popular beach draws huge crowds on hot summer days. The 2-mi-long stretch extends from the north entrance of Mission Bay to Pacific Beach. A wide boardwalk paralleling the beach is popular with walkers, joggers, roller skaters, bladers, and bicyclists. Surfers, swimmers, and volleyball players congregate at the south end. Thinly clad volleyball players practice on Cohasset Court year-round. Toward its north end, near the Belmont Park roller coaster, the beach narrows and the water becomes rougher. The crowds grow thicker and somewhat rougher as well. For parking you can try for a spot on the street, but your best bet are the two big lots at Belmont Park. ☒ *Exit I–5 at Grand Ave. and head west to Mission Blvd. Turn south and look for parking near roller coaster at West Mission Bay Dr., Mission Beach.*

Pacific Beach/North Pacific Beach. The boardwalk of Mission Beach turns into a sidewalk here, but there are still bike paths and picnic tables along the beachfront. Pacific Beach runs from the north end of Mission Beach to Crystal Pier. North Pacific Beach extends from the pier north. The scene here is particularly lively on weekends. There are designated surfing areas, and fire rings are available. Parking can be a challenge, but there are plenty of restrooms, showers, and restaurants in the area. ☒ *Exit I–5 at Grand Ave. and head west to Mission Blvd. Turn north and look for parking, Pacific Beach.*

La Jolla

The beaches of La Jolla combine unusual beauty with good fishing, scuba diving, and surfing. On the down side, they are crowded and have limited parking. Don't think about bringing your pet; dogs aren't even allowed on the sidewalks above some beaches here.

SURFING SAN DIEGO

SURFING MAY HAVE originated in Hawaii, but modern surfing culture is inextricably linked to the Southern California lifestyle. From the Malibu settings of Beach Blanket Bingo and Gidget to the surf-city sounds of Jan and Dean and the Beach Boys, the entertainment industry brought a California version of surfing to the landlocked, and in the process created an enduring mystique.

Today the billion-dollar surfing industry centered around Orange and San Diego counties sells the California surfing "dude" image worldwide. However, surfing is not just for dudes anymore. Women are entering the sport at a rate twice that of men, a trend that represents a return to surfing's Hawaiian origins, when it was enjoyed by people of both genders and all ages.

Surfing is a demanding sport that requires great reflexes, endurance, and balance. But besides being a strong athlete, a good surfer must be part oceanographer and part meteorologist in order to understand the subtle nuances of the ocean. Waves suitable for surfing are generated by the intense winds of offshore storms blowing across large expanses of water. When the waves reach the shallow water of the coast, they stand up and break. Because the quality and size of waves at any given spot is subject to many variables, including the contour of the ocean bottom, tides, and local winds, even the best spots may not be consistent. But with a little knowledge and luck, a surfer can fulfill his or her quest for the perfect wave.

Watching surfing from the shore can be a test of patience. Surfers spend a lot of time paddling into position and waiting to "take off" on the next wave. When someone takes off, look for one of two types of surfing: longboarding and shortboarding. Longboarders tend to ride boards more than 8 feet in length with rounded noses. Shortboarders ride the lightweight, high-performance boards from 5 to 7 feet in length with pointed noses. A great longboarder will have a smooth, fluid style and will shuffle up and down the board, maybe even riding on the nose with the toes of both feet on the very edge ("hanging ten"). Shortboarders tend to surf faster and more aggressively. The best shortboarders surf vertical to the wave face and may even break free of the wave—known as "aerials" or "catching air." Nonsurfers are often most impressed and amused by the mistakes. "Wipeouts," the sometimes spectacular falls, inevitably happen to all surfers.

In San Diego the biggest waves usually occur in winter, although good-size swells can come any time of the year. Generally, swells come from a northerly direction in winter, while in summer they tend to come from the south. Certain surf spots are better on different swells. In winter try beaches like Swami's in Encinitas or Black's Beach near La Jolla. Summer spots are Windansea in La Jolla and nearby Tourmaline Surfing Park.

Another good place for watching surfers is any municipal pier, which gives you a much closer vantage point on the action. To get a feel for the surfing culture at large, spend some time in the laid-back shops and restaurants of towns like Ocean Beach, Pacific Beach, and Encinitas. The truly adventurous can seek instruction from a qualified surf school and soon understand the stoke that one feels after shredding clean epic peaks during a dawn patrol (or, in plain English, feeling the elation of surfing good waves during an early morning surf session).

–Rob Aikins

Tourmaline Surfing Park. This is one of the area's most popular beaches for surfing and sailboarding year-round. No swimming is allowed and surfing etiquette is strongly enforced by the locals in and out of the water. There's a 175-space parking lot at the foot of Tourmaline Street that normally fills to capacity by midday. ⊠ *Take Mission Blvd. north (it turns into La Jolla Blvd.) and turn west on Tourmaline St., La Jolla.*

Windansea Beach. If the scenery here seems familiar, it's because Windansea and its habitués were the inspiration for Tom Wolfe's satirical novel *The Pump House Gang*, about a group of surfers who protect their surf-turf from outsiders. The beach's sometimes towering waves (caused by an underwater reef) are truly world class. With its incredible views and secluded sunbathing spots set among sandstone rocks, Windansea is also one of the most romantic of West Coast beaches, especially at sunset. ⊠ *Take Mission Blvd. north (it turns into La Jolla Blvd.) and turn west on Nautilus St., La Jolla.*

Marine Street Beach. Wide and sandy, this strand of beach often teems with sunbathers, swimmers, walkers, and joggers. The water is known as a great spot for bodysurfing, although the waves break in extremely shallow water and you'll need to watch out for riptides. ⊠ *Accessible from Marine St., off La Jolla Blvd., La Jolla.*

Children's Pool. Because of the pool's location at the tip of the La Jolla peninsula, you can actually look east back over the peninsula for unmatched panoramic views of the coastline and ocean. This shallow cove, protected by a seawall, has small waves and no riptide. The area just outside the pool is popular with scuba divers who explore the offshore reef when the surf is calm. Groups of harbor seals and sea lions often hang out along the beach, and there's a reserve called Seal Rock a short ways offshore. Many people come just to watch these cute but unfriendly pinnipeds wallow in the sand. ⊠ *Follow La Jolla Blvd. north. When it forks, stay to left, then turn right onto Coast Blvd., La Jolla.*

Shell Beach. North of Children's Pool is a small cove, accessible by stairs, with a relatively secluded beach. The exposed rocks off the coast have been designated a protected habitat for sea lions; you can watch them sun themselves and frolic in the water. ⊠ *Continue along Coast Blvd. north from Children's Pool, La Jolla.*

FodorśChoice **La Jolla Cove.** This is one of the prettiest spots on the West Coast. A palm-
★ lined park sits on top of cliffs formed by the incessant pounding of the waves. At low tide the tide pools and cliff caves provide a destination for explorers. Divers, snorkelers, and kayakers can explore the underwater delights of the San Diego–La Jolla Underwater Park Ecological Reserve. The cove is also a favorite of rough-water swimmers. ⊠ *Follow Coast Blvd. north to signs, or take La Jolla Village Dr. Exit from I–5, head west to Torrey Pines Rd., turn left, and drive downhill to Girard Ave. Turn right and follow signs, La Jolla.*

★ ☺ **La Jolla Shores.** On summer holidays all access routes are usually closed, so get here early—this is one of San Diego's most popular beaches. The lures are an incredible view of La Jolla peninsula, a wide sandy beach, an adjoining grassy park, and the most gentle waves in San Diego. In fact, several surf schools teach here and kayak rentals are nearby. A concrete boardwalk parallels the beach. Arrive early to get a parking spot in the lot at the foot of Calle Frescota. ⊠ *From I–5 take La Jolla Village Dr. west and turn left onto La Jolla Shores Dr. Head west to Camino del Oro or Vallecitos St. Turn right, La Jolla.*

Black's Beach. The powerful waves at this beach, officially known as Torrey Pines City Park Beach, attract world-class surfers, and its relative isolation appeals to nudist nature lovers (although by law nudity is prohibited) as well as gays and lesbians. Access to parts of the shore coincides with low tide. There are no lifeguards on duty, and strong rip currents are common—only experienced swimmers should take the plunge. Storms have weakened the cliffs in the past few years; they're dangerous to climb and should be avoided. Part of the fun here is watching hangliders and paragliders ascend from the glider port atop the cliffs. ⊠ *Take Genesee Ave. west from I–5 and follow signs to glider port; easier access, via a paved path, available on La Jolla Farms Rd., but parking is limited to 2 hrs, La Jolla.*

Del Mar

★ **Torrey Pines State Beach and Reserve.** One of San Diego's best beaches encompasses 1,750 acres of bluffs and bird-filled marshes. A network of meandering trails leads to the sandy shoreline below. Along the way enjoy the rare Torrey Pine trees, found only here and on Santa Rosa Island offshore. The large parking lot is rarely full. Lifeguards patrol the beach occasionally, and guided tours of the nature preserve here are offered on weekends. Torrey Pines tends to get crowded in summer, but more isolated spots under the cliffs are a short walk in either direction. ⊠ *Take Carmel Valley Rd. Exit west from I–5, turn left on Rte. S21, Del Mar* ☎ *858/755–2063* ⊠ *Parking $6.*

Del Mar Beach. The numbered streets of Del Mar, from 15th north to 29th, end at a wide beach popular with volleyball players, surfers, and sunbathers. Parking can be a problem on nice summer days, but access is relatively easy. The portions of Del Mar south of 15th Street are lined with cliffs and rarely crowded. Leashed dogs are permitted on most sections of the beach year-round; from October through May, dogs may run free at Rivermouth, Del Mar's northernmost beach. During the annual summer meeting of the Del Mar Thoroughbred Club, horse players sit on the beach in the morning, working on the *Daily Racing Form* before heading across the street to the track. ⊠ *Take Via de la Valle Exit from I–5 west to Rte. S21 (also known as Camino del Mar in Del Mar) and turn left, Del Mar.*

Solana Beach

Most of the beaches in this little city are nestled under cliffs, and access is limited to private stairways. However, at the west end of Lomas Santa Fe Drive (at an area known as Pillbox because of the bunkerlike structures on top of the cliffs), you'll find access to a small beach, known locally as **Fletcher Cove.** Also here are restrooms and a large parking lot. During low tide it's an easy walk under the cliffs to nearby beaches. High tide can make some of the beach impassable. Tides and surf conditions are posted at a kiosk on top of the bluffs. ⊠ *From I–5 take Lomas Santa Fe Dr. west, Solana Beach.*

Cardiff-by-the-Sea

Cardiff State Beach. This beach, popularly known as George's, begins at the parking lot immediately north of the cliffs at Solana Beach. A reef break draws surfers, although this cobbly beach otherwise is not particularly appealing. However, a walk south will give you great access to some of the secluded coves of Solana Beach. Pay attention to the incoming tide or you may have to wade or swim back to the parking lot. ⊠ *From I–5 turn west on Lomas Santa Fe Dr. to Rte. S21 (Old Hwy. 101) and turn right, Cardiff-by-the-Sea* ☎ *760/753–5091* 🅿 *Parking $4.*

San Elijo State Beach. There are **campsites** (☎ 800/444–7275 for reservations) atop a scenic bluff at this park, which also has a store and shower facilities plus beach access for swimmers and surfers. Sites run $12–$25. ⊠ *From I–5 turn west on Lomas Santa Fe Dr. to Rte. S21 (Old Hwy. 101) and turn right, Cardiff-by-the-Sea* ☎ *760/753–5091* 🅿 *Parking $4 per car, or park free nearby on U.S. 101.*

Encinitas

Swami's. Palms and the golden lotus-flower domes of the nearby Self-Realization Center ashram earned this picturesque beach its name. Extreme low tides expose tide pools that harbor anemones, starfish, and other sea life. Remember to look but don't touch; all sea life here is protected. The beach is also a top surfing spot; the only access is by a long stairway leading down from the cliff-top park. On big winter swells, the bluffs are lined with gawkers watching the area's best surfers take on, and be taken down by, one of the best big waves in the county. ⊠ *Follow Rte. S21 north from Cardiff, or exit I–5 at Encinitas Blvd., go west to Rte. S21, and turn left, Encinitas.*

Moonlight State Beach. Large parking areas and lots of facilities make this beach, tucked into a break in the cliffs, an easy getaway. To combat erosion sand is trucked in every year. The volleyball courts on the north end attract many competent players, including a few professionals who live in the area. ⊠ *Take Encinitas Blvd. Exit from I–5 and head west to 3rd St. Turn left. Parking lot is on your right at top of hill, Encinitas.*

Carlsbad

Carlsbad State Beach/South Carlsbad State Beach. Erosion from winter storms has made the southern Carlsbad beaches rockier than most beaches in Southern California. This is particularly true of South Carlsbad, a stretch of which is named in honor of Robert C. Frazee, a local politician and civic booster. Still, it's a good swimming spot, there are fine street- and beach-level promenades outside downtown Carlsbad, and for self-contained RVs there's **overnight camping** (☎ 800/444–7275). No overnight camping is allowed at Carlsbad State Beach, farther to the north, but there's a fishing area and a parking lot. ⊠ *Exit I–5 at La Costa Ave. and head west to Rte. S21. Turn north and follow coastline, Carlsbad* ☎ *760/438–3143* 🅿 *Free at both beaches.*

Oceanside

Swimmers, surfers, and U.S. Marines (from nearby Camp Pendleton) often come to play on **Oceanside's beaches.** The surf is good around the Oceanside Pier near the foot of Mission Avenue and on either side of the two jetties. Self-serve RV camping is permitted in the parking lot at the northernmost end of Harbor Beach for $15 per 24-hour period (you can stay for up to five days). There's no tent camping. There are plenty of pay lots and meters around the pier and also in the Oceanside Harbor area. ☒ *Take Vista Way west from I–5 to Rte. S21 (Coast Hwy.) and turn right. Best access points are from Cassidy St., Oceanside Pier, and Oceanside Harbor area. For direct access to Oceanside Harbor, take Harbor Dr. Exit from I–5 and follow signs, Oceanside.*

Bicycling

On any given summer day **Route S21** from La Jolla to Oceanside looks like a freeway for cyclists. It's easily the most popular and scenic bike route around, never straying more than a quarter-mile from the beach. Although the terrain is fairly easy, the long, steep Torrey Pines grade, heading south just past Del Mar, is world famous for weeding out the weak. Experienced cyclists follow **Lomas Santa Fe Drive** in Solana Beach east into Rancho Santa Fe, perhaps even continuing east on Del Dios Highway, past Lake Hodges, to Escondido. These roads can be narrow and winding in spots. For more leisurely rides, **Mission Bay, San Diego Harbor,** and the **Mission Beach boardwalk** are all flat and scenic. San Diego also has a **velodrome** in the Morley Field section of Balboa Park. Often thought of as only for racing, this ⅓-km, light-banked, elliptical cycling track is often more like a lap pool for bicyclists of all types who come for community, not competition. For those who want to take their biking experience to the extreme, the **Magdalena Ecke Family YMCA Skate Park** (☒ 200 Saxony Rd., Encinitas ☎ 760/942–9622) has set times when BMXers can rip it up on the same wood vert ramp and street courses that skateboarders use.

Bicycle Barn (☒ 746 Emerald St., Pacific Beach ☎ 858/581–3665) rents a variety of bikes—from mountain bikes to beach cruisers and tandems—to get you cruising the boardwalk in no time. **Cheap Rentals Mission Beach** (☒ 3221 and 3685 Mission Blvd., Mission Beach ☎ 858/488–9070 or 800/941–7761 ⊕ www.cheap-rentals.com) is right on the boardwalk. **Wheel Fun Rentals** (☒ 1355 N. Harbor Dr., Downtown ☎ 619/342–7244), at the downtown Holiday Inn, rents surreys, cruisers, mountain bikes, tandems, and electric bicycles. Once you're off the boat at Coronado Ferry Landing, explore the charming community with a bike from **Bikes & Beyond** (☒ 1201 1st Ave., Coronado ☎ 619/435–7180).

Bullfighting

The **California Academy of Tauromaquia** (☒ Point Loma ☎ 619/709–0664 ⊕ www.bullfightschool.com) opened in 1997 as the first bullfighting school in the United States. Year-round, the school offers a weeklong (Tuesday through Saturday) course in San Diego that finishes with a trip to a working bullranch in northern Baja California. An intensive (12 hours of instruction) weekend course beginning on Friday in San Diego and moving to the bullranch in Baja on Saturday takes place once or twice monthly year-round. A weekend intensive course in central Mexico and a one or two annual field trips to Spain are also part of the syllabus.

Diving

Enthusiasts the world over come to San Diego to snorkel and scuba-dive off La Jolla and Point Loma. At La Jolla Cove you'll find the **San Diego–La Jolla Underwater Park Ecological Preserve.** Because all sea life is protected here, it's the best place to see large lobster, sea bass, and sculpin, as well as numerous golden garibaldi, the state marine fish. It's common to see hundreds of beautiful (and harmless) leopard sharks schooling on the north end of the cove, near La Jolla Shores, especially in summer. Farther north, off the south end of Black's Beach, the rim of **Scripps Canyon** lies in about 60 feet of water. The canyon plummets to more than 900 feet in some sections.

The HMCS *Yukon,* a decommissioned Canadian warship, was intentionally sunk off **Mission Beach** to create a diving destination. A mishap caused it to settle on its side, creating a surreal, M. C. Escher–esque diving environment. Beware and exercise caution: even experienced divers have become disoriented inside the wreck. Another popular diving spot is **Sunset Cliffs** in Point Loma, where the sea life and flora are relatively close to shore. Strong rip currents make it an area best enjoyed by experienced divers, who mostly prefer to make their dives from boats. It's illegal to take any wildlife from the ecological preserves in La Jolla or near Cabrillo Point. Spearfishing requires a license (available at most dive stores), and it's illegal to take out-of-season lobster and game fish. The *San Diego Union–Tribune* includes diving conditions on its weather page. For recorded diving information, contact the **San Diego City Lifeguard Service** (☎ 619/221–8824).

San Diego Divers Supply (✉ 4004 Sports Arena Blvd., Sports Arena ☎ 619/224–3439 ⊕ www.oceanenterprises.com) provides equipment and instruction, as well as boat trips and maps of local wrecks and attractions. **Ocean Enterprises Scuba Diving** (✉ 7710 Balboa Ave., Clairemont Mesa ☎ 858/565–6054), a sister location of San Diego Divers Supply, provides the same full range of services. **Diving Locker** (✉ 1020 Grand Ave., Pacific Beach ☎ 858/272–1120 ⊕ www.divinglocker.com) has been a fixture in San Diego since 1959, making it the city's longest-running dive shop. **Scuba and Kayak San Diego** (✉ 1775 E. Mission Bay Dr., Mission Bay ☎ 619/260–1880 or 800/586–3483 ⊕ www.scubasandiego.com) is well-regarded for its top-notch instruction and certification programs as well as for guided dive tours of La Jolla Cove, La Jolla Canyon, and several sunken ships off city waters. Not for the faint of heart, **San Diego Shark Diving Expeditions** (✉ 6747 Friar's Rd., Suite 112, Mission Valley ☎ 619/299–8560 or 888/737–4275 ⊕ www.sdsharkdiving.com) will chum the water with blood and lower you in a cage to the frenzy below the surface. They do not offer instruction and cater to experienced divers only.

Fishing

Live out your deep-water fishing fantasies of wrestling with a bluefin tuna or hauling in a shark from a local pier. San Diego's waters are home to a plethora of game species and you never know what you'll hook into. Depending on the season, a half- or full-day ocean charter trip could bring in a yellowfin, dorado, sea bass, or halibut. Longer trips to Mexican waters can net you bigger game like a marlin or a bigeye tuna. Pier fishing doesn't offer as much potential excitement, but it's the cheapest ocean fishing option available. No license is required to fish from a public pier, such as the Ocean Beach, Imperial Beach, and Oceanside piers. Public lakes are frequently stocked with a variety of trout and large-mouth bass, but also have resident populations of bluegill and catfish. A fishing license from the **South Coast Department of Fish and Game** (✉ 4949 Viewridge Ave., San Diego 92123 ☎ 858/467–4201), available at most bait-and-tackle and sporting-goods stores, is required for fishing from the shoreline. Nonresidents can purchase an annual license or a 10-day, 2-day, or 1-day short-term license. Children under 16 do not need a license.

County-operated **Lake Jennings** (✉ 10108 Bass Rd., Lakeside ☎ 619/478–5473) and **Lake Morena** (✉ 2550 Lake Morena Dr., Campo ☎ 619/478–5473) are popular for fishing and camping. City-operated reservoirs, like **Sutherland** (✉ Sutherland Dam Rd.) and **San Vicente** (✉ Moreno Ave.) are good spots for catching trout and bass, but have no campgrounds. For information, call 619/668–3274. Three freshwater lakes—**Dixon, Hodges,** and **Wohlford**—surround the North County city of Escondido. On the south shore of Lake Wohlford, camping is allowed at the **Oakvale RV Park** (☎ 760/749–2895); there's a supply store and a boat ramp. On the north shore, there's camping at **Lake Wohlford Resort** (☎ 760/749–2755), complete with stores selling food, drinks, bait, tackle, and camping supplies. Boats can be rented at the boat ramp. **Dixon Lake Campground** (☎ 760/741–3328, 760/839–4680 ranger station) is city-administered and offers similar amenities as the areas at Wohlford.

Fisherman's Landing (✉ 2838 Garrison St., Point Loma ☎ 619/221–8500 ⊕ www.fishermanslanding.com) has a fleet of luxury vessels from 57 feet to 124 feet long, offering long-range multiday trips in search of yellowfin tuna, yellowtail, and other deep-water fish. Whale-watching and sometimes whale-petting trips are also available. **H&M Landing** (✉ 2803 Emerson St., Point Loma ☎ 619/222–1144 ⊕ www.hmlanding.com) schedules fishing trips, plus whale-watching excursions from December through March. **Seaforth Boat Rentals** (✉ 1641 Quivira Rd., Mission Bay ☎ 619/223–1681 ⊕ www.seaforthboatrental.com) can take you out on Mission Bay in a rowboat or power skiff or can arrange a charter for an ocean adventure. **Helgren's Sportfishing** (✉ 315 Harbor Dr. S, Oceanside ☎ 760/722–2133 ⊕ www.helgrensportfishing.com) is your best bet in North County, offering the full assortment of trips from Oceanside Harbor.

Fitness

Most major hotels have full health clubs, with weight machines, cardio equipment, and hot tubs and saunas. Several hotels have elaborate spas that offer spa-and-fitness programs for nonguests; typically, if you purchase a treatment or service at a hotel spa, you're entitled to use the hotel's fitness and athletic facilities for the day.

The spa at **Hotel Del Coronado** (✉ 1500 Orange Ave., Coronado ☎ 619/522–8100) offers body treatments and massages including the Ayurveda Bindi Herbal Body Treatment and the Del Massage. **L'Auberge Del Mar Resort and Spa** (✉ 1540 Camino Del Mar, Del Mar ☎ 858/793–6493) has a full European-inspired spa with services that range from single treatments to full-day affairs. Facials are custom-blended to each client's needs, with no two being alike. Buena Vista Spa at the tony **Rancho Bernardo Inn** (✉ 17550 Bernardo Oaks Dr., Rancho Bernardo ☎ 858/675–8471) is known for its holistic massages, aloe wraps (great for skin damage from excessive sun), and its superb fitness center. Day-spa packages at the **Rancho Valencia Resort** (✉ 5921 Valencia Circle, Rancho Santa Fe ☎ 858/756–1123) include deep-tissue massage, shiatsu, and aromatherapy facials. The **Coronado Island Marriott Spa** (✉ 2000 2nd St., Coronado ☎ 619/435–3000) has pampering packages that include the use of fitness facilities and admission to exercise classes. The **Chopra Center for Well Being** (✉ Costa Del Mar Rd., Carlsbad ☎ 760/438–9111), which is at the glitzy La Costa Resort and Spa, was founded by New Age guru Dr. Deepak Chopra to teach and treat guests according to his holistic view of life. Day spa treatments and multiday packages are available. Spa Terre at Mission Bay's **Paradise Point Resort & Spa** (✉ 1404 Vacation Rd. Mission Bay ☎ 858/274–4630) offers soothing salt glows, seaweed body masks, hot-stone massage, skin-hydration treatments, and other state-of-the-art services.

Frog's Athletic & Racquet Club (✉ 901 Hotel Circle S, Hotel Circle ☎ 619/291–3500) has a weight room, saunas, and tennis and racquetball courts. Anyone can use the splendid facilities at the **Sporting Club at Aventine** (✉ 8930 University Center La., La Jolla ☎ 858/552–8000). The **24 Hour Fitness Centers** (✉ 5885 Rancho Mission Rd., Mission Valley ☎ 619/281–5543 ✉ 1 Horton Plaza, Downtown ☎ 619/232–4024 ✉ 7514 Girard Ave., Unit 3, La Jolla ☎ 858/551–7800 ✉ 3965 5th Ave., Hillcrest ☎ 619/683–2424 ✉ 909 Garnet Ave., Pacific Beach ☎ 858/270–6024) welcome nonmembers for a fee. **Gold's Gym** (✉ 3156 Sports Arena Blvd., Sports Arena ☎ 619/226–9500) allows drop-ins.

Football

The **San Diego Chargers** (✉ 9449 Friars Rd., Mission Valley ☎ 619/280–2121 or 877/242–7437 ⊕ www.chargers.com) of the National Football League fill Qualcomm Stadium from August through December. Games with AFC West rivals the Oakland Raiders and Denver Broncos are particularly intense.

The **San Diego State University Aztecs** (☎ 619/283–5808 ⊕ www.goaztecs. com) compete in the Mountain West Conference and attract the most loyal fans in town, with attendance rivaling and sometimes surpassing that of the NFL Chargers. The biggest game of the year is always a show-down with Brigham Young University. Like the Chargers, the Aztecs also play their home games at Qualcomm Stadium. The **Holiday Bowl** (619/283–5808), one of college football's most watched playoff games, takes place in Qualcomm Stadium around the end of December.

Frisbee Golf

This is like golf, except it's played with Frisbees. A course, laid out at Mor-ley Field in Balboa Park, is open seven days a week from dawn to dusk. Equipment and playing times can be arranged with the Disc Golf Club on a first-come, first-served basis. Rules are posted. Directions to the field are available from the **Balboa Park Disc Golf Course** (☎ 619/692–3607).

Golf

On any given day, it would be difficult to find a better place to play golf than San Diego. The climate—generally sunny, without a lot of wind—is perfect for the sport, and there are courses in the area to suit every level of expertise. Experienced golfers can play the same greens as PGA-tournament participants, and beginners or rusty players can book a week at a golf resort and benefit from expert instruction. You'd also be hard-pressed to find a locale that has more scenic courses—everything from sweeping views of the ocean to verdant hills inland.

During busy vacation seasons it can be difficult to get a good tee-off time. Call in advance to see if it's possible to make a reservation. You don't necessarily have to stay at a resort to play its course; check if the one you're interested in is open to nonguests. Most public courses in the area provide a list of fees for all San Diego courses. The **Southern California Golf Association** (☎ 818/980–3630 ⊕ www.scga.org) pub-lishes an annual directory ($15) with detailed and valuable information on all clubs. Another good resource for golfers is the **Public Links Golf Association of Southern California** (☎ 714/994–4747 ⊕ www.plga.org), which details the region's public courses on its Web site.

The PGA **Buick Invitational** (☎ 619/281–4653) brings the pros to the Tor-rey Pines Golf Course in late January. The PGA's **Accenture Match Play Championship** (☎ 866/942–2672) is held at the La Costa Resort in late February.

Courses

The following is not intended to be a comprehensive list but provides suggestions for some of the best places to play in the area. The greens fee is included for each course; carts (in some cases mandatory), instruction, and other costs are additional.

The **Balboa Park Municipal Golf Course** (✉ 2600 Golf Course Dr., Bal-boa Park ☎ 619/239–1660) is in the heart of Balboa Park, making it convenient for downtown visitors. Greens fee: $36–$41.

Carmel Mountain Ranch Country Club (✉ 14050 Carmel Ridge Rd., Poway ☎ 858/487–9224 ⊕ www.clubcmr.com) has 18 holes, a driving range, and equipment rentals. A challenging course with many difficult holes, Carmel Mountain Ranch is not particularly scenic: it's in a suburban area and runs through a housing development. Greens fee: $83–$105.

Coronado Municipal Golf Course (✉ 2000 Visalia Row, Coronado ☎ 619/435–3121) has 18 holes, a driving range, equipment rentals, and a snack bar. Views of San Diego Bay and the Coronado Bridge from the back nine holes on this course make it popular—but rather difficult to get on unless you reserve tee time. Greens fee: $25–$40.

Cottonwood at Rancho San Diego Golf Club (✉ 3121 Willow Glen Rd., El Cajon ☎ 619/442–9891 or 800/455–1902 ⊕ www.cottonwoodgolf.com) has a driving range, rentals, a restaurant, and two 18-hole courses. The Monte Vista course is the easier of the two. Ivanhoe often hosts tournaments. Both are good walking courses, and have nice practice putting greens. Greens fee: $30–$47.

Eastlake Country Club (✉ 2375 Clubhouse Dr., Chula Vista ☎ 619/482–5757) has 18 holes, a driving range, equipment rentals, and a snack bar. A fun course for golfers of almost all levels of expertise, it's not overly difficult despite the water hazards. Greens fee: $52–$72.

Encinitas Ranch (✉ 1275 Quail Gardens Dr., Encinitas ☎ 760/944–1936), tucked away in the former flower fields of coastal North County, is a hilly course that offers beautiful views of the Pacific as you play its championship 18 holes. Greens fee: $52–$72.

Mission Bay Golf Resort (✉ 2702 N. Mission Bay Dr., Mission Bay ☎ 858/490–3370) has 18 holes, a driving range, equipment rentals, and a snack bar. A not-very-challenging executive (par 3 and 4) course, Mission Bay is lighted for night play with final tee time at 8 PM. Greens fee: $19–$23.

Mount Woodson Golf Club (✉ 16422 N. Woodson Dr., Ramona ☎ 760/788–3555) has 18 holes, equipment rentals, a golf shop, and a snack bar. This heavily wooded course in the mountains outside San Diego has scenic views and wooden bridges. Greens fee: $59–$85.

Fodor'sChoice ★ **Torrey Pines Golf Course** (✉ 11480 N. Torrey Pines Rd., La Jolla ☎ 800/985–4653 ⊕ www.torreypinesgolfcourse.com) has 36 holes, a driving range, and equipment rentals. One of the best public golf courses in the United States, Torrey Pines has views of the Pacific from every hole. The par-72 South Course receives rave reviews from the touring pros. Designed by acclaimed course designer Rees Jones, it has more length and more challenges than the North Course and, fittingly, commands higher greens fees. It's not easy to get a good tee time here as professional brokers buy up the best ones. Check the yellow pages for broker's numbers. Out-of-towners are better off booking the instructional Golf Playing Package, which includes cart, greens fee, and a golf-pro escort for the first three holes. Greens fee: $140–$205.

Resorts

★ **Aviara Golf Club** (✉ 7447 Batiquitos Dr., Carlsbad ☎ 760/603–6900) is a top-quality course with 18 holes (designed by Arnold Palmer), a driving range, equipment rentals, and views of the protected adjacent Batiquitos Lagoon and the Pacific Ocean. Carts fitted with GPS systems that tell you the distance to the pin, among other features, are included in the cost. Greens fee: $195–$225.

Barona Creek (⊠ 1000 Wildcat Canyon Rd., Lakeside ☎ 619/443–2300) in East County is one of the newer resorts in the area. Hilly terrain and regular winds add to the challenge. Fast greens will test your finesse. If your game is on, you can always see if your luck holds in the adjacent casino. Greens fee: $80–$100.

Carlton Oaks Lodge and Country Club (⊠ 9200 Inwood Dr., Santee ☎ 619/448–4242 ⊕ www.carltonoaksgolf.com) has 18 holes, a driving range, equipment rentals, a clubhouse, a restaurant, and a bar. Many local qualifying tournaments are held at this difficult Pete Dye–designed course with lots of trees and water hazards. Carts are included. Greens fee: $55–$80.

Carmel Highland Doubletree Golf and Tennis Resort (⊠ 14455 Peñasquitos Dr., Rancho Peñasquitos ☎ 858/672–9100), a fairly hilly, well-maintained course in inland North County, has 18 holes, a driving range, equipment rentals, and a clubhouse with restaurant. Greens fee: $60–$80.

La Costa Resort and Spa (⊠ 2100 Costa del Mar Rd., Carlsbad ☎ 760/438–9111 or 800/854–5000 ⊕ www.lacosta.com) has two 18-hole PGA-rated courses, a driving range, a clubhouse, equipment rentals, an excellent golf school, and a pro shop. One of the premier golf resorts in Southern California, it hosts the Accenture Match Play Championship each February. After a full day on the links you can wind down with a massage, steam bath, and dinner at the exclusive spa resort that shares this verdant property. None of this is cheap, but then again, how many courses will send a limo to pick you up at the airport? Greens fee: $185–$195.

Morgan Run Resort and Club (⊠ 5690 Cancha de Golf, Rancho Santa Fe ☎ 858/756–2471 ⊕ www.morganrun.com), a very popular walking course near polo grounds and stables, has 27 holes (for members and resort guests only) that can be played in three combinations of 18; a driving range; equipment rentals; and a pro shop. Greens fee: $100–$120.

Rancho Bernardo Inn and Country Club (⊠ 17550 Bernardo Oaks Dr., Rancho Bernardo ☎ 858/675–8470 Ext. 1 ⊕ www.ranchobernardoinn.com) has an 18-hole course, driving range, equipment rentals, and a restaurant; the course is managed by JC Golf, which has a golf school as well as seven other respected courses throughout Southern California (including Encintas Ranch and Mount Woodson Golf Club, both described above), which guests of Rancho Bernardo Inn have access to. The restaurant here lays out one of the best Sunday brunches in the county. Greens fee: $90–$115.

Redhawk (⊠ 45100 Redhawk Pkwy., Temecula ☎ 909/310–3850 or 800/451–4295 ⊕ www.redhawkgolfcourse.com) has 18 holes in an arboretumlike setting, a driving range, a putting green, and a restaurant. The par-72 course offers enough challenges to have earned a four-star rating from *Golf Digest* and a top 10 ranking from *California Golf Magazine*. Greens fee: $60–$80.

Sycuan Resort & Casino (✉ 3007 Dehesa Rd., El Cajon ☎ 619/442–3425) came into being in 1955 as the Singing Hills Country Club. Now owned by the Sycuan Tribal Development Corp., it comes highly recommended by anyone who's played here and is one of *Golf Digest*'s favorites. There are 54 holes, a driving range, equipment rentals, tennis courts, a lodge, and restaurants. Hackers will love the executive par-3 course; seasoned golfers can play the championship courses. Greens fee: $39–$45.

Hang Gliding & Paragliding

The **Torrey Pines Glider Port** (✉ 2800 Torrey Pines Scenic Dr., La Jolla ⊕ www.flytorrey.com), perched on the cliffs overlooking the ocean north of La Jolla, is one of the most spectacular spots to hang glide in the world. However, it's definitely for experienced pilots only. Hang gliding and paragliding lessons and tandem rides for inexperienced gliders are available from the **Hang Gliding/Paragliding Center** (☎ 858/452–9858) based here.

Hiking & Nature Trails

San Diego has plenty of open space for hiking. From beachside bluffs and waterfront estuaries to the foothills and trails of the nearby Laguna mountains and the desert beyond, the county has several vegetation and climate zones. Those who lack the time to explore the outskirts will find a day hike through the canyons and gardens of Balboa Park a great way to escape to nature without leaving the city. A list of scheduled walks appears in the Night and Day section of the Thursday *San Diego Union-Tribune* and in the *Reader* weekly.

Guided hikes are conducted regularly through Los Peñasquitos Canyon Preserve and the Torrey Pines State Beach and Reserve.

The **San Dieguito River Park** (✉ 21 mi north of San Diego on I–5 to Lomas Santa Fe Dr., east 1 mi to Sun Valley Rd., north into park, Solana Beach ☎ 858/664–2270) is a 55-mi corridor that begins at the mouth of the San Dieguito River in Del Mar and heads from the riparian lagoon area through coastal sage scrub and mountain terrain to end in the desert just east of Volcan Mountain near Julian. The **Tijuana Estuary** (✉ 301 Caspian St., Exit I–5 at Coronado Ave., head west to 3rd St., turn left onto Caspian, which leads into estuary parking lot, Imperial Beach ☎ 619/575–3613), mostly contained within Border Field State Park, is one of the last extant riparian environments in Southern California. The freshwater and saltwater marshes give refuge to migrant and resident waterfowl. The visitor center has an amphitheater for interpretive talks. **Mission Trails Regional Park** (✉ 1 Father Junípero Serra Trail, Mission Valley ☎ 619/668–3275 ⊕ www.mtrp.org), which encompasses nearly 6,000 acres of mountains, wooded hillsides, lakes, and riparian streams, is only 8 mi northeast of downtown. Trails range from easy to difficult; they include one with a superb view of the city from Cowles Mountain and another along a historic missionary path.

Horse Racing

For a few short weeks in summer, during the annual summer meeting of the **Del Mar Thoroughbred Club** (⊠ Take I–5 north to Via de la Valle exit, Del Mar ☎ 858/755–1141) on the Del Mar Fairgrounds, racing forms and racing fans can be seen all over Del Mar. The track attracts the best horses and jockeys in the country. Racing begins in July—tradition dictates that women wear a hat on opening day—and continues through early September, every day except Tuesday. At the entrance to the track's parking lot, open Wednesday through Sunday, is the **Surf-side Race Place at Del Mar** (☎ 858/755–1167), where you can bet on races at tracks throughout the country, shown on TV via satellite.

Horseback Riding

Bright Valley Farms (⊠ 12310 Campo Rd., Spring Valley ☎ 619/670–1871) offers lessons and rents horses to ride on the winding trails of the Sweetwater River Valley. **Happy Trails Horse Rentals** (⊠ 12115 Black Mountain Rd., Miramar ☎ 858/271–8777) offers guided trail rides through the Los Peñasquitos Reserve.

Sandi's Rental Stable (⊠ 2060 Hollister St., Imperial Beach ☎ 619/424–3124) leads rides through Border Field State Park. They offer lessons for beginners and will accommodate more advanced riders. Be sure to tell them your needs before you saddle up.

Ice Hockey

The five-time Taylor Cup champion **San Diego Gulls** (⊠ 3500 Sports Arena Blvd., Sports Arena ☎ 619/224–4625 ⊕ www.sandiegogulls.com) of the minor-league ECHL take to the ice from late October through March at the San Diego Sports Arena.

Ice-Skating

La Jolla Icetown (⊠ University Towne Centre, 4545 La Jolla Village Dr., La Jolla ☎ 858/452–9110) offers open skating, group and private figure skating lessons, hockey lessons, pickup hockey, and hockey leagues. You can watch from the mall's food court above the rink. **Iceoplex** (⊠ 555 N. Tulip St., Escondido ☎ 760/489–5550) has two Olympic-size rinks, a fitness center, a heated swimming pool, a sauna, and a restaurant. It offers public skate sessions, figure skating and ice-hockey lessons, pickup hockey, and hockey leagues. The **San Diego Ice Arena** (⊠ 11048 Ice Skate Pl., Mira Mesa ☎ 858/530–1825) has public skate sessions with skate rental, group and private figure-skating lessons, hockey lessons, and youth and adult pickup games.

Jet Skiing

Jet Skis can be launched from most ocean beaches, although you must ride beyond surf lines, and some beaches have special regulations governing their use. The only freshwater lake that allows Jet Skis is **El Capitan Reservoir,** 30 mi northeast of the city near Lake Jennings. Take I–8 north to Lake Jennings Park Road, head east on El Monte Road, and follow signs; there's a day-use fee of $5 per person. Waveless Mission Bay and the small **Snug Harbor Marina** (✉ 4215 Harrison St. Carlsbad ☎ 760/434–3089), east of the intersection of Tamarack Avenue and I–5 in Carlsbad, are favorite spots. **H2O Jet Ski Rentals** (✉ 1617 Quivira Rd., Mission Bay ☎ 619/226–2754) rents Jet Skis for use on Mission Bay. **San Diego Jet Ski Rentals** (☎ 619/851–8141) rents Jet Skis and will deliver them to you anywhere in the city.

Jogging

Almost any beach in the county is great for running at low tide. Make sure to consult the tide charts in the local newspaper or your run may turn into a swim. The most popular run downtown is along the **Embarcadero,** which stretches for 2 mi around the bay. There are uncongested sidewalks all through the area, but the alternative in the downtown area is to head east to **Balboa Park,** where trails snake through the canyons. Joggers can start out from any parking lot, but it's probably easiest to start anywhere along the 6th Avenue side. Entry to the numerous lots is best where Laurel Street connects with 6th Avenue. There's also a fitness circuit course in the park's **Morley Field** area. **Mission Bay** is renowned among joggers for its wide sidewalks and basically flat landscape. Trails head west around Fiesta Island, providing distance as well as a scenic route. **Del Mar** has the finest running trails along the bluff; park your car near 15th Street and run south along the cliffs for a gorgeous view of the ocean. The **Mission Beach boardwalk** is a great place to run while soaking up the scenery and beach culture. Organized runs occur almost every weekend. They're listed in *Competitor* magazine, which is available free at bike and running shops. **Roadrunner Sports** (✉ 5553 Copley Dr., San Diego ☎ 619/693–6377) has all the supplies and information you'll need for running in San Diego. Don't run in bike lanes!

Over-the-Line

As much a giant beach party as a sport, this game is a form of beach softball played with three-person teams. Every July the world championships are held on Fiesta Island, with two weekends of wild beer drinking and partying. Some good athletes take part in the games, too. Admission is free, but parking is impossible and traffic around Mission Bay can become unbearable. Contact the **Old Mission Beach Athletic Club** (☎ 619/688–0817 ⊕ www.ombac.org) for more information.

Rock Climbing

San Diego offers a variety of indoor and outdoor climbing options for beginners through experts. **Mission Trails Regional Park** (✉ 1 Father Junípero Serra Trail, Mission Valley ☎ 619/668–3281 ⊕ www.mtrp. org) has a huge quantity of bouldering, top-roping, and single-pitch climbs. With plenty of belay stations and holds that are regularly changed, the three locations of **Solid Rock Gym** (✉ 2074 Hancock St., Old Town ☎ 619/299–1124 ✉ 13026 Stowe Rd., Poway ☎ 858/748–9011 ✉ 992 Rancheros Dr., San Marcos ☎ 619/299–1124) appeal to all skill levels. **Vertical Hold Sport Climbing Center** (✉ 9580 Distribution Ave., Mira Mesa ☎ 858/586–7572) is the largest full-service indoor rock-climbing gym in Southern California. It offers lessons, rentals, and party packages. The Web site of the **San Diego Climbers' Coalition** (⊕ www. giantsoftware.com/sdcc) lists numerous resources, including real and manmade rock-climbing areas and gyms in the region.

Rollerblading & Roller-Skating

The sidewalks at **Mission Bay** are perfect for Rollerblading and skating; you can admire the sailboats and kites while you get some exercise. **Bicycle Barn** (✉ 746 Emerald St., Pacific Beach ☎ 858/581–3665) rents blades for leisurely skates along the Pacific Beach boardwalk. **Bikes and Beyond** (✉ 1201 1st Ave., Coronado ☎ 619/435–7180) is the place to go to rent skates, blades, and bikes to cruise the beachwalk of Coronado. **Mission Beach Club** (✉ 704 Ventura Pl., Mission Beach ☎ 858/488–5050) is right next to the Mission Beach boardwalk; its black, castle-like facade is easy to spot. You can also rent lockers, skateboards, and almost everything else a beachgoer could need. **Skateworld** (✉ 6907 Linda Vista Rd., Linda Vista ☎ 858/560–9349) has several public sessions daily, in addition to private group sessions for bladers and skaters.

Sailing & Boating

The city's history is full of seafarers, from the ships of the 1542 Cabrillo expedition to the America's Cup that once had a home here. Winds in San Diego are consistent, especially in winter. You can rent a slip at one of several marinas, if you're bringing your own boat. If not, you can rent vessels of various sizes and shapes—from small paddleboats to sleek 12-meters and kayaks to Hobie Cats—from specialized vendors. In addition, most bay-side resorts rent equipment for on-the-water adventures. Most of what's available from these outlets is not intended for the open ocean, which is wise, considering the potential danger for the inexperienced. The **Bahia Resort Hotel** (✉ 998 W. Mission Bay Dr., Mission Bay ☎ 858/488–2582) and its sister location, the **Catamaran Resort Hotel** (✉ 3999 Mission Blvd., Mission Beach ☎ 858/488–2582) rent paddleboats, kayaks, Waverunners, and sailboats from 14 feet to 22 feet. The Bahia also rents out a ski boat. **Harbor Sailboats** (✉ 2040 Harbor Island Dr., Suite 104, Harbor Island ☎ 619/291–9568 or 800/854–6625 ⊕ www.harborsailboats.com) rents sailboats from 22 feet to 46 feet long for open-ocean adventures. **Coronado Boat Rentals** (✉ 1715 Strand Way, Coronado ☎ 619/437–1514) has kayaks, Jet Skis, fishing skiffs, and power boats from 10 feet to 20 feet in length as well as sailboats from 14 feet to 30 feet. They also can hook you up with a skipper. **Seaforth Boat Rentals** (✉ 1641 Quivira Rd., Mission Bay ☎ 619/223–1681 ⊕ www. seaforthboatrental.com) rents Jet Skis, paddleboats, sailboats, and skiffs. **Downtown Boat Rental** (✉ Marriott Hotel & Marina, 333 W. Harbor Dr., Gate 1, Downtown ☎ 619/239–2628) is your downtown source for sailboats and other watercraft. **Carlsbad Paddle Sports** (✉ 2002 S. Coast Hwy., Oceanside ☎ 760/434–8686 ⊕ www.carlsbadpaddle.com) handles kayak sales, rentals, and instruction for coastal North County.

Contact **California Cruisin'** (✉ 1450 Harbor Island Dr., Downtown ☎ 619/296–8000 or 800/449–2248 ⊕ www.californiacruisin.com) for yachting charter excursions. **Hornblower Dining Yachts** (✉ 1066 N. Harbor Dr., Embarcadero ☎ 619/686–8700 or 888/467–6256 ⊕ www. hornblower.com) operates sunset cocktail and dining cruises, plus whale-watching excursions and yacht charters. **San Diego Harbor Excursion** (✉ 1050 N. Harbor Dr., Embarcadero ☎ 619/234–4111 or 800/442–7847 ⊕ www.harborexcursion.com) has one- and two-hour narrated harbor tours, as well as dinner and brunch cruises and a ferry to Coronado. **Classic Sailing Adventures** (✉ 2051 Shelter Island Dr., Shelter Island ☎619/224–0800 or 800/659–0141 ⊕www.classicsailingadventures. com) will take you on their 38-foot sailboat for champagne sunset cruises in summer, or daytime whale-watching in winter. In Coronado, sailboat and powerboat charters and cruises can be arranged through the **Charter Connection** (✉1715 Strand Way, Coronado ☎619/437–8877). For information, including tips on overnight anchoring, contact the **Port of San Diego Mooring Office** (☎ 619/686–6227). For additional information contact the **San Diego Harbor Police** (☎ 619/686–6272).

Skateboard Parks

Skateboarding culture has always thrived in San Diego, and recent changes in liability laws have encouraged a jump in the number of skateparks. A good number of top pro skateboarders live in San Diego and often practice and perfect new moves at local skate parks. Pads and helmets (always a good idea anywhere) are required at all parks.

Escondido Sports Center (✉ 3315 Bear Valley Pkwy., Escondido ☎ 760/738–5425) has a miniramp, street course, and vertical ramp. Serving the southern part of the area, **South Bay Family YMCA** (✉ 1201 Paseo Magda, Chula Vista ☎ 619/421–8805) has an elaborate layout and offers lessons. ★ **Magdalena Ecke Family YMCA** (✉ 200 Saxony Rd., Encinitas ☎ 760/942–9622) is very popular among the many pros in this beach town. It has a competition street course, two cement pools, and a classic vertical ramp from the 2003 X games. **Ocean Beach Skatepark at Robb Field** (✉ 2525 Bacon St., Ocean Beach ☎ 619/525–8486) is the largest park in the city. It has a huge street plaza, bowls, ledges, grind rails, and quarterpipes.

Surfing

If you're a beginner, consider paddling in the waves off Mission Beach, Pacific Beach, Tourmaline Surfing Park, La Jolla Shores, Del Mar, or Oceanside. More experienced surfers usually head for Sunset Cliffs, the La Jolla reef breaks, Black's Beach, or Swami's in Encinitas. All necessary equipment is included in the cost of all surfing schools. **Kahuna Bob's Surf School** (☎760/721–7700 or 800/524–8627 ⊕www.kahunabob.com) conducts two-hour lessons in coastal North County seven days a week. **San Diego Surfing Academy** (☎ 760/230–1474 or 800/447–7873 ⊕ www. surfsdsa.com) has surf camps and lessons at South Carlsbad State Beach. **Surf Diva Surf School** (✉ 2160 Avenida de la Playa, La Jolla ☎ 858/454–8273 ⊕ www.surfdiva.com) offers clinics, surf camps, surf trips, and private lessons especially formulated for women. Clinics and trips are for women only, but guys can book private lessons from the nationally recognized staff.

Many local surf shops rent both surf and bodyboards. **Cheap Rentals Mission Beach** (✉ 3221 and 3685 Mission Blvd., Mission Beach ☎ 858/488–9070 or 800/941–7761 ⊕ www.cheap-rentals.com) is right on the boardwalk, just steps from the waves. **Star Surfing Company** (✉ 4652 Mission Blvd., Pacific Beach ☎ 858/273–7827 ⊕ www.starsurfingco.com) can get you out surfing around the Crystal Pier. **La Jolla Surf Systems** (✉ 2132 Avenida de la Playa, La Jolla ☎ 858/456–2777 ⊕ www.lajollasurfsystems.com) takes care of your needs if you want to surf the reefs or beachbreaks of La Jolla. **Hansen's** (✉ 1105 S. Coast Hwy. 101, Encinitas ☎ 760/753–6595 ⊕ www.hansensurf.com) is just a short walk from Swami's beach.

Swimming

Built in 1925, Belmont Park's 58-yard-long **Plunge** (✉ 3115 Ocean Front Walk, Mission Beach ☎ 858/488–3110) is the largest heated indoor swimming pool in California. The **Copley Family YMCA** (✉ 3901 Landis St., North Park ☎ 619/283–2251) has a pool on the eastern edge of the city. The **Bud Kearns Memorial Pool** (✉ 2229 Morley Field Dr., Balboa Park ☎ 619/692–4920) is operated year-round by the City of San Diego.

The pools at the **Downtown YMCA** (✉ 500 W. Broadway Ave., Suite B ☎ 619/232–7451) are close to the Gaslamp Quarter and Balboa Park. The **Magdalena Ecke Family YMCA** (✉ 200 Saxony Rd., Encinitas ☎ 760/942–9622) is convenient for swimming in North County.

Tennis

Most of the more than 1,300 courts around the county are in private clubs, but a few are public. The **Balboa Tennis Club at Morley Field** (✉ 2221 Morley Field Dr., Balboa Park ☎ 619/295–9278 ⊕ www.balboatennis.com) has 25 courts, 19 of them lighted. Courts are available on a first-come, first-served basis for a daily $5-per-person fee. Heaviest usage is 9 AM–11 AM and after 5 PM; at other times you can usually arrive and begin playing. The **La Jolla Tennis Club** (✉ 7632 Draper Ave., La Jolla ☎ 858/454–4434 ⊕ www.ljtc.org) has nine public courts near downtown La Jolla; five are lighted; the daily fee is $5. The 12 lighted courts at the privately owned **Peninsula Tennis Club** (✉ Robb Field, Ocean Beach ☎ 619/226–3407) are available to the public for $4 per person daily.

Several San Diego resorts have top-notch tennis programs staffed by big-name professional instructors. **Rancho Bernardo Inn** (✉ 17550 Bernardo Oaks Dr., Rancho Bernardo ☎ 858/675–8500 ⊕ www.ranchobernardoinn.com) has 12 tennis courts and packages that include instruction, accommodations, and meals. **Rancho Valencia Resort** (✉ 5921 Valencia Circle, Rancho Santa Fe ☎ 858/756–1123 ⊕ www.ranchovalencia.com), which is among the top tennis resorts in the nation, has 18 hard courts and several instruction programs. **La Costa Resort and Spa** (✉ Costa Del

Mar Rd., Carlsbad ☎ 760/438–9111 ⊕ www.lacosta.com), where the annual Acura Tennis Classic is held, has 19 courts, seven of them lighted, plus professional instruction, clinics, and workouts.

Volleyball

Ocean Beach, South Mission Beach, Del Mar Beach, Moonlight Beach, and the western edge of Balboa Park are major congregating points for volleyball enthusiasts. These are also the best places to find a pickup game. Contact the **San Diego Volleyball Club** (☎ 858/486–6885 ⊕ www. sdvolleyballclub.org) to find out about organized games and tournaments.

Waterskiing

Mission Bay is one of the most popular waterskiing areas in Southern California. It's best to get out early, when the water is smooth and the crowds are thin. Boats and equipment can be rented from **Seaforth Boat Rentals** (✉ 1641 Quivira Rd., Mission Bay ☎ 619/223–1681 ⊕ www. seaforthboatrental.com). The private **San Diego and Mission Bay Boat & Ski Club** (✉ 2606 N. Mission Bay Dr. ☎ 858/270–0840 ⊕ www. sdmbbsc.org) operates a slalom course and ski jump in Mission Bay's Hidden Anchorage. Permission from the **Mission Bay Harbor Patrol** (☎ 619/221–8985) is required.

Windsurfing

Also known as sailboarding, windsurfing is a sport best practiced on smooth waters, such as Mission Bay or the Snug Harbor Marina at the intersection of I–5 and Tamarack Avenue in Carlsbad. More experienced windsurfers will enjoy taking a board out on the ocean. Wave jumping is especially popular at the Tourmaline Surfing Park in La Jolla and in the Del Mar area, where you can also occasionally see kiteboarders practice their variation on the theme. Sailboard rentals and instruction are available at the **Bahia Resort Hotel** (✉ 998 W. Mission Bay Dr., Mission Bay ☎ 858/488–2582). The **Catamaran Resort Hotel** (✉ 3999 Mission Blvd., Mission Beach ☎ 858/488–1081), a sister location of the Bahia Resort Hotel, offers similar services. Head to **Windsport** (✉ 844 W. Mission Bay Dr., Mission Bay ☎ 858/488–4642) to see Mission Bay from a sailboard. The **Snug Harbor Marina** (✉ 4215 Harrison St., Carlsbad ☎ 760/434–3089) has rentals and instruction and can advise those looking to windsurf on Agua Hedionda lagoon.

Shopping

6

WORD OF MOUTH

"Horton Plaza . . . is an unusual mall in downtown San Diego. It looks somewhat like a Dr. Seuss children's book with stairways branching off in every direction, vivid colors and designs. Definitely worth seeing."

—San_Diego_Mom

Updated by
Lenore Greiner

A MÉLANGE OF HISTORIC DISTRICTS, homey villages, funky neighborhoods, megamalls, and chic suburbs make up the shopping areas of San
Diego. Malls and shopping areas are outdoors; the architecture, such
as that of Horton Plaza or Seaport Village, is often creative and you can
enjoy the legendary sunny weather at the same time. In the beach towns,
cruising the shops provides a break from the surf and sun. Hillcrest and
the Gaslamp Quarter are known for their hip stores, La Jolla's Prospect
Street and Girard Avenue for world-class boutiques, and the quaint village of Coronado for its gift shops. If you poke around some of the smaller
neighborhoods—Del Mar, Solana Beach's Cedros Design District, Carlsbad's upscale outlet mall, and Julian—you may turn up some real finds.

Most major malls, many in the Westfield Shoppingtown chain (and that
includes Horton Plaza, although locals still refer to it as Horton Plaza
rather than as Westfield Shoppingtown Horton Plaza), offer merchandise you can find nearly anywhere. For San Diego–related memorabilia,
browse the gift shops at attractions like the zoo, Wild Animal Park, and
the Plaza del Pasado and Bazaar del Mundo Shops in Old Town. You
can also pick up a real-live San Diego keepsake at the flower nurseries
around Carlsbad and Encinitas, and along inland farm trails.

Establishments are usually open daily 10–6; department stores and
shops within the larger malls stay open until 9 on weekdays. Just about
all will ship your purchase for you domestically or internationally. Sales
are advertised in the *San Diego Union-Tribune* and in the *Reader,* a free
weekly that comes out on Thursday. Also, check out the Web sites
⊕ www.signonsandiego.com and ⊕ www.sandiegoinsider.com for more
details on local shops and sales. Click on the San Diego Convention &
Visitors Bureau's Web site (www.sandiego.org) for shopping coupons.

Coronado

Shopping Center

Fodor's Choice **Ferry Landing Marketplace.** A staggering view of San Diego's downtown
★ skyline across the bay, 30 boutiques, and a Tuesday afternoon Farm-
ers' Market provide a delightful place to shop while waiting for a ferry.
Lavender Gift Shop (☎ 619/522–9868) stocks a sweet-smelling selection of herbs and soaps as well as vintage-inspired gifts and antiques.
Men's Island Sportswear (☎ 619/437–4696) has hats, tropical sportswear,
and accessories. ✉ *1201 1st St., at B Ave., Coronado.*

Specialty Stores

Friendly shopkeepers make the boutiques lining **Orange Avenue,** Coronado's main drag, a good place to browse.

BOOKS **Bay Books.** This old-fashioned bookstore is the spot to sit, read, and sip
★ coffee on an overcast day by the sea. International travelers will love
the large selection of foreign-language magazines and newspapers, children the section in the back is devoted to children's books and games.
There are plenty of secluded reading nooks and a sidewalk reading area
with coffee bar. ✉ *1029 Orange Ave., Coronado* ☎ *619/435–0070*
🖷 *619/435–2755* ⊕ *www.baybookscoronado.com.*

GOURMET FOODS **In Good Taste.** Come here for smooth-as-silk chocolates and fudge, specialty cheeses, wine, truffles, and fresh bread. ✉ *1146 Orange Ave., Coronado* ☎ *619/435–8356.*

HOME
ACCESSORIES &
GIFTS
The Attic. The Attic is stocked with lots of Victoriana, white-painted furniture, quilts, and linens. ✉ *1011 Orange Ave., Coronado* ☎ *619/435–5432.*

Forget-Me-Not. This relatively tacky gift shop has a few surprises, including reasonably priced glass baubles and miniature figures by Eickholt, Glass Eye Studio, and Goebel. ✉ *1009-A Orange Ave., Coronado* ☎ *619/435–4331.*

Hotel Del Coronado. At the 20 gift shops within the peninsula's main historic attraction, you can purchase everything from sportwear to designer handbags, jewelry, and antiques. ✉ *1500 Orange Ave., Coronado* ☎ *619/435–6611.*

La Provencale. The shop carries imported linens, tableware, fashion accessories, and paintings, all in sunny colors. A line of remarkable French-made acrylic trays and salad bowls are filled with dried herbs and flowers by Amalgam. ✉ *1122 Orange Ave., Coronado* ☎ *619/437–8881.*

Seaside Home. Sophisticated bedding, crystal, porcelain, and home accessories are sold here. ✉ *1053 B Ave., Coronado* ☎ *619/435–8232* ⊕ *www.seasidehomecoronado.com.*

Seaside Paperie. This sister store of Seaside Home offers a selection of high-end wedding invitations, greeting cards, wrapping papers, and luxury personal stationery. ✉ *1162 Orange Ave., Coronado* ☎ *619/435–5565* ⊕ *www.seasidepapery.com.*

WOMEN'S &
MEN'S CLOTHING
Dale's Swim Shop. Something is bound to catch your eye in this shop crammed with swim suits, hats, sunglasses, and sunscreen. ✉ *1150 Orange Ave., Coronado* ☎ *619/435–7301.*

Kippys. The horse and rodeo sets come here for fine leather shirts, chaps, skirts, belts, and bags, most trimmed with gold and silver spangles and beads. ✉ *1114 Orange Ave., Coronado* ☎ *619/435–6218.*

Pollack's Men's Shop. The fine men's sportswear here includes many sweaters and a line of colorful Hawaiian shirts by Reyn Spooner. ✉ *1162 Orange Ave., Coronado* ☎ *619/435–3203.*

Downtown

Shopping Centers

Seaport Village. Horse and carriage rides, an 1895 Looff carousel, and frequent public entertainment are the side attractions to this waterfront complex of more than 50 shops and restaurants. There's a parking lot and the Seaport is within walking distance of hotels and the San Diego Convention Center. **Discover Nature** (☎ 619/231–1299) is where you can find gifts for the office, table-top fountains, wind chimes, and jewelry. **Magic Shop** (☎ 619/236–1556) specializes in magic, games, and gifts. **Seaport Village Shell Company** (☎ 619/234–1004) carries shells, coral, jewelry, and craft items. **Latitudes** (☎ 619/235–0220) sells casual beachwear. **Wyland Galleries** (☎ 619/544–9995) offers the marine life art of Wyland; there's another branch in La Jolla. ⊠ *W. Harbor Dr. at Kettner Blvd., Embarcadero* ☎ 619/235–4014 ⊕ *www.spvillage.com.*

Westfield Shoppingtown Horton Plaza. Within walking distance of most downtown hotels, the Horton Plaza is bordered by Broadway, 1st Avenue, G Street, and 4th Avenue. The multilevel shopping, dining, and entertainment complex is an open-air visual delight, with a terra-cotta color scheme and flag-draped facades. There are department stores, including Macy's, Nordstrom, and Mervyn's; fast-food counters; upscale restaurants; the Lyceum Theater; cinemas; and 140 other stores. Park in the plaza garage and any store where you make a purchase will validate your parking ticket, good for three free hours. The **San Diego City Store** (☎ 619/238–2489) sells city artifacts and memorabilia, such as street signs and parking meters. The yellow SURFING OK sign is a typical San Diego–inspired souvenir. ⊠ *Gaslamp Quarter* ☎ 619/238–1596.

Gaslamp Quarter

Within the Victorian buildings and renovated warehouses along 4th and 5th avenues in the historic heart of San Diego are fine restaurants catering to conventioneers and partying locals, plus some fantastic shops. The art galleries, antiques, and specialty stores in this area tend to close early, starting as early as 5 PM.

Specialty Stores

ANTIQUES **Olde Cracker Factory.** The historic home of the Bishop Cracker Factory now houses a collection of antique shops. **Bobbie's Paper Dolls** (☎ 619/233–0055) displays Victorian paper goods. **Bert's Antiques** (☎ 619/239–5531) specializes in military memorabilia. ⊠ *448 W. Market, Gaslamp Quarter* ☎ 619/233–1669.

San Diego Hardware. If you've been hunting for a piece of reproduction Victorian hardware, this store dating to 1892 may have that piece you've been seeking. ⊠ *840 5th Ave., Gaslamp Quarter* ☎ 619/232–7123.

CLOTHING & **Jacques Lelong.** You'll find everything from formal dresses to T-shirts and
ACCESSORIES jeans, with the shoes, jewelry, scarves, and accessories to go with them. ⊠ *635 5th Ave., Gaslamp Quarter* ☎ 619/234–2583.

La Femme. The filmiest, finest European lingerie can be found here. ⊠ *437 Market St., Gaslamp Quarter* ☎ 619/233–4443.

Le Travel Store. Among the travel accessories sold here are luggage, totes, guidebooks, and maps. ⊠ *745 4th Ave., Gaslamp Quarter* ☎ 619/544–0005.

Splash Wearable Art. The reasonably priced clothing includes one-of-a-kind things not found at the malls, such as dresses crafted from Balinese fabrics and a fine collection of hand-beaded evening wear. ⊠ *376 5th Ave., Gaslamp Quarter* ☎ 619/233–5251.

SHOPPING BLITZ TOUR

A shopping safari in San Diego means casting a wide net, so give yourself plenty of time to navigate the freeways to the malls and to spot parking places. Exact store addresses can be found in the listings below.

Gifts

Charge yourself with a fortifying espresso at **Caffe Italia** in Little Italy and then set off on India Street, where **Bella Stanza, Simply Italian,** and **The Art Store** sell handmade wares. Charming boutiques make up the **Fir Street Cottage Shops,** between India and Columbia streets.

In the nearby Gaslamp Quarter, you'll find **Le Travel Store,** with accessories that travelers love (and sometimes forget to pack), and the **Lucky Dog Pet Boutique,** where you can indulge your four-footed friends.

Bargains

Join the locals on Friday, Saturday, and Sunday at **Kobey's Swap Meet** in Point Loma. Then head to Mission Valley to the **Park in the Valley Center** for discounts at Saks Fifth Avenue's outlet, OFF 5th. Across the street in the **Westfield Shoppingtown Mission Valley,** comb the men's and women's clothing racks at Loehmann's and Nordstrom's Rack for inexpensive basics to designer items.

Galleries

The intersection of Prospect and Girand streets in La Jolla is one of the most glamourous places to shop. Overlooking the ocean is **La Mano** a small shop jam-packed with artful, hand-made Venetian-style Carnival masks in leather, ceramic, and papier-mâché. **Gallery Eight** has lovely hand-blown glass vases and bowls. **Fingerhut Gallery** hangs works by local artists—such as the whimsical lithographs of La Jolla's own Dr. Seuss—along with those by Chagall and Lautrec.

Western Hat Works. Western Hat Works has been selling every kind of hat from fedora to Stetson on this corner since 1922. ✉ 868 5th Ave., Gaslamp Quarter ☎ 619/234–0457.

GALLERIES **Many Hands Crafts Gallery.** This cooperative crafts gallery showcases local pottery, glass, woodwork, photography, fibers, and basketry. ✉ 302 Island Ave., Gaslamp Quarter ☎ 619/557–8303.

Opium Gallery. Furniture and accessories from the world over are sold here. ✉ 425 Market St., Gaslamp Quarter ☎ 619/234–2070.

GIFTS **Cuban Cigar Factory.** Master Cuban cigarmakers hand-roll the goods for
★ this factory, the largest maker of hand-rolled cigars on the West Coast. Its walk-in humidor also carries cigars from Nicaragua, Dominican Republic, and many other countries. They'll ship domestically and internationally. Retail outlets are at the Horton Plaza and Fashion Valley malls. ✉ 551 5th Ave., Gaslamp Quarter ☎ 619/238–2496.

La Paperie. Where paper is art. Fine stationery, cards, and papers from around the world are here, including papyrus, banana paper from the Philippines, and silkscreens from India. ✉ 363 5th Ave., Gaslamp Quarter ☎ 619/234–5457.

Lucky Dog Pet Boutique. If nothing is too good for Fifi or Fido, prove it with a fashionable sweater, raincoat, or pair of shoes. The dog gifts here even include hats, bags, and perfume. ⊠ *557 4th Ave., Gaslamp Quarter* ☎ *619/696–0364.*

San Diego Wine & Culinary Center. Promoting the bountiful produce, wine, food, and chefs of San Diego, the center offers cooking classes and wine tastings. Stock up on locally made olive oils, jams, and sauces to take home. ⊠ *200 Harbor Dr. in Harbor Club Towers, Gaslamp Quarter* ☎ *619/241–2304* ⊕ *www.sdwineculinary.com.*

Splash Bath and Body. Fresh, handmade bath products, such as Milk and Honey Sugar Scrub, After Workout Bath Bomb, or Mary Jane hemp soap complete with seeds—don't worry, this is the legal kind. ⊠ *226 5th Ave., Gaslamp Quarter* ☎ *619/236–9003.*

Little Italy

Italians arrived here in the 1920s to work in the city's once-massive tuna industry. Their working-class neighborhood has turned into a lively urban village, hip and cozy, artsy and bohemian, noted for its bold architecture. Little Italy is bound by the waterfront, Interstate–5 to the east, and Laurel and Ash streets; its heart is India Street, between Cedar and Grape streets. This main thoroughfare has a collection of creative restaurants, boutiques, and art galleries. Take a break from shopping at **Caffe Italia** (⊠ 1804 India St., Little Italy ☎ 619/234–6767), where you can catch up on fashion trends and news at the extensive magazine and newspaper rack.

Specialty Stores

GALLERIES **Boomerang for Modern.** Thoroughly mid-20th century modern design is celebrated here. Aficionados will discover now-classic furniture and accessories produced by Charles and Ray Eames and George Nelson. Small exhibitions showcase vintage and recent works in the modernist spirit, many by local artists. ⊠ *2040 India St., Little Italy* ☎ *619/239–2040* ⊕ *www.boomerangformodern.com.*

2400 Kettner Street. Several fine art galleries are in this building, including **Candy Kuhl** (☎ 619/696–7230) and **David Zapf Gallery** (☎ 619/232–5004). ⊠ *2400 Kettner Blvd., Little Italy.*

GIFTS **The Art Store.** Beside supplying artists with their tools, the Art Store also carries fine stationery, beautiful leather-bound journals, and a fine selection of art books. ⊠ *1844 India St., Little Italy* ☎ *619/687–0050.*

Bella Stanza. The elegant Italian handmade gifts for the home include a large collection of colorful ceramics, glass, and art pieces. ⊠ *1501 India St., No. 120, Little Italy* ☎ *619/239–2929.*

Fir Street Cottage Shops. These colorful cottages hold upscale boutiques. **Cathedral Home** (☎ 619/255–5861), just like its Hillcrest outpost, has fragrant candles, tall Japanese floral vases, and astrologically themed body lotions. Visit **Sorella Boutique** (☎ 619/232–9322) for dresses, separates, accessories, handbags, and jewelry by designers whose labels you won't see in all the malls. ⊠ *600 block of Fir St., between India and Columbia Sts., Little Italy.*

Simply Italian. The fine selection of furniture and accessories for the home hand-crafted by Italian artisans includes Murano glass chandeliers and lava stone and maiolica tables from Naples. ⊠ *1646 India St., Little Italy* ☎ *619/702–7777.*

Hillcrest, North Park, Uptown & Mission Hills

Although their boundaries blur, each of these four established neighborhoods north and northeast of downtown contains a distinct urban village with shops, many ethnic restaurants and cafés, and entertainment venues. Most of the activity is in Hillcrest, on University Avenue and Washington Street, and along the side streets connecting the two.

Gay-popular and funky Hillcrest, northwest of Balboa Park, has many gift, book, and music stores. East of Hillcrest, in North Park, retro rules: nostalgia shops along Park Boulevard and University Avenue at 30th Street carry clothing, accessories, furnishings, wigs, and bric-a-brac of the 1920s–1960s. East of North Park, you'll find the Uptown District, an open-air shopping center on University Avenue that includes several furniture, gift, and specialty stores. Sophisticated, old monied elegance is the tone in the well-heeled Mission Hills neighborhood, west of Hillcrest.

Specialty Stores

BOOKSTORE **Obelisk.** The shelves here hold a bounty of gay and lesbian literature, cards, and gifts. ⊠ *1029 University Ave., Hillcrest* ☎ *619/297–4171.*

GOURMET FOOD **Henry's Marketplace.** This market is a San Diego original for fresh produce, bulk grains, nuts, snacks, dried fruits, and health foods. ⊠ *4175 Park Blvd., North Park* ☎ *619/291–8287.*

Original Paw Pleasers. At this bakery for dogs and cats you'll find oatmeal "dogolate" chip cookies, carob brownies, and "itty bitty kitty treats." ⊠ *1220 Cleveland Ave., Hillcrest* ☎ *619/670–7297.*

Trader Joe's. This shop stocks an affordable and eclectic selection of gourmet foods and wines from around the world. ⊠ *1090 University Ave., Hillcrest* ☎ *619/296–3122.*

HOME **Auntie Helen's.** The nonprofit thrift shop sells heirlooms, collectibles, sea-
ACCESSORIES & sonal items, furniture, and brand-name clothing. Proceeds provide med-
GIFTS ical equipment, clothing, and laundry service to people with AIDS. ⊠ *4028 30th St., North Park* ☎ *619/584–8438.*

Babette Schwartz. This zany pop-culture store sells toys, books, T-shirts, and magnets. ⊠ *421 University Ave., Hillcrest* ☎ *619/220–7048.*

California Fleurish. This perfumery has lots of extras: silk scarves, delicate Japanese pottery, and fine vinegars and soaps. ⊠ *4011 Goldfinch St., Mission Hills* ☎ *619/291–4755.*

Cathedral. Voted the "Best Place to Smell" in a local poll, this store is worth a sniff around. As does its Little Italy sister, it specializes in candles and home and bath goods. You can find creative combinations, such as in the cocoa-hazelnut spice candles, coriander-lavender bath foams, and Asian pear–and–ginger body scrubs. ✉ *435 University Ave., Hillcrest* ☎ *619/296–4046.*

Hillcrest Hardware. Don't let the name fool you. Hardware carries hard-to-find, expensive holiday decorative accessories. ✉ *1007 University Ave., Hillcrest* ☎ *619/291–5988.*

Maison en Provence. There really is a house in Provence and you can rent it from the French proprietors, Pascal and Marielle Giai, who bring sunny fabrics and pottery from the region. There's also fine soaps, antique postcards, and bottles of flower syrups to mix with champagne. ✉ *820 Fort Stockton Dr., Mission Hills* ☎ *619/298–5318.*

Metropolis. This store specializes in reproduction Arts and Crafts items, antiques, and decorative accessories. ✉ *1003 University Ave., Hillcrest* ☎ *619/220–0632.*

P. B. Home & Garden. If you don't make it south of the border, this is a good resource for Mexican pottery and folk art. ✉ *3795 4th Ave., Hillcrest* ☎ *619/295–4851.*

Pomegranate Home Collection. Housed in one of Hillcrest's oldest buildings, the Pomegranate has gifts, cards, and home accessories along with contemporary furnishings. ✉ *1037 University Ave., Hillcrest* ☎ *619/220–0225.*

WOMEN'S & MEN'S CLOTHING   **Le Bel Age Boutique.** Owners Valerie Lee and Michala Lawrence design the women's silk hostess pants and jewelry themselves. ✉ *1607 W. Lewis St., Mission Hills* ☎ *619/297–7080.*

Wear It Again Sam. Among the trendy men's and women's vintage clothes are 1960s ballgowns, panama hats, and collectible cowboy shirts. ✉ *3823 5th Ave., Hillcrest* ☎ *619/299–0185.*

La Jolla

A shopper's dream, this seaside village blends a European resort atmosphere with sunny Southern California characteristics. Chic boutiques, art galleries, and gift shops line narrow twisty streets that are often celebrity soaked. Parking is tight in the village and store hours vary widely, so it's wise to call in advance. Most shops on Prospect Street stay open until 10 PM on weeknights to accommodate evening strollers. On the east side of I–5 office buildings surround Westfield Shoppingtown UTC, where you'll find department stores and chain stores.

Shopping Center

Westfield Shoppingtown UTC. This handy outdoor mall east of La Jolla village has 155 shops, a cinema, and 25 eateries, plus an ice-skating rink. Department stores include Nordstrom, Robinsons-May, Macy's, and Sears Roebuck. **Charles David** (☎ 858/625–0275) sells high-fashion women's shoes. **Chuao Chocolatier** (☎858/546-1463 ⊕www.chuaochocolatier.com), pronounced "chew-wow," is an artisanal chocolate factory named after a region in Venezuela that produces the world's most prized cacao beans. **Royal Nursery** (☎ 858/450–1317) sells sophisticated clothing and accessories for babies. **Papyrus** (☎ 858/458–1399) carries a collection of San Diego postcards, whimsical notecards, gifts, and fine stationery. ⊠ *La Jolla Village Dr., between I–5 and I–805, La Jolla* ☎ *858/546–8858.*

Specialty Stores

Shops in the **Coast Walk Plaza** on Prospect Street, feature designer clothing and handmade crafts amid stunning Pacific Ocean views.

Green Dragon Colony. A loose collection of galleries and boutiques occupy these old buildings, which once served as a retreat for writers, actors, musicians, and other artists. The colony dates back to 1895, when the first structures were built by Anna Held, a German-born woman who came to California as the governess of Ulysses S. Grant Jr.'s children. ⊠ *Prospect St. near Ivanhoe St., La Jolla.*

ANTIQUES **Glorious Antiques.** Profits from the sale of the truly glorious antiques, fine china, silver, crystal, and fine art benefit the San Diego Humane Society. ⊠ *7616 Girard Ave., La Jolla* ☎ *858/459–2222.*

BOOKSTORE **Warwick's.** An upscale bookstore and La Jolla fixture since 1896, Warwick's often hosts big-name author signings. ⊠ *7812 Girard Ave., La Jolla* ☎ *858/454–0347.*

CHILDREN'S **Gap Kids.** The area's best bet for children's togs is this international chain.
CLOTHING ⊠ *7835 Girard Ave., La Jolla* ☎ *858/454–2052.*

FINE ART & **Africa and Beyond.** This gallery carries Shona stone sculpture, textiles,
CRAFTS crafts, masks, and jewelry. ⊠ *1250 Prospect St., La Jolla* ☎ *858/454–9983.*

The Artful Soul. Jewelry, handbags, and gifts by more than 130 contemporary crafts artists, many local. ⊠ *1237-C Prospect St., La Jolla* ☎ *858/459–2009.*

Fingerhut Gallery. Fingerhut carries the art of Dr. Seuss and Grace Slick alongside works by Peter Max and etchings and lithographs by Picasso, Chagall, and Lautrec. ⊠ *1205 Prospect St., La Jolla* ☎ *858/456–9900.*

Gallery Eight. Hand-blown glass, quilted silk jackets from India, and ceramics with a botanical motif are on display. ⊠ *7464 Girard Ave., La Jolla* ☎ *858/454–9781.*

Prospect Place Fine Art. Etchings and lithographs by 19th- and 20th-century masters include works by Miró, Matisse, Rufino Tamayo, and Chagall. ⊠ *1268 Prospect St., La Jolla* ☎ *858/459–1978.*

Wyland Galleries. California artist Wyland is famous for his art works depicting whales and other marine life. The gallery showcases his bronzes, original paintings, and limited-edition work. There's also a gallery in Seaport Village. ⊠ *1025 Prospect St., Suite 100, La Jolla* ☎ *858/459–8229.*

HOME **Alexander Perfumes and Cosmetics.** Products rarely seen in the United States
ACCESSORIES & are available in this European-style perfumery, which claims to have the
GIFTS largest selection of fragrances in California. Its cosmetic lines include Lancaster, Darphin, and Orlane. ⊠ *7914 Girard Ave., La Jolla* ☎ *858/454–2292.*

Bo Danica. The tantalizing selection includes contemporary tabletops, Lynn Chase jungle-motif china, Orrefors crystal, and handmade decorator items. ⊠ *7722 Girard Ave., La Jolla* ☎ *858/454–6107.*

Everett Stunz. This store stocks the finest in luxury home linens, robes, and sleepwear in cashmere, silk, or Swiss cotton. ⊠ *7624 Girard Ave., La Jolla* ☎ *800/883–3305.*

★ **La Mano.** Save yourself a trip to La Serenissima and explore the wide selection of delightful papier-mâché and ceramic Venetian Carnival masks, many handmade. You'll also find the traditional Carnival costumes, including black hooded capes, for rent. ⊠ *1298 Prospect St., La Jolla* ☎ *858/ 454–7732.*

JEWELRY   **Fogel's Antique Beads.** Among the European precious beads from the 1920s are dazzling Austrian and Czech crystal beads. Restringing is done here. ⊠ *1128 Wall St., La Jolla* ☎ *858/456–2696.*

Philippe Charriol Boutique. Charriol's U.S. flagship store features the limited-edition La Jolla watch, an 18-karat white gold bracelet that opens to reveal a mother-of-pearl face on a black satin strap, and also sells watches, necklaces, and bracelets in the Swiss brand's stainless steel and Celtic cable designs. There are fine leather goods and writing instruments as well. It's open noon–6 daily. ⊠ *1227 Prospect St., La Jolla* ☎ *858/ 551–4933 or 800/872–0172.*

Pomegranate. Antique and estate jewelry is paired here with fashions by Eileen Fisher and Harari. ⊠ *1152 Prospect St., La Jolla* ☎ *858/459– 0629.*

WOMEN'S &   **Ascot Shop.** The classic Ivy League look is king in this traditional haber-
MEN'S CLOTHING   dashery that sells menswear by Kenneth Gordon and Talbott, but also gives you the option of loosening up with a Hawaiian shirt. Local stockbrokers are the biggest customers of this store, where professional shoeshines by La Jolla village fixture, Gene Williams, are offered afternoons in the back of the shop. ⊠ *7750 Girard Ave., La Jolla* ☎ *858/454–4222.*

Gentleman's Quarter. This high-end specialist in European-designed suits and sportswear is known for its excellent customer service. The shop also specializes in bespoke Armani, Canali, and Zegna suits made with European specifications and fabrics. ⊠ *1200 Prospect St., La Jolla* ☎ *858/459–3351.*

La Jolla Surf Systems. One block from La Jolla Shores Beach, this La Jolla institution for vivid California beach and resort wear has been in business since 1979. Tame the waves with surfboards by Olas or Tuberville and boogie boards by BZ and Morey. This shop also rents surfboards and boogie boards, beach chairs, umbrellas, and snorkel gear. ⊠ *2132 Avenida de la Playa, La Jolla* ☎ *858/456–2777.*

Rangoni of Florence. This boutique carries its own house brand, Rangoni of Florence, as well as other, medium-price European men's and women's footwear brands including Amalfi, Donald Pliner, and Cole Haan, all fashioned in Italy. ⊠ *7870 Girard Ave., La Jolla* ☎ *858/459–4469.*

Sigi Boutique. Fashionistas seeking very high-end European designer fashions and accessories will discover Italian lines such as Loro Piana for cashmere pieces and Max Mara for sportswear. ✉ *7888 Girard Ave., La Jolla* ☎ *858/454–7244.*

Mission Valley–Hotel Circle Area

The Mission Valley–Hotel Circle area, northeast of downtown near I–8 and Route 163, has two major shopping centers, plus a number of smaller shopping centers that cater to residents.

Shopping Centers

Fodor'sChoice **Fashion Valley.** San Diego's best and most upscale mall has a contem-
★ porary Mission theme, lush landscaping, and more than 200 shops and restaurants. To get here, you can use the San Diego Trolley; many hotels also provide complimentary shuttle service. The major department stores are Macy's, Neiman Marcus, Nordstrom (which also provides a shuttle from various hotels), Robinsons-May, and Saks Fifth Avenue; there's even a Tiffany's here. **April Cornell** (☎ 619/298–8482) carries designer home decor items. **Na Hoku** (☎ 619/294–7811), a Hawaiian jewelry store, has Tahitian black pearls and pendants fashioned as exotic flowers. **Smith & Hawkin** (☎ 619/298–0441) stocks fancy gardening supplies, teak furniture, and gifts. ✉ *7007 Friars Rd., Mission Valley.*

Park in the Valley Center. This U-shape strip mall is across the street from Westfield Shoppingtown Mission Valley. It's anchored by **OFF 5th** (☎ 619/296–4896), where fashions by Ralph Lauren, Armani, and Burberry seen last season in Saks Fifth Avenue are now sold at Costco prices. ✉ *1750 Camino de la Reina, Mission Valley.*

Westfield Shoppingtown Mission Valley. The discount stores at San Diego's largest outdoor mall sometimes reward shoppers with the same merchandise as in Fashion Valley, the mall up the road, but at lower prices. Shops include Macy's Home Store; Loehmann's; Bed, Bath and Beyond; Nordstrom Rack; Charlotte Russe; and Fredericks of Hollywood. ✉ *1640 Camino del Rio N, Mission Valley.*

Specialty Stores

BOOKSTORE **Prince & the Pauper Collectible Children's Books.** You'll find some old friends here, ones you can introduce to your kids. Snaking bookcases in the 4,000-square-foot store reveal 75,000 books. Most titles are gently used hardbacks, some rare and many collectible, and there are out-of-print, first edition, and signed volumes, too, the reason why prices range from one buck to a thousand. The rarer and more valuable volumes are kept under glass. Contemporary titles, like the popular (and hilarious) Captain Underpants books are also available. ✉ *3201 Adams Ave., Normal Heights* ☎ *619/283–4380.*

Ocean Beach, Mission Beach & Pacific Beach

Among the T-shirt shops, yogurt stands, and eateries that line the coast within San Diego proper are a few stores worthy of a browse.

★ **Anna Brazil Brazilian Bikinis.** Anna really hails from Brazil and her shop is the hub of the local Brazilian community. Her rainbow of bikinis range from the teeniest of thongs to bikinis substantial enough to stay on while surfing. She also offers fun sportswear, beach cover-ups, sarongs, and sexy, girly lingerie. ⊠ *954 Garnet Ave., Pacific Beach* ☎ *858/273–3032.*

Great News Discount Cookware. Cooks drool over the discount kitchen tools and gadgets, especially over the mandolines and chinois. There's a cooking school in the back, an extensive selection of cookbooks, and excellent customer service. ⊠ *1789 Garnet Ave., Pacific Beach* ☎ *858/270–1582.*

Mallory's OB Attic. Mallory's handles collectibles and antique and used furniture. ⊠ *4921 Newport Ave., Ocean Beach* ☎ *619/223–5048.*

Pilar's Beach Wear. Come to Pilar's for one of California's largest selections of major-label swimsuits. ⊠ *3745 Mission Blvd., Mission Beach* ☎ *858/488–3056.*

Trader Joe's. Snacks on the beach are as necessary as sunscreen, so stop here for gourmet food and dried fruits and nuts, and for wine and cheese for the evening. ⊠ *1211 Garnet Ave., Pacific Beach* ☎ *858/272–7235.*

Old Town San Diego

North of downtown, off I–5, the colorful Old Town San Diego historic district recalls a Mexican marketplace—maybe a little touristy but with an authentic Latin flavor. Adobe architecture, flower-filled plazas, tiled fountains, and courtyards decorate the shopping areas of Plaza del Pasado, Old Town Esplanade, and Bazaar del Mundo shops, where you'll find international goods, toys, souvenirs, and arts and crafts.

Shopping Centers

Bazaar del Mundo Shops. A new arcade with a Mexican villa theme shares the corner of Taylor and Juan with the Guadalajara Restaurant and offers a variety of gift shops such as the **Ariana Shop,** for ethnic and artsy women's fashions; **Artes de Mexico,** which has a fine array of handmade Latin American crafts and Guatamalan weavings; and **The Gallery** which has handmade jewelry, Native American crafts, collectible glass, and original seriographs by John August Swanson. The **Laurel Burch Galleria** carries the complete collection of this northern California artist's signature jewelry, accessories, and totes. Use the main number for all. ⊠ *4133 Taylor St., Old Town* ☎ *619/296–3131.*

Kobey's Swap Meet. Not far from Old Town is San Diego's premier flea market. The open-air weekend event seems to expand every week, with sellers displaying everything from futons to fresh strawberries. The back section, with secondhand goods, is a bargain-hunter's delight. The swap meet is open Friday–Sunday 7–3; admission is 50¢ on Friday and $1 on weekends; parking is free. ⊠ *San Diego Sports Arena parking lot, 3500 Sports Arena Blvd., Sports Arena* ☎ *619/226–0650.*

Plaza del Pasado. This San Diego institution, formerly known as the Bazaar del Mundo, acquired new management in mid-2005. A collection of boutiques and eateries around a flower-filled courtyard, it resembled a colonial Mexican square in its previous incarnation, but plans are to restore it to a look more in keeping with Old Town's early California days, from 1821 to 1872, and for its shops to stock items reminiscent of that era. Among the planned 11 shops are the **Tienda del Pasado,** selling housewares, linens, and crafts replicating those of the period; **Casa de Serrano,** selling earthenware and ceramics; **Casa de Moreno-Marron,** selling jewelry; **La Roperia,** a clothing store; and **Rudolph Schiller's Books and Journals,** selling quill pens, inkwells, and the like. Many of these were already open at presstime, as was a restaurant, Casa de Reyes, serving Mexican food. Note that a number of the shops previously at this location are now in the Bazaar del Mundo Shops complex at Taylor and Juan streets. Shops are open daily 9–10. ☒ *2754 Calhoun St., Old Town* ☎ *619/297–3100* ⊕ *www.plazadelpasado.com.*

Specialty Shops

FINE ART & **Circa a.d.** The eclectic collection of gifts and home decor includes items
CRAFTS from Asia and Europe such as Japanese tea chests, Thai spirit houses, Russian icons, and Indonesian puppets. ☒ *5355 Grant St., Mission Hills* ☎ *619/293–3328* ⊕ *www.circaad.com.*

★ **Gallery Old Town.** The rare collection of photojournalism by Alfred Eisenstaedt, Margaret Bourke-White, and Gordon Parks occupies a historic building on one of San Diego's oldest streets. ☒ *2513 San Diego Ave., Old Town* ☎ *619/296–7877.*

Studio Gallery of Old Town. This gallery, often crowded at night with after-dinner strollers, is devoted to the extensive animation art of the late Chuck Jones, cartoon director at Warner Bros. from 1938 to 1962 and creator of the Road Runner and Wile E. Coyote among other characters. ☒ *2501 San Diego Ave., Old Town* ☎ *619/294–9880.*

GIFT SHOPS **Apache Indian Arts Center.** Southwestern Indian jewelry, paintings, sculpture, and Pueblo baskets are sold here. ☒ *2425 San Diego Ave., Old Town* ☎ *619/296–9226.*

Earth, Wind & Fire. Now at a new location, this shop sells decorative fountains, ceramics, wind chimes, and cacti. ☒ *2539 Congress St., Old Town* ☎ *619/294–2028.*

Maidhof Bros. This is one of California's oldest and largest dealers in nautical and brass items. ☒ *1891 San Diego Ave., Old Town* ☎ *619/574–1891.*

Ye Olde Soap Shoppe. This shop carries hand-fashioned soaps, as well as a full line of soap-making supplies including kits, herbs, and vegetable bases. ☒ *2497 San Diego Ave., Old Town* ☎ *619/543–1300.*

North County & Environs

WORD OF MOUTH

"I just spent a day in Carlsbad—wandered through all the shops, found a place to do some wine tasting, walked over to the beach, and spent some time there—it was great!!"

—sunbum1944

"The drive through the desert and up [Palomar Mountain] is spectacular: orchards and bougainvillea down low, fields of ferns at the top. There are a lot of good picnic areas both en route and at the mountaintop."

—Gary

"Go see the races in Del Mar!"

—jomomma92024

THE SAN DIEGO NORTH COAST
FROM DEL MAR TO OCEANSIDE

Updated by

Bobbi Zane

ONCE UPON A TIME, TO SAY THAT THE NORTH COAST OF SAN DIEGO COUNTY WAS DIFFERENT from the city of San Diego would have been an understatement. From the northern tip of La Jolla up to Oceanside, a half-dozen small communities developed separately from urban San Diego—and from one another. Del Mar, because of its 2.5 mi of wide beaches, splendid views, and Thoroughbred horse-racing complex, was the playground of the rich and famous. Up the road, agriculture played a major role in the development of Solana Beach and Encinitas.

Carlsbad, too, rooted in the old Mexican rancheros, has agriculture in its past, as well as the entrepreneurial instinct of German immigrant John Frazier, who in the late 19th century promoted the area's water as a cure for common ailments and constructed a replica of a German mineral-springs resort. Oceanside was a beachside getaway for inland families until its economic fortunes changed with the construction of Camp Pendleton as a Marine Corps base during World War II.

What these towns shared was at least a half-century's worth of Southern California beach culture—think Woodies (wood-bodied cars), surfing, the Beach Boys, alternate lifestyles—and the road that connected them, U.S. Highway 101, which nearly passed into oblivion with the advent of Interstate 5.

Then began an explosion of development in the 1980s, and the coast north of San Diego has come to resemble a suburban extension of the city itself. Once-lovely hillsides and canyons have been bulldozed and leveled to make room for bedroom communities in Oceanside, Carlsbad, and even in such high-price areas as Rancho Santa Fe and La Jolla. As suburbanization continues, the towns are reinventing themselves—Carlsbad, for instance, is morphing from a farming community into a tourist destination with Legoland California, several museums, an up-scale outlet shopping complex, and the Four Seasons Resort Aviara.

Still, if you venture off the freeway and head for the ocean, you'll discover remnants of the old beach culture surviving in sophisticated towns where the arts, fine dining, and elegant lodgings rule. The historic U.S. Highway 101—now designated Highway S21 on most maps—is once again marked by its old black-and-white signs most of the way, thanks to the efforts of dedicated preservationists. It connects the beach towns of Del Mar, Solana Beach, Cardiff-by-the-Sea, Encinitas, Leucadia, Carlsbad, and Oceanside, though the road is known by a different name in each one. (Signs say Highway 101 in Solana Beach and Oceanside; in Del Mar it's called Camino del Mar; and in Carlsbad, Carlsbad Boulevard.) Whatever the alias, it's a delightfully scenic drive up the coast past fragile bluffs, rare Torrey pines, and ever-present surfers bobbing in the blue waters.

Numbers in the margin correspond to points of interest on the San Diego North County map.

Del Mar

23 mi north of downtown San Diego on I–5, 9 mi north of La Jolla on Rte. S21.

Del Mar is best known for its quaint old section west of Interstate 5 marked with a glamorous racetrack, half-timber buildings, chic shops, tony restaurants, celebrity visitors, and wide beaches. Its new face is the Del Mar Gateway business complex with high-rise hotels and fast-food outlets east of the interstate at the entrance to Carmel Valley. Access to Del Mar's beaches is from the streets that run east–west off Coast Boulevard; access to the business complex is via Highway 56. Along with its collection of shops, **Del Mar Plaza** also contains outstanding restaurants and landscaped plazas and gardens with Pacific views. The shops and restaurants are pricey, but the view—best enjoyed from the upper level benches and chairs—is free.

Summer evening concerts take place at the west end of **Seagrove Park** (⌧ 15th St., Del Mar), a small stretch of grass overlooking the ocean.

❶ The Spanish mission–style **Del Mar Fairgrounds** is the home of the **Del Mar Thoroughbred Club** (⌧ 2260 Jimmy Durante Blvd., Del Mar ☎ 858/755–1141 ⊕ www.delmarracing.com). Crooner Bing Crosby and his Hollywood buddies—Pat O'Brien, Gary Cooper, and Oliver Hardy, among others—organized the club in the 1930s, primarily because Crosby wanted to have a track near his Rancho Santa Fe home. Del Mar soon developed into a regular train stop for the stars of stage and screen. Even now the racing season here (usually July–September, Wednesday–Monday, post time 2 PM) is one of the most fashionable in California. One of the best places to see and be seen is in the Paddock, where you can watch horses being saddled and the jockeys mount and get ready to trot out to the track. If you're new to horse racing, stop by the Plaza de Mexico where you'll find a table staffed by an employee who can explain how to place a bet on a horse. The track also hosts free Four O'Clock Friday concerts following the races. During off-season, horse players can bet on races at other California tracks televised via satellite at the Surfside Race Place. Times vary, depending on which tracks in the state are operating. Del Mar Fairgrounds hosts more than 100 different events each year, including the Del Mar Fair (San Diego County), which draws more than a million visitors annually, plus a number of horse shows. ⌧ *Head west at I–5 Via de la Valle Rd. Exit* ☎ *858/793–5555* ⊕ *www.sdfair.com.*

☾ **Freeflight,** a small exotic-bird training aviary adjacent to the Del Mar Fairgrounds, is open to the public. You're allowed to handle the birds—a guaranteed child pleaser. ⌧ *2132 Jimmy Durante Blvd., Del Mar* ☎ *858/481–3148* ⊕ *www.animalandbirdhospital.com* ⌦ *$1* ☾ *Daily 10–4.*

Where to Stay & Eat

$$$–$$$$ ✕ **J. Taylor's.** Jacob Taylor built the first hotel in Del Mar early in the 20th century, and nearly a century later the posh Auberge Del Mar Resort and Spa did him the honor of naming its dining room after him.

7

Beaches
Locals stake out their favorite sunning, surfing, bodyboarding, and walking territories at the easily accessible beaches of Coronado, Del Mar, Solana Beach, Encinitas, Carlsbad, and Oceanside.

Desert Adventures
Anza-Borrego Desert State Park encompasses more than 600,000 acres, most of it wilderness. Springtime, when the wildflowers are in full bloom, is a good season to visit. In the sandstone canyons you can walk in the footsteps of prehistoric camels, zebras, and giant ground sloths.

Dining
Dining out is a pleasure wherever you go in the San Diego area, beginning with the array of restaurants in the Gaslamp Quarter and extending north through La Jolla, Del Mar, Solana Beach, and Carlsbad, all of which hold artfully designed restaurants featuring innovative cuisine created by celebrity chefs. By contrast, casual dining is the rule in the beach towns, inland mountain towns, and desert communities.

	WHAT IT COSTS				
	$$$$	$$$	$$	$	¢
AT DINNER	over $30	$23–$30	$16–$22	$10–$15	under $10

Prices are for a main course at dinner, excluding 7.75% tax.

Flowers
The North County is a prolific flower-growing region. Nurseries, some open to the public, line the hillsides on both sides of I–5 in Encinitas, Leucadia, and Carlsbad. Most of the poinsettias sold in the United States get their start here. Quail Botanical Gardens in Encinitas displays native and exotic plants year-round. The gardens at the San Diego Wild Animal Park attract nearly as many people as the animals do.

Lodging
If you stay overnight in the North County, your choices are diverse, from stylish hotels providing solicitous, traditional service to basic motels catering to the beach crowd. Tennis and golf resorts and health-oriented spas abound, and some fine bed-and-breakfast inns are tucked into wooded hillsides around Julian.

	WHAT IT COSTS				
	$$$$	$$$	$$	$	¢
FOR 2 PEOPLE	over $250	$176–$250	$121–$175	$90–$120	under $90

Prices are for a standard double room in high (summer) season, excluding 9 to 10.5% tax.

San Diego North County

Temecula

15

79

Fallbrook

Pala

Palomar
Mountain
6

76

S13

Bonsall

Mission
San Luis Rey **4**

76

S13

Vista

S12

San Diego
Wild
Animal
Park **5**

Anza-Borrego
Desert
State Park

56

S21

78

Oceanside

S11

San
Marcos

15

Escondido

7

Legoland
California **3**

S12

San Pasqual
Valley Rd.

78

Ramona

Carlsbad

5

S10

Rancho Pkwy.

S6

TO JULIAN →

Batiquitos ◆
Lagoon

Quail Botanical
Gardens **2**

Encinitas Blvd.

Lake
Hodges

West
Bernardo Dr.

TO CUYAMACA →
RANCHO STATE PARK

Rancho
Bernardo
Rd.

Leucadia

S9

Encinitas

S11

Rancho
Santa Fe

Rancho
Bernardo

67

Cardiff-by-the-Sea
San Elijo Lagoon Reserve ◆

S8

55

54

Solana Beach

S6

Black Mtn Rd.

15

Poway Rd.   Poway

Del Mar
Fairgrounds **1**

Ted Williams Freeway

Scripps Poway Pkwy.

Pomerado Rd.

Del Mar

56

Mira Mesa

Mira Mesa Blvd.

805

Miramar Rd.

52

La Jolla

163

Mission Gorge Rd.

TO ALPINE →

La Mesa

El Cajon

5

8

125

94

Ocean Beach

94

SAN DIEGO

15

National City

Coronado

805

Chula Vista

5

San Ysidro

905

P A C I F I C   O C E A N

0 ————— 10 miles
0 ————— 15 km

Elegant but relaxed, it offers some of the best cooking in town. Breakfast and lunch, including an all-day Sunday brunch, are excellent, but the dinner menu truly takes off with such appetizers as a "steak" of fresh foie gras with huckleberry sauce, followed by entrées like citrus caramel lacquered duck breast with confit smashed potatoes. ⊠ *1540 Camino del Mar, Del Mar* ☎ *858/259–1515* ▤ *AE, D, DC, MC, V.*

$$–$$$$ ✕ **Arterra Restaurant & Bar.** The name of this hot dining spot created by celebrity chef Bradley Ogden and tucked inside the San Diego Marriott Del Mar hotel means "art of the earth." You can find just that in gorgeous plates of hors d'oeuvres such as Maine lobster cakes with a roasted beet salad or Fuji persimmon salad with goat cheese soufflé and in entrées such as bigeye tuna stacked on wild baby leeks or Moroccan spiced squab. The menu changes daily to reflect what's fresh. A sushi bar is open nightly. The extensive wine list is all-American. ⊠ *11966 El Camino Real* ☎ *858/369–6032* ▤ *AE, D, MC, V* ⊘ *No lunch Sat. and Sun.; sushi bar closed Sun.*

$$–$$$$ ✕ **Jake's Del Mar.** This enormously popular oceanfront restaurant has a close-up view of the water and a menu of simple but well-prepared fare that ranges from an appetizer of mussels steamed in aromatic saffron broth to a mustard-crusted lamb rack with port-flavored garlic sauce. A menu note reminds that the legendary, ice cream–stuffed hula pie is "what the sailors swam ashore for in Lahaina." ⊠ *1660 Coast Blvd., Del Mar* ☎ *858/755–2002* ⌒ *Reservations essential* ▤ *AE, D, MC, V* ⊘ *No lunch Mon.*

$$–$$$$ ✕ **Pacifica Del Mar.** This lovely restaurant overlooks the sea from the plush precincts of Del Mar Plaza. Highly innovative, the restaurant frequently rewrites the menu to show off such show-stoppers as a barbecue sugar-spice salmon with mustard sauce and mustard catfish with Yukon Gold potato–corn succotash; the menu also lists low-carb items. The crowd ranges from young hipsters at the bar to well-dressed businesspeople on the terrace, where glass screens block any hint of a chilly breeze. ⊠ *Del Mar Plaza, 1515 Camino del Mar, Del Mar* ☎ *858/792–0476* ▤ *AE, D, MC, V.*

$$–$$$$ ✕ **Ruth's Chris Steak House.** In a spacious, handsomely decorated setting with a vast outdoor sculpture installation and a narrow view of the Pacific, this outpost of the upscale chain serves oversize portions family style on red-hot metal plates. You might open with lobster bisque, a shrimp cocktail, or a fancy salad. Steaks range in size from a petite filet to a huge "cowboy" rib eye. Maine lobsters start at 2½ pounds. Although ordering dessert may seem improbable after consuming such massive quantities, keep the bread pudding with whiskey sauce in mind. ⊠ *11582 El Camino Real, Del Mar* ☎ *858/755–1454* ▤ *AE, D, DC, MC, V* ⊘ *No lunch.*

$$–$$$$ ✕ **Scalini.** The site of San Diego's most notable singles bar, with dancing the first Wednesday of each month, Scalini overlooks the playing fields of the region's most exclusive polo club from the second floor of a shopping center. The otherwise sedate eatery offers pizza for those who must; for the rest, the menu concentrates on fine pastas, such as the linguine *frutti di mare,* (seafood) and on entrées such as Italian-style bouillabaisse and rack of lamb on a bed of black olive risotto. ⊠ 3790 Via de la Valle, Del Mar ☎ 858/259–9944 ☰ AE, D, DC, MC, V ⊗ No lunch.

$–$$$ ✕ **Epazote.** The menu changes seasonally at this casual-chic eatery. Innovative Southwestern-style dishes range from carne asada salad with organic greens and goat cheese dressed with chile vinaigrette to chile-seared rare ahi tuna with tequila-citrus butter and house-smoked chicken. The hand-shaken margaritas are on the expensive side but superb. There's an ocean view from the patio, which gets busy on weekend nights and during Sunday brunch. ⊠ Del Mar Plaza, 1555 Camino del Mar, Suite 322, Del Mar ☎ 858/259–9966 ☰ AE, D, DC, MC, V.

★ **$–$$$** ✕ **Fish Market.** There's no ocean view at the North County branch of downtown's waterfront restaurant, but this eatery remains popular with residents and tourists for its simple preparations of very fresh fish and shellfish from a menu that changes daily. The oyster bar here is popular. The scene is lively, crowded, and noisy, a great place to bring the kids. ⊠ 640 Via de la Valle, Del Mar ☎ 858/755–2277 ☰ AE, D, DC, MC, V.

$–$$$ ✕ **Nugent's Seafood Grille.** The view of the lagoon is a draw, and if you get here weekdays from 4:30 to 6, when the early-bird menu is in force, you can enjoy it when entrées are about half price. The kitchen respects the integrity of old-style seafood favorites, especially from the owner–chef's native East Coast. Choose from clam chowder and lightly breaded, deep-fried shellfish (served in baskets with spiced french fries), steamed Maine lobster and Chesapeake Bay–style crab cakes, and seafood pastas. ⊠ 2282 Carmel Valley Rd., Del Mar ☎ 858/792–6100 ☰ AE, D, MC, V ⊗ No lunch weekends.

$–$$ ✕ **Barone's Trattoria del Mare.** True to its name, this is a lively, small, Italian seafood restaurant with an outdoor terrace. On the southern rim of town, Barone's specializes in good service and a sizable menu of amply portioned dishes; you are expected to be hungry, and you will be after you scan the list of crab-stuffed mushrooms, linguine with assorted shellfish, grilled swordfish, grilled beef fillet, and other dishes. Light eaters can request half portions of pasta. ⊠ 2234 Carmel Valley Rd., Unit A, Del Mar ☎ 858/259–9063 ☰ AE, MC, V ⊗ No lunch Wed. and Sun.

$–$$ ✕ **Elijah's Delicatessen.** San Diegans are known to complain about the scarcity of decent, East Coast–type delicatessens. Well, this comfortable, no-frills establishment fits the bill. The vast menu extends to all the Jewish deli classics, including blintzes, chopped liver, smoked fish platters, skyscraping sandwiches, and baked beef brisket with potato pancakes. As a plus—this is Del Mar, after all—you can be served on a pleasant outdoor terrace. ⊠ 2638 Del Mar Heights Rd., Del Mar ☎ 858/259–4880 ☰ AE, D, MC, V.

$–$$ ✕ **Villa Capri.** This suave, reasonably priced Italian bistro in Carmel Valley serves out-of-the-ordinary fare, with appetizers like thinly sliced smoked duck breast dressed with truffle oil and shavings of Parmesan. The pasta list shines with such offerings as penne with Italian sausage and artichoke hearts in a pink tomato sauce. Among the entrées, consider the seabass sautéed with tomatoes, onions, capers and black olives, or an unusual veal scaloppine with raspberries flamed in cognac. There's a special children's menu. ⊠ 3870 Valley Center Dr., Del Mar ☎ 858/720–8777 ☰ AE, MC, V ⊗ No lunch weekends.

$ ✕ **Le Bambou.** Small, carefully decorated, and more elegant than any Vietnamese restaurant in San Diego proper, Le Bambou snuggles into the corner of a neighborhood shopping center and is easy to overlook. Those in the know, however, seek it out for authoritative versions of such classics as ground shrimp grilled on sugar cane; Imperial rolls generously stuffed with shrimp, noodles, and bamboo shoots; and cooked-at-the-table beef dishes. ⊠ *2634 Del Mar Heights Rd., Del Mar* ☎ *858/259–8138* ⊟ *MC, V* ⊙ *Closed Mon.*

$ ✕ **Milton's Delicatessen, Grill, Bakery.** There's a bunkerlike quality to this cavernous, semi-underground, Flower Hill Mall restaurant. It was built so that sunlight cascades down the walls, which are decorated with vintage magazine covers. Milton's offers belly-busting portions of traditional deli fare. The vast menu lists some 50 sandwiches, from a simple egg salad on rye to a pork chop sandwich with grilled onions. Entrée salads such as the Cobb and the grilled steak salad easily serve two. The traditional "poor man's meal" in Germany, *hoppel poppel,* an egg scramble of salami, peppers, onions, and potatoes, makes a filling breakfast. ⊠ *2660 Via de la Valle, Del Mar* ☎ *858/792–2225* ⊕ *www.miltonsbaking.com* ⊟ *AE, MC, V.*

¢–$$ ✕ **Taste of Thai.** Tucked into a corner at the east end of the Flower Hill Mall, this informal café is a crowd-pleaser. Flashing lights in the ceiling and other artistic tricks delight young and old as they await plates of savory mee krob noodles, minced beef salad flavored with mint and chilies, and batter-fried calamari with sweet chili sauce. After these substantial snacks diners get down to business with carefully prepared Thai curries, noodle dishes, and such house specialties as crisp-skin duck in garlic sauce and grilled freshwater prawns in mild curry sauce. ⊠ *15770 San Andreas Rd., Del Mar* ☎ *858/793–9695* ⊟ *AE, MC, V.*

$$$$ ▦ **L'Auberge Del Mar Resort and Spa.** Although it looks rather like an upscale condominium complex, L'Auberge is modeled on the Tudor-style hotel that once stood here, a playground for the early Hollywood elite. Today's inn has a relaxed elegance, fitting for the repeat celebrity guests. The beach is a three-minute walk downhill, and the outdoor Pacific Terrace provides a glimpse of the ocean horizon between pine trees. Rooms are done in pink-and-green pastels and have marble bathrooms; most have balconies and gas fireplaces. The resort's own J. Taylor 's restaurant is one of Del Mar's best, and across the street are restaurants and boutiques at Del Mar Plaza. ⊠ *1540 Camino del Mar, Del Mar 92014* ☎ *858/259–1515 or 800/901–9514* ⊟ *858/755–4940* ⊕ *www.laubergedelmar.com* ⇌ *112 rooms, 8 suites* △ *Restaurant, room service, minibars, cable TV with movies, in-room broadband, in-room data ports, 2 tennis courts, 2 pools, gym, outdoor hot tub, massage, sauna, spa, steam room, bar, meeting room, parking (fee); no smoking* ⊟ *AE, D, DC, MC, V.*

$$$ ▦ **San Diego Marriott Del Mar.** Within walking distance of AMN Healthcare, Peregrine, Fair Isaacs, and other companies in the Carmel Valley Corporate Center, this is convenient for business travelers. It's adjacent to two freeways and apt to be noisy outside. However, guest rooms are quiet and services include two-line phones, voice mail, and weekday newspaper delivery. Public areas are homey, with comfortable sofas and fireplaces in the lobby and on a patio outside the Arterra restaurant. Parking in an adjacent structure is $16 per night. ⊠ *11966 El Camino Real, San Diego 92130* ☎ *858/523–2700* 🖷 *858/523–1355* ⊕ *www.marriott. com* 🛏 *281 rooms, 3 suites* ⚪ *Restaurant, room service, cable TV with movies, in-room broadband, in-room data ports, Web TV, Wi-Fi, pool, gym, outdoor hot tub, bar, shop, babysitting, dry cleaning, laundry service, concierge, concierge floor, business services, meeting rooms, car rental, parking (fee), no-smoking rooms* ▤ *AE, D, DC, MC, V.*

$$–$$$ 🏨 **Best Western Stratford Inn of Del Mar.** During racing season this equestrian-themed inn hosts horse owners and jockeys. Spacious rooms, many with ocean views or kitchenettes, are surrounded by six lushly landscaped acres. There's a European day spa, Spa Cucina, on the property. The staff is multilingual. Continental breakfast is included in the price. ⊠ *710 Camino del Mar, Del Mar 92014* ☎ *858/755–1501 or 800/446-7228* 🖷 *858/794–4055* ⊕ *www.bestwestern.com* 🛏 *63 rooms, 31 suites* ⚪ *Some kitchenettes, refrigerators, cable TV, Wi-Fi, 2 pools, outdoor hot tub, spa, laundry service, business services, meeting room, free parking, no-smoking rooms* ▤ *AE, D, DC, MC, V* ⦿l *CP.*

$$ 🏨 **Clarion Del Mar Inn.** Del Mar's Tudor theme prevails at this hotel with steep gabled roofs and colorful English gardens. The inn is within walking distance of the beach, shopping, restaurants, and a local fitness center, which you can use at no charge. A continental breakfast and afternoon tea are included in the room rate. ⊠ *720 Camino del Mar, Del Mar 92014* ☎ *858/755–9765 or 800/451–4515* 🖷 *858/792–8196* ⊕ *www.delmarinn.com* 🛏 *81 rooms* ⚪ *Some kitchenettes, some microwaves, refrigerators, cable TV, pool, outdoor hot tub, library, dry cleaning, laundry facilities, business services, meeting rooms, free parking; no smoking* ▤ *AE, D, DC, MC, V* ⦿l *CP.*

Shopping

The tiered, Mediterranean-style **Del Mar Plaza** (⊠ 15th St. and Camino Del Mar, Del Mar ☎ 858/792–1555) has flower-filled courtyards, fountains, a spectacular view of the Pacific, and some fine restaurants. Some businesses validate parking, which is underground. **White House/Black Market** (☎ 858/794–0355) stocks fashionable apparel for women, mainly in basic black and white. **Georgiou** (☎ 858/481–1964) specializes in designer women's fashions. **San Diego Harley Davidson** (☎ 858/259–7037) stocks signature fashions and gifts for Harley riders.

Thinker Things (⊠ 2670 Via de la Valle, Del Mar ☎ 858/755–4488) carries children's dolls, puppets, crafts, and games.

Solana Beach

1 mi north of Del Mar on Rte. S21, 25 mi north of downtown San Diego on I–5 to Lomas Santa Fe Dr. west.

Once-quiet Solana Beach is *the* place to look for antiques, collectibles, and contemporary fashions and artwork. The Cedros Design District, occupying four blocks south of the Amtrak station, contains shops, galleries, designers' studios, restaurants, and a popular performance venue, the Belly Up Tavern. The tavern and businesses surrounding it occupy a group of World War II–style Quonset huts standing side by side. Solana

Beach is known for its excellent restaurants, but most area lodging is in the adjacent towns of Del Mar and Encinitas. In September, 2003, the city became the first in California to ban smoking on its beaches.

Where to Stay & Eat

★ $$$–$$$$ ✕ **Pamplemousse Grille.** Justly celebrated as one of North County's best restaurants, the "Grapefruit Grill," across the street from the racetrack, offers French-country dining California style. Chef-proprietor Jeffrey Strauss brings a caterer's sensibilities to the details, like a mix-or-match selection of sauces—wild mushroom, grey mustard, or peppercorn—to complement the simple but absolutely top-quality grilled meats and seafood. Appetizers can be very clever, like the huge wild mushroom ravioli. The comfortable rooms are painted with murals of bucolic country scenes, and the service is quiet and professional. ⊠ 514 Via de la Valle, Solana Beach ☎ 858/792–9090 ⊟ AE, D, DC, MC, V ⊗ No lunch Sat.–Thurs.

$$–$$$$ ✕ **Red Tracton's.** Across the street from the Del Mar racetrack, this deluxe steak and seafood house is a high-roller's heaven. Everyone from the bar pianist to the exceptional waitresses is well aware that smiles and prompt service can result in tips as generously sized as the gigantic Australian lobster tails that the menu demurely lists at "market price." Tracton's serves simple but good food, and the menu highlights roasted prime rib in addition to prime New York sirloin and filet mignon, top-grade pork back ribs, panfried scallops, and such starters as lobster bisque and "jumbo" shrimp on ice. ⊠ 550 Via de la Valle, Solana Beach ☎ 858/755–6600 ⟐ Reservations essential ⊟ AE, D, DC, MC, V ⊗ No lunch Sun.

¢–$$ ✕ **Pizza Port.** Local families flock to the port for its casual ambiance, great pizza, and hand-crafted brews. Pick a spot at one of the long picnic-type tables, choose traditional or whole grain beer crust for your pie and any original topping—such as the Monterey, with pepperoni, onions, mushrooms, and artichoke hearts—and tip back a brew from one of the longest boutique lists in San Diego. Even dessert reeks of hops: beer floats with homemade ice cream for the over-21 set and made with root beer for everyone else. ⊠ 135 N. Hwy. 101, Solana Beach ☎ 858/481–7332 ⊠ 571 Carlsbad Village Dr., Carlsbad ☎ 760/720–7007 ⟐ Reservations not accepted ⊟ AE, MC, V.

¢–$ ✕ **Don Chuy.** Small, family-run, unassuming, and utterly charming, Don Chuy serves authentic Mexican cuisine to Southern Californians who, before dining here, may have tasted only a pale version of the real thing. The flavors are savory and convincing, and the portions sufficient to banish hunger until the following day. For something straight from the soul of Mexican home cooking, try the *nopales con chorizo y huevos,* a scramble of tender cactus leaves, crumbled spicy sausage, and eggs; this is served with piles of rice and beans as well as a warm tortilla and the palate-warming house salsa. ⊠ 650 Valley Ave., Solana Beach ☎ 858/794–0535 ⊟ AE, D, MC, V.

$$–$$$ ▥ **Holiday Inn Express.** Straddling the border between Del Mar and Solana Beach, this modern hotel offers good value in a pricey area, par-

ticularly in the cool off-season. Simply furnished rooms have balconies with pool views and coffeemakers. A continental breakfast is included in the room rate. ⊠ *621 S. Coast Hwy. 101, Solana Beach 92075* ☎ *858/350–0111* 🖷 *858/481–9177* ⊕ *www.hinnexpress.com* ↩ *64 rooms, 16 suites* ⚘ *Microwaves, refrigerators, cable TV with movies, Wi-Fi, pool, gym, outdoor hot tub, meeting rooms, free parking, no-smoking rooms* ▭ *MC, V* ⦿ *CP.*

Nightlife

Belly Up Tavern (⊠ 143 S. Cedros Ave., Solana Beach ☎ 858/481–9022), a fixture on local papers' "best of" lists, has been drawing crowds of all ages since it opened in the mid-'70s. The "BUT's" longevity attests to the quality of the eclectic entertainment on its stage. Within converted Quonset huts, critically acclaimed artists play everything from reggae and folk to—well, you name it.

Shopping

★ The **Cedros Design District** (⊕ www.cedrosdesigndistrict.com) is a collection of nearly 100 shops that specialize in interior design and gifts.

Antique Warehouse (⊠ 212 S. Cedros Ave. ☎ 858/755–5156) carries American and European antiquities, art, books, glass, dolls, and jewelry. **Birdcage** (⊠ 143 S. Cedros Ave., Suite J ☎ 858/793–6263) specializes in unusual home accessories. At **Frangipani, Resort Wear** (⊠ 130 S. Cedros Ave., No. 130 ☎ 858/259–0288), you can find sarongs and aloha shirts, as well as south seas fragrances, hats, and shoes. You'll find cool accessories such as designer beds and totes for *haute* dogs and cats at **Muttropolis** (⊠ 227 S. Cedros Ave. ☎ 858/755–3647). **Trios Gallery** (⊠ 130 S. Cedros Ave. ☎ 858/793–6040) showcases the work of local artists, including James Hubbell, and designer jewelry.

Rancho Santa Fe

4 mi east of Solana Beach on Rte. S8, Lomas Santa Fe Dr., 29 mi north of downtown San Diego on I–5 to Rte. S8 east.

Groves of huge, drooping eucalyptus trees cover the hills and valleys of exclusive Rancho Santa Fe. East of I–5 on Via de la Valle Road, Rancho Santa Fe is horse country. It's common to see entire families riding the many trails that crisscross the hillsides.

The town, modeled after a Spanish village, was designed by Lillian Rice, one of the first women to graduate with a degree in architecture from the University of California. Her first structure, a 12-room house built in 1922, evolved into the Inn at Rancho Santa Fe, which became a gathering spot for celebrities such as Bette Davis, Errol Flynn, and Bing Crosby. The challenging Rancho Santa Fe Golf Course, the original site of the Bing Crosby Pro-Am and considered one of the best courses in Southern California, is open only to members of the Rancho Santa Fe community and guests of the inn.

Where to Stay & Eat

★ $$$–$$$$ ✕ **Mille Fleurs.** Mille Fleurs is a winner, from its location in the heart of wealthy, horsey Rancho Santa Fe to the warm Gallic welcome extended by proprietor Bertrand Hug and the talents of chef Martin Woesle. The quiet dining rooms are decorated like a French villa. Menus are written daily to reflect the market and Woesle's mood, but sometimes feature a soup of *musque de Provence* (pumpkin with cinnamon croutons), sautéed *lotte* (monkfish) with pink grapefruit, medallions of antelope with apples and spaetzle, and oven-roasted baby lamb with summer vegetable ratatouille. ☒ *Country Squire Courtyard, 6009 Paseo Delicias, Rancho Santa Fe* ☎ 858/756–3085 ⚏ *Reservations essential* ▤ *AE, DC, MC, V* ☉ *No lunch weekends.*

$$$$
Fodor's Choice
★

🏨 **Rancho Valencia Resort.** One of Southern California's hidden treasures has luxurious accommodations in Spanish-style casitas scattered on 40 acres of landscaped grounds. Suites have corner fireplaces, luxurious Berber carpeting, and shuttered French doors leading to private patios. Twelve suites also have steam showers, private outdoor hot tubs, and wall-mounted plasma flat screen TVs. Rancho Valencia is one of the nation's top tennis resorts and is adjacent to three well-designed golf courses. Its first-rate restaurant ($$$$) has a seasonal menu that might include maple-glaze cedar plank salmon, beef rib eye with green peppercorn Armagnac sauce, or an array of fresh vegetables from the famed Chino Family Farm. ☒ *5921 Valencia Circle, Rancho Santa Fe 92067* ☎ *858/756–1123 or 800/548–3664* ⎙ *858/756–0165* ⊕ *www.ranchovalencia.com* ⇖ *49 suites* ⚏ *Restaurant, room service, in-room safes, some in-room hot tubs, minibars, refrigerators, cable TV with movies, in-room broadband, 18 tennis courts, 2 pools, health club, 3 outdoor hot tubs, spa, bicycles, croquet, hiking, bar, shops, business services, meeting rooms, free parking, no-smoking rooms* ▤ *AE, DC, MC, V.*

★ **$$$–$$$$**

🏨 **Inn at Rancho Santa Fe.** Understated elegance is the theme of this genteel old resort in the heart of the Spanish colonial revival–style village of Rancho Santa Fe. Guest rooms are in red-tile cottages spread around the property's 23 lushly landscaped acres. Many have private patios and woodburning fireplaces. The inn provides guests with membership at the exclusive Rancho Santa Fe Golf Club and privileges at five other nearby, exclusive courses. ☒ *5951 Linea del Cielo, Rancho Santa Fe 92067* ☎ *858/756–1131 or 800/843–4661* ⎙ *858/759–1604* ⊕ *www.theinnatrsf. com* ⇖ *73 rooms, 5 suites, 8 private 1-, 2-, and 3-bedroom cottages* ⚏ *Restaurant, room service, in-room safes, some kitchens, minibars, microwaves, cable TV with movies, in-room broadband Wi-Fi, 3 tennis courts, pool, exercise equipment, croquet, bar, library, piano, meeting rooms, free parking, some pets allowed; no smoking* ▤ *AE, DC, MC, V.*

Shopping

Tony boutiques here cater to the ultrawealthy. However, a couple of shops are worthy of note, even if you don't have a fat wallet. **Country Friends** (☒ 6030 El Tordo ☎ 858/756–1192) is a great place for unusual gifts. Operated by a nonprofit foundation, it carries collectibles, silver, and antiques donated or consigned by the community's residents. The **Vegetable Shop** (☒ 6123 Calzada del Bosque ☎ 858/756–3184) is the place to buy the same premium (and very expensive) fruits and rare baby vegetables that the Chino Family Farm grows for many of San Diego's upscale restaurants and for such famed California eateries as Chez Panisse in Berkeley and Spago in Los Angeles.

Encinitas

6 mi north of Solana Beach on Rte. S21, 7 mi west of Rancho Santa Fe on Rte. S9, 28 mi north of downtown San Diego on I–5.

Flower breeding and growing has been the major industry in Encinitas since the early part of the 20th century; the town now calls itself the Flower Capital of the World due to the large number of nurseries operating here. The city, which encompasses the coastal towns of Cardiff-by-the-Sea and Leucadia as well as inland Olivenhain, is home to Paul Ecke Poinsettias (open only to the trade), which tamed the wild poinsettia in the 1920s and today is the largest producer and breeder of the Christmas blossom in the world. During the spring blooming season some commercial nurseries east of I–5 are open to the public. The palms and the golden domes of the Self-Realization Fellowship Retreat and Hermitage mark the southern entrance to downtown Encinitas.

U.S. 101—now Route S21—was the main route connecting all the beach towns between southern Orange County and San Diego before the I–5 freeway was constructed to the east of Encinitas. Local civic efforts are bringing back the historic California–U.S. 101 signs and restoring the boulevard's historic character.

Quail Botanical Gardens displays more than 4,000 rare, exotic, and endangered plants on 30 landscaped acres. Displays include plants from Central America, Africa, Australia, the Middle East, the Mediterranean, the Himalayas, Madagascar, and more; the largest collection of bamboo in North America; California native plants; and subtropical fruits. Kids can roll around in the Seeds of Wonder garden, explore a baby dinosaur forest, discover a secret garden, or play in a playhouse. An Under the Sea Garden, opened in 2004, is actually a rock garden of succulents that uncannily mimics an underwater environment. ⊠ *230 Quail Gardens Dr., Encinitas* ☎ *760/436–3036* ⊕ *www.qbgardens. com* ⊡ *$8* ⊙ *Daily 9–5.*

The **San Elijo Lagoon Reserve,** between Solana Beach and Encinitas, is the most complex of the estuary systems in San Diego North County. A network of trails surrounds the area, where more than 189 species of birds, 300 species of plants, and many fish and migrating birds live. Docents offer free public walks here; call for dates and times. ⊠ *2710 Manchester Ave., Encinitas* ☎ *760/436–3944* ⊕ *www.sanelijo.org* ⊡ *Free* ⊙ *Daily dawn–dusk.*

The **Self-Realization Fellowship Retreat and Hermitage** was founded in 1936 as a retreat and place of worship by Paramahansa Yogananda, author of the classic *Autobiography of a Yogi.* Two beautiful meditation gardens open to the public have sweeping views of the Pacific. The gardens are planted with flowering shrubs and trees and contain a series of ponds connected by miniature waterfalls populated by tropical fish. Wandering through this peaceful place, you may encounter a couple exchanging wedding vows against the backdrop of the Pacific Ocean. ⊠ *215 K St., Encinitas* ☎ *760/753–2888* ⊕ *www.encinitastemple.org* ⊡ *Free* ⊙ *Tues.–Sun. 9–5.*

BOUNTIFUL BEAUTY

SOUTHERN CALIFORNIA'S FAMOUS WARM, SUNNY CLIMATE has blessed this corner of the continent with an ever-changing, year-round palette of natural color. It's hard to find a spot anywhere around the globe that produces as spectacular a scene as San Diego does in spring—from the native plant gardens found tucked away in mountain canyons and streambeds to the carpets of wildflowers on the desert floor. You'll have to see it yourself to believe just how alive the deceptively barren desert really is.

Spring debuts in late February or early March. Heavy winter rains always precede the best bloom seasons. And good blooms also bring even more beauty—a bounty of butterflies. A further boon: here in this generally temperate climate, the bloom season lasts nearly all year.

Some drought-tolerant plants rely on fire to germinate, and the years following wildfires generally produce a profusion of plantlife not normally seen. Although wildfires in the Cuyamaca and Laguna mountains in 2002 and 2003 destroyed much of the ancient forest, subsequent years saw brilliant and unusual wildflower displays as a result, and these should continue. Look for rare western redbud trees erupting into a profusion of crimson flowers, sometimes starting as early as February. Native California lilacs (ceanothus) blanket the hillsides throughout the backcountry with fragrant blue-and-white blossoms starting in May and showing until August.

Native varieties of familiar names show up in the mountain canyons and streambeds. A beautiful white western azalea would be the star in anyone's garden. A pink California rose blooms along streambeds in spring and summer. Throughout the year three varieties of native dogwood show off white blooms and beautiful crimson fall foliage. The Cuyamaca Mountains usually put on a display of fall color as the native oaks turn gold and red. By winter the rare toyon, known as the California Christmas tree, shows off its red berries alongside the roads.

You can get a good introduction to mountain wildflowers by visiting Julian in early May, when the Women's Club puts on its annual Wildflower Show. For more than seven decades members have collected and displayed native plants and flowers from hillsides, meadows, and streambeds surrounding the mountain town. For information on exact dates call the Julian Chamber of Commerce (☎ 760/765–1857).

Farther east in the Anza-Borrego Desert State Park, the spring wildflower display can be spectacular: carpets of pink, purple, white, and yellow verbena and desert primrose as far as the eye can see. Rocky slopes yield clumps of beavertail cactus topped with showy pink blossoms, clumps of yellow brittlebush tucked among the rocks, and crimson-tip ocotillo trees. For a good introduction to desert vegetation, explore the visitor center demonstration garden, adjacent to the park's underground headquarters.

For a vivid view of both the mountain and desert spring flora, take Interstate 8 east to Route 79, go north to Julian, and then east on Route 78 into Anza-Borrego park.

San Diego County is a leading flower supplier to the nation, with dozens of nurseries turning out poinsettias, ranunculus, bromeliads, orchids, begonias, and other subtropical plants. Many can be seen and visited in the coastal area of the county. In spring, tour the brilliant acres of ranunculus blooms at the Flower Fields at Carlsbad Ranch (Palomar Airport Road, east of I–5, ☎ 760/431–0352, www.theflowerfields.com).

☺ The **Magdalena Ecke Family YMCA Skate Park,** completed in June 2004, holds a 25,000-square-foot street course with quarter pipes, bank ramps, roll-in ramps, pyramids, hips, handrail stations, slider boxes, a 12-foot vert wall, and a little kids' course. Ask your nearest 13-year-old what these things mean. There are two classic cement pools, one kidney-shape and the other clover-shape. A new 120-foot-wide ramp was used by the X Games in 2003. One or two times a week, the street course and vert ramp are co-opted for the exclusive use of BMX bikers (this depends on demand and policy may change in the future). Even if you don't skate or ride it's exciting just to sit and watch. ⊠ *200 Saxony Rd., Encinitas* ☎ *760/942–9622* ⊕ *ecke.ymca.org* ⊠ *$10* ⊙ *Weekdays 2:30–5, weekends 9–5.*

Where to Stay & Eat

$$–$$$$ ✕ **La Bonne Bouffe.** A longtime North County favorite, this tiny storefront restaurant offers expertly prepared classic French fare, including a delicious beef bourguignonne, roast duckling in green peppercorn sauce, Dover sole, and frogs' legs. With lace curtains, white tablecloths, and bistro chairs, you can pretend you're dining in France. ⊠ *471 Encinitas Blvd., Encinitas* ☎ *760/436–3081* ⚏ *Reservations essential* ⊟ *AE, D, DC, MC, V* ⊙ *Closed Sun. and Mon. No lunch.*

$–$$ ✕ **Hershel's.** Morning, noon, and night, this cheerful deli and restaurant is packed with diners who flock here for the enormous omelets, lox and bagel noshes, and overstuffed sandwiches that range from four variations on the Reuben to kippered salmon salad. Breakfast is served all day, and Hershel's serves a small selection of dinner specials, too. Beware—the desserts are more than enough for two. Give yourself some time to peruse the menu; it's enormous. ⊠ *1486 Encinitas Blvd., Encinitas* ☎ *760/942–9655 or 888/656–3354* ⊟ *AE, D, DC, MC, V.*

¢–$$$ ✕ **Italian Market.** A gregarious Franco-Italian couple, Jean and Rosanna, run this small restaurant in old Encinitas. At lunch there are great deli sandwiches on homemade bread (try the prosciutto and provolone on focaccia) and excellent pizzas. The dinner menu lists osso buco and veal chop. There are a few tables inside and several more on the front and back patios. ⊠ *806 S. Coast Hwy., U.S. 101, Encinitas* ☎ *760/942–0738* ⊟ *AE, D, DC, MC, V.*

¢–$$ ✕ **La Especial Norte.** Casual to the point of funkiness, this Mexican café is a great hit with locals who flock here to slurp up large bowls of delicious homemade soups. Try the chicken, beans, and rice, or the Seven Seas fish soup accompanied by tortillas and a dish of cabbage salad. You can also order renditions of the standard burrito, enchilada, and taco, and premium margaritas. ⊠ *644 N. Coast Hwy., Encinitas* ☎ *760/942–1040* ⊟ *AE, D, MC, V.*

$$–$$$ ▥ **Best Western Encinitas Inn and Suites at Moonlight Beach.** This hotel, tucked into a hillside west of I–5 with ocean or city views from all rooms, offers a great deal. Unusually spacious rooms are well equipped for business travelers. Most rooms have private balconies. There's an attractive swimming pool area and a popular Japanese restaurant, Tomiko. Continental breakfast is complimentary. ⊠ *85 Encinitas Blvd., Encinitas 92024* ☎ *760/942–7455* ⊞ *760/632–9481* ⊕ *www.bestwestern.com* ◁ *60 rooms, 34 suites* ⚭ *Restaurant, in-room safes, refrigerators, cable TV with movies, in-room* *broadband, in-room data ports, pool, outdoor hot tub, sauna, bar, laundry service, concierge, business services, meeting room, airport shuttle, free parking, no-smoking rooms* ⊟*AE, D, DC, MC, V* ⋔❘ *CP.*

★ **$–$$** 🏨 **Country Inn by Ayers.** Just off I–5, this inn has a European ambience. Rooms are decorated with reproduction French antiques including pencil point beds and mahogany armoires. The large lobby resembles a living room with a huge fireplace. Breakfast and afternoon refreshments (mid-week) are included in the room rate. ✉ *1661 Villa Cardiff Dr., Cardiff by the Sea 92007* 🕾 *760/944–0427 or 800/322-9993* 🖷 *760/944–7708* ⊕ *www.ayershotel.com* ⮡ *100 rooms* ⚒ *Refrigerators, cable TV, in-room data ports, pool, outdoor hot tub, business services, meeting room, free parking, no-smoking rooms* ⊟ *AE, D, DC, MC, V* ⋔❘ *CP.*

$–$$ 🏨 **Ocean Inn.** Across from the train tracks on the main drag through town, this lodging is apt to be somewhat noisy. The simple guest rooms are done in soft pink and blue floral fabrics, except for the Lego-themed suite that has a bold primary color scheme. In the afternoon you can share a *cuppa* in the hotel's cheery tea room. Continental breakfast is included in the price. ✉ *1444 N. Coast Hwy. 101, Encinitas 92024* 🕾 *760/436–1988 or 800/546–1598* 🖷 *760/436–3921* ⊕ *www.oceaninnhotel.com* ⮡ *50 rooms* ⚒ *Some in-room hot tubs, kitchenettes, microwaves, refrigerators, cable TV, laundry facilities, free parking, no-smoking rooms* ⊟ *AE, D, MC, V* ⋔❘ *CP.*

$ 🏨 **Moonlight Beach Motel.** This folksy, laid-back motel is a short walk from the beach. Rooms are basic but spacious and clean, and most have balconies and ocean views. ✉ *233 2nd St., Encinitas 92024* 🕾 *760/753–0623 or 800/323–1259* 🖷 *760/944–9827* ⮡ *24 rooms* ⚒ *Kitchenettes, cable TV, free parking, no-smoking rooms; no a/c* ⊟ *AE, D, DC, MC, V.*

Shopping

Souvenir items are sold at shops along U.S. 101 and in the Lumberyard Shopping Center. Encinitas also abounds in commercial plant nurseries where you can pick up a bit of San Diego to take home. Look for cut flowers, seeds, bulbs, starter cuttings, unusual small plants, and cactus in nursery gift shops.

Anderson's La Costa Nursery (✉ 400 La Costa Ave., Encinitas 🕾 760/ 753–3153) offers rare and hard-to-find orchids, bromeliads, cactus, and succulents. **Bailey's–That Cat Place** (✉ 162 S. Rancho Santa Fe Rd., Encinitas 🕾 760/944–5783), caters to cat-lovers with feline toys and supplies and cat-themed human apparel, jewelry, and gifts. **Hansen's** (✉ 1105 S. Coast Hwy. 101, Encinitas 🕾 760/753–6595 ⊕ www. hansensurf.com), one of San Diego's oldest surfboard manufacturers, is owned by Don Hansen, surfboard shaper extraordinaire, who came here from Hawaii in 1962. The store, about a block south of the Lumberyard Shopping Center, also stocks a full line of recreational clothing and casual wear.

Weideners' Gardens (✉ 695 Normandy Rd., Encinitas 🕾 760/436–2194) carries begonias, fuchsias, and other flowers. It's closed sporadically in fall and winter; call for hours.

Carlsbad

6 mi from Encinitas on Rte. S21, 36 mi north of downtown San Diego on I–5.

The opening of the Legoland California theme park in 2000 marked a turning point for once laid-back Carlsbad, a Bavarian-inspired coastal community that has long been popular with beachgoers and sun seekers. On a clear day you can take in sweeping ocean views that stretch from La Jolla to Oceanside by walking along a 2-mi-long seawalk that runs between the Encina power plant and Pine Street. En route, you'll find several stairways leading to the beach and quite a few benches. The advent of Legoland California has moved much of the area's visitor appeal inland east of I–5: the park is at the center of a tourist complex that includes resort hotels, a discount shopping mall, golf courses, and colorful spring-blooming Flower Fields at Carlsbad Ranch. Until the mid-20th century, when suburban development began to sprout on the hillsides, farming was the main industry in Carlsbad, with truckloads of avocados, potatoes, and other vegetables shipped out year-round. Some agriculture remains. Carlsbad strawberries are still among the sweetest you'll find in Southern California; in spring you can pick them yourself in fields on both sides of I–5. Area farmers develop and grow new varieties of flowers including the ranunculus that transform a hillside into a rainbow each spring.

Carlsbad village owes its name and Bavarian look to John Frazier, who lured people to the area a century ago with talk of the healing powers of mineral water bubbling from a coastal well. The water was found to have the same properties as water from the German mineral wells of Karlsbad—hence the name of the new community. Remnants from this era, including the original well and a monument to Frazier, are found at the **Alt Karlsbad Mineral Water Spa** (⊠ 2802 Carlsbad Blvd., Carlsbad ☎ 760/434–1887), a stone building that houses a small day spa and the Carlsbad Water Company, a 21st-century version of Frazier's waterworks.

Development has destroyed many of the lagoons and saltwater marsh wildlife habitats that used to punctuate the North County coastline, but **Batiquitos Lagoon,** one of the few remaining tidal wetlands in Southern California, has been restored to support fish and bird populations. A stroll along the 1.5 mi trail along the north shore of the lagoon reveals nesting sites of the red-wing blackbird, lagoon birds such as the great blue heron, the great egret, and the snowy egret, and life in the mud flats. This is a quiet spot for contemplation or a picnic. ⊠ *Batiquitos Dr. S, east of I–5's Poinsettia La. Exit, Carlsbad* ☎ *760/931–0800* ⊕ *www.batiquitosfoundation.org* ☉ *Tours on weekends and Fri.; call ahead.*

ⓒ ❸ **Legoland California,** the centerpiece of a development that includes re-
FodorsChoice sort hotels and a designer discount shopping mall, offers a full day of
★ entertainment for pint-size fun-seekers and their parents. The mostly outdoor experience is best appreciated by kids ages 2 to 10, who often beg to ride the mechanical horses around the Royal Joust again and again

or to take just one more turn through the popular Volvo Jr. Driving School. Miniland USA, an animated collection of U.S. cities and other areas constructed entirely of Lego blocks, captures the imaginations of all ages. Dads beg to be taken to Miniland Florida, which has a diminutive race course where they can race remote-controlled Lego brick cars. Also in Miniland USA is the Block of Fame, a collection of busts of famous people such as George Washington and Marilyn Monroe, created from Lego bricks. Kids get a chance to dig for buried fossils on Dino Island, which holds the Dig Those Dinos paleontological play area as well as the Coastearaurus, a junior roller coaster. At the Fun Town Fire Academy, families compete at fire fighting by racing in a model fire truck and hosing down a simulated burning building. Also in Fun Town, besides the driving school, with miniature cars, is the Skipper School, with miniature boats. Other Legoland attractions include a castle; a power tower with an ocean view; a waterworks operated by joysticks; and Aquazone Wave Racers, the first power-ski water ride in North America. Stage shows and restaurants with kid-friendly buffets are also part of the mix. ⊠ *1 Lego Dr., exit I–5 at Cannon Rd. and follow signs east ¼ mi, Carlsbad* ☎ *760/918–5346* ⊕ *www.legolandca.com* ⊠ *$44.95, kids $37.95* ☉ *Days, hrs vary. Mid-Sept.–mid-June, daily 10–5; mid-June–Labor Day, daily 10–8.*

In spring the hillsides are abloom at **Flower Fields at Carlsbad Ranch,** the largest bulb production farm in Southern California. Here, from mid-March through mid-May, you can walk through fields planted with thousands of Giant Tecolote ranunculus—a stunning 50-acre display of color against the backdrop of the blue Pacific Ocean. Also to be seen are the rose gardens—including the miniature rose garden and the walk of fame garden, lined with examples of every All-American Rose Selection award-winner since 1940—and demonstration gardens created by artists who normally work with paint and easel. The unusually large and well-stocked Armstrong Garden Center at the exit carries plants, garden accessories, and ranunculus bulbs. ⊠ *5704 Paseo del Norte, east of I–5, Carlsbad* ☎ *760/431–0352* ⊕ *www.theflowerfields.com* ⊠ *$8* ☉ *Mar.–May, daily 9–6.*

Take an interactive journey through 100 years of popular music at the **Museum of Making Music,** which displays more than 450 vintage instruments and samples of memorable tunes from the past century. Hands-on activities include playing a digital piano, drums, guitar, and electric violin. ⊠ *5790 Armada Dr., east of I–5, Carlsbad* ☎ *760/438–5996* ⊕ *www.museumofmakingmusic.org* ⊠ *$5* ☉ *Tues.–Sun. 10–5.*

The **Leo Carrillo Ranch Historic Park** was a real working ranch with 600 head of cattle owned by actor Leo Carrillo, who played Pancho in the Cisco Kid television series in the 1950s. Before Carrillo bought the spread in 1937, the rancho, occupying portions of a Spanish land grant, was the home of a band of Luiseno Indians. Carrillo's hacienda and other buildings have been restored to reflect the life of the star when he hosted his Hollywood friends for long weekends in the country. Four miles of trails take visitors through colorful native gardens to the cantina, wash

CloseUp

SPAS

SAN DIEGO CAN CLAIM ONE OF THE largest concentrations of European-style spa resorts in the United States.

Hollywood freshens up at *Cal-a-Vie Spa* (✉ 29402 Spa Havens Way, Vista ☎ 760/945–2055 or 866/772–4283 ⊕ www.cal-a-vie.com), an intimate destination spa in the hills near Escondido. Sharon Stone, Russell Crowe, and Oprah Winfrey have come to this French country–style estate to hike, work out, attend health and nutrition lectures, be massaged and wrapped, and devour delicious, nutritionally balanced meals. When new owners early in the 21st century acquired what was already one of the best spas in California, they added European antiques and elegant touches to the 24 individual cottages. They also built a light-filled, frescoed Turkish–style bathhouse with travertine marble tile. Guests can play golf or tennis; a fitness facility opened in 2005 with a calendar full of celebrity instructors. The chef even teaches you how to cook your healthy gourmet meals at home. All this comes at a price of course, which ranges from $5,795 to $6,295 per week.

The spa and fitness center at **Four Seasons Resort Aviara** (✉ 7100 Four Seasons Point, Carlsbad ☎ 760/603–6800 ⊕ www. fourseasons.com/aviara) holds 25 treatment rooms including a Couple's Suite with side-by-side massage tables, a lounge with marble fireplace and double shower, and a private patio with whirlpool. There's also a Zen garden with five outdoor massage cabanas. Facilities include a fitness center with machines and free weights, plus an indoor solarium with fireplace whirlpools. The spa offers a full menu of massages, scrubs, body wraps, facials, and bath rituals. Indigenous Southern California treatments include a hydrating avocado body wrap. There's also a José Eber Salon on the premises offering a range of hair, skin-care, and nail services.

The venerable spa at **La Costa Resort and Spa** (✉ 2100 Costa Del Mar Rd., Carlsbad ☎ 760/931–7570 or 800/ 729–4772 ⊕ www.lacosta.com) was transformed into an elegant sanctuary in 2004 after joining with the Chopra Center to add therapies for the body and mind, including medical consultation, yoga, meditation, and ayurvedic oil, herb, and aroma treatments. La Costa's new spa services are available à la carte or packaged as one-day themed Day Spa Journeys for individuals or VIP Spa Journeys for couples. Services include massages, mineral baths and water therapies, scrubs and wraps, and facials. Feng shui-inspired facilities include 42 treatment rooms, a shoulder-pounding Roman Waterfall, sunbathing areas, outdoor pool and Jacuzzi, and an outdoor aromatic–herbal steam gazebo. There's also a full-service Athletic Club, a Yamaguchi Salon offering a complimentary feng shui beauty consultation along with hair, manicure, and pedicure services.

Spa at Torrey Pines (✉ 11480 N. Torrey Pines Rd., La Jolla ☎ 858/453–4420 ⊕ www.spatorreypines.com) focuses on ancient rituals and techniques from four distinct cultures. Choose from the Ancient Oceans Ritual, the Indian aruryvedic Ayoma Ritual, a Scen Tao Ritual with shiatsu and acupressure, and the Aboriginal Australian Li'Tya Sacred Earth Ritual. Each lasts 140 minutes and features massage, wraps, facials, herbs, and essential oils. Also offered is a full menu of group fitness classes, yoga, meditation, and Pilates. Skin-care treatments include mud facials, body masks, and wraps. An intimate full-service facility, the spa has 14 treatment rooms, saunas, herbal-infused steam rooms, and aromatherapy inhalation rooms.

–Bobbi Zane

house, pool and cabana, barn, and stable that Carrillo used. After his death in 1961, the ranch remained in the family until the 1990s, when part of the acreage was acquired by the city for a park. ⊠ *7200 Flying C La., Carlsbad* ☎ *760/476–1042* ⊕ *www.carrillo-ranch.org* 🎟 *Free* ⊗ *Tues.–Sat. 9–5, Sun. 11–5.*

☉ The **Children's Discovery Museum of North County** provides playful, hands-on activities that teach children about science and the environment. Kids can assemble art projects to take home, play color games, and discover the world of sound. ⊠ *2787 State St., Carlsbad* ☎ *760/720–0737* ⊕ *www.museumforchildren.org* 🎟 *$6* ⊗ *Tues.–Sat. 10–4, Sun. noon–4.*

Where to Stay & Eat

☉ **$$$$**
Fodor'sChoice
★ 🏨 **Four Seasons Resort Aviara.** This hilltop resort sitting on 30 acres overlooking Batiquitos Lagoon is one of the most luxurious in the San Diego area, with gleaming marble corridors, original artwork, crystal chandeliers, and enormous flower arrangements. Rooms have every possible amenity: oversize closets, private balconies or garden patios, and marble bathrooms with double vanities and deep soaking tubs. The resort is exceptionally family friendly, providing a wide selection of in-room amenities designed for the younger set. The kids also have their own pool, nature walks with wildlife demonstrations, and video and board games. ⊠ *7100 Four Seasons Point, Carlsbad 92009* ☎ *760/603–6800 or 800/332–3442* 🖷 *760/603–6801* ⊕ *www.fourseasons.com/aviara* 🛏 *285 rooms, 44 suites* ♿ *4 restaurants, room service, in-room safes, minibars, cable TV with movies and video games, in-room DVD/VCR, in-room broadband, in-room data ports, Web TV, 18-hole golf course, 6 tennis courts, 2 pools, health club, 2 hot tubs, massage, sauna, spa, steam room, bicycles, hiking, volleyball, shops, babysitting, children's programs (ages 5–12), laundry service, concierge, business services, meeting room, airport shuttle, car rental, parking (fee), some pets allowed (fee); no smoking* ⊟ *AE, D, DC, MC, V.*

$$$$
🏨 **La Costa Resort and Spa.** This famous resort, a collection of low-slung buildings on more than 400 tree-shaded acres, is surprisingly low-key. Unusually large rooms, totally redecorated in a major renovation in 2003–2004, have a traditional look with lots of dark wood and opulent marble bathrooms. Also revamped is the legendary spa, now the home of the Chopra Center, which integrates medical consultations and spa services. The resort also has one of the most comprehensive sports programs in the area. There are two PGA championship golf courses and a large tennis center. ⊠ *2100 Costa del Mar Rd., Carlsbad 92009* ☎ *760/438–9111 or 800/854–5000* 🖷 *760/438–3758* ⊕ *www.lacosta.com* 🛏 *397 rooms, 77 suites* ♿ *2 restaurants, room service, in-room safes, minibars, some refrigerators, cable TV with movies, in-room broadband, driving range, 2 18-hole golf courses, putting green, 19 tennis courts, pro shop, 4 pools, health club, hair salon, 3 outdoor hot tubs, sauna, spa, steam room, bicycles, croquet, hiking, lounge, nightclub, shops, babysitting, children's programs (ages 5–12), dry cleaning, laundry service, concierge, business services, meeting rooms, car rental, no-smoking rooms* ⊟ *AE, D, DC, MC, V.*

☉ **$$$–$$$$**
🏨 **Carlsbad Inn Beach Resort.** Gable roofs, half-timber walls, and stone supports are among the architectural elements of note at this sprawling

inn and time-share condominium complex, steps from the beach. Rooms, which range from cramped to large, are furnished European fashion, with pencil-post beds and wall sconces. Many have ocean views and kitchenettes; some also have fireplaces and hot tubs. With sprawling, landscaped grounds the inn is well-equipped to accommodate families. Kids are included in a number of the resort's scheduled activities. ⊠ *3075 Carlsbad Blvd., Carlsbad 92008* ☎ *760/434–7020 or 800/235–3939* 🖷 *760/729–4853* ⊕ *www.carlsbadinn.com* ❧ *61 rooms, 1 suite* ⑃ *Some in-room hot tubs, some kitchenettes, cable TV, in-room data ports, pool, gym, outdoor hot tub, sauna, bicycles, shops, playground, laundry facilities, laundry service, business services, meeting rooms, free parking, no-smoking rooms* ⊟ *AE, D, DC, MC, V.*

$$ 🔁 **Inns of America Suites.** An excellent choice to stay with your family on a trip to Legoland, this hotel is less than a mile from the park. You can buy tickets at the hotel and catch a free shuttle to the entrance. Despite proximity to I–5, the suites are very quiet, and all are equipped with kitchenettes or full kitchens. A Mexican fountain in the marble lobby and details like granite counters and hand-painted ceramic sinks complete the picture. Included in the price, breakfast is served in a pleasant, south-of-the-border-style room. ⊠ *5010 Avenida Encinas, Carlsbad 92008* ☎ *760/929–8200* 🖷 *760/929–8219* ⊕ *www.innsofamerica.com* ❧ *73 rooms, 25 suites* ⑃ *Some kitchenettes, microwaves, refrigerators, cable TV with movies and video games, in-room broadband, pool, gym, outdoor hot tub, laundry facilities, business services, meeting rooms, free parking, no-smoking rooms* ⊟ *AE, D, MC, V* ⑂❶ *CP.*

$–$$$ 🔁 **Pelican Cove Inn.** Two blocks from the beach and surrounded by palm trees and mature colorful gardens with secluded nooks, this two-story bed-and-breakfast has spacious rooms with gas fireplaces, feather beds, and private entrances. The innkeepers provide beach chairs and towels and can make arrangements for biplane rides or balloon excursions. Breakfast is included in the price. ⊠ *320 Walnut Ave., Carlsbad 92008* ☎ *760/434–5995 or 888/735–2683* ⊕ *www.pelican-cove.com* ❧ *10 rooms* ⑃ *Some in-room hot tubs, cable TV, in-room broadband, free parking; no a/c, no phones in some rooms, no smoking* ⊟ *AE, MC, V* ⑂❶ *BP.*

Shopping

★ **Carlsbad Premium Outlets** (⊠ 5620 Paseo Del Norte, Carlsbad ☎ 760/ 804–9000 or 888/790–7467 ⊕ www.premiumoutlets.com/carlsbad) is the only upscale designer factory outlet in the San Diego area. Within this attractively landscaped complex you can find Wedgwood, Lennox, Donna Karan Company Store, and Polo Ralph Lauren. **Thousand Mile Outdoor Wear** (☎ 760/804–1764) makes the bathing suits used by most lifeguards in Southern California and also has a line of outerwear manufactured from recycled soft-drink bottles. **Barney's New York** (☎ 760/929–9600) carries a large selection of designer women's and men's fashions. You can find home accessories at the **Crate & Barrel Outlet** (☎ 760/692–2100). **Dooney & Bourke** (☎ 760/476–1049) sells their popular handbags and accessories at discounted prices.

Oceanside

8 mi north of Carlsbad on Rte. S21, 37 mi north of downtown San Diego on I–5.

California Welcome Center Oceanside offers complete state travel information, foreign language assistance, and a concierge service inside a mission-style, white-arched building. You can buy discount tickets to many Southern California attractions. ⊠ *928 Coast Hwy., Oceanside 92054* ☎ *760/721–1101 or 800/350–7873* ⊕ *www.californiawelcomecenter. org* ⊙ *Daily 9–5.*

With 900 slips, **Oceanside Harbor** (☎ 760/435–4000) is North County's fishing, sailing, and watersports center. **Helgren's Sportfishing** (⊠ 315 Harbor Dr. S, Oceanside ☎ 760/722–2133) schedules daily ocean fishing trips and whale-watching coastal excursions. South of the Harbor, **Oceanside Pier**, at 1,942 feet, is one of the longest on the West Coast. A restaurant, Ruby's Diner, stands at the end of the wooden pier's long promenade.

California Surf Museum displays a large collection of surfing memorabilia, photos, vintage boards, apparel, and accessories. ⊠ *223 N. Coast Hwy., Oceanside* ☎ *760/721–6876* ⊕ *www.surfmuseum.org* ⊒ *Free* ⊙ *Daily 10–4.*

Camp Pendleton, the nation's largest amphibious military training complex, encompasses 17 mi of Pacific shoreline. It's not unusual to see herds of tanks and flocks of helicopters maneuvering through the dunes and brush alongside I–5. You may also see herds of sheep keeping the bushland down and fertile fields growing next to the Pacific coastline.

☺ ❹ **Mission San Luis Rey** was built by Franciscan friars in 1798 under the diFodor'sChoice rection of Father Fermin Lasuen to help educate and convert local Na-
★ tive Americans. Once a location for filming Disney's *Zorro* TV series, the well-preserved mission is still owned by Franciscan friars. The San Luis Rey was the 18th and largest and most prosperous of California's missions. The *sala* (parlor), the kitchen, a friar's bedroom, a weaving room, and a collection of religious art convey much about early mission life. Retreats are still held here, but a picnic area, a gift shop, and a museum (which has the most extensive collection of old Spanish vestments in the United States) are also on the grounds, as are sunken gardens and the *lavanderia* (open-air laundry). Self-guided and docent-led tours are available. The mission's retreat center has limited, inexpensive dormitory-style overnight accommodations. ⊠ *4050 Mission Ave., Oceanside* ☎ *760/ 757–3651* ⊕ *www.sanluisrey.org* ⊒ *$5* ⊙ *Daily 10–4.*

Oceanside Museum of Art, housed in the old City Hall designed by architect Irving Gill, presents changing exhibits of local artwork and exhibitions on loan from major art museums. Recent exhibits have included photography, art books, and works of regional artists. ⊠ *704 Pier View Way, Oceanside* ☎ *760/721–2787* ⊕ *www.oma-online.org* ⊒ *$5* ⊙ *Tues.–Sat. 10–4, Sun. 1–4.*

The **Wave Waterpark** is a 3-acre waterpark run by the City of Vista. It's also one of the few places in the country with a flow-rider, a type of standing wave that allows riders on bodyboards to turn, carve, and slash almost as though they were surfing on a real wave. If you haven't learned how to do that, you can tube down the park's own river or slip down the 35-foot water slide. ⊠ *161 Recreation Dr., Vista* ☎ *760/940–9283* 🖙 *$11.50* ☉ *Memorial Day–Labor Day, daily 10:30 to 5:30; weekends only until last weekend of Sept. 11–5.*

Where to Stay & Eat

$–$$$ ✕ **A Taste of Europe.** French with a German accent is the theme at this comfortable little restaurant where candlelight, white table linens, and attentive service prevail. You can dine on such well-prepared entrées as rack of lamb Provençale, steak *au poivre vert* (with green pepper), or Wiener schnitzel. There's a good wine list featuring Californian and imported vintages. ⊠ *1733 S. Coast Hwy., Oceanside* ☎ *760/722–7006* ▤ *AE, D, DC, MC, V* ☉ *Closed Mon. No lunch.*

$$ ✕ **Monterey Bay Cannery.** A pleasant place to dine while watching small fishing and pleasure boats moving through the Oceanside Harbor, this restaurant has tables outside and inside. The menu lists chowders, halibut, steamed clams, grilled ahi, and steak. The Sunday brunch here is a popular event. There's entertainment most nights. ⊠ *1325 N. Harbor Dr.* ☎ *760/722–3474* ▤ *AE, DC, MC, V.*

¢–$$ ✕ **Jolly Roger.** This casual restaurant is a good choice for waterside dining. You can watch traffic move through the harbor while savoring nicely prepared salmon, halibut, ahi, or even teriyaki steak or prime rib. The dining room is a bit old-fashioned, with leather-lined booths and laminate-topped tables. Entertainment is presented on weekends. ⊠ *1900 N. Harbor Dr.* ☎ *760/722–1831* ▤ *AE, D, MC, V.*

¢ ✕ **101 Cafe.** A diner dating back to 1928, this is both a local hangout and the headquarters of the historic Highway 101 movement. You'll find all kinds of Highway 101 memorabilia here along with breakfast, lunch, and dinner. The menu lists burgers, sandwiches, and salads for lunch, and biscuits and gravy, chicken-fried steak, spaghetti, and meat loaf for dinner. ⊠ *631 S. Coast Hwy.* ☎ *760/722–5220* 🖙 *Reservations not accepted* ▤ *No credit cards.*

★ $$$–$$$$ 🏨 **Oceanside Marina Suites.** Of all the oceanfront lodgings in North County towns, this motel occupies the best location—a spit of land surrounded by water and cool ocean breezes on all sides. The rooms are unusually large and have fireplaces and expansive balconies; all have either ocean or harbor views. There are barbecues for guest use. A free boat shuttles you to the beach in summer. Continental breakfast is included in the price. ⊠ *2008 Harbor Dr. N, Oceanside 92054* ☎ *760/722–1561 or 800/252–2033* 🖶 *760/439–9758* ⊕ *www.omihotel.com* 🖙 *51 suites* ♿ *Kitchens, cable TV with movies, in-room DVDs, in-room data ports, pool, hot tub, sauna, fishing, Ping-Pong, volleyball, laundry facilities, free parking; no a/c, no smoking* ▤ *AE, MC, V* ❌ *CP.*

$ 🏨 **Marina Comfort Suites.** Convenient to I–5 and Route 76 but also noisy at times, this Mediterranean-style, all-suite hotel is close to the marina, the beach, and downtown Oceanside. A morning newspaper, continental breakfast, and afternoon refreshments are included. ✉ *888 N. Coast Hwy., Oceanside 92054* 🕿 *760/722–8880 or 800/228–5150* ⊕ *www.choicehotels.com* 🖷 *760/722–7280* 🛏 *47 rooms, 25 suites* ♿ *Fans, some in-room hot tubs, microwaves, refrigerators, cable TV with movies, in-room data ports, pool, gym, laundry service, meeting room, free parking; no smoking* ⊟ *AE, D, DC, MC, V* ⊠ *CP.*

¢–$$ 🎮 **Best Western Marty's Valley Inn.** This attractive family-owned motel, east of I–5, is a good choice for families. Rooms are ample with contemporary furniture; some rooms have fireplaces. Children under 12 stay free. Continental breakfast is included. ✉ *3240 E. Mission Ave., Oceanside 92054* 🕿 *760/757–7700 or 800/747–3529* 🖷 *760/439–3311* ⊕ *www.bwmartys.com* 🛏 *108 rooms, 2 suites* ♿ *Some microwaves, some refrigerators, cable TV with movies, in-room broadband, in-room data ports, pool, gym, outdoor hot tub, business services, meeting rooms, free parking, no-smoking rooms* ⊟ *AE, D, DC, MC, V* ⊠ *CP.*

¢–$ 🎮 **Guesthouse Inn & Suites.** This is a convenient, but noisy location, just steps from I–5 and the railroad tracks. The hotel is close to the marina and convenient to Camp Pendleton. There's an on-site restaurant, the Flying Bridge, and a breakfast room, where a complimentary continental breakfast is served. ✉ *1103 N. Coast Hwy., Oceanside 92054* 🕿 *760/722–1904 or 800/914–2230* 🖷 *760/722–1168* ⊕ *www.guesthouseintl.com* 🛏 *80 rooms* ♿ *Restaurant, microwaves, refrigerators, cable TV, pool, business services, meeting room, free parking, no-smoking rooms* ⊟ *AE, D, DC, MC, V* ⊠ *CP.*

Shopping

Oceanside Photo & Telescope (✉ 918 Mission Ave., Oceanside 🕿 760/722–3348 ⊕ www.optcorp.com) is the place to pick up a telescope or binoculars to view San Diego County's dazzling night sky; call for information about stargazing parties the store holds regularly.

San Diego North Coast A to Z

To research prices, get advice from other travelers, and book travel arrangements, visit www.fodors.com

AIR TRAVEL

McClellan Palomar Airport is run by the county of San Diego. America West Express has passenger service from here to Phoenix Sky Harbor Airport and United Express has flights to Los Angeles International Airport.

🚩 Airport Information **McClellan Palomar Airport** ✉ 2198 Palomar Airport Rd., Carlsbad 🕿 760/431–4646 ⊕ www.co.san-diego.ca.us/dpw/airports/mcpal.htm.

BUS TRAVEL

The San Diego Transit District covers the city of San Diego up to Del Mar. The North County Transit District serves San Diego County from Del Mar north.

🚩 Bus Information The **North County Transit District** 🕿 800/266–6883 ⊕ www.sdcommute.com. **San Diego Transit District** 🕿 619/233–3004 ⊕ www.sdcommute.com.

CAR TRAVEL

Interstate 5 is the main freeway artery connecting San Diego to Los Angeles. Running parallel west of I–5 is Route S21, also known and sometimes indicated as Highway 101, Old Highway 101, or Coast Highway 101, which never strays too far from the ocean.

TRAIN TRAVEL

Amtrak stops in Solana Beach and Oceanside. Coaster operates commuter rail service between San Diego and Oceanside, stopping in Old Town, Sorrento Valley, Solana Beach, Encinitas, and Carlsbad en route. The last Coaster train leaves San Diego at about 7 each night (9 on Friday; the last arrival is about midnight).

🚆 **Train Information Amtrak** ☎ 760/722-4622 in Oceanside, 800/872-7245 ⊕ www. amtrakcalifornia.com. **Coaster** ☎ 800/262-7837 ⊕ www.sdcommute.com.

TOURS

Civic Helicopters gives whirlybird tours of the area along the beaches for about $100 per person per half hour. Barnstorming Adventures conducts excursions aboard restored 1920s-vintage open-cockpit biplanes and military-style Top Dog air combat flights on prop-driven Varga VG-21s. Flights are from McClellan Palomar Airport and start at $129 per couple.

🚆 **Tour Companies Barnstorming Adventures** ☎ 760/438-7680 or 800/759-5667 ⊕ www.barnstorming.com. **Civic Helicopters** ⊠ 2192 Palomar Airport Rd., Carlsbad ☎ 760/438-8424 ⊕ www.civichelicopters.com.

VISITOR INFORMATION

🚆 **Carlsbad Convention and Visitors Bureau** 🖘 400 Carlsbad Village Dr., Carlsbad 92008 ☎ 760/434-6093 or 800/227-5722 ⊕ visitcarlsbad.com. **Del Mar Regional Chamber of Commerce** ⊠ 1104 Camino del Mar, Del Mar 92014 ☎ 858/755-4844 ⊕ www.delmarchamber.org. **Oceanside Welcome Center** ⊠ 928 N. Coast Hwy., Oceanside 92054 ☎ 760/721-1101 or 800/350-7873 ⊕ www.californiawelcomecenter.org. **San Diego North Convention and Visitors Bureau** ⊠ 360 N. Escondido Blvd., Escondido 92025 ☎ 760/745-4741 or 800/848-3366 ⊕ www.sandiegonorth.com.

INLAND NORTH COUNTY

RANCHO BERNARDO, ESCONDIDO, FALLBROOK & TEMECULA

Long regarded as San Diego's beautiful backyard, replete with green hills, quiet lakes, and citrus and avocado groves, inland San Diego County is now one of the fastest-growing areas in Southern California. Subdivisions, many containing palatial homes, now fill the hills and canyons around Escondido and Rancho Bernardo, and even extend north into Temecula, the wine-making area of southern Riverside County. Growth notwithstanding, the area still has such natural settings as the San Diego Wild Animal Park, Rancho Bernardo, and the Welk Resort Center.

Numbers in the margin correspond to points of interest on the San Diego North County map.

Rancho Bernardo

23 mi northeast of downtown San Diego on I–15.

Rancho Bernardo straddles a stretch of I–15 between San Diego and Escondido and technically is a neighborhood of San Diego. Originally sheep and cattle grazing land, it was transformed in the early 1960s into a planned suburban community, one of the first, and a place where many wealthy retirees settled down. It's now home to a number of high-tech companies, the most notable of which is Sony. It's the location of the Rancho Bernardo Inn, one of San Diego's most delightful resorts.

Where to Stay & Eat

$$–$$$$
Fodor'sChoice
★
✕ **El Bizcocho.** Wealthy locals rate this restaurant at the Rancho Bernardo Inn tops for style and cuisine. The tranquil setting features candle-lighted tables, plush banquettes, and quiet, live music. Chef Gavin Kaysen, who took over the kitchen in 2004, has updated the classic menu with sublime renditions of seared Spanish turbot on a bed of baby bok choy, Black Angus filet mignon with horseradish-infused roasted potatoes, and butternut squash risotto with brussels sprout leaves. A tasting menu ($65 per person) offers a succulent selection based on what's fresh. The wine list has more than 1,000 wines, including rare vintages. ⊠ *Rancho Bernardo Inn, 17550 Bernardo Oaks Pkwy., Rancho Bernardo* ☎ *800/267–5662 or 858/675–8500* ⌂ *Reservations essential* 🏛 *Jacket and tie* ⊟ *AE, D, DC, MC, V* ⊗ *No lunch, no dinner Sun.*

$$–$$$$
✕ **Carver's Steak House.** Dried-leaf and bark arrangements adorn the entrance to this upscale restaurant whose walls and tables are made of finished wood. House specialties here include prime rib and filet mignon. Seafood and chicken are also available. ⊠ *11940 Bernardo Plaza Dr., Rancho Bernardo* ☎ *858/485–1262* ⌂ *Reservations essential* ⊟ *AE, D, DC, MC, V* ⊗ *No lunch weekends.*

$$–$$$
✕ **Bernard'O.** Intimate despite its shopping center location, Bernard'O is the choice for a romantic dinner. Sit fireside in the small dining room, dine by candlelight, and savor contemporary versions of classic rack of lamb, grilled king salmon on a bed of gnocchi, or seared scallops with Julian apples. An extensive wine list includes rare old vintages from California and France along with well-priced newer bottles. ⊠ *12457 Rancho Bernardo Rd., Rancho Bernardo* ☎ *858/487–7171* ⊟ *AE, D, DC, MC, V* ⊗ *No lunch Sat. through Tues.*

$$–$$$
✕ **French Market Grille.** The Grille's flower-decked dark-wood dining room and patio with twinkling lights will help you forget that you're eating in a shopping center. The French fare changes with the seasons; typical entrées include grilled beef tenderloin, roasted scallops Dijonnaise, or roasted chicken with fresh herbs. On Tuesday night, local and guest artists present opera. ⊠ *15717 Bernardo Heights Pkwy., Rancho Bernardo* ☎ *858/485–8055* ⊟ *AE, D, DC, MC, V.*

$–$$$
✕ **Cafe Luna.** The setting is low-key and intimate in this candlelit café with exposed brick. The house specialty is tournedos gorgonzola—two petit filets mignon, pan-seared with a cabernet demi-glace and topped with mushroom caps and gorgonzola. Pastas and desserts are homemade daily. ⊠ *11040 Rancho Carmel Dr., Carmel Mountain Ranch* ☎ *858/*

673–0077 ᐸ *Reservations essential* ▤ *AE, D, DC, MC, V* ⊙ *Closed Sun. No lunch Mon. and Tues.*

$–$$$ ✕ **Chin's Szechwan Cuisine.** Locals pick Chin's for special occasions. It feels rich, with dark-red walls, blooming orchids everywhere, and heavy wooden furnishings. The extensive menu lists popular items such as Kung Pao chicken, sizzling beef and scallops, and lamb à la Mandarin. ⊠ *15721 Bernardo Heights Pkwy. Rancho Bernardo* ☎ *858/676–0166* ▤ *AE, MC, V.*

$–$$ ✕ **Passage to India.** One of a growing number of ethnic restaurants in North County, Passage to India offers an extensive menu divided into tandoori sizzlers and chicken, lamb, seafood, and vegetarian entrées. Sauces and preparation are similar in each category—the price difference is in the meat. Look for masalas, bhunas, kormas, and tikkas to go with your garlic naan. You can sample all of it at the buffet lunch or weekend brunch. ⊠ *16411 Bernardo Center Dr., Rancho Bernardo* ☎ *858/674–7500* ▤ *AE, D, MC, V.*

¢–$ ✕ **Spices Thai Cafe.** One of the North County's most stylish ethnic restaurants, this is part of a collection of ethnic eateries in a small mall just off I–15. Among the beautiful Thai dishes is the traditional pad thai, a feast of shrimp, bean sprouts, bean curd, and noodles. Interesting seafood specialties include the prawn and crab hot pot, soft shell crab in yellow curry, and steamed fresh seafood with three sauces. ⊠ *16441 Bernardo Center Dr., Rancho Bernardo* ☎ *858/674–4665* ▤ *AE, D, DC, MC, V.*

★ ♨ $$$$ ▦ **Rancho Bernardo Inn.** This gem of a resort is on 265 oak-shaded acres surrounded by a well-established residential community. The two-story, red-roof adobe buildings are complemented by bougainvillea-decked courtyards adorned with original art. Public areas are a collection of small sitting rooms where Spanish mission–style sofas and chairs invite you to linger with a good book. There are fireplaces everywhere, overstuffed furniture, and Oriental rugs on tile floors. Rooms inside are ample, but simply furnished and appointed with early California and Mexican art. All have private patios or balconies with views. Suites have fireplaces. Seasonal children's activities include science and sports instruction. ⊠ *17550 Bernardo Oaks Dr., Rancho Bernardo 92128* ☎ *858/675–8500 or 877/517–9342* ⊟ *858/675–8501* ⊕ *www.ranchobernardoinn. com* ⇆ *272 rooms, 15 suites* ᐸ *2 restaurants, room service, in-room safes, minibars, refrigerators, cable TV with movies and video games, in-room broadband, in-room data ports, driving range, 18-hole golf course, 27-hole golf course, putting green, 12 tennis courts, 2 pools, fitness center, 7 outdoor hot tubs, sauna, spa, steam room, bicycles, volleyball, 2 bars, sports bar, shops, children's programs (ages 5–13), concierge, business services, meeting rooms, no-smoking rooms* ▤ *AE, D, DC, MC, V.*

Shopping

A trip to **Bernardo Winery** (⊠ 13330 Paseo Del Verano Norte, Rancho Bernardo ☎ 858/487–1866 ⊕ www.bernardowinery.com) feels like traveling back to early California days; some of the vines on the former Spanish land-grant property have been producing grapes for more than 100 years. The winery was founded in 1889 and has been operated by the Rizzo family since 1928. Besides the wine-tasting room, selling cold-pressed olive oil and other gourmet goodies, there's a restaurant, the Cafe Merlot, serving lunch daily except Monday. About a dozen shops offer apparel, home-decor items, and arts and crafts. If you're lucky, the glassblowing artist will be working at the outdoor furnace. The winery is open daily 9–5; the shops are open Tuesday–Sunday 10–5.

Escondido

8 mi north of Rancho Bernardo on I–15, 31 mi northeast of downtown San Diego on I–15.

Escondido and the lovely rolling hills around it were originally a land grant bestowed on Juan Bautista Alvarado in 1843 by Mexican Governor Manuel Micheltorena. The Battle of San Pasqual, a bloody milestone in California's march to statehood, took place just east of the city. For a century and a half, the hills supported citrus and avocado trees, plus large grape vineyards. The rural character began to change when the San Diego Zoo established its Wild Animal Park in the San Pasqual Valley east of town in the 1970s. By the late 1990s, suburban development had begun to transform the hills into housing tracts. The California Center for the Arts, opened in 1993, now stands as the downtown centerpiece of a burgeoning arts community that includes a branch of the Mingei Folk Art Museum and a collection of art galleries along Grand Avenue. Despite its urbanization, Escondido still supports several pristine open-space preserves that attract nature-lovers, hikers, and mountain bikers.

⑤ **FodorśChoice** **★** **San Diego Wild Animal Park** is an extension of the San Diego Zoo, 35 mi to the south. The 1,800-acre preserve in the San Pasqual Valley is designed to protect endangered species from around the world. Exhibit areas have been carved out of the dry, dusty canyons and mesas to represent the animals' natural habitats in North, South, and East Africa, the Heart of Africa, the Australian rain forest, the Asian swamps, and the Asian plains.

The best way to see these preserves is to take the 60-minute, 5-mi monorail ride on the Wgasa Bushline Railway (included in the price of admission). As you pass in front of the large, naturally landscaped enclosures, you can see animals bounding through prairies and mesas as they would in the wild. More than 3,500 animals of more than 400 species roam or fly above the expansive grounds. Predators are separated from prey by deep moats, but only the elephants, tigers, lions, and cheetahs are kept in isolation. Photographers with zoom lenses can get spectacular shots of zebras, gazelles, and rhinos (a seat on the right-hand side of the monorail is best for viewing). In summer, when the park stays open late, the trip is especially enjoyable in the early evening, when the heat has subsided and the animals are active and feeding. When the monorail travels through the park after dark, sodium-vapor lamps illuminate the active animals.

The park is as much a botanical garden as a zoo, and botanists collect rare and endangered plants for preservation. Unique gardens include cacti and succulents from Baja California, a bonsai collection, fuchsia display, native plants, protea, and water-wise plantings. The park sponsors a number of garden events throughout the year, including a winter camellia show and a spring orchid show.

Lion Camp, the lion exhibit opened in 2004, gives you a close-up view of the king of beasts in a slice of African wilderness complete with sweeping plains and rolling hills. You walk through this encounter to an observation station where you can watch the giant cats lounging around through a 40-foot-long window. The last stop is a research station where you can see the cats all around you through glass panels.

The 1¼-mi-long **Kilimanjaro Safari Walk** winds through some of the park's hilliest terrain in the East Africa section, with observation decks overlooking the elephants and lions. A 70-foot suspension bridge spans a steep ravine, leading to the final observation point and a panorama of the entire park and the San Pasqual Valley.

The ticket booths at **Nairobi Village,** the park's center, are designed to resemble the tomb of an ancient king of Uganda. Animals in the **Petting Kraal** here affectionately tolerate tugs and pats and are quite adept at posing for pictures with toddlers. At the **Congo River Village** 10,000 gallons of water pour each minute over a huge waterfall into a large lagoon. **Hidden Jungle,** an 8,800-square-foot glass house, houses creatures that creep, flutter, or just hang out in a tropical habitat. Gigantic cockroaches and bird-eating spiders share the turf with colorful butterflies and hummingbirds and oh-so-slow-moving two-toed sloths. **Lorikeet Landing,** simulating the Australian rain forest, holds 75 of the loud and colorful small parrots—you can buy a cup of nectar at the aviary entrance to induce them to land on your hand. Along the trails of 32-acre **Heart of Africa** you can travel in the footsteps of an early explorer through forests and lowlands, across a floating bridge to a research station where an expert is on hand to answer questions; finally you arrive at Panorama Point for an up-close-and-personal view of cheetahs, a chance to feed the giraffes, and a distant glimpse of the expansive savanna where rhinos, impalas, wildebeest, oryx, and beautiful migrating birds reside. At **Condor Ridge,** the Wild Animal Park, which conducts captive breeding programs to save rare and endangered species, shows off one of its most successful efforts, the California condor. The exhibit, perched like one of the ugly black vultures it features, occupies nearly the highest point in the park, and affords a sweeping view of the surrounding San Pasqual Valley. Also on exhibit here is a herd of rare desert bighorn sheep.

Frequent Flyers, the newest bird show at the Benbough Amphitheater, offers a behind-the-scenes look at some of the park's free flight birds. All the park's animal shows are entertainingly educational. The gift shops here offer wonderful merchandise, much of it limited-edition items. Rental camcorders, strollers, and wheelchairs are available. Serious shutterbugs might consider joining one of the special Photo Caravan Safari tours ($90–$130, plus park admission). You can also see a cheetah sprint by signing on to a Cheetah Safari ($69, plus park admission), overnight in the park in summer on a Roar and Snore Camp-Over (adults $110, kids 8–11 $90, plus admission), and celebrate the holidays during the annual Festival of Lights. ☒ *15500 San Pasqual Val-*

ley Rd., Escondido, Take I–15 north to Via Rancho Pkwy. and follow signs, 6 mi ☎ 760/747–8702 ⊕ www.sandiegozoo.org/wap ⊠ $28.50 includes all shows and monorail tour; a $54.45 combination pass grants entry, within 5 days of purchase, to San Diego Zoo and San Diego Wild Animal Park; parking $8 ⊙ Mid-June–Labor Day, daily 9–8; Mid-Sept.–mid-June, daily 9–4 ▤ D, MC, V.

🜂 The **California Center for the Arts,** an entertainment complex with two theaters, an art museum, and a conference center, presents operas, musicals, plays, dance performances, and symphony and chamber-music concerts. Performers conduct free workshops for children; check the Web site for dates. The museum, which focuses on 20th-century art, occasionally presents blockbuster exhibits such as the glass art of Dale Chihuly and photos by Ansel Adams, making a side trip here worthwhile. ⊠ 340 N. Escondido Blvd., Escondido ☎ 800/988–4253 box office, 760/839–4100 ⊕ www.artcenter.org ⊠ Museum price varies ⊙ Museum hrs vary.

The outdoor **Heritage Walk Museum** is adjacent to the California Center for the Arts, in Grape Day Park. The museum, operated by the Escondido Historical Society, consists of several historic buildings moved here to illustrate local development from the late 1800s, when grape growing and gold mining supported the economy. Exhibits include the 1888 Santa Fe Depot, Escondido's first library, the Bandy Blacksmith shop, a furnished 1890 Victorian house, and other 19th-century buildings. ⊠ 321 N. Broadway, Escondido ☎ 760/743–8207 ⊕ www.escondidohistoricalsociety.com ⊠ $3 ⊙ Thurs.–Sat. 1–4.

The **Escondido Municipal Gallery** showcases works by local artists. The Arts Bazaar gift shop carries locally crafted jewelry, blown glass, and textiles. ⊠ 142 W. Grand Ave., Escondido ☎ 760/480–4101 ⊙ Tues.–Sat. 11–4.

The **Mingei International Museum North County,** a satellite of the larger facility in San Diego's Balboa Park, occupies a former JCPenney store at the foot of Escondido's emerging arts district. All the Mingei art is classified as folk art; collections include pre-Columbian items, ceramics, textiles, glass, and a variety of Japanese arts of daily life. ⊠ 155 W. Grand Ave. ☎ 760/735–3355 ⊕ www.mingei.org ⊠ $6 ⊙ Tues.–Sun. 1–4.

🜂 A 3,058-acre conservation area and historic ranch site, **Daley Ranch** holds 20 mi of multipurpose trails for hikers, mountain bikers, and equestrians. The 2.4-mi Boulder Loop affords sweeping views of Escondido, and the 2.5-mi Ranch House Loop passes two small ponds, the Daley family ranch house built in 1928, and the site of the original log cabin. Private motorized vehicles are prohibited on the ranch, but a Sunday shuttle service is provided from the parking area to the entrance. ⊠ 3024 La Honda Dr., Escondido 92027 ☎ 760/839–4680 ⊕ www.ci.escondido.ca.us ⊠ Free ⊙ Dawn–dusk daily.

> **off the beaten path**

Lavender Fields – In spring a visit to this organic lavender farm is worth a detour. A self-guided walking tour takes you through 6 acres planted with 28 varieties of lavender and to an area where plants are distilled into essential oils. A gift shop sells lavender products and plants. ⊠ 12460 Keys Creek Rd., Valley Center

☎ 760/742–1489 ⊕ *www.thelavenderfields.com* ☞ *Free*
⊙ *Weekends May and June 10–5.*

Orfila Vineyards offers tours and tastings of award-winning Syrah, Sangiovese, and Viognier produced from grapes harvested from the 10,000-acre vineyard. The Rose Arbor has a picnic area and there's a gift shop with wine-related merchandise. ✉ *13455 San Pasqual Valley Rd., Escondido* ☎ *760/738–6500* ⊕ *www.orfila.com* ⊙ *Daily 10–6, guided tours at 2.*

🄲 The last work by sculptor Niki de Saint Phalle (1930–2002), **Queen Califia's Magical Circle** is a sculpture garden consisting of eight totemic figures up to 21 feet tall. Adorned with stylized monsters, protective deities, geometric symbols, crests, human skulls and animals, they evoke ancient tales and legends. Saint Phalle designed the garden for the entertainment of children, who can scramble around and on the giant fanciful figures. ✉ *Kit Carson Park, Bear Valley Pkwy. and Mary La., Escondido* ☎ *760/839-4691* ⊕ *www.queencalifia.org* ☞ *Free* ⊙ *9–dusk daily except when raining.*

🄲 **San Dieguito River Park** maintains several hiking and walking trails in the Escondido area. These are part of an intended 55-mi-long Coast to Crest Trail that will eventually link the San Dieguito Lagoon near Del Mar with the river's source on Volcan Mountain, north of Julian. Among the existing trails are three that circle Lake Hodges: the **North Shore Lake Hodges Trail;** the **Piedras Pintadas Trail,** which informs about native American Kumeyaay lifestyles and uses for native plants; and the **Highland Valley Trail,** the first half mile of which is the Ruth Merrill Children's Walk. Three trails in **Clevenger Canyon** lead to sweeping views of the San Pasqual Valley. Visit the Web site for a list of upcoming guided hikes. ✉ *18327 Sycamore Creek Rd., Escondido* ☎ *858/674–2270* ⊕ *www.sdrp.org* ☞ *Free* ⊙ *Dawn–dusk daily.*

San Pasqual Battlefield State Historic Park and Museum commemorates an important moment in the Mexican-American War. On December 6, 1846, a contingent of Americans, including famous frontier scout Kit Carson, suffered defeat by a group of Californios (Spanish-Mexican residents of California). This was the Californios' most notable success during the war, but the Americans, with support from Commodore Stockton in San Diego, regained control of the region. A historic battle reenactment is held every December. ✉ *15808 San Pasqual Valley Rd., Escondido* ☎ *760/737–2201* ⊕ *www.sanpasqual.org* ☞ *Free* ⊙ *Weekends 10–3.*

Where to Stay & Eat

★ **$$–$$$$** ✕ **150 Grand Cafe.** This pretty storefront restaurant lies a block from the California Center for the Arts. It consists of a collection of individually decorated dining rooms, all with a garden ambience, and a sidewalk dining area. The seasonal menu might feature miso-braised salmon on a bed of long grain wild rice, barbecued pork loin with coffee molasses and bourbon sauce, or chicken sausage penne with lemon vodka cream. Reservations are essential on weekends ✉ *150 W. Grand Ave., Escondido* ☎ *760/738–6868* ▤ *AE, D, DC, MC, V* ⊙ *Closed Sun.*

$$–$$$$ ✕ **Vincent's Sirinos.** Here's an excellent choice for dining before attending an event at the nearby California Center for the Arts. Original paintings decorate the walls and crisp white tablecloths cover the tables, adorned with fresh flowers. The menu changes frequently; offerings might include Muscovy duck legs with garlic sauce, a grilled portobello mushroom with Parmesan, or veal prosciutto ravioli. The wine list is serious, as are the desserts. The service is friendly and attentive. ⊠ *113 W. Grand Ave., Escondido* ☎ *760/745–3835* 🖃 *AE, D, MC, V* ☾ *Closed Mon. No lunch weekends.*

$$$ 🏨 **Welk Resort Center.** Sprawling over 600 acres of rugged, oak-studded hillside, this resort, built by bandleader Lawrence Welk in the 1960s, recently underwent a complete makeover. Now one and two-bedroom villas have replaced outdated motel-style units. Fully furnished and appointed, villas are actually time-share units that are rented to nonowners when available. Amenities in some units include fireplaces and hot tubs. The resort complex is family friendly with abundant children's activities, although parents must supervise. A museum displays Welk memorabilia and a theater presents Broadway-style musicals year-round. ⊠ *8860 Lawrence Welk Dr., Escondido 92026* ☎ *760/749–3000 or 800/ 932–9355* 🖷 *760/749–6182* ⊕ *www.welkresort.com/sandiego* ⋈ *286 suites* ⚹ *Restaurant, kitchens, cable TV, some in-room DVD/VCR, in-room data ports, 2 18-hole golf courses, 5 tennis courts, 6 pools, 7 hot tubs, gym, lake, fishing, bicycles, basketball, billiards, horseshoes, table tennis, volleyball, bar, theater, video game room, shops, free parking, no-smoking rooms* 🖃 *AE, D, MC, V.*

$–$$$ 🏨 **Castle Creek Inn Resort and Spa.** European touches and unusually lush gardens mark this small resort tucked into a canyon just north of Escondido. Public areas feature antique armoires, gilded mirrors, and crystal chandeliers. Rooms, all with patios or balconies affording garden or golf-course views, are simply appointed with antique chairs and desks, hand-painted wall stenciling, and down comforters. ⊠ *29850 Circle R Way, 92026* ☎ *760/ 751–8800 or 800/253–5341* 🖷 *760/751–8787* ⊕ *www.castlecreekinn.com* ⋈ *30 rooms, 1 suite* ⚹ *Microwaves, refrigerators, cable TV, in-room broadband, golf privileges, pool, gym, 4 outdoor hot tubs, sauna, spa, meeting room, free parking; no smoking* 🖃 *AE, D, DC, MC, V.*

¢–$ 🏨 **Holiday Inn Express.** This basic motel, right off I–15, is one of the closest to the Wild Animal Park, about 6 mi away. It's on a busy thoroughfare, but close to the California Center for the Arts and a large strip mall where you can find everything from Target to many fast food outlets. Simply decorated rooms sport a vague African theme. Continental breakfast is included in the price. ⊠ *1250 W. Valley Pkwy., 92029* ☎ *760/741–7117* 🖷 *760/839–1601* ⊕ *www.hiexescondido.com* ⋈ *84 rooms, 35 suites* ⚹ *Some kitchenettes, cable TV with movies, in-room broadband, pool, gym, exercise equipment, outdoor hot tub, dry cleaning, laundry facilities, concierge, business services, meeting rooms, free parking, no-smoking rooms* 🖃 *AE, DC, MC, V* ⚏ *CP.*

Shopping

Although farmland began to give way to suburbs in the 1990s, and the area's fruit, nut, and vegetable bounty has diminished, you can still find overflowing farmstands in the San Pasqual Valley and in Valley Center, just east of the city. These days Escondido has begun to look to the arts to sustain its economy. The downtown streets surrounding the California Center for the Arts are getting makeovers, attracting mid-to-high-end art galleries and restaurants to replace the thrift stores and diners.

Bates Nut Farm (⊠ 15954 Woods Valley Rd., Valley Center ☎ 760/749–3333 ⊕ www.batesfarm.com) is the home of San Diego's largest pumpkin patch in fall, where you might find 200-pound squash. The 100-acre farm, in the Bates family for five generations, sells locally grown pecans, macadamia nuts, and almonds. There's a petting zoo holding farm animals, a picnic area, and gift shop. **Canterbury Gardens** (⊠ 2402 S. Escondido Blvd., Escondido ☎ 760/746–1400 ⊕ www.canterburygardens.com) occupying an old winery, specializes in giftware and seasonal decorative accessories for the home, plus a year-round selection of Christmas ornaments and collectibles from Christopher Radko, Mark Robert's Fairies, and Department 56.

The **Lillian Berkley Collection** (⊠ 128 E. Grand Ave., Escondido ☎ 760/480–9434 ⊕ www.lillianberkley.com) presents colorful paintings by several contemporary Russian artists including Vachagan Narazyan and Vigen Sogomonyan. **Rave Reviews** (⊠ 120 W. Grand Ave., Escondido ☎ 760/743–0056) carries high-end vintage clothing and accessories from the 1940s, '50s, and '60s. The **Woodcrafter Design Gallery** (⊠ 135 E. Grand Ave., Escondido ☎ 760/741–0124) offers handmade one-of-a-kind wood products ranging from small bowls and cutting boards to exquisite desks and chairs.

Palomar Mountain

6 *35 mi northeast of Escondido on I–15 to Rte. 76 to Rte. S6, 66 mi northeast of downtown San Diego on Rte. 163 to I–15 to Rte. 76 to Rte. S6.8*

Palomar Mountain has the distinction of being the home of one of the world's most significant astronomical observation sites, Palomar Observatory, installed in 1947. Before that, the mountain played a role in San Diego County's rich African-American history and culture. One of many who migrated to the area in the mid-19th century was Nathan Cole, a former slave who owned a large swath property on the mountain where he farmed and raised cattle, the significance of which is just being revealed through archaeological excavations conducted by local university students. According to local historians, Cole and other former slaves made up a majority of the backcounty population until about 1900.

Palomar Observatory, atop Palomar Mountain, is owned and operated by the California Institute of Technology, whose astronomy faculty conducts research here. The observatory houses the 200-inch Hale Telescope, as well as 60-inch, 48-inch, 18-inch, and Snoop telescopes. Some of the most important astronomical discoveries of the 20th century have been made here, and already in this century, in November, 2003, a tiny planetoid, Sedna, the most distant object in the solar system, was discovered through the observatory's 48-inch telescope. The small museum contains photos of some of these discoveries, as well as photos taken by NASA's Hubble Space Telescope and from recent NASA-European Space Agency missions to Mars and Saturn. A park with picnic areas surrounds the observatory. ⊠ *Rte. S6, north of Rte. 76, east of I–15, Palomar Mountain* ☎ *760/742–2119* ⊕ *www.astro.caltech.edu/ palomar* ⊠ *Free* ☉ *Observatory for self-guided tours daily 9–4, except Dec. 24 and 25.*

🅒 **Mission San Antonio de Pala** is a living remnant of the mission era. Built in 1816 to serve Native American Indians, it still ministers to the Native American community—the only original Spanish mission still serving its initial purpose. The old jail and cemetery are part of the original mission. ⊠ *Pala Mission Rd. off Rte. 76, 6 mi east of I–15, Pala* ☎ *760/ 742–1600* ⊠ *$2* ☉ *Museum and gift shop Wed.–Sun. 10–4.*

🅒 One of the few areas in Southern California with a Sierra-like atmosphere, **Palomar Mountain State Park** holds a forest of pines, cedars, western dogwood, native azalea, and other plants. Wildflower viewing is good in spring. **Boucher Lookout,** on one of several nature–hiking trails, affords a sweeping view to the west. There's trout fishing in Doane Pond. The campground holds 31 sites with tables, firepits, and flush toilets. ⊠ *Off Hwy. S6 at Hwy. S7, Palomar Mountain* ☎ *760/742–3462 ranger station, 800/444–7275 campsite reservations* ⊕ *www.palomar.statepark. org* ⊠ *$4, camping $15–$19.*

Fallbrook

19 mi northwest of Escondido on I–15 to Mission Rd., Rte. S13, to Mission Dr.

With 6,000 hillside acres planted, Fallbrook bills itself as the avocado capital of the world. Citrus and macadamia nuts are grown in the region, too. Historic Old Main Street, a few antiques malls, and agriculture are the attractions in this small walkable town. During the annual spring Avocado Festival in April you can sample great guacamole or even avocado ice cream.

Under the 20-foot ceilings with exposed beams, spacious **Fallbrook Art and Cultural Center** hosts local and regional art shows of watercolors, oils, glass sculpture, bronzework, ceramics, and even gourd art. ⊠ *103 S. Main St.* ☎ *760/728–1414 or 800/919–1159* ⊠ *$5* ☉ *Open days vary with exhibit; call ahead.*

Where to Stay & Eat

$–$$$ ✕ **Bistro Restaurant.** In summer you can eat on the patio or upstairs in the casual indoor dining room. Rack of lamb, black pepper filet mignon, duck, and shrimp are part of the continental menu. ⊠ *119 N. Main Ave.* ☎ *760/723–3559* ⊟ *AE, D, DC, MC, V* ☉ *Closed Sun. and Mon.*

★ $$–$$$$ ▦ **Pala Mesa Resort.** This two-story resort, tucked into a canyon right off I–15 midway between Temecula and Escondido, offers excellent value and is popular with convention groups. It was built in the 1970s, but fully renovated in 2004, and boasts a championship golf course. All guest rooms have golf-course or foothills views, and many have balconies or private patios; some have private outdoor hot tubs. The resort offers a free golf clinic midweek. Locals flock to the AcquaTerra Restaurant and Oyster Bar for fresh seafood and sushi. ⊠ *2001 Old Hwy. 395, 92028* ☎ *760/728–5881 or 800/722–4700* 🖷 *760/723–8292* ⊕ *www.palamesa. com* ➷ *133 rooms* ⚭ *Restaurant, room service, refrigerators, cable TV with movies, in-room broadband, driving range, 18-hole golf course, putting green, 4 tennis courts, pool, fitness center, outdoor hot tub, massage, bar, business services, meeting rooms, free parking, no-smoking rooms* ▤ *AE, D, DC, MC, V.*

¢–$ 🏨 **Fallbrook Country Inn.** This motel-like building wraps around a swimming pool. Decor is country style with fluffy floral bedspreads and overstuffed chairs. Each room has a private balcony. Breakfast is included in the price. ⊠ *1425 S. Mission Rd., 92028* ☎ *760/728–1114* 🖷 *760/ 731–6754* ⊕ *www.pinnaclehotelsusa.com* ➷ *28 rooms* ⚭ *Fans, some kitchenettes, some microwaves, some refrigerators, cable TV, in-room data ports, pool, outdoor hot tub, free parking, no-smoking rooms* ▤ *AE, D, MC, V* ⦿⧠ *CP.*

¢–$ 🏨 **La Estancia Inn.** This Italian-style lodge offers a convenient, but not glamorous, stop right alongside the freeway. Rooms are small and somewhat dark. Grounds support mature landscaping with plenty of flowers year-round to decorate the many weddings held here. The restaurant is open daily. ⊠ *3135 Hwy. 395 S, 92028* ☎ *760/723–2888* 🖷 *760/ 451–3528* ⊕ *www.laestanciainn.com* ➷ *40 rooms, 4 suites* ⚭ *Restaurant, some in-room safes, some in-room hot tubs, some kitchenettes, some microwaves, some refrigerators, cable TV, in-room data ports, pool, outdoor hot tub, free parking, no-smoking rooms* ▤ *AE, D, MC, V.*

Temecula

29 mi from Escondido, 60 mi from San Diego on I–15 north to Rancho California Rd. east.

Once an important stop on the Butterfield Overland Stagecoach route and a market town for the huge cattle ranches in the surrounding hillsides, Temecula (pronounced teh-*mec*-yoo-la) is Southern California's only developed wine region. Premium wineries, most of which allow tasting for a small fee, can be found along Rancho California Road as it snakes through oak-studded hills. Temecula draws thousands of people to its Balloon and Wine Festival held in the spring. Hot-air-balloon excursions are a good choice year-round. **Grape Escape Balloon Adventure** (☎ 800/965–2122 ⊕ www.hotairtours.com) has morning lift-offs.

Temecula is home to some 20 wineries. The **Temecula Valley Winegrowers Association** (⊠ 34567 Rancho California Rd., Temecula ☎ 951/699–6586 or 800/801–9463 ⊕www.temeculawines.org ⊙Weekdays 8:30–4:30) distributes brochures and sells tickets to special wine events. **Thornton Winery** (⊠32575 Rancho California Rd., Temecula ☎951/699–0099 ⊕www. thorntonwine.com) produces several varieties of wine, including sparkling white wine; it offers weekend tours and daily tastings. **Callaway Vineyard**

& Winery (✉ 32720 Rancho California Rd., Temecula ☎ 800/472–2377 ⊕ www.callawaycoastal.com) produces several lines of wines made from grapes grown along the coast including cabernet sauvignon, chardonnay, and merlot. It offers tastings, tours, and a gift shop. **Maurice Car'rie Vineyard & Winery** (✉ 34225 Rancho California Rd., Temecula ☎ 951/676–1711 ⊕ www.mauricecarriewinery.com) produces 16 varietal wines. It has a tasting room, a gift shop, and a picnic area.

Once a hangout for cowboys, **Old Town Temecula** still looks the part. Park on Front Street and walk along the six-block stretch past the large 19th-century wooden buildings; several antiques shops here specialize in local and Wild West memorabilia.

☺ **Temecula Valley Museum,** adjacent to Sam Hicks Monument Park, focuses on Temecula Valley history, including early–Native American life, Butterfield stage routes, and the ranchero period. A hands-on interactive area for children holds a general store, photographer's studio, and ride-a-pony station. Outside there's a playground and picnic area. ✉ 28314 Mercedes St., Temecula ☎ 951/694–6450 ✉ $2 donation requested ☉ Tues.–Sat. 10–5, Sun. 1–5.

☺ The **Santa Rosa Plateau Ecological Reserve** provides a glimpse of what this countryside was like before the developers took over. Trails wind through oak forests and past vernal pools and rolling grassland. A visitor and operations center has interpretive displays and maps; some of the reserve's hiking trails begin here. No pets allowed. ✉ Take I–15 south to Clinton Keith Rd. exit and head west 5 mi, Murrieta ☎ 951/677–6951 ⊕ www.santarosaplateau.org ✉ $2 ☉ Daily dawn–dusk.

Where to Stay & Eat

$$–$$$$ ✕ **Café Champagne.** The Thornton Winery's airy country restaurant, whose big windows overlook the vineyards, serves contemporary cuisine. Menu highlights include grilled eggplant with portobello mushroom Napoleon, pan roasted pork chops with sweet potatoes, apple hash, and honey lavender sauce, osso buco with fettuccine, and grilled Colorado lamb with polenta and pomegranate reduction. If you're in the mood for something small, pick one of the appetizers as your main course. ✉ 32575 Rancho California Rd., Temecula ☎ 951/699–0088 ▤ AE, D, MC, V.

$$$–$$$$ ✕ **Temet Grill.** The lovely brass-and-glass room at the Temecula Creek Inn has wall-to-wall views of the resort's golf courses. Dinner entrées change from time to time; typical options include filet mignon with blue cabernet demi-glace, grilled pork tenderloin with potato gratin, and angel hair pasta with shrimp and lobster. ✉ 44501 Rainbow Canyon Rd. ☎ 951/587–1465 ▤ AE, D, DC, MC, V.

☺ ¢–$ ✕ **Bank of Mexican Food.** Flautas—shredded beef or chicken rolled in a flour tortilla and deep fried—crab enchiladas, and other south-of-the-border dishes are served in this building that started out as a bank in 1913. For an authentic experience request the table set in the vault. There's also a ceramic-tile patio if you want to eat outside. Meals come with beans and rice, and there's a kids' menu, too. ✉ 28645 Front St. ☎ 951/676–6160 ▤ MC, V.

$$$ ☒ **Temecula Creek Inn.** This upscale golf resort occupies a hillside adjacent to I–15 and is a short distance from the wine-touring area. Rooms are in a collection of low-slung buildings (those facing the freeway are apt to be noisy) and are unusually large and bright, nicely appointed with double vanity areas and expansive windows revealing a tranquil golf-course view (which you also get from a private balcony or patio). Decorated in soft desert colors, rooms contain interesting displays of Native American pottery, basket remnants, and antique tribal weavings. ✉ *44501 Rainbow Canyon Rd., Temecula 92592* ☎ *951/694–1000 or 877/517–1823* ⊕ *www.temeculacreekinn.com* ⤳ *130 rooms* △ *Restaurant, café, room service, in-room safes, cable TV with movies, refrigerators, in-room broadband, in-room data ports, driving range, 27-hole golf course, putting green, 2 tennis courts, pool, gym, outdoor hot tub, in-room, massage, croquet, hiking, horseshoes, volleyball, piano bar, meeting room, no-smoking rooms* ▭ *AE, D, DC, MC, V.*

$–$$$ ☒ **Loma Vista Bed and Breakfast.** This mission-style inn has tranquil views of vineyards, citrus groves, and gardens. Most rooms have private balconies or outdoor sitting areas; some have private entrances or fireplaces. A full breakfast, with champagne, is included in the price. ✉ *33350 La Serena Way, Temecula 92592* ☎ *951/676–7047* ⤳ *10 rooms* △ *Some in-room hot tubs, outdoor hot tub; no room phones, no room TVs, no smoking* ¶○¶ *BP* ▭ *MC, V.*

Inland North County A to Z

To research prices, get advice from other travelers, and book travel arrangements, visit www.fodors.com

BUS TRAVEL
☷ Bus Information **North County Transit District** ☎ 800/266–6883.

CAR TRAVEL
Escondido sits at the intersection of Route 78, which heads east from Oceanside, and I–15, the inland freeway connecting San Diego to Riverside, which is 30 minutes north of Escondido. Del Dios Highway winds from Rancho Santa Fe through the hills past Lake Hodges to Escondido. Route 76, which connects with Interstate 15 north of Escondido, veers east to Palomar Mountain. Interstate 15 continues north to Fallbrook and Temecula.

TOURS
Several companies offer individual and group tours of the Temecula wine country with departures from San Diego and Temecula. Some include lunch or refreshments as part of the package.
☷ Limousine Tours **Destination Temecula** ☎ 951/695–1232 or 800/584–8162 ⊕ www. destem.com. **Grapeline Wine County Shuttle** ☎ 951/693–5463 ⊕ www.gogrape.com.

VISITOR INFORMATION
☷ **Escondido Chamber of Commerce** ✉ 135 W. Mission Ave., #104, Escondido 92025 ☎ 760/745–2125 ⊕ www.escondidochamber.org. **Fallbrook Chamber of Commerce** ✉ 233 E. Mission Rd., Fallbrook 92028 ☎ 760/728–5845 ⊕ www.fallbrookchamber. com. **Rancho Bernardo Chamber of Commerce** ✉ 11650 Iberia Pl., Suite 220, San Diego

92128 ☎ 858/487-1767 ⊕ www.rbchamber.com. **San Diego North Convention and Visitors Bureau** ✉ 360 N. Escondido Blvd., Escondido 92025 ☎ 760/745-4741 ⊕ www.sandiegonorth.com. **Temecula Valley Convention and Visitors Bureau** ✉ 26790 Ynez Ct., Temecula 92591 ☎ 951/676-5090 or 866/676-5090 ⊕ www.temecula.org.

EAST COUNTY

San Diego's East County, the area that extends directly east of the city to the Anza-Borrego Desert, bills itself as the sunny side of San Diego, because seasonal summer fog, prevelant along the coast, is rarely seen here. The area is one vast outdoor playground, holding the alpinelike Cuyamaca, Laguna, and Volcan mountains, where camping, hiking, birding, and stargazing are popular pursuits, and lakes and reservoirs that lure boaters and fishermen. The East County is the least developed area of San Diego County, but development pressures are visible not only in the area's major cities, but also along major highways such as Interstate 8, which bisects the region in an east–west direction.

El Cajon

18 mi from San Diego, on I–8.

El Cajon nestles in a valley surrounded by hills or mountains on four sides, hence its name, which means the big Box Valley. Now home to 95,000 people, El Cajon was part of a Mexican land grant where agriculture was the main activity. Following the discovery of gold to the east in Julian in 1869, it became a waystation for commerce and travelers. The city holds a satellite government for the East County, a major regional shopping center, an arts complex, and a downtown that is rediscovering its heritage. The area is a growing East County hub, home to two casino complexes.

The theater of the **East County Performing Arts Center** has 1,142 seats and good sight lines. George Winston, Olivia Newton John, Marvin Hamlish, and the San Diego Symphony Orchestra have all appeared here. ✉ *210 E. Main St.* ☎ *619/440–2277* ⊕ *www.ecpac.com.*

Aircraft intended for display at the San Diego Aerospace Museum in Balboa Park are restored at **Gillespie Field,** a small general aviation airport in the East County. Recent projects have included restoration of a Convair F102A Delta Dagger, which was first built at the Convair facility in San Diego. ✉ *Off Hwy. 67 at Prospect Ave.* ☎ *619/234–8291* ⊕ *www.aerospacemuseum.org/gillespie* ☼ *Mon., Wed., and Fri. 8–3.*

off the beaten path

The **Santee Drive-In** (✉ 10990 N. Woodside Ave., Santee ☎ 619/448-7447 ☼ Mon.–Thurs. 7:30 PM, Fri. and Sat. 8 PM) is one of the last drive-in theaters in the county and the only one that operates year-round. Many viewers bring lawn chairs or blankets and set up just in front or to the sides of their cars.

The **Heritage of the Americas Museum** is dedicated to the natural and human history of the Americas, which it displays in a variety of forms, including meteorites, tribal tools, and jewelry. The museum overlooks the Cuyamaca Community College campus. ⊠ *12110 Cuyamaca College Dr. W* ☎ *619/670–5194* ⊡ *$3* ⊘ *Tues.–Fri. noon–4, Sat. noon–5.*

The storefront **Olaf Wieghorst Museum** celebrates the work of western artist Olaf Wieghorst, who lived in El Cajon during the mid-20th century and produced lifelike bronzes, paintings, and watercolors that focus on the beauty and strength of horses. Many western film celebrities including Gene Autry, John Wayne, and Clint Eastwood have acquired Wieghorst works for their private collections. ⊠ *131 Rea Ave.* ☎ *619/590–3431* ⊕ *www.wieghorstmuseum.org* ⊡ *Donation* ⊘ *Tues.–Fri. 10–3.*

At **Summers Past Farms** you can stroll among the many herb and flower gardens, learn about fairies, flowers, and gardening, or just play with the resident birds, dogs, cats, and rabbits that make this a great place for kids and adults to spend an idyllic afternoon. ⊠ *16502 Olde Hwy. 80, Flinn Springs* ☎ *619/390–1523* ⊕ *www.summerspastfarms.com* ⊡ *Free* ⊘ *Wed.–Sat. 8–5, Sun. 10–5.*

Cajon Speedway is a ⅜-mi professional track of the NASCAR Southwest Region, where a variety of NASCAR-rated stock cars compete. Races are generally scheduled on Saturday evenings, with qualifying laps starting at 5:15 and the first race at 6:45. There are occasional Friday and Sunday races. ⊠ *1888 Wing Ave., at Denny Ave., El Cajon* ☎ *619/448–8900* ⊕ *www.cajonspeedway.com* ⊡ *$10.*

off the beaten path

SIMPSON'S GARDEN TOWN NURSERY AND CAR BARN – More than just a place to buy potted plants, these 25 acres also have barnyard animals, a small historic museum, and 50 antique automobiles. All this ambience makes the long drive from San Diego worthwhile. ⊠ *13925 Hwy. 94, Jamul* ☎ *No phone* ⊕ *www. simpsonsnursery.com* ⊡ *Free* ⊘ *Daily 8:30–5.*

Where to Stay & Eat

$–$$$$ ✕ **Jasmine Bistro.** Flavors from China, Singapore, and Thailand mingle in every lovely dish that comes from the open kitchen at this restaurant tucked into Westfield Shoppingtown. Specialties include Crouching Tiger Hidden Dragon (sautéed lobster tail and tiger prawns), Malay prawns and scallops, and Thai hot basil shrimp. You can dine inside or out, but the patio has a view of the parking lot. ⊠ *315 Parkway Plaza* ☎ *619/588–8228* ▭ *AE, D, DC, MC, V.*

¢–$ ✕ **Por Favor.** A popular dining spot in El Cajon's up-and-coming downtown, Por Favor presents a variety of interesting entrées including a chile relleno filled with shrimp, carne asada made with dried beef, and several versions of fajitas. Soup-bowl–size margaritas are a specialty. You can dine indoors or out in the large patio area. ⊠ *148 E. Main St.* ☎ *619/440–8228* ▭ *AE, D, MC, V.*

$–$$ ▥ **Sycuan Resort & Casino.** Established on 425 acres in 1955 as the Singing Hills Country Club, this is considered one of most challenging championship golf facilities in the San Diego area. It was acquired in 2001 by the Sycuan Tribal Development Corp. and renamed in 2004, when hotel operations were joined with a tribe-operated casino nearby. Guest rooms are fairly basic, but have views of the mountains, the Dehesa Valley, and golf courses. ✉ *3007 Dehesa Rd., 92019* ☎ *619/442–3425 or 800/457–5568* 🖷 *619/442–9574* ⊕ *www.sycuanresort.com* ⇨ *102 rooms* ⚭ *Restaurant, room service, some microwaves, refrigerators, 3 golf courses, 3 putting greens, 11 tennis courts, 2 pools, gym, outdoor hot tub, massage, bar, laundry facilities, business services, no-smoking rooms* ☰ *AE, D, MC, V.*

¢–$ ⊞ **Best Western Continental Inn.** This modern motel is easily accessed off I–8 in downtown El Cajon. Bright rooms are simply furnished. Continental breakfast is included in the price. ✉ *650 N. Mollison Ave., 92021* ☎ *619/442–0601, 800/882–3781* 🖷 *619/442–0152* ⊕ *www. bestwestern.com* ⇨ *98 rooms, 2 suites* ⚭ *Some in-room hot tubs, some kitchenettes, microwaves, refrigerators, cable TV, broadband, in-room data ports, pool, gym, outdoor hot tub, business services, meeting room, free parking, no-smoking rooms* ☰ *AE, D, DC, MC, V* ⎆ *CP.*

Shopping

Not your typical outlet mall, **Viejas Outlet Center,** operated by the Viejas tribe, occupies a beautifully landscaped setting with an Indian theme. There are 57 stores including Big Dog, Gap, Nike, and Tommy Hilfinger; eight food outlets include Rubio's and McDonalds. There's free entertainment here throughout the year. ✉ *5005 Willows Rd., Alpine* ☎ *619/659–2070* ⊕ *www.shopviejas.com* ☉ *Mon.–Sat. 10–9, Sun. 10–7.*

Literary adventures await kids who venture into **The Yellow Book Road** (✉ 8315 La Mesa Blvd., La Mesa ☎ 619/463–4900 ⊕ www. yellowbookrd.com), a huge surprise-filled bookstore. If you're lucky, you may meet an author of a popular children's book at this venue, which hosts signings and readings on a regular basis.

East County A to Z

To research prices, get advice from other travelers, and book travel arrangements, visit www.fodors.com

PUBLIC TRANSPORTATION

San Diego Transit provides bus and trolley service to East County cities including La Mesa, El Cajon, and Santee. The Northeast Rural Bus System has service from the El Cajon Transit Center to Alpine, Harbison Canyon, and points east.

🚍 Bus Information Northeast Rural Bus System (NERBS) ☎ 800/858-0291. San Diego Transit ☎ 619/233-3004, 619/234-5005 TTY/TDD ⊕ www.sdcommute.com.

VISITOR INFORMATION

The Web site of the La Mesa Village Merchant's Association has information about seasonal events and festivals, such as the three-day Oktoberfest, which takes place in La Mesa and is East County's oldest and biggest celebration.

🚍 La Mesa Village Merchant's Association ⊕ www.lmvma.com. San Diego East County Visitors Bureau ✉ 5005 Willows Rd., #208, Alpine 91901 ☎ 619/445-0180 or 800/463-0669 ⊕ www.visitsandiegoeast.com

THE BACKCOUNTRY & JULIAN

The Cuyamaca and Laguna mountains to the east of Escondido—sometimes referred to as the backcountry by county residents—are favorite weekend destinations for hikers, nature lovers, stargazers, and apple-pie fanatics. Most of the latter group head to Julian, a historic mining town now better known for apple pie than for the gold once extracted from its hills. Nearby Cuyamaca Rancho State Park, once a luscious ancient oak and pine forest, was temporarily closed after it burned in a 2003 fire. Now many of its ancient oak trees are coming back to life, hiking and horse trails have been repaired, and some campgrounds are open with new facilities.

The **Sunrise National Scenic Byway,** in the Cleveland National Forest, is the most dramatic approach to Julian—its turns and curves reveal amazing views of the desert from the Salton Sea all the way to Mexico. You can spend an entire day roaming these mountains; an early-morning hike to the top of Garnet Peak (mile marker 27.8) is the best way to catch the view. Springtime wildflower displays are spectacular, particularly along Big Laguna Trail from Laguna Campground. There are picnic areas along the highway at Desert View and Pioneer Mail.

On summer weekends you can view the heavens through a 21-inch telescope in the **Mount Laguna Observatory** (✉ Morris Ranch Rd., off Sunrise Scenic Byway, Mt. Laguna ☎ 619/594–6182), which sits on Mount Laguna at an altitude of 6,100 feet. It's operated by San Diego State University.

Cuyamaca Mountains

An alternative route into the mountains is through **Cuyamaca Rancho State Park** (✉ 12551 Rte. 79, Descanso 92016 ☎ 760/765–0755 ⊕ www.cuyamaca.statepark.org), which spreads over 24,677 acres of open meadows, oak woodlands, and mountains. Cuyamaca Peak rises to 6,512 feet. Much of the park, including all of its infrastructure, burned during a wildfire in 2003. Local volunteers have been rebuilding the 120 mi of hiking and nature trails, picnic areas, campgrounds, and museum, and much has been completed. However, even three years later a drive through the park will reveal nature's healing processes as abundant seasonal wildflowers and other native plants emerge from the blackened earth in a breathtaking display. For an inspirational desert view, stop at the lookout about 2 mi south of Julian on Route 79; on a clear day you can see several mountain ranges in hues ranging from pink to amber stepped back behind the Salton Sea.

C Behind a dam constructed in 1888, the 110-acre **Lake Cuyamaca** offers fishing, boating, picnicking, nature hikes, and wildlife watching. Anglers regularly catch trout, smallmouth bass, and sturgeon. A shaded picnic area occupies the lakeshore. Families can rent small motorboats, rowboats, canoes, and paddleboats by the hour. Free guided nature walks take place the first Sunday of the month along the 3.5-mi perimeter trail. Free fishing classes for kids are held Saturday at 10 AM. Fishing licenses and advice are available at the tackle shop. Two rental condominiums, 40 RV campsites with hookups, and 10 tent sites are available at Chambers Park on a first-come, first-served basis. ⊠ *15027 State Hwy. 79, Julian* ☎ *760/765–0515* ⊕ *www.lakecuyamaca.org* ➶ *$6* ⊘ *Daily dawn–dusk.*

Where to Eat

$–$$ ✕ **Lake Cuyamaca Restaurant.** This tidy, lace-curtained lakefront café specializes in Austrian fare, highlights of which include a selection of schnitzels and wursts, plus several chicken and steak entrées. Austrian beers are on tap. The restaurant, as well as the adjacent food market, is popular with anglers and locals. ⊠ *15027 Rte. 79, Julian* ☎ *760/765–0700* ▤ *AE, D, DC, MC, V.*

Julian, Santa Ysabel & Wynola

62 mi from San Diego to Julian, east on I–8 and north on Rte. 79.

Gold was discovered in the Julian area in 1869 and gold-bearing quartz a year later. More than $15 million worth of gold was taken from local mines in the 1870s. Local history and old photos reveal that the Julian area held a large population of African-Americans in the years following the Civil War. Indeed the gold was discovered by Fred Coleman, who was black, and the Julian Hotel was founded and operated by Albert and Margaret Robinson, who were also black. Today many of the buildings along Julian's Main Street and the side streets date back to the gold-rush period; others are reproductions.

When gold and quartz became scarce the locals turned to growing apples and pears. During the fall harvest season you can buy fruit, sip cider, eat apple pie, and shop for local original art, antiques and collectibles. But spring is equally enchanting (and less congested), as the hillsides explode with wildflowers, thousands of daffodils, lilacs, and peonies. More than 50 artists have studios tucked away in the hills surrounding Julian; they often show their work in local shops and galleries. The Julian area comprises three small crossroads communities: Santa Ysabel, Wynola, and historic Julian. You can find bits of history, shops, and dining options in each community. Most visitors come to spend a day in town, but the hillsides support many small bed-and-breakfast establishments for those who want to linger longer.

The rundown-looking **Banner Queen Trading Post Gallery** is a remnant of an old gold mine dug into a hillside on Banner Grade, 5 mi east of Julian. A step inside what was the mine superintendent's home reveals a wealth of contemporary art. Five rooms are filled with paintings, photos, sculpture, ceramics, stained glass (even some fire glass), and woven pieces by Julian artists. Prices range from $30 or less for photos and pottery to hundreds for paintings and sculptures by widely recognized artists such as James Hubbell and Bob Verdugo. ⊠ *36766 Hwy. 78, Julian* ☎ *760/765–2168* ⊘ *Fri.–Sun. 1–5.*

★ ☾ One of the few places in North America where you can get an up-close view of the gray wolves that once roamed much of the continent lies

CloseUp

SAN DIEGO COUNTY'S CASINO COUNTRY

SAN DIEGO COUNTY IS THE INDIAN GAMING CAPITAL OF CALIFORNIA, with 12 tribes currently operating casinos in the region's rural backcountry. The casinos range from sprawling Las Vegas–style resorts, with big-name entertainment and golf courses, to small card rooms tucked away on rural crossroads. Although the gaming options may resemble what you might find in Las Vegas, the action is definitely different. The casinos stand alone on back roads, so it's not practical to travel from one to another. The big casinos—Viejas, Barona and Sycuan—are popular with local seniors, some Asian visitors to San Diego, and the tour bus crowd from the Los Angeles area. These three are described below, followed by another found on a North County backroad. More are on their way. Many casinos offer bus transport, so call before visiting and save on gas. Also, note that the gambling age is 21 years and over.

Viejas Casino (✉ 5000 Willows Rd., Alpine ☎ 619/445-5400 ⊕ www. viejas.com) is a massive Native American–themed entertainment–shopping complex with the largest casino in San Diego County, but it has no hotel. It's just east of El Cajon and Lakeside off I-8. Viejas has 2,240 slot machines, plus blackjack, poker, bingo, pai gow, and off-track wagering. There are five restaurants and a cocktail lounge, and the Dream Catcher Showroom presents top-of-the-line entertainment. Weekends have Top 40 bands, Sunday is Big Band night, and big names include George Thorogood and Big Bad Voodoo Daddy. The Viejas Outlet Center, a factory outlet mall across from the casino, has 57 shops, restaurants, and a landscaped amphitheater where evening shows are presented.

Barona Valley Ranch Resort and Casino (✉ 1000 Wildcat Canyon Rd., Lakeside ☎ 619/443-2300 ⊕ www.barona.com) is an all-in-one western-style destination with gaming, hotel, restaurants, and golf course. In the casino you can find 2,000 video slot machines including progressives like Wheel of Fortune, 70 gaming tables including blackjack, a bingo hall, a poker room, and off-track betting. There are three restaurants including Barona Oaks Steakhouse, Branding Iron Cafe, and the Ranch House buffet. The 400-room Barona Valley Ranch hotel has a fitness center, day spa, pool and outdoor whirlpool tub, business center, and meeting rooms. Adjacent is the well-regarded 18-hole Barona Creek Golf Club.

More compact than other area casinos, **Sycuan Casino** (✉ 5469 Dehesa Rd., El Cajon ☎ 619/445-6002 ⊕ www.sycuan.com) has 2,000 slot machines, table games such as blackjack, poker, and pai gow, a bingo parlor, and off-track betting. The Showcase Theatre hosts top name acts such as Little Richard and Wayne Newton. On-site restaurants include Wachena Falls Café and Paipa's Oasis buffet. The tribe also owns the nearby Sycuan Resort.

Tropically themed **Casino Pauma** (✉ 777 Pauma Reservation Rd., Pauma Valley ☎ 760/742-2177 ⊕ www.casinopauma.com), a huge tent surrounded by orange orchards in the Pauma Valley, has 850 slot machines, 24 gaming tables for Las Vegas–style craps and roulette, blackjack, and pai gow. There's a café, and two bar-lounges with entertainment. In 2005 the tribe announced an agreement with Harrah's to enlarge the casino and build a hotel.

–Bobbi Zane

just outside Julian. The **California Wolf Center,** which is dedicated to the preservation of the endangered North American gray wolf and participates in breeding programs, houses several captive packs, including some rare Mexican grays, a subspecies of the North American gray wolf that came within seven individuals of extinction in the 1970s. The animals are kept secluded from public view in 3-acre pens, but some may be seen by visitors during weekly educational tours. Private tours are available by appointment. ⊠ *Hwy. 79 at KQ Ranch Rd., Julian* ☎ *760/765–0030* ⊕ *www.californiawolfcenter.org* ✍ *$8, reservations required* ⊙ *Tour Sat. 2 PM.*

☮ At the **Eagle Mining Company,** five blocks east of the center of Julian, you can take an hour-long tour of an authentic Julian gold mine. A small rock shop and gold-mining museum are also on the premises. ⊠ *C St., Julian* ☎ *760/765–0036* ✍ *$10* ⊙ *Daily 10–3, weather permitting.*

☮ In Julian's heyday, it was invaded by mobs of gold miners, who left when the mines played out, leaving behind discarded mining tools and empty houses. Today the **Julian Pioneer Museum,** a 19th-century brewery, displays remnants of that time, including pioneer clothing, a collection of old lace, and old photographs of the town's historic buildings and mining structures. ⊠ *4th and Washington Sts.* ☎ *760/765–0227* ✍ *$2* ⊙ *Apr.–Nov., daily 10–4; Dec.–Mar., weekends 10–4.*

off the beaten path

JULIAN OPEN STUDIOS – A group of professional artists can arrange private visits to the studios of member artists. Most studios are along Julian's scenic backroads. Advance reservations are required. ⊠ *Julian* ☎ *760/765–1774* ⊕ *www.julianstudios.org.*

The 1¼-mi trail through **Volcan Mountain Wilderness Preserve** passes through Engleman oak forest, native manzanita, and rolling mountain meadows to a panoramic viewpoint extending north all the way to Palomar Mountain. On a clear day you can see Point Loma in San Diego. At the entrance you pass through gates designed by James Hubbell, a local artist known for his ironwork, wood carving, and stained glass. ⊠ *From Julian take Farmer Rd. to Wynola Rd., go east a few yards, and then north on Farmer Rd.* ☎ *760/765–2300* ⊕ *www.volcanmt.org* ✍ *Free* ⊙ *Open daily.*

The Santa Ysabel Valley, where three Native American tribes live, looks pretty much the way the backcountry appeared a century ago, with sweeping meadows surrounded by oak-studded hillsides. The Indians operate small farms and run cattle here, although the valley's beautiful pasturelands have been threatened by development in recent years. However, in 2000 the Nature Conservancy acquired large portions of the valley to set aside as a nature preserve. The village of **Santa Ysabel,** 7 mi west of Julian, has several interesting shops. West of Santa Ysabel, tiny **Mission Santa Ysabel** (⊠ 23013 Hwy. 79 ☎ 760/765–0810) is a late-19th-century adobe mission that continues to serve several local Native American communities.

Where to Stay & Eat

$–$$$ ✕ **Julian Grille.** The menu at this casual restaurant inside one of Julian's historic homes appeals to a variety of tastes, including vegetarian. Chicken dishes are popular, as are steaks and the smoked pork chops served with applesauce. Lunch options include good burgers, whopping sandwiches, and soups. There's a tree-shaded dining area that is heated on cool evenings. ⊠ *2224 Main St., Julian* ☎ *760/765–0173* ▤ *AE, D, MC, V* ☾ *No dinner Mon.*

$–$$ ✕ **Romano's Dodge House.** You can gorge on huge portions of antipasto, pizza, pasta primavera, sausage sandwiches, and seafood in a cozy old house. This is a casual, red-checkered tablecloth kind of place. ⊠ *2718 B St., Julian* ☎ *760/765–1003* ▤ *No credit cards* ☾ *Closed Tues.*

¢–$ ✕ **Julian Tea and Cottage Arts.** Sample finger sandwiches, scones topped with whipped cream, and lavish sweets during afternoon tea inside the Clarence King House, built by Will Bosnell in 1898. Regular sandwiches, soups, salads, and a children's tea are also available. ⊠ *2124 3rd St., Julian* ☎ *760/765–0832* ☾ *No dinner* ⩥ *Reservations required* ▤ *AE, D, MC, V.*

¢–$ ✕ **Wynola Pizza Express.** Locals come to this casual indoor–outdoor restaurant for delicious, single portion pizzas such as pesto pizza, Thai chicken pizza, and tostada pizza. Other items include chili, lasagna, and sandwiches. Entertainers usually perform on weekends in the adjacent Red Barn, or in fine weather, outdoors. ⊠ *4355 Hwy. 78, Wynola* ☎ *760/ 765–1004* ▤ *AE, MC, V.*

★ $ ✕ **Julian Pie Company.** The apple pies that made Julian famous come from the Smothers family bakery in a one-story house on Main Street. In pleasant weather you can sit on the front patio and watch the world go by while savoring a slice of hot pie—from Dutch Apple to Apple Mountain Berry Crumb—topped with homemade cinnamon ice cream. The Smothers family has been making pies in Julian since 1986; by 1988 they had bought their own orchard, and by 1992, they had built a larger bakery in Santa Ysabel. At lunchtime the Julian location also serves soup and sandwiches. The Santa Isabel bakery just makes pies. ⊠ *2225 Main St., Julian* ☎ *760/765–2449* ⊠ *21976 Hwy. 79, Santa Ysabel* ☎ *760/ 765–2400* ⊕ *www.julianpie.com* ▤ *MC, V.*

★ $$$–$$$$ ▦ **Orchard Hill Country Inn.** On a hill above town, this lodge and five Craftsman-style cottages have a sweeping view of the countryside. The luxurious backcountry accommodations are decorated with antiques, original art, and handcrafted quilts. The cottage suites have see-through fireplaces, double whirlpool tubs, and wet bars—even private patios or balconies. Guests gather in the evening for wine and hors d'oeuvres in the Great Room, where a fire blazes in the stone fireplace. Breakfast is included. Dinner is served nightly except Monday and Wednesday to guests only at an extra charge. ⊠ *Washington St., Julian 92036* ☎ *760/ 765–1700 or 800/716–7242* ⊟ *760/765–0290* ⊕ *www.orchardhill. com* ⇨ *10 rooms, 12 suites* ⅄ *Dining room, some in-room hot tubs, some minibars, cable TV, in-room VCRs, in-room data ports, bicycles, hiking, wine bar, meeting room; no smoking* ▤ *AE, MC, V* ⅃⊙⅃ *BP.*

$$ ▦ **Butterfield Bed and Breakfast.** Built in the 1930s, this inn on a 4-acre hilltop is cordial and romantic with knotty pine ceilings, Laura Ashley accents, and a gazebo in the backyard. Rooms, ranging from small to ample, have fireplaces or woodstoves, VCRs and CD players, and private entrances. The property is beautifully landscaped with terraced rose gardens. The innkeepers can arrange for a horse and carriage to take you to Julian for dinner or sightseeing. Full breakfast and afternoon refreshments are included. ⊠ *2284 Sunset Dr., Julian 92036* 🕾 *760/765–2179 or 800/379–4262* 🖷 *760/765–1229* ⊕ *www.butterfieldbandb.com* 📤 *5 rooms* ♿ *Dining room, cable TV, in-room VCR; no a/c* 🖃 *AE, D, MC, V* ⫟◯⫟ *BP.*

\$\$ ▥ **Wikiup Bed and Breakfast.** Best known for its herd of 16 llamas, Wikiup appeals to animal lovers. There are angora goats, a donkey, and a parrot, plus assorted dogs and cats to keep you company. The inn consists of a main contemporary cedar-and-brick structure with cedar paneling, modern Danish furnishings, and high, open-beam ceilings holding sky lights. Guest rooms in the main house and a pair of cottages have private entrances, fireplaces, and outdoor hot tubs for stargazing. The innkeepers offer full and half-day llama treks to guests. A full breakfast is included in the price. ⊠ *1645 Whispering Pines Dr., 92036* 🕾 *760/765–1890 or 800/526–2725* 🖷 *760/765–1512* ⊕ *www.wikiupbnb.com* 📤 *4 rooms* ♿ *In-room hot tubs, microwaves, refrigerators, library, no-smoking rooms; no room phones, no room TVs* 🖃 *AE, MC, V.*

\$–\$\$\$ ▥ **Julian Gold Rush Hotel.** Built in 1897 by freed slave Albert Robinson and his wife Margaret, the over 100-year-old hotel is Julian's only designated national landmark. Current owners Steve and Gig Ballanger have brought the old place into the 21st century, but the ambience is thoroughly Victorian. Smallish rooms hold antique furnishings and colorful quilts. Cottage accommodations have private entrances and fireplaces. The innkeepers serve afternoon tea and invite guests to sit on the porch. Full breakfast is included in the price. ⊠ *2032 Main St., Julian 92036* 🕾 *760/765–0201 or 800/734–5854* ⊕ *www.julianhotel.com* 📤 *14 rooms, 2 suites* ♿ *Fans, lobby lounge; no a/c, no room phones, no room TVs* 🖃 *AE, MC, V.*

¢–\$ ▥ **Apple Tree Inn.** This basic motel is set along busy Highway 78 in the Wynola area, about 3 mi west of Julian. Simply furnished ground-floor rooms with private entrances surround a parking lot and swimming pool with gazebo. ⊠ *4360 Rte. 78, Wynola 92070* 🕾 *760/765–0222* 🖷 *760/765–0206* ⊕ *www.julianappletreeinn.com* 📤 *16 rooms* ♿ *Cable TV, in-room VCRs, pool, pets allowed* 🖃 *AE, MC, V.*

¢–\$\$ ▥ **Julian Lodge.** A replica of a late-19th-century Julian hotel, this two-story lodge calls itself a bed-and-breakfast. The rooms and public spaces are furnished with antiques; on chilly days you can warm yourself at the large stove in the small lobby. Buffet-style continental breakfast is included in the price. ⊠ *4th and C Sts., Julian 92036* 🕾 *760/765–1420 or 800/542–1420* ⊕ *www.julianlodge.com* 📤 *23 rooms* ♿ *Cable TV, library, piano, no-smoking rooms* 🖃 *AE, MC, V* ⫟◯⫟ *CP.*

Shopping

Julian, Wynola, and Santa Ysabel have a number of unique shops that are open weekends, but midweek hours vary considerably. In autumn locally grown apples, pears, nuts, and cider are available in town and at a few roadside stands. The best apple variety produced here is a Jonagold, a hybrid of Jonathan and Golden Delicious.

The **Birdwatcher** (⊠ 2775 B St., Julian ☎ 760/765–1817) offers items for wild-bird lovers, including birdhouses, birdseed, hummingbird feeders, plus bird-themed accessories such as jewelry, apparel, novelties, and guidebooks for serious birders. The **Falcon Gallery** (⊠ 2015A Main St., Julian ☎ 760/765–1059), in a replica of one of Julian's original hotels, has works by local artists, books about area history including Native American history, and a small but tantalizing collection of books and art and science kits for kids. The **Julian Bell, Book and Candle** (⊠ 2007 Main St., Julian ☎ 760/765–1377) displays an unusual collection of hand-crafted candles and accessories.

Once Upon a Time (⊠ Rte. 78 and Rte. 79, Santa Ysabel ☎ 760/765–1695) comprises three tiny cottages, each devoted to antiques, florals, gifts, and Christmas decorations. **Santa Ysabel Art Gallery** (⊠ Rte. 78 and Rte. 79, Santa Ysabel ☎ 760/765–1676) shows watercolors, stained glass, sculptures, and other creations by local artists.

★ ☙ **King Leo Chocolate Factory and Store** (⊠ 4510 Rte. 78, Wynola ☎ 760/765–2264) makes and sells creamy chocolates and fudges, including seasonal items such as apple pie and butterscotch fudge. Factory tours are also available. **Meyer Orchards** (⊠ 3962 Rte. 78, Wynola ☎ 760/765–0233) carries different kinds of local apples, including a few heirloom varieties such as Northern Spy and Arkansas Black.

The Backcountry & Julian A to Z

To research prices, get advice from other travelers, and book travel arrangements, visit www.fodors.com

CAR TRAVEL

A loop drive beginning and ending in San Diego is a good way to explore this area. You can take the Sunrise National Scenic Byway (sometimes icy in winter) from I–8 to Route 79 and return through Cuyamaca Rancho State Park (also icy in winter). If you're only going to Julian (a 75-minute trip from San Diego in light traffic), take either the Sunrise Byway or Route 79, and return to San Diego via Route 78 past Santa Ysabel to Ramona and Route 67; from here I–8 heads west to downtown.

VISITOR INFORMATION

🛈 Julian Chamber of Commerce ⊠ 2129 Main St., Julian 92036 ☎ 760/765–1857 ⊕ www.julianca.com.

THE DESERT

In most spring seasons the stark desert landscape east of the Cuyamaca Mountains explodes with colorful wildflowers. The beauty of this spectacle, as well as the natural quiet and blazing climate, lures many tourists and natives each year to Anza-Borrego Desert State Park, less than a two-hour drive from central San Diego.

For hundreds of years the only humans to linger here were Native Americans of the Cahuilla and Kumeyaay tribes, who made their winter homes in the desert. It was not until 1774, when Mexican explorer Captain Juan Bautista de Anza first blazed a trail through the area seeking a shortcut from Sonora, Mexico, to San Francisco, that Europeans had their first glimpse of the oddly enchanting terrain.

The desert is best visited from October through May to avoid the extreme summer temperatures. Winter temperatures are comfortable, but nights (and sometimes days) are cold, so bring a warm jacket.

Numbers in the margin correspond to points of interest on the San Diego North County map.

Anza-Borrego Desert State Park

❼ *88 mi from downtown San Diego (to park border due west of Borrego Springs), east on I–8, north on Rte. 67, east on Rte. S4 and Rte. 78, north on Rte. 79, and east on Rtes. S2 and S22. Alternately take I–8 east to Hwy. 79, follow Hwy. 79 to Julian, where it intersects with Hwy. 78, take Hwy. 78 east to Yaqui Pass Rd., which will take you to Borrego Springs.*

Today more than 600,000 acres are included in the Anza-Borrego Desert State Park, one of the few parks in the country where you can follow a trail and pitch a tent wherever you like. No campsite is necessary. Rangers and displays at an excellent underground **Visitors Information Center** (✉ 200 Palm Canyon Dr., Borrego Springs ☎ 760/767–5311, 760/767–4684 wildflower hotline ⊕ www.anzaborrego.statepark.org ☉ Oct.–May, daily 9–5; June–Sept., weekends and holidays 9–5) can point you in the right direction.

Five hundred miles of paved and dirt roads traverse the park, and you are required to stay on them so as not to disturb its ecological balance. There are also 110 mi of hiking and riding trails that allow you to explore canyons, capture scenic vistas, and tip-toe through fields of wildflowers in spring. In addition, 28,000 acres have been set aside in the eastern part of the desert near Ocotillo Wells for off-road enthusiasts. General George S. Patton conducted field training in the Ocotillo area to prepare for the World War II invasion of North Africa.

Many of the park's sites can be seen from paved roads, but some require driving on dirt roads. Rangers recommend using four-wheel-drive vehicles when traversing dirt roads. Carry the appropriate supplies: shovel and other tools, flares, blankets, and plenty of water. Canyons are susceptible to flash flooding; inquire about weather conditions before entering.

Wildflowers, which typically begin to bloom in January and are at their peak in mid-March, attract thousands of visitors each spring. A variety of factors including rainfall and winds determine how extensive the bloom will be in a particular year. However, good displays of low-growing sand verbena can be found along Airport Road and DiGeorgio Road. Most of the desert plants can also be seen in the demonstration desert garden at the visitor center.

Narrows Earth Trail, off Route 78 east of Tamarisk Grove, is a short walk that reveals the many geologic processes involved in forming the desert canyons. Water, wind, and faulting created the commanding vistas along **Erosion Road,** a self-guided, 18-mi auto tour along Route S22. The **Southern Emigrant Trail** follows the route of the Butterfield Stage Overland Mail through the desert.

At **Borrego Palm Canyon,** a few minutes west of the Visitors Information Center, a 1½-mi trail leads to a small oasis with a waterfall and palms. The Borrego Palm Canyon campground is one of only two developed campgrounds with flush toilets and showers in the park. (The other is Tamarisk Grove Campground, at the intersection of Route 78 and Yaqui Pass Road; sites at both are $20, $29 with hookup at Borrego Palm Canyon.)

Geology students from all over the world visit the Fish Creek area of Anza-Borrego to explore a famous canyon known as **Split Mountain** (⊠ Split Mountain Rd., south from Rte. 78 at Ocotillo Wells), a narrow gorge with 600-foot perpendicular walls that was formed by an ancestral stream. Fossils in this area indicate that a sea covered the desert floor at one time. A 2-mi nature trail west of Split Mountain rewards hikers with a good view of shallow caves created by erosion.

Borrego Springs

31 mi from Julian, east on Rte. 78 and Yaqui Pass Rd., and north on Rte. S3.

A quiet town with a handful of year-round residents, Borrego Springs is set in the heart of the Anza-Borrego Desert State Park and is emerging as a laid-back destination for desert-lovers. From September through June, temperatures hover in the 80s and 90s, and you can enjoy activities such as hiking, nature study, golf, tennis, horseback riding, and mountain-bike riding. Even during the busier winter season, Borrego Springs feels quiet. There are five golf resorts, two bed-and-breakfast inns, and a growing community of winter residents, but the laid-back ambience prevails. If winter rains cooperate, Borrego Springs puts on some of the best wildflower displays in the low desert.

Where to Stay & Eat

$$–$$$$ ✕ **Krazy Coyote Bar & Grill.** The theme at this café is trendy mid-'50s, with dark-red walls adorned with movie posters and other memorabilia. But the menu is strictly contemporary, listing entrées such as Santa Fe crab cakes, sesame-garlic grilled pork tenderloin, and seared ahi. ⊠ *2220 Hoberg Rd.* ☎ *760/767–7788* ⌕ *Reservations required* ⊟ *AE, D, DC, MC, V* ☉ *Closed July–Sept. No lunch.*

$–$$$ ✕ **Carlee's Bar & Grill.** The local watering hole, Carlee's is the place to go any night of the week. A large dimly-lighted room holds both bar and dining tables. The menu lists pasta and pizza in addition to old-fashioned entrées such as liver and onions and mixed grill. Dinners come with soup or salad. ⊠ *660 Palm Canyon Dr.* ☎ *760/767–3262* ⊟ *AE, D, MC, V.*

¢–$$ ✕ **Bernard's.** In a single large room with a wall of windows overlooking the collection of shops and restaurants known as the Mall in Borrego Springs, chef-owner Bernard offers casual dining with a unique Alsatian flavor (Alsace is a region in northeast France, along the border with Germany). Try sauerkraut Alsatian style, or daily duck, pork, or other meat dishes with an Alsatian slant. ✉ *501 Palm Canyon Dr.* ☎ *760/767–5666* ▤ *AE, D, MC, V* ⊘ *Closed Sun.*

★ ¢–$ ✕ **Red Ocotillo.** The only indication that this Quonset hut on the east side of town is a restaurant is the "Eat" sign out front. Inside, the menu says "Congrats you found us," making it clear that they know how good they are, as you will too, as soon as your food arrives. This casual place serves breakfast and lunch only—omelets, pancakes, eggs Benedict, breakfast burritos, soups, sandwiches, burgers, and salads, plus a few desserts—but the food is absolutely outstanding. A delightful courtyard out back has tables for dining, and the wait staff is friendly. ✉ *818 Palm Canyon Dr.* ☎ *760/767–7400* ▤ *AE, D, DC, MC, V* ⊘ *No dinner, closes at 3.*

$$$$ ▦ **La Casa del Zorro.** This serene resort owned by San Diego's prominent **Fodor's**Choice Copley family pampers guests with spectacular desert scenery, luxurious ★ accommodations, and gracious and superb service. You need walk only a few hundred yards from your room to find yourself in a quiet desert garden surrounded by ocotillo and cholla or alone under the stars at night. Accommodations range from ample standard rooms to private casitas with their own pools or private outdoor hot tubs. The elegant restaurant puts on a good Sunday brunch. La Casa schedules wine, jazz, and astronomy weekends throughout the year. In summer, prices are deeply discounted. ✉ *3845 Yaqui Pass Rd., Borrego Springs 92004* ☎ *760/767– 5323 or 800/824–1884* 📠 *760/767–5963* ⊕ *www.lacasadelzorro.com* ⇨ *48 rooms, 12 suites, 19 1- to 4-bedroom casitas* ♨ *2 restaurants, room service, BBQs, fans, some in-room hot tubs, minibars, microwaves, cable TV with movies, in-room VCRs, in-room data ports, Wi-Fi, putting green, 6 tennis courts, 5 pools, health club, hair salon, 3 outdoor hot tubs, massage, bicycles, archery, boccie, croquet, hiking, horseback riding, horseshoes, Ping-Pong, shuffleboard, volleyball, lounge, children's programs (ages 7–12), concierge, business services, meeting rooms, airport shuttle, free parking, no-smoking rooms* ▤ *AE, D, MC, V.*

★ $$–$$$ ▦ **Borrego Valley Inn.** Desert gardens of mesquite, ocotillo, and creosote surround the adobe buildings of this southwestern-style inn. Spacious rooms with plenty of light are decorated in Indian-design fabrics and hold original art. Furnishings include lodgepole beds with down comforters and sarape-stripe bedspreads, double futons facing corner fireplaces, and walk-in showers with garden views. Every room opens out to its own enclosed garden with chaises, chairs, and table. Friendly innkeepers serve a tasty continental breakfast and invite guests to enjoy the courtyard desert garden while dining. The inn is very pet friendly; the innkeepers even have bowls of water in the lobby. ✉ *405 Palm Canyon Dr., Borrego Springs 92004* ☎ *760/767–0311 or 800/333–5810* 📠 *760/ 767–0900* ⊕ *www.borregovalleyinn.com* ⇨ *14 rooms, 1 suite* ♨ *Some kitchenettes, microwaves, refrigerators, cable TV, in-room data ports, Wi-Fi, 2 pools, 2 hot tubs, some pets allowed (fee); no smoking* ▤ *D, MC, V* ⧒�‖ *CP.*

$$–$$$ ⌂ **Palms at Indian Head.** Spectacular desert views of the Anza-Borrego Desert State Park can be had from this small romantic hotel. Large guest rooms are furnished with hand-crafted, Southwest lodgepole furniture and original art by local artists. Two poolside rooms have fireplaces. When it was called the Old Hoberg Resort, celebrities Marilyn Monroe, Bing Crosby, and Lon Chaney Jr., among others, vacationed here. Continental breakfast is included in the price. ✉ *2220 Hoberg Rd., 92004* ☎ *760/767–7788 or 800/519–2624* 🖷 *760/767–9717* ⊕ *www. thepalmsatindianhead.com* ➪ *12 rooms* ⚭ *Restaurant, microwaves, refrigerators, cable TV, Wi-Fi, pool, outdoor hot tub, bar, shop; no room phones, no smoking* ⊟ *AE, D, DC, MC, V* ⟦◯⟧ *CP.*

$$ ⌂ **Palm Canyon Resort.** One of the largest properties around Anza-Borrego Desert State Park includes a hotel, an RV park, a restaurant, and recreational facilities. Decor is western style and some rooms have balconies. ✉ *221 Palm Canyon Dr., Borrego Springs 92004* ☎ *760/767–5341 or 800/222–0044* 🖷 *760/767–4073* ⊕ *www.pcresort.com* ➪ *60 rooms, 1 suite* ⚭ *Restaurant, refrigerators, cable TV with movies, in-room broadband, in-room data ports, pool, gym, outdoor hot tub, lounge, shop, laundry facilities, meeting room, no-smoking rooms* ⊟ *AE, D, DC, MC, V.*

$–$$ ⌂ **Borrego Springs Resort and Country Club.** This low-key resort is surrounded by expansive desert views, visible from every room. Rooms are simply furnished with contemporary oak and upholstered pieces; amenities include hair dryers and in-room coffeemakers. The restaurant on premises serves lunch and dinner daily except Monday. ✉ *1112 Tilting T Dr., Borrego Springs 92004* ☎ *760/767–5700 or 888/826–7734* 🖷 *760/767–5710* ⊕ *www.borregospringsresort.com* ➪ *66 rooms, 34 suites* ⚭ *Restaurant, some kitchenettes, microwaves, refrigerators, in-room data ports, 27-hole golf course, putting green, 6 tennis courts, 2 pools, exercise equipment, outdoor hot tub, bar, laundry, meeting rooms, free parking, some pets allowed, no-smoking rooms* ⊟ *AE, D, MC, V.*

Sports & the Outdoors

The 27-hole course at **Borrego Springs Resort and Country Club** (☎ 769/ 767–5700) is open to the public. The greens fee ranges from $59 to $69, including mandatory cart; discounts may be available to foursomes midweek. The 18-hole **Rams Hill Country Club** (☎ 760/767–5000) course is open to the public. The greens fee is $150, which includes a mandatory cart. The **Roadrunner Club** (☎ 760/767–5374) has an 18-hole par-3 golf course. The greens fee is $20, cart $14.

Smoketree Institute and Ranch (☎ 760/767–5850) offers a variety of equine encounters—guided desert rides on Arabian or quarter horses, pony rides for kids, and a nonriding human-to-horse communication experience similar to horse-whispering.

⎧ off the beaten path ⎫ **OCOTILLO WELLS STATE VEHICULAR RECREATION AREA –** The sand dunes and rock formations at this 78,000-acre haven for off-road enthusiasts are fun and challenging. Camping is permitted throughout the area, but water is not available. The only facilities are in the small town (really no more than a corner) of Ocotillo Wells. ✉ *Rte. 78, 18 mi east from Borrego Springs Rd., Ocotillo Wells* ☎ 760/767–5391.

The Desert A to Z

To research prices, get advice from other travelers, and book travel arrangements, visit www.fodors.com

BUS TRAVEL

The Northeast Rural Bus System connects Julian, Borrego Springs, Agua Caliente, and many other small communities with La Mesa, 15 mi east of downtown San Diego. There's no service Sunday or Monday.
🚌 Bus Information **Northeast Rural Bus System** (NERBS) ☎ 800/858-0291.

CAR TRAVEL

From downtown San Diego, take I–8 east to Route 67 north, to Route 78 east, to Route 79 north, to Routes S2 and S22 east.

VISITOR INFORMATION

🚌 **Anza-Borrego Desert State Park** ✉ 200 Palm Canyon Dr., Borrego Springs 92004 ☎ 760/767-5311 ⊕ www.anzaborrego.statepark.org. **Borrego Springs Chamber of Commerce** ✉ 622 Palm Canyon Dr., Borrego Springs 92004 ☎ 760/767-5555 ⊕ www. borregosprings.org. **State Park Reservations** ☎ 800/444-7275 ⊕ www.reserveamerica. com. **Wildflower Hotline** ☎ 760/767-4684.

NORTH OF THE BORDER
CHULA VISTA & SAN YSIDRO

Chula Vista and San Ysidro are the southernmost communities in San Diego County. Chula Vista is transforming itself from a small town with limited attractions into a much larger community well known for its U.S. Olympic Training Center. The border town of San Ysidro, where thousands cross back and forth to and from Mexico daily, is working to lose its shady image with construction of the Las Americas shopping/hotel/dining complex.

Numbers in the margin correspond to points of interest on the San Diego North County map.

Chula Vista

10 mi south of San Diego via I–5.

This suburban San Diego community of more than 200,000 residents is the second largest city in San Diego County and one of the fastest growing cities in the nation. Consisting of 52 square mi, the city, whose name means "beautiful view" in Spanish, stretches from the southern shore of San Diego Bay east to the San Miguel Mountains. It has bayside parks, a harbor with two marinas, coastal wetlands, master planned communities, the outdoor Coors Amphitheatre, and the crowning U.S. Olympic Training Center. It's one of several towns along I–5 that link downtown San Diego with Tijuana, just across the Mexican border.

The **U. S. Olympic Training Center** is a year-round, warm-weather facility with sport venues and support facilities for eight Olympic sports on its

155 acres: archery, canoe–kayak, cycling, field hockey, rowing, soccer, softball, and track and field. The Copley Visitor Center relates the history of the Olympics using displays and videos. Free tours by golf cart are offered every day during business hours. The tour follows the Conrad N. Hilton Olympic Path, an elevated visitor promenade from which you can see athletes in training for the Olympic gold. A gift shop is also on-site. ✉ *2800 Olympic Pkwy., Chula Vista 91915* ☎ *619/482–6222* ⊕ *www.usolympicteam.com* ✍ *Free* ☉ *Mon.–Sat. 10–3, Sun. 11–3.*

☾ **Chula Vista Nature Center.** Plants and animals native to the San Diego Bay can be seen at this zoo and aquarium in the 316-acre Sweetwater Marsh National Wildlife Refuge. Major displays include the Shark and Ray Experience, consisting of a 4,000-gallon touch-tank containing five species of sharks and rays; a free-swimming tank with underwater viewing areas; and a number of hands-on displays. Eagle Mesa holds both golden eagles and a bald eagle. Hands-on exhibits focus on marine life as well as other animal life typical of salt marshes; there's a walk-through shore bird aviary, as well as six aviaries of other native birds, including hawks, owls, and falcons. One and a half miles of trails lead to San Diego Bay. Free interpretive tours are given on Wednesday, Saturday, and Sunday at 2 PM. Park in the small lot off I–5 at E St. and get the free shuttle to the center. ✉ *1000 Gunpowder Point Dr., Chula Vista* ☎ *619/409–5900* ⊕ *www.chulavistanaturecenter.org* ✍ *$5; includes round-trip shuttle* ☉ *Tues.–Sun. 10–5. Shuttle runs 10–4.*

Knott's Soak City U.S.A. is a 32-acre waterpark with 22 water rides including four high-speed slides, six tube slides, and six body slides for action-packed fun. There are also plenty of wading pools, a family raft ride, and tamer slides for the littlest visitors. You can even choose to just lounge around in a deck chair or an innertube. Food is readily available. Be certain to bring sunscreen. ✉ *2252 Entertainment Circle, Chula Vista* ☎ *619/661–7373* ⊕ *www.knotts.com/soakcity* ✍ *$24.95* ☉ *Daily 10 AM–6 PM* ☉ *Closed in winter.*

Rohr Park cuts a green swath between Chula Vista and Bonita. It boasts open space for picnicking, a playground, an equestrian ring, a 3.3-mi hiking trail, and a working, scale model miniature steam engine that you can ride the second weekend of each month. The Chula Vista Live Steamers club operates it 1 PM–3 PM. ✉ *4548 Sweetwater Rd., Chula Vista* ☎ *619/267–5675* ✍ *Free* ☉ *Daily dawn–dusk.*

Where to Stay & Eat

☾ **$–$$** ✕ **Galley at the Marina.** The view is the attraction at this popular seafood eatery, but there are also bargains on the eclectic menu. The restaurant offers all-you-can-eat fish-and-chips on Thursday night and spaghetti on Tuesday night. Other options include Jamaican chicken with mango sauce and chicken fried steak. A children's menu is available, too. ✉ *550 Marina Pkwy.* ☎ *619/422–5714* ▤ *AE, D, MC, V.*

$–$$ 🏨 **Holiday Inn Express.** This southwest-style motel just west of I–805 at the southern end of Chula Vista is 4 mi from the Mexican border at San Ysidro. Continental breakfast is included in the price. ✉ *4450 Main St., 91911* ☎ *619/422–2600* 📠 *619/425–4605* ⊕ *www.holiday-inn.com*

↻ *118 rooms* ⟨ *Microwaves, refrigerators, cable TV with movies, Wi-Fi, pool, outdoor hot tub, laundry facilities, no-smoking rooms; no a/c* ⊟ *AE, D, DC, MC, V* ⍟ *CP.*

San Ysidro

19 mi south of San Diego via I–5.

San Ysidro is California's southernmost community, just across the border from Tijuana, Mexico. This is the busiest border-crossing point in the world, with more than 104 million crossings each year. The town is busy, somewhat dirty, and just a bit scary, with unsavory looking characters and a heavy Border Patrol and law enforcement presence. In the early 20th century, San Ysidro was called the Little Landers Colony after a "back to the land" settlement begun by William Smythe, which eventually included 150 inhabitants. It was renamed in honor of the patron saint of farmers, San Ysidro, who was, according to legend, a virtuous farmer whose fields were plowed by angels.

The easiest, most convenient way to get to San Ysidro is via the San Diego Trolley, which takes about 30 minutes from downtown San Diego and stops just short of the footbridge that crosses the border into Mexico; you'll be steps from downtown Tijuana when you get to the other side. If you're driving, you can park at one of several secure lots or at Las Americas (see below), where you can catch a shuttle bus to take you to the border.

★ Set right against the international border in San Ysidro, **Las Americas** is an open-air multicultural retail and entertainment complex with 120 shops, including two duty-free outlets, a clutch of fast-food outlets, and three sit-down restaurants. A final phase of this development project, which will eventually include a library and cultural center, a hotel, and the International Gateway—a new footbridge over the Tijuana River directly into Mexico—is scheduled for completion in 2006 or 2007. One of the largest outlets in the world, the **Nike Factory Store** (☎ 619/428–8849) sells shoes, clothing, and accessories. You can find trendy fashions at **Guess Factory Store** (☎ 619/934–7216). Clothing and fragrances are among the finds at **Tommy Hilfiger Company Store** (☎ 619/934–7182). ✉ *4211 Camino de la Plaza* ☎ *619/934–8400* ⊕ *www.lasamericas.com* ☑ *Free* ⊘ *Weekdays 10–9, Sat. 10–8, Sun. 10–6.*

North of the Border A to Z

To research prices, get advice from other travelers, and book travel arrangements, visit www.fodors.com

BUS TRAVEL
🚌 **Bus Information Chula Vista Transit** ☎ 619/233–3004 ⊕ www.sdcommute.com.

CAR TRAVEL
Both Chula Vista and San Ysidro can be reached by car. For Chula Vista take I–5 south from San Diego 8 mi to Highway 54. Go east to reach downtown and the Otay Lakes area. To reach the Chula Vista Nature

Center, continue south on I–5 to E Street and turn west to the gate. To reach San Ysidro, continue south on I–5 8 mi; follow signs to the international border.

TROLLEY TRAVEL

The San Diego Trolley Blue Line offers a convenient means of reaching the international border. You can catch the trolley at any downtown San Diego location for the 30-minute ride to the border. The last north-bound trolley leaves San Ysidro at 1 AM nightly.

🚩 San Diego Trolley **San Diego Transit** ☎ 619/233-3004 ⊕ www.sdcommute.com.

VISITOR INFORMATION

🚩 **Chula Vista Chamber of Commerce** ✉ 750 E St., 91910 ☎ 619/425-4444 ⊕ www. chulavistaconvis.org. **San Ysidro Chamber of Commerce** ✉ 663 E. San Ysidro Blvd., 92173 ☎ 619/428-1281 ⊕ www.sanysidrochamber.org.

Tijuana, Playas de Rosarito & Ensenada

WORD OF MOUTH

"Tijuana is very third-world and border waits can be a problem, but it is an interesting slice of life."
—San_Diego_Mom

"Tijuana is dirty, filled with t-shirt shops, bars, liquor stores, and lots of pharmacies selling all sorts of medications and "supplements" only available by prescription in US."

—Gail

"I have driven to Ensenada more than thirty times. Nearly all of the journey offers spectacular views of the Pacific. Yes, you do see some poverty, but [that] is one of the provocative parts of travel."

—Joe

By Maribeth
Mellin

Updated by
Tina Randall

SEPARATED FROM MAINLAND MEXICO by the Sea of Cortez, the Baja California peninsula stretches 1,625 km (1,000 mi) from Tijuana to Los Cabos. Baja (meaning lower) California is only 21 km (13 mi) across at its narrowest point and 193 km (120 mi) at its widest. Its desert landscape harbors isolated fishing retreats, Prohibition-era gambling palaces, and world-class golf courses. Adventurers who visit the area delight in kayaking alongside migrating gray whales, diving with hammerhead sharks, and hiking to hidden cave paintings.

The peninsula is divided into two states—Baja California (also called Baja Norte, meaning North Baja) and Baja California Sur (South). Baja Norte is densely populated. Tijuana, 29 km (18 mi) south of San Diego across one of the busiest international borders in the world, is home to more than 2 million people and is the peninsula's largest city. It's also the most popular destination for day-trippers from San Diego, who come for the souvenir shopping, to attend sports events, and engage in some sophisticated Mexican dining.

Travelers in search of a more laid-back Mexican experience bypass Tijuana and take the Carretera Transpeninsular (Transpeninsular Highway, or Mexico Highway 1) south along the Pacific coast of Baja Norte to the beach communities of Playas de Rosarito (29 km [18 mi] south of Tijuana) and Ensenada (75 km [47 mi] south of Rosarito). Here, English is spoken as freely as Spanish, and the dollar is as readily accepted as the peso. Between Baja's towns, the landscape is unlike any other, with cacti growing beside the sea, and stark mountains and plateaus rising against clear blue skies.

It's possible to visit all three cities in a long, busy day. Begin by heading past Tijuana straight for the toll road to Playas de Rosarito, a less than 20-mi drive south. Stop at the Rosarito Beach Hotel for breakfast, take a walk on the beach in front of the hotel, and check out a few of the shops on Boulevard Benito Juárez. Return to the toll road south of the hotel and continue south to Ensenada. Take your time along this stretch of road, and exit at Salsipuedes and El Mirador to admire the view.

In Ensenada, park at the Plaza de Marina on the waterfront and do your exploring on foot. Spend an hour or two wandering along Avenida López Mateos and its side streets, where you may find bargains on leather goods and jewelry in high-quality shops. Culture-seekers should tour the Riviera del Pacifico, a former gambling palace built in the 1920s. Return to the waterfront for a quick run through the fish market, and try to be back on the road by early afternoon. On the way, stop for a lobster lunch in Puerto Nuevo, south of Rosarito.

If you finish lunch by mid-afternoon, you'll be able to reach Tijuana by evening. Once in the city, park in a lot by Calle 2A, the road that ties the highway to the border; walk up Calle 2A to Avenida Revolución, finish your souvenir shopping, and have dinner at a restaurant on the way back to your car. It's smart to wait until after 7 to cross the border, when rush-hour traffic has diminished.

A more leisurely tour would include an overnight stay in Playas de Rosarito. By doing so, you can spend the morning in Tijuana seeing the sights and pricing possible purchases. Check into your hotel in the early afternoon, and then visit the beach or the shops. Dine in town or in Puerto Nuevo, get to bed early, and start off to Ensenada in the morning. Spend a half day there, and then head back to Tijuana, where you can pick up that last tacky souvenir from a vendor along the border traffic lines.

Exploring Tijuana, Playas de Rosarito & Ensenada

Border city Tijuana has close ties to the southwestern United States, while Playas de Rosarito and Ensenada, on Baja's northern Pacific coast, are practically extensions of southern California. South of Ensenada the natural side of Baja appears in desolate mountain ranges and fields of cacti and boulders.

If you plan to drive the peninsula, you must have Mexican auto insurance. Always carry water, and make sure your vehicle is in good condition. Keep your gas tank at least half full at all times—remote stations may be out of gas just when you need it. For the most part, the Carretera Transpeninsular is well maintained, although some areas are marred by potholes or gravel and rocks. In addition, the route often has only two lanes, and sharing them with semis and speeding buses can be unnerving.

About the Restaurants

As a rule restaurants in Baja California are low-key and casual, though in Tijuana and Ensenada you're as apt to find upscale continental dining rooms as you are *taquerías* (taco stands). Dress is accordingly informal, and reservations aren't generally required. Moderate prices prevail, though some places add a 15% service charge to the bill.

About the Hotels

You can find great deals at small, one-of-a-kind hostelries. A few out-of-the-way and budget-price hotels don't accept credit cards; some of the more lavish places add a 10%–20% service charge to your bill. Most properties also raise their rates for the December–April high season (and raise them even higher for the days around Christmas). Expect to pay 25% less during the off-season. Many hotels offer midweek discounts.

WHAT IT COSTS				
	$$$$	**$$$**	**$$**	**$**	**¢**
RESTAURANTS	over $25	$15–$25	$10–$15	$5–$10	under $5
HOTELS	over $250	$150–$250	$75–$150	$50–$75	under $50

Restaurant prices are for a main course at dinner excluding tax and tip. Hotel prices are for two people in a standard double room in high season, based on the European Plan (EP, with no meals) and excluding service and 17% tax.

Timing

Baja's climate is extreme, thanks to its desert locale. Temperatures in Tijuana, Ensenada, and Rosarito are similar to those in southern California.

TIJUANA

29 km (18 mi) south of San Diego.

Tijuana is the only part of Mexico many people see—unfortunately, it provides a distorted view of a country with a rich heritage. Before the city became a gigantic recreation center for southern Californians, it was a ranch populated by a few hundred Mexicans. In 1911 a group of Americans invaded the area and attempted to set up an independent republic; they were quickly driven out by Mexican soldiers. When Prohibition hit the United States in the 1920s and the Agua Caliente Racetrack and Casino opened (1929), Tijuana boomed. Americans seeking alcohol and gambling flocked across the border, spending freely and fueling the region's growth. Tijuana became the entry port for what some termed a "sinful, steamy playground" frequented by Hollywood stars.

Then Prohibition was repealed, Mexico outlawed gambling, and Tijuana's fortunes declined. The flow of travelers from the north slowed to a trickle, although Tijuana still captivated those in search of the sort of fun not allowed back home, and drivers heading into Baja's wilderness continued to pass through downtown Tijuana, stopping along Avenida Revolución and its side streets for supplies and souvenirs.

When the toll highway to Ensenada was finished in 1967, travelers bypassed the city. But Tijuana began attracting residents from throughout Latin America at the same time, and its population mushroomed from a mere 300,000 in 1970 to more than 2 million today. As the government struggles to keep up with the growth and demand for services, thousands live without electricity, running water, or adequate housing in squatters' villages along the border. Petty crime is a significant problem; moreover, the area has become headquarters for serious drug cartels, and violent crime—reaching the highest levels of law enforcement and business—is booming. You're unlikely to witness a shooting or some other frightening situation, but be mindful of your surroundings, stay in the tourist areas, and guard your belongings.

City leaders, realizing that tourism creates jobs and bolsters Tijuana's fragile economy, are working hard to attract visitors. Avenida Revolución, the main street in the commercial Centro district, is lined with shopping arcades, restaurants, and bars. The Zona Río district—with its impressive Centro Cultural Tijuana, several shopping complexes, fine restaurants, and fashionable discos—competes with Avenida Revolución for your attention. A massive 10-story-high cathedral dedicated to the Virgin of Guadalupe is under construction in this neighborhood. The Avenida Paseo de los Héroes, one of the city's main thoroughfares, cuts through the Zona Río, running parallel to the dry Río Tia Juana (Tia Juana River). The avenue is notable for its large statues of historic figures, including Abraham Lincoln.

A word about shopping. From the moment you cross the border, people will approach you and insist that you look at their wares. If you drive, workers will run out from auto-body shops to bid on new paint or upholstery for your car. All along Avenida Revolución and its side streets, shops sell everything from tequila to Tiffany-style lamps. If you intend to buy food in Mexico, get the U.S. customs list of articles that are illegal to bring back so that your purchases won't be confiscated.

What to See

➋ Avenida Revolución. This infamous strip, lined with shops and restaurants that cater to uninhibited travelers, has long been Tijuana's main tourism zone. Shopkeepers call out from doorways, offering low prices for garish souvenirs and genuine folk art treasures. Many shopping arcades open onto Avenida Revolución; inside the front doors are mazes of stands with low-price pottery and other crafts.

★ ☙ ➏ **Centro Cultural Tijuana (CECUT).** The cultural center was designed by architects Manuel Rosen and Pedro Ramírez Vásquez, who also created Mexico City's Museo Nacional de Antropología. The stark, low-slung, tan buildings fronted by the globelike Omnimax Theater are beloved landmarks. The center's Museo de las Californias provides an excellent overview of Baja's history, geography, and flora and fauna. The Omnimax shows films on a rotating schedule; some are in English. The film *Marine Oasis: The Riches of the Sea of Cortez* has fabulous underwater scenes. Exhibitions on art and culture change frequently, and the center's stage hosts performances by international groups. ⊠ *Paseo de los Héroes and Av. Mina, Zona Río* ☎*664/687–9600* ⊕*www.cecut.gob.mx* ⊠*Museum $2, museum and Omnimax Theater $4* ☉ *Tues.–Sun. 10–6.*

➍ **L.A. Cetto Winery.** Most of Baja's legendary wineries are in the Ensenada region, but Tijuana does have this branch of one of Mexico's finest wineries. You can tour the bottling plant and sample the wines while watching a video on operations in the Guadalupe Valley. The shop's prices are far lower than those in regular liquor stores. ⊠ *Cañon Johnson 2108, at Av. Constitución Sur, Centro* ☎*664/685–3031 or 664/685–1644* ⊠*$2 for tour and wine tasting* ☉ *Weekdays 10–5:30, Sat. 10–4.*

➌ **El Palacio Frontón.** For many years, the magnificent Moorish-style Jai Alai Palace hosted fast-paced jai alai games. The sport declined in popularity, however, and the games are no more. The palacio has been turned into a convention center, and is also used for concerts. ⊠ *Av. Revolución, at Calle 7, Centro* ☎*664/634–3213* ☉ *Open only for special events.*

➑ **Playas de Tijuana.** Along the oceanfront is this mix of modest and expensive residential neighborhoods, with a few restaurants and hotels. The isolated beaches are visited mostly by residents.

➒ **Plaza Monumental.** Also known as the "Bullring by the Sea," this is at the northwest corner of the beach area near the U.S. border. Besides summer bullfights (April through October), it's occasionally used for summer concerts. ☎ *664/688–0125.*

➎ **Plaza Río Tijuana.** Across from the Centro Cultural Tijuana, the area's largest shopping complex has good restaurants, department stores, hundreds of shops, and a multiplex theater that usually shows English-language films. Shade trees and flowers line the sidewalks that lead from here to the cultural center. ⊠ *Paseo de los Héroes 96 and 98, Zona Río* ☏ *664/684–0402.*

❼ Pueblo Amigo. This entertainment center resembles a colonial village, with stucco facades and tree-lined paths leading to a domed gazebo. The complex includes a hotel, several restaurants and clubs, a huge grocery store, and a large branch of the Caliente Race Book, where gambling on televised sporting events is legal. Things get lively at night. ⊠ *Paseo de Tijuana, between Puente Mexico and Av. Independencia, Zona Río.*

❶ San Ysidro Border Crossing. Locals and tourists jostle each other along the pedestrian walkway through the Viva Tijuana dining and shopping center and into the center of town. Artisans' stands line the walkway and adjoining streets, offering a quick overview of the wares to be found all over town.

Where to Stay & Eat

$$–$$$ ✕ **El Faro de Mazatlán.** Fresh fish prepared simply is the hallmark of one of Tijuana's best seafood restaurants. This is the place to try ceviche, abalone, squid, and lobster without spending a fortune. Frequented by professionals, the dining room is a peaceful spot for a long, leisurely lunch.

Appetizers and soup are included in the price of the meal. ✉ *Blvd. Sánchez Taboada 9542, Zona Río* ☎ *664/684–8883* ☰ *MC, V.*

$–$$$ ✕ **Cien Años.** In this Spanish colonial–style restaurant, dishes include crepes
Fodor'sChoice filled with *huitlacoche* (fungus that grows on corn), shrimp with nopal
★ cactus, and tender beef with avocado and cheese. An unusual blend of flavors—tamarind, Mexican oregano, mango, poblano chilies—distinguishes the taste of each dish, including the *queso fundido* (melted cheese wrapped in tortillas). ✉ *Blvd. Sánchez Taboada 10451, Zona Río* ☎ *664/634–7262* ☰ *AE, MC, V.*

★ **¢–$** ✕ **La Especial.** At the foot of the stairs that run down to an underground shopping arcade you can find the best place in the tourist zone for home-style Mexican cooking. The gruff, efficient waiters shuttle platters of carne asada, enchiladas, and burritos, all with a distinctive flavor found only at this busy, cavernous basement dining room. ✉ *Av. Revolución 718, Centro* ☎ *664/685–6654* ☰ *MC, V.*

$$–$$$ ✕ 🏨 **Real Del Mar Residence Inn by Marriott.** Golfers and escapists relish this all-suites hotel a short drive south of Tijuana. The suites' living rooms have vaulted brick ceilings, fireplaces, and kitchens. The on-site Rincón de San Román restaurant ($–$$$) is excellent, attracting diners from Tijuana and Rosarito. It nods to both France and Mexico; for instance, you could have beef with either an escargot garlic sauce or a chipotle chili sauce. The spa provides ample diversion for nongolfers. ✉ *Ensenada toll road, Km 19.5, 22710* ☎ *661/631–3670, 800/803–6038 in U.S.* 🖷 *661/631–3677* ⊕ *www.realdelmar.com.mx* ⇔ *75 suites* � ⅃ *2 restaurants, snack bar, room service, in-room safes, some refrigerators, cable TV, 18-hole golf course, pool, gym, massage, spa, bar, laundry service, meeting rooms, no-smoking rooms* ☰ *AE, MC, V* ◯ *CP.*

$$–$$$ 🏨 **Lucerna.** Once one of the most charming hotels in Tijuana, the Lucerna is now showing its age. Still, the lovely gardens, large pool surrounded by palms, touches of tile work, and folk art lend the hotel a distinct Mexican character. ✉ *Paseo de los Héroes 10902, at Av. Rodríguez, Zona Río, 22320* ☎ *664/633–3900, 800/582–3762 in U.S.* 🖷 *664/634–2400* ⊕ *www. hotel-lucerna.com.mx* ⇔ *156 rooms, 9 suites* ⅃ *Restaurant, coffee shop, room service, cable TV, pool, gym, nightclub, laundry service, Internet, business services, meeting rooms, travel services* ☰ *AE, MC, V.*

¢–$ 🏨 **La Villa de Zaragoza.** This brown stucco motel's strong suit is location; it's near El Palacio Frontón and around the corner from Avenida Revolución. The neighborhood can be noisy, though, so request a room at the back. Some rooms have kitchenettes; the guarded parking lot is a major plus. The motel is used by tour groups, so book ahead for holidays and weekends. ✉ *Av. Madero 1120, Centro, 22000* ☎ *664/685–1832* 🖷 *664/ 685–1837* ⊕ *www.hotellavilla.biz* ⇔ *66 rooms* ⅃ *Restaurant, room service, cable TV, some kitchenettes, bar, no-smoking rooms* ☰ *MC, V.*

Nightlife & the Arts

Nightlife

Tijuana has toned down its Sin City image, but there are still plenty of boisterous bars on Avenida Revolución. Locals prefer the classier nightclubs in the Zona Río. Tijuana's discos usually have strict dress codes—no T-shirts, jeans, or sandals allowed.

Baby Rock (✉ Calle Diego Rivera 1482, Zona Río ☎ 664/634–1313), an offshoot of a popular Acapulco disco, attracts a young, hip crowd. The **Hard Rock Cafe** (✉ Av. Revolución 520, between Calles 1 and 2, Centro ☎ 664/685–0206) has the same menu and decor as other branches of the ubiquitous club.

Businessmen (there's a definite shortage of women here) favor **María Bonita** (✉ Camino Real hotel, Paseo de los Héroes 10305, Zona Río ☎ 664/633–4000). Designed after the L'Opera bar in Mexico City, this small clublike tavern serves several brands of fine tequila along with beer and mixed drinks. You're encouraged to play dominoes, chess, and card games at the tables.

★ Tijuana has its own brand of beer, thanks to the Czech brew master at **Tijuana Brewery Company/La Cervecería** (✉ Blvd. Fundadores 2951, Centro ☎ 664/638–8662). The European-style pub serves Tijuana Claro and Tijuana Oscura, the light and dark beers brewed in the glassed-in brewery beside the bar. *Botanes,* or appetizers, include chiles rellenos and smoked tuna. Bands play some nights.

The Arts
Tijuana's cultural scene is thriving, with visiting music and theater groups from around the world performing at the Centro Cultural Tijuana. **El Lugar del Nopal** (✉ Callejón Cinco de Mayo, at Calle 6, Centro ☎ 664/685–1264) hosts evening performances by jazz groups, classical guitarists, and other performers. You can usually reach an English speaking person on the phone.

Sports & the Outdoors
Bullfighting
Skilled matadors from throughout Mexico and Spain face down bulls in Tijuana. Admission to bullfights varies, depending on the fame of the matador and the location of your seat—try for one in the shade. Bullfights are held downtown at the **Toreo de Tijuana** (✉ Blvd. Agua Caliente, Zona Río ☎ 664/686–1510 ⊕ www.bullfights.org) from May through early August, most Sundays at 4:30. Ticket prices are $15–$75. In August the fights move from the downtown Toreo de Tijuana to the **Plaza Monumental** (✉ Ensenada Hwy., Playas de Tijuana ☎ 664/686–1219 ⊕ www.bullfights.org), also known as the Bullring-by-the-Sea; fights take place here on Sunday at 4:30, through October. Expect to pay $15–$75.

Shopping
All along Avenida Revolución and its side streets stores sell everything from tequila to crafts and curios and Tiffany-style lamps. This shopping area spreads across Calle 2 to a pedestrian walkway leading from the border. Begin by checking out the stands along this walkway. You may find that the best bargains are closer to the border; you can pick up your piñatas and serapes on your way out of town. Bargaining is expected on the streets and arcades, but not in the finer shops.

More than 40 stands display crafts from around Mexico at **Bazaar de Mexico** (⊠ Av. Revolución, at Calle 7, Centro). High-quality furnishings and art are tastefully displayed at **Mallorca** (⊠ Calle 4, at Av. Revolución, Centro ☎ 664/688–3502). **El Vaquero** (⊠ Av. Revolución 1006, Centro ☎ 664/685–5236) is a dependable place to buy leather jackets, boots, and saddles.

You can find great buys on fashionable clothing and shoes at the **Plaza Río Tijuana** (⊠ Paseo de los Héroes 96 and 98, Zona Río ☎ 664/684–0402), across from the center. **Sanborns** (⊠ Av. Revolución at Calle 8, Centro ☎ 664/688–1462) has beautiful crafts from throughout Mexico, an excellent bakery, and chocolates from Mexico City. The nicest folk-art store, **Tolán** (⊠ Av. Revolución 1471, between Calles 7 and 8, Centro ☎ 664/688–3637), carries everything from antique wooden doors to ceramic miniature village scenes.

Market
★ The **Mercado Hidalgo** (⊠ Av. Independencia, at Av. Sánchez Taboada, 5 blocks east of Av. Revolución, Zona Río) is Tijuana's municipal market, with rows of fresh produce, some souvenirs, and Baja's best selection of piñatas.

PLAYAS DE ROSARITO

29 km (18 mi) south of Tijuana.

What was once a suburb of Tijuana has become a separate self-governed municipality. The region attracted considerable attention in the mid-1990s when 20th Century Fox built a permanent movie-production studio on the coastline south of town to film the mega-success *Titanic*. Today, the complex doubles as a theme park and a working studio.

Meanwhile, Rosarito's population, now about 100,000, has been growing steadily. The main drag, alternately known as the Old Ensenada Highway and Boulevard Benito Juárez, reflects the unrestrained growth and speculation that have both helped and harmed Rosarito. The street is packed with restaurants, bars, and shops in a jarring juxtaposition of building styles. The building boom has slowed, however, and the town's boosters are attempting to beautify the boulevard.

Southern Californians use Rosarito as a weekend getaway, and the crowd is far from subdued—the town's on the spring break circuit. The police do their best to control the revelers, but spring and summer weekend nights can be outrageously noisy. But hedonism shares the bill with healthier pursuits. Surfers, swimmers, and sunbathers enjoy the beach, which stretches from the power plant at the north end of town to about 8 km (5 mi) south. Horseback riding, jogging, and strolling are popular along this uninterrupted strand, where whales swim within viewing distance on their winter migration.

Sightseeing consists of strolling along the beach or down Boulevard Benito Juárez's collection of shopping arcades, restaurants, and motels. Nearly everyone stops at the landmark Rosarito Beach Hotel. It was built during Prohibition and has huge ballrooms, tiled fountains and stair-ways, murals, and a glassed-in pool deck overlooking the sea. A wooden pier stretches over the ocean; on calm days, there's no better place to watch the sun set than from the café tables along its glassed-in edges.

Foxploration. Fox Studios Baja—created in 1996 for the filming of the blockbuster *Titanic* and still a full-fledged production facility—has expanded its operation to include a film-oriented theme park. You learn how films are made by visiting one set that resembles a New York street scene and another filled with *Titanic* props. Exhibits on filming, sound-and-light effects, and animation are both educational and entertaining, and Fox's most famous films are shown in the large state-of-the-art theater. The park includes a children's playroom where kids can shoot thousands of foam balls out of air cannons, a food court with U.S. franchises, and a large retail area. ⊠ *Old Ensenada Hwy., Km 32.8* ☎ *661/614–9444, 866/369–2252 in U.S.* ⊕ *www.foxploration.com* ☞ *$9–$12* ☉ *Wed.–Fri. 9–5:30, weekends 10–6:30.*

Galería Giorgio Santini. Baja's finest painters and sculptors display their work in this architecturally stunning gallery. Stop by for a glass of wine or an espresso in the coffee shop, and learn something about Baja's vibrant art scene. ⊠ *Old Ensenada Hwy., Km 40* ☎ *661/614–1459* ⊕ *www.giorgiosantini.com* ☞ *Free* ☉ *Daily 10–6.*

Where to Stay & Eat

$–$$$ ✕ **El Nido.** A dark, wood-paneled restaurant with leather booths and a large central fireplace, this is one of Rosarito's oldest eateries. Diners unimpressed with newer, fancier places come here for mesquite-grilled steaks and grilled quail from the owner's farm in the Baja wine country. ⊠ *Blvd. Juárez 67* ☎ *661/612–1430* ▤ *No credit cards.*

$–$$$ ✕ **El Patio.** Although it's amid the bustle of the Festival Plaza hotel-restaurant-entertainment complex, this tasteful, colonial-style restaurant is the best spot for a relaxed, authentic Mexican meal. The aromas of chilies, mole, and grilled meats spark the appetite. Try the grilled quail, shrimp crepes, or chicken with poblano sauce. The bar is a good place to enjoy a cocktail away from the street-side crowds. ⊠ *Festival Plaza, Blvd. Juárez 1207* ☎ *661/612–2950* ▤ *MC, V.*

$$–$$$ 🏨 **Rosarito Beach Hotel and Spa.** Charm rather than comfort is the main reason for staying here. The rooms in the oldest section have hand-painted wooden beams and heavy, dark furnishings. The more modern rooms in the tower have air-conditioning and pastel color schemes. ⊠ *Blvd. Juárez s/n, south end of town* ☎ *Box 430145, San Diego, CA 22710* ☎ *661/612–0144, 800/343–8582 in U.S.* ⊕ *www.rosaritobeachhotel. com* ⇆ *180 rooms, 100 suites* ♦ *2 restaurants, in-room safes, tennis court, 2 pools, gym, spa, beach, racquetball, bar, shops, playground, laundry service; no a/c in some rooms* ▤ *MC, V.*

$$ 🏨 **Las Rocas.** This white hotel with blue-tile domes would be the most romantic lodging in town if only it were renovated. The least expensive rooms are small; larger quarters have fireplaces and microwaves. All rooms have ocean views, and the pool and whirlpool seem to spill into the Pa-

cific. An excellent spa offers reasonably priced state-of-the-art treatments. ⊠ *Old Ensenada Hwy., Km 38.5, 22710* ☎ *661/614–0357, 888/527–7622 in U.S.* 🖷 *661/614–0360* ⊕ *www.lasrocas.com* ➷ *40 rooms, 34 suites* ৬ *2 restaurants, some kitchenettes, cable TV, 2 pools, exercise equipment, hot tub, massage, spa, beach, 2 bars* ⊟ MC, V.

Nightlife

Rosarito's many restaurants keep customers entertained with live music, piano bars, or *folklórico* (folk music and dance) shows, and the bar scene is hopping as well. Drinking-and-driving laws are stiff. If you drink, take a cab or assign a designated driver. The police also enforce laws that prohibit drinking in the streets; confine your revelry to the bars.

Festival Plaza (⊠ Blvd. Juárez 1207 ☎ 661/612–2950, 661/612–2950 cantina), a hotel with more than a dozen restaurants, bars, and clubs, presents live concerts on its courtyard stage most weekends. Among the nightspots are El Museo Cantina, dedicated to the art of imbibing tequila and stocked with more than 130 brands of the fiery drink, and Rock & Roll Taco, an on-site taco stand that's also the town's largest (and most rambunctious) dancing and drinking hangout.

Papas and Beer (⊠ On beach off Blvd. Juárez near Rosarito Beach Hotel ☎ 661/612–0444) draws a young, energetic crowd for drinking and dancing on the beach and small stages.

Sports & the Outdoors

Golf

The **Real Del Mar Golf Resort & Country Club** (⊠ 18 km [11 mi] south of border on Ensenada toll Rd. ☎ 661/631–3670) has 18 holes overlooking the ocean. Greens fees are $59 Monday through Thursday and $69 Friday through Sunday. Golf packages are available at some Playas de Rosarito hotels.

Shopping

Shopping is far better in Rosarito than in most Baja cities, especially for pottery, wooden furniture, and high-end household items favored by condo owners in nearby expat clusters. Curio stands and open-air artisans' markets line Boulevard Juárez both north and south of town. Major hotels have shopping arcades with decent crafts stores.

★ **Apisa** (⊠ Blvd. Juárez 2400 ☎ 661/612–0125) sells contemporary furnishings and iron sculptures from Guadalajara. At **Casa la Carreta** (⊠ Old Ensenada Hwy., Km 29 ☎ 661/612–0502) you can see woodcarvers shaping elaborate desks, dining tables, and armoires. **Casa Torres** (⊠ Rosarito Beach Hotel Shopping Center, Blvd. Juárez s/n ☎ 661/612–1008) sells imported perfumes.

The **Mercado de Artesanías** (⊠ Blvd. Juárez 306 ☎ No phone) is a great place to find manufactured souvenirs—everything from sombreros to serapes. Resembling a colonial church with its facade of hand-painted tiles, **La Misión del Viejo** (✉ Blvd. Juárez 139 ☎ 661/612–1576) purveys hand-carved chairs, tin lamps shaped like stars, and glazed pottery.

Puerto Nuevo

12 km (7½ mi) south of Rosarito.

Southern Californians regularly cross the border to indulge in the classic Puerto Nuevo meal: lobster fried in hot oil and served with refried beans, rice, homemade tortillas, salsa, and lime. At least 30 restaurants are packed into this village; nearly all offer the same menu. In most places prices are based on size; a medium lobster will cost you about $15.

Though the fried version is the Puerto Nuevo classic, some restaurants offer steamed or grilled lobsters, which are actually more flavorful. Each October, to mark the start of the season (which ends in March), the town holds a wine and lobster festival.

Where to Eat

$$–$$$$ ✕ **La Casa de la Langosta.** Seafood soup and grilled fish are options in this large, noisy dining room, but lobster is the star. It's served in omelets and burritos or steamed with a wine sauce. Most tables are covered with platters of fried or grilled lobster and all the standard accompaniments. There's an actual wine list here, and it has several Baja wines. ✉ *Tiguron, at Azuelo* ☎ *661/664–4102* ▤ *MC, V.*

$$–$$$$ ✕ **Ortega's Patio.** Spend a sunny afternoon on the upstairs deck; try for a table with a sea view. Brightly striped serapes hanging about provide some shade, and pots of bougainvillea add color. Diners tend to converse between tables as they slowly devour their lobster and well-chilled margaritas. ✉ *Chinchorro 12* ☎ *661/664–1411* ▤ *MC, V.*

ENSENADA

75 km (47 mi) south of Rosarito.

In 1542 Juan Rodríguez Cabrillo first discovered the seaport that Sebastián Vizcaíno named Ensenada-Bahía de Todos Santos (All Saints' Bay) in 1602. Since then the town has drawn a steady stream of explorers and developers. First came ranchers, who made their homes on large plots along the coast and into the mountains. Gold miners followed in the late 1800s, but after the mines were depleted, the area settled back into a bucolic state. The harbor gradually grew into a major port for shipping agricultural goods, and today Baja's third-largest city (with a population of 369,000, it follows Tijuana and Mexicali, Baja California's capital) is one of Mexico's largest seaports. It also has a thriving fishing fleet and fish-processing industry. The center of Mexico's fledgling wine industry is just east of Ensenada, in the Guadalupe Valley.

There are no beaches in Ensenada proper, but sandy stretches north and south of town are satisfactory for swimming, sunning, surfing, and camping. Estero Beach is long and clean, with mild waves; the Estero Beach Hotel takes up much of the oceanfront, but the beach is public. Surfers populate the strands off Carretera 1 north and south of Ensenada, particularly San Miguel, Tres Marías, and Salsipuedes; scuba divers prefer Punta Banda, by La Bufadora. Lifeguards are rare, so be cautious. The tourist office in Ensenada has a map that shows safe diving and surfing beaches.

Many cruise ships stop for at least a few hours in Ensenada to clear Mexican customs; thus, Ensenada is called Baja's largest cruise-ship port. Both the waterfront and downtown's main street are pleasant places to stroll. If you're driving, be sure to take the Centro exit from the highway, since it bypasses the commercial port area.

What to See

⑪ Las Bodegas de Santo Tomás. Once part of the Mission of St. Thomas Aquinas, whose priests first planted grapes in Baja in the late 18th century, the Bodegas de Santo Tomás dates from 1888, making it Baja's oldest winery. Tours and tastings take place at its downtown winery and bottling plant. The restaurant, La Embotelladora Vieja, in a room once used to age wines, is one of Baja's finest. The winery also operates La Esquina de Bodegas, a café, shop, and gallery in a bright-blue building across Avenida Miramar. ⊠ *Av. Miramar 666, Centro* ☎ *646/174–0836 or 646/174–0829* ☜ *$2* ☉ *Tours, tastings daily at 11, 1, and 3.*

⑰ Catedral Nuestra Señora de Guadalupe. The city's largest cathedral is named for the country's patron saint and is the center of celebrations on December 12, the feast of the Virgin of Guadalupe. Though modest in comparison to mainland cathedrals, the church does have impressive stained-glass windows. ⊠ *Av. Floresta, at Av. Juárez, Centro.*

★ **⑫ Mercado de Mariscos.** At the northernmost point of Boulevard Costero, the main street along the waterfront, is an indoor-outdoor fish market where row after row of counters display piles of shrimp, tuna, dorado, and other fish caught off Baja's coasts. Outside, stands sell grilled or smoked fish, seafood cocktails, and fish tacos. You can pick up a few souvenirs, eat well for very little money, and take some great photographs. The original fish taco stands line the dirt path to the fish market. If your stomach is delicate, try the fish tacos at the cleaner, quieter Plaza de Mariscos in the shadow of the giant beige Plaza de Marina that blocks the view of the traditional fish market from the street.

⑬ Muelle de Pescador. Fishing and whale-watching boats depart from this pier. The area around it has been remodeled, and a broad *malecón* (seaside walkway) with park benches and palms runs along the waterfront. ⊠ *Blvd. Costero, at Av. Alvarado, Centro.*

⑩ Parque Revolución. Revolution Park is Ensenada's most traditional plaza, with a bandstand, playground, and plenty of benches in the shade. The plaza is festive on weekend evenings, when neighbors congregate here to chat and children chase seagulls. ⊠ *Av. Obregón, between Calles 6 and 7, Centro.*

⑮ Paseo Calle Primera. Formerly known as Avenida López Mateos, this is the center of Ensenada's traditional tourist zone. High-rise hotels, souvenir shops, restaurants, and bars line the avenue for eight blocks, from its beginning at the foot of the Chapultepec Hills to the dry channel of the Arroyo de Ensenada. The avenue also has cafés and most of the town's souvenir shops. Businesses use one or both street names for their addresses, though most stick with López Mateos. Locals shop for furniture, clothing, and other necessities a few blocks inland on Avenida Juárez, in Ensenada's downtown area.

⑭ Plaza Cívica. This block-long concrete park—with sculptures of Mexican heroes Benito Juárez, Miguel Hidalgo, and Venustiano Carranza—feels more like a monument than a gathering spot. Still, there are benches and horse-drawn carriages at the ready. ⊠ *Blvd. Costero, at Av. Riveroll, Centro.*

⑯ Riviera del Pacífico. Officially called the Centro Social, Cívico y Cultural de Ensenada, the Riviera is a rambling, white, hacienda-style mansion built in the 1920s. An enormous gambling palace, hotel, restaurant, and bar, the glamorous Riviera was frequented by wealthy U.S. citizens and Mexicans, particularly during Prohibition. When gambling was outlawed in Mexico and Prohibition ended in the United States, the palace lost its raison d'être. You can tour some of the elegant ballrooms and halls, which occasionally host art shows and civic events. The gardens alone are worth visiting, and the building houses a museum on Baja's history.

✉ *Blvd. Costero, at Av. Riviera, Centro* ☎ 646/177–0594 ⌨ *Bldg. and gardens free; museum donations requested* ⊙ *Daily 9:30–2 and 3–5.*

off the beaten path

LA BUFADORA – Seawater splashes up to 75 feet in the air, spraying sightseers standing near this impressive tidal blowhole (*la bufadora* means the buffalo snort) in the coastal cliffs at Punta Banda. Legend has it that the blowhole was created by a whale or sea serpent trapped in an undersea cave; both these stories, and the less romantic scientific facts, are posted on a roadside plaque here. The road to La Bufadora along Punta Banda—an isolated, mountainous point that juts into the sea—is lined with stands selling olives, tamales, strands of chilies and garlic, and terra-cotta planters. The drive gives you a sampling of Baja's wilderness. There are public restrooms as well as a few restaurants, including the extremely popular Gordo's, which is open Friday through Sunday. There's a small fee to park near the blowhole. A public bus runs from the downtown Ensenada station to Maneadero, the nearest town on the highway to La Bufadora. Here you can catch a minibus labeled Punta Banda that goes to La Bufadora. ✉ *Carretera 23, 31 km (19 mi) south of Ensenada, Punta Banda.*

Where to Stay & Eat

★ **$$–$$$$** ✕ **El Rey Sol.** From its chateaubriand *bouquetière* (garnished with a bouquet of vegetables) to the savory chicken chipotle, this family-owned French restaurant sets a high standard. Louis XIV–style furnishings and an attentive staff make it both comfortable and elegant. The side-walk tables are a perfect place to dine and people-watch. The small café in the front sells pastries, all made on the premises. ✉ *Av. López Mateos 1000, Centro* ☎ 646/178–1733 ⊟ *AE, MC, V.*

$–$$$ ✕ **La Embotelladora Vieja.** This elegant restaurant was once the wine-aging room of the Santo Tomás winery. The Baja French menu could include smoked tuna, grilled lobster in cabernet sauvignon sauce, or quail with sauvignon blanc sauce. Some dishes are available without alcohol-enhanced sauces. ✉ *Av. Miramar 666, Centro* ☎ 646/178–1660 ⊟ *AE, MC, V* ⊙ *Closed Mon.*

$–$$ ✕ **Hacienda Del Charro.** Hungry patrons hover over platters of chiles rel-
Fodor'sChoice lenos, enchiladas, and fresh chips and guacamole at heavy wooden pic-
★ nic tables. Plump chickens slowly turn over a wood-fueled fire by the front window, and the aroma of simmering beans fills the air. ✉ *Av. López Mateos 454, Centro* ☎ 646/178–2114 ⊟ *No credit cards.*

☾ **$$** 🏨 **Estero Beach Resort.** Families love this long-standing resort on Ensenada's top beach. The best rooms (some with kitchenettes) are by the sand; the worst are by the parking lot. Be sure to check out the outstanding collection of folk art and artifacts in the resort's small museum. Mid-week winter rates are a real bargain. There's also an on-site RV park; its 38 sites have hookups for water, sewer, and electricity. ✉ *Mexico Carretera 1, 10 km (6 mi) south of Ensenada, Estero Beach* ⌂ *482 W. San Ysidro Blvd., San Ysidro, CA 92173* ☎ 646/176–6230 or 646/176–6235 ⎙ 646/176–6925 ⊕ *www.hotelesterobeach.com* ⇥ *94 rooms, 2 suites*

⚙ *Restaurant, some kitchenettes, cable TV, 4 tennis courts, pool, horse-back riding, volleyball, bar, shops, playground* ☰ MC, V.

$$ ⌂ **Hotel Coral & Marina.** This all-suites resort is enormous. It has a spa, tennis courts, a water-sports center, and marina with slips for 350 boats and customs-clearing facilities. All guest quarters have refrigerators and coffeemakers. Suites in the two eight-story towers are done in burgundy and dark green; most have waterfront balconies, seating areas, and international phone service. ⊠ *Mexico Carretera 1, Km 103, Zona Playitas 22860* ☎ *646/175–0000, 800/862–9020 in U.S.* ≣ *646/175–0005* ⊕ *www.hotelcoral.com* ⊅ *147 suites* ⚙ *Restaurant, room service, refrigerators, cable TV, 2 tennis courts, 3 pools (1 indoor), gym, hot tub, massage, spa, boating, marina, fishing, bar, laundry service, meeting rooms* ☰ MC, V.

$$
Fodor'sChoice
★ ⌂ **Las Rosas.** All rooms in this intimate hotel north of Ensenada face the ocean and pool; some have fireplaces and hot tubs, and even the least expensive are lovely. The atrium lobby has marble floors, mint-green-and-pink couches that look out at the sea, and a glass ceiling that glows at night. Make reservations far in advance. ⊠ *Mexico Carretera 1, north of Ensenada, Zona Playitas* ⊕ *374 E. H St., Chula Vista, CA 91910* ☎ *646/174–4320 or 646/174–4360* ≣ *646/174–4595* ⊕ *www.lasrosas. com* ⊅ *48 rooms* ⚙ *Restaurant, 2 tennis courts, pool, hot tub, gym, massage, spa, bar, laundry service* ☰ AE, MC, V.

$$ ⌂ **Posada El Rey Sol.** A glass elevator rises three floors to rooms that have comfy armchairs, sculpted headboards, and carpeting. The rooms are the loveliest in the downtown area, and the proximity to restaurants and shops is a big plus. Room service is provided by the El Rey Sol restaurant across the street. ⊠ *Av. Blancarte 130, Centro, 22860* ☎ *646/178–1641, 888/315–2378 in U.S.* ≣ *646/174–0005* ⊕ *www.posadaelreysol. com* ⊅ *52 rooms* ⚙ *Restaurant, room service, in-room data ports, in-room safes, minibars, pool, hot tub, bar, laundry service, meeting room, no-smoking rooms* ☰ MC, V.

Nightlife

Ensenada is a party town for college students, surfers, and other young tourists, though it's also possible to enjoy a mellow evening out. **La Capilla** (⊠ Hotel El Cid, Paseo Calle Primera 993, Centro ☎ 646/178–2401 Ext. 104) attracts an older crowd that enjoys romantic ballads in a relaxed setting and dancing to live Cuban music (Wednesday–Sunday). ★ **Hussong's Cantina** (⊠ Av. Ruíz 113, Centro ☎ 646/178–3210) has been an Ensenada landmark since 1892 and has changed little since then. A security guard stands by the front door to handle the often rowdy crowd—a mix of locals and visitors of all ages over 18. The noise is usually deafening, pierced by mariachi and ranchera musicians and the whoops and hollers of the pie-eyed. **Papas and Beer** (⊠ Av. Ruíz 102, Centro ☎ 646/174–0145) attracts a collegiate crowd.

Sports & the Outdoors

Whale-Watching & Fishing

Boats leave the Ensenada sportfishing pier for whale-watching trips from December through February. The gray whales migrating from the north to bays and lagoons in southern Baja pass through Todos Santos Bay, often close to shore. Binoculars and cameras with telephoto capabilities come in handy. The trips last about three hours. Vessels are available from several outfitters at the sportfishing pier. A three-hour tour costs about $30.

The best angling is from April through November, with bottom fishing good in winter. Charter vessels and party boats are available from several outfitters along Avenida López Mateos and Boulevard Costero and off the sportfishing pier. Mexican fishing licenses for the day or year are available at the tourist office or from charter companies.

Ensenada Clipper Fleet (⊠ Sportfishing Pier, Blvd. Costero at Av. Alvarado, Centro ☎ 646/178–2185) has charter and group boats. The fee for a day's fishing is $50, including a fishing license. **Sergio's Sportfishing** (⊠ Sportfishing Pier, Blvd. Costero at Av. Alvarado, Centro ☎ 646/178–2185 ⊕ www.sergios-sportfishing.com), one of the best sportfishing companies in Ensenada, has charter and group boats as well as boat slips for rent. The fee for a day's fishing is $50 per person on a group boat, including the cost of a license.

Shopping

Most of the tourist shops are along Avenida López Mateos beside the hotels and restaurants. There are several two-story shopping arcades, some with empty shops. Dozens of curio shops line the street, all selling similar selections of pottery, serapes, and more.

Artes Don Quijote (⊠ Av. López Mateos 503, Centro ☎ 646/174–4082) has carved wood doors, huge terra-cotta pots, and crafts from Oaxaca. It's closed on Tuesday. **Bazar Casa Ramirez** (⊠ Av. López Mateos 510, Centro ☎ 646/178–8209) sells high-quality Talavera pottery and other ceramics, wrought-iron pieces, and papier-mâché figurines. Be sure to check out the displays upstairs. At **Los Castillo** (⊠ Av. López Mateos 1076, Centro ☎ 646/178–2335) the display of silver jewelry from Taxco is
★ limited but of excellent quality. The **Centro Artesenal de Ensenada** has a smattering of galleries and shops. By far the best shop there is **Galería Pérez Meillón** (⊠ Blvd. Costero 1094–39, Centro ☎ No phone), with its museum-quality Casas Grandes pottery and varied folk art by indigenous northern Mexican peoples.

La Esquina de Bodegas (⊠ Av. Miramar at Calle 6, Centro ☎ 646/178–3557) is an innovative gallery, shop, and café run by Baja's oldest winery, Bodegas de Santo Tomás. **Los Globos** (⊠ Calle 9, 3 blocks east of Reforma, Centro ☎ No phone) is a daily open-air swap meet. Vendors and shoppers are most abundant on weekends. **Mario's Silver** (⊠ Calle Primera 1090-6, Centro ☎ 646/178–2451) has several branches along the main street tempting shoppers with both silver and gold jewelry. **La Mina de Salomón** (⊠ Av. López Mateos 1000, Centro ☎ 646/178–1733) carries elaborate jewelry in a tiny gallery next to El Rey Sol restaurant. It also has a pastry shop.

TIJUANA, PLAYAS DE ROSARITO & ENSENADA A TO Z

To research prices, get advice from other travelers, and travel arrange-ments, visit www.fodors.com.

BUS TRAVEL

Greyhound buses head to Tijuana from downtown San Diego several times daily. Buses to San Diego and Los Angeles depart from Tijuana 14 times a day. Fares to Tijuana are $7 one-way from San Diego (round-trip $9) and $21 from Los Angeles (round-trip $30). Mexicoach runs border shut-tle buses from the San Diego Trolley stop in San Ysidro and the large parking lot on the U.S. side of the border to the Tijuana Tourist Termi-nal at Avenida Revolución between Calles 6 and 7. These shuttles make the circuit every 15 minutes between 8 AM and 9 PM; the fare is $1.50.

Buses to destinations in Baja and mainland Mexico depart from Tijuana's Central Camionera de Tijuana (Central Bus Station), at Calz. Lázaro Cárdenas and Blvd. Arroyo Alamar. Buses connect all the towns in Baja Norte and are easy to use. Autotransportes de Baja California covers the entire Baja route. Tijuana's Central de Autobuses de la Linéa (Bor-der Bus Station) has service to Rosarito, Ensenada, and other Baja points, along with city buses to downtown Tijuana. The Central de Au-tobuses Centro (Downtown Bus Station), at Calle 1a and Avenida Madero, also has service to Rosarito and Ensenada. To catch the bus back to the border from downtown, go to Calle Benito Juárez (also called Calle 2a) between Avenidas Revolución and Constitución. Buses to Rosarito stop at a small terminal on Boulevard Juárez across from the Rosarito Beach Hotel; there's no official bus station here.

🚍 Bus Lines **Autotransportes de Baja California** ☎ 664/686-9010. **Greyhound** ☎ 664/686-0697, 664/688-0165 in Tijuana, 01800/710-8819 in Mexico, 800/231-2222 in U.S. ⊕ www.greyhound.com. **Mexicoach** ☎ 664/685-1440, 619/428-9517 in U.S. ⊕ www.mexicoach.com.

🚍 Bus Stations **Ensenada** ✉ Av. Riveroll 1075, between Calles 10 and 11, Centro, En-senada ☎ 646/178-6680. **San Diego** ✉ 120 W. Broadway ☎ 619/239-2366. **Tijuana Border Bus Station** ✉ Centro Comercial Viva Tijuana, Vía de la Juventud Oriente 8800, Zona Río, Tijuana ☎ 664/621-2982. **Tijuana Central Bus Station** ✉ Calz. Lázaro Cár-denas, at Blvd. Arroyo Alamar, La Mesa, Tijuana ☎ 664/621-2982. **Tijuana Downtown Bus Station** ✉ Calle 1a, at Av. Madero, Centro, Tijuana ☎ 664/621-2982.

CAR RENTAL

Many U.S. car-rental companies don't allow you to drive their cars into Mexico. Avis permits its cars to go from San Diego into Baja as far as 724 km (450 mi) south of the border. You must declare your intention to take the car into Mexico and buy Mexican auto insurance; one-way rentals into Mexico are not permitted, and the person who rents the car must be the one to return it in San Diego. California Baja Rent-A-Car rents four-wheel-drive vehicles, convertibles, and sedans for use through-out Mexico (the only company to do this).

Fiesta Rent-a-Car and Hertz have offices in Ensenada. The larger U.S. rental agencies have offices at Tijuana's Aeropuerto Abelardo L. Rodriguez as well as other locations in Tijuana.

🏧 **Alamo** ✉ Blvd. R. Sánchez Taboada 10401, Zona Río, Tijuana ☎ 664/686-4040 ⊕ www. alamo.com. **Avis** ✉ Blvd. Cuauhtémoc 1705, Zona Río, Tijuana ☎ 664/683-0603 ⊕ www.avis.com. **Budget** ✉ Paseo de los Héroes 77, Zona Río, Tijuana ☎ 664/634-3303 ⊕ www.budget.com. **California Baja Rent-A-Car** ✉ 9245 Jamacha Blvd., Spring Valley, CA 91977 ☎ 619/470-7368, 888/470-7368 in U.S. ⊕ www.cabaja.com. **Fiesta Rent-a-Car** ✉ Hotel Corona at Blvd. Costero, Centro, Ensenada ☎ 646/176-3344. **Hertz** ✉ Av. Blancarte, between Calles 1 and 2, Centro, Ensenada ☎ 646/178-2982 ⊕ www. hertz.com. **Hertz** ✉ Paseo Centenario 9575, Zona Río, Tijuana ☎ 664/607-3950 ⊕ www.hertz.com. **National Car Rental** ✉ Av. Nezahuatcoyotl 1640, Zona Río, Tijuana ☎ 664/683-5500 ⊕ www.nationalcar.com.

CAR TRAVEL

The best way to thoroughly tour Baja Norte is by car, although the driving can be complicated. If you're just visiting Tijuana, it's easiest to park on the U.S. side of the border and walk across.

From San Diego, U.S. 5 and I–805 end at the San Ysidro border crossing; Highway 905 leads from I–5 and I–805 to the Tijuana border crossing at Otay Mesa. U.S. 94 from San Diego connects with U.S. 188 to the border at Tecate, 57 km (35 mi) east of San Diego. I–8 from San Diego connects with U.S. 111 at Calexico—203 km (126 mi) east—and the border crossing to Mexicali.

To head south into Baja from Tijuana, follow the signs for Ensenada Cuota, the toll road (also called Carretera 1 and, on newer signs, the Scenic Highway) that runs south along the coast. There are two clearly marked exits for Rosarito, and one each for Puerto Nuevo and Ensenada. The road is excellent, although it has some hair-raising curves atop the cliffs and is best driven in daylight (the stretch from Rosarito to Ensenada is one of the most scenic drives in Baja). Tollbooths accept U.S. and Mexican currency; tolls are about $3. Restrooms are available near toll stations. The alternative free road—Carretera 1D or Ensenada Libre—may be difficult for first-timers to navigate. (The entry to the 1D is on a side street in a congested area of downtown Tijuana, and the highway is quite curvy.) Carretera 1 continues south of Ensenada to the border between Baja California and Baja California Sur and on to the southernmost point of the peninsula; there are no tolls past Ensenada.

The combination of overpopulation, lack of infrastructure, and heavy winter rains makes many of Tijuana's streets difficult to navigate by automobile. It's always best to stick to the main thoroughfares. Most of Rosarito proper can be explored on foot, which is a good idea on weekends, when Boulevard Juárez has bumper-to-bumper traffic. To reach Puerto Nuevo and other points south, continue on Boulevard Juárez (also called Old Ensenada Highway and Ensenada Libre) through town. Most of Ensenada's attractions are within five blocks of the waterfront; it's easy to take a long walking tour of the city. A car is necessary to reach La Bufadora and most of the beaches.

PARKING Large lots stretch on both sides of I–5 at San Ysidro, close to the border. The charge is $8 to $12 per day; though most have an attendant, they're not actually guarded, so don't leave any valuables in your car. In Tijuana, there are lots along Avenida Revolución and at most major attractions. There's plenty of waterfront parking along Avenida Costera in Ensenada. Parking spaces are harder to find in Rosarito; try the large lot on Avenida Juárez by the Commercial Mexicana grocery store.

🏴 Mexican Customs Office ⊠ Inside San Ysidro border crossing ☎ 664/682-3439 or 664/684-7790.

CHILDREN IN MEXICO

Mexico has a very strict policy about children entering the country. All children, including infants, must have proof of citizenship (a birth certificate) for travel to Mexico. All children up to age 18 traveling with a single parent must also have a notarized letter from the other parent stating that the child has his or her permission to leave their home country. If the other parent is deceased or the child has only one legal parent, a notarized statement saying so must be obtained as proof.

CONSULATES

🏴 Canadian Consulate ⊠ Calle Germán Gedovius 10411, Zona Río, Tijuana ☎ 664/684-0461. **U.K. Consulate** ⊠ Av. Salinas 1500, Fracc. Aviación, Tijuana ☎ 664/686-5320. **U.S. Consulate** ⊠ Tapachula 96, Tijuana ☎ 664/622-7400 ⊕ www.usembassy-mexico.gov/tijuana/Tenglish.htm.

EMERGENCIES

In an emergency anywhere in Baja Norte, dial 066. The operators speak at least a bit of English. For tourist assistance with legal problems, accidents, or other incidents dial the Tourist Information and Assistance hotline at 078.

The Tijuana government publishes a small guide to crime for tourists, available at information desks. It lists the agencies to contact if you've been involved in a crime, and lists the crimes that tourists most often commit (carrying weapons, purchasing illegal drugs, public drunkenness). Victims of a crime should contact the State District Attorney's Office or the U.S. Consulate General.

🏴 State District Attorney ☎ 664/638-5206.

ENTRY REQUIREMENTS

U.S. citizens must prove citizenship by showing a valid passport, certified copy of a birth certificate, or voter-registration card (the last two must be accompanied by a government-issued photo ID). However, a passport is the best option, and after December 31, 2006, U.S. citizens will be required to show a passport when reentering the U.S. by air or sea from Mexico. After December 31, 2007, a passport will be needed to return by land. Minors traveling with one parent need notarized permission from the absent parent. *See* Children in Mexico.

TELEPHONES

The country code for Mexico is 52. When calling a Mexico number from abroad, dial any necessary international access code, then the country code and then all of the numbers listed for the entry. (From the United States, for instance, dial 011-52, plus the city area code and the local seven digit number. The city area code for Tijuana is 664, for Rosarito 661, and for Ensenada 646.)

Directory assistance is 040 nationwide. For assistance in English, dial 090 first for an international operator; tell the operator in what city, state, and country you require directory assistance, and he or she will connect you.

TOURS & PACKAGES

Baja California Tours has comfortable, informative bus trips throughout northern Baja. Seasonal day and overnight trips focus on whale-watching, fishing, shopping, wineries, sports, dude ranches, and art and cultural events in Tijuana, Rosarito, and Ensenada. Cali-Baja Tours runs bus trips to La Bufadora from Ensenada. Five Star Tours runs a daily Tijuana shuttle and tours to Rosarito Beach, Puerto Nuevo, and Ensenada. San Diego Scenic Tours offers half- and full-day bus tours of Tijuana, with time allowed for shopping.

Baja California Tours ✉ 7734 Herschel Ave., Suite O, La Jolla, CA 92037 ☎ 858/454-7166 or 800/336-5454 ⊕ www.bajaspecials.com. **Cali-Baja Tours** ✉ Av. Macheros at Blvd. Costero, Centro, Ensenada, BC 92037 ☎ 646/178-1641. **Five Star Tours** ✉ 1050 Kettner Blvd., San Diego, CA 92101 ☎ 619/232-5049 ⊕ www.efivestartours.com. **San Diego Scenic Tours** ✉ 2255 Garnet Ave., San Diego, CA 92109 ☎ 858/273-8687 ⊕ www.sandiegoscenictours.com.

VISITOR INFORMATION

Baja tours, Mexican auto insurance, a monthly newsletter, discounts, and lectures are available through Discover Baja, which is a membership club for Baja travelers.

Baja's largest cities have tourism offices operated by different agencies. These offices are usually open weekdays 9–7 (although some may close in early afternoon for lunch) and weekends 9–1. Some of the smaller areas don't have offices. The excellent Baja California State Secretary of Tourism distributes information on the entire state.

Of Ensenada's two tourist bureaus, the one on Boulevard Costero has the most information. Tijuana has both a Baja California State Secretary of Tourism office and the Tijuana Convention and Tourism Bureau. The latter has two locations, one within the San Ysidro border crossing and one on Avenida Revolución. The Tijuana Tourist Trust operates an office in the Zona Río. Rosarito also has a tourist office.

Baja California State Secretary of Tourism ✉ Paseo de los Héroes 10289, Zona Río, Tijuana ☎ 664/634-6330 ⊕ www.discoverbajacalifornia.com. **Discover Baja** ✉ 3089 Clairemont Dr., San Diego, CA 92117 ☎ 619/275-4225 or 800/727-2252 ⊕ www.discoverbaja.com. **Ensenada Tourism** ✉ Blvd. Costero 1477, Centro, Ensenada ☎ 646/172-3022 ⊕ www.ensenada-tourism.com. **Ensenada Tourism Board** ✉ Blvd. Cárdenas 609, Centro, Ensenada ☎☎ 646/178-8578 or 800/025-3991 in Mexico, 800/310-9687 in U.S. ⊕ www.enjoyensenada.com. **Rosarito Tourist Board** ✉ Blvd. Juárez 907, Oceana Plaza Shopping Center, Rosarito ☎ 624/612-0396 ⊕ www.rosarito.org. **Tijuana Convention and Tourism Bureau** ✉ Inside the San Ysidro border crossing, Border, Tijuana ☎ 664/683-1405 ✉ Av. Revolución, between Calles 3 and 4, Centro, Tijuana ☎ 664/684-0481 or 664/688-0555 ⊕ www.tijuanaonline.org. **Tijuana Tourist Trust** ✉ Paseo de los Héroes 9365-201, Zona Río, Tijuana ☎ 664/684-0537, 888/775-2417 in U.S. ⊕ www.seetijuana.com.

UNDERSTANDING SAN DIEGO

SAN DIEGO AT A GLANCE

Fast Facts

Type of government: Mayor elected every four years, but must share power with City Manager appointed by City Council, composed of eight members elected from within their council districts.
Population: 1,294,032 million (city), 3,017,204 million (region)
Population Density: 3,771.9 people per square mi (city), 670 per square mi (region)
Median age: 33.7
Ethnic groups: White 60.18%; African American 7.86%; Native American 0.62%; Asian 13.65%; Pacific Islander 0.48%; other (and two or more) races 17.22%. People of Hispanic or Latino origin of any race 25.40%

Geography & Environment

Latitude: 33° N (same as Charleston, South Carolina; Casablanca, Morocco; Dallas, Texas; Jerusalem, Israel; Shanghai, China)
Longitude: 117° W (same as Beijing, China; Perth, Australia)
Elevation: 85 feet
Land area: 342.5 square mi (city), 4,261 square mi (region)
Terrain: Seventy miles of beaches along the west coast, with elevations rising eastward through gentle foothills to forested mountains and desert beyond. The 600,000-acre Anza-Borrego Desert State Park straddles San Diego County and Imperial County to the east
Natural hazards: Earthquakes, heavy surf, and riptides at some beaches, landslides, wildfires in dry eastern desert
Environmental issues: Urban runoff and sewage spills close most beaches during wet weather; summer droughts are a persistent problem; wildlife and plant preservation as the city continues robust growth, particularly with new home building; concerns over the effects of San Onofre, a nuclear power plant, on the Pacific Ocean and local residents' long-term safety

Economy

Per capita income: $32,515
Unemployment: 4.7%
Work force: 1.5 million; services (business/health/tourism) 29.8%; government 18.1%; trade 16.7%; goods producing (including mining and construction) 15.3%; manufacturing 9.3%; retail trade 9%; other 3.8%
Major industries: Aerospace, bio-tech, electronics, manufacturing, oceanography, shipbuilding, software, telecommunications, tourism

Did You Know?

• A recent study ranked San Diego as one of the least segregated cities in the nation.

• Scientist Kurt Benirschke coined the phrase "extinct is forever" when doing work with endangered species at the San Diego Zoo.

• After the New York Yacht Club lost the America's Cup for the first time in 132 years in 1983, it was the San Diego Yacht Club, representing the U.S., that won it back from Australia in 1987 and successfully defended it in 1988 and 1992.

• San Diego gained 215,000 legal and illegal immigrants in the 1990s, increasing its foreign-born population to more than 600,000.

• San Diego County consists of 18 incorporated cities and 17 unincorporated communities and is about the same size as the state of Connecticut.

• San Diego skateboarder Danny Way, who already held world records for dis-

tance and height on a skateboard, set a new world record on July 9, 2005, when he became the first person to jump over the Great Wall of China without the use of a motorized vehicle and live to tell the tale.

• A recent U.S. report estimated that more than 20 million gallons of untreated sewage was being discharged near Tijuana and carried by currents onto U.S. beaches, many in San Diego.

• Among the things kept at the San Diego Supercomputer Center at UCSD is the largest single repository of protein structure data on earth and one of the world's top 20 supercomputers, capable of doing more than 1.7 trillion calculations per second.

• One of La Jolla's most famous residents was Theodor Seuss Geisel, better known as Dr. Seuss. The author once said that his greatest work was the Lion Wading Pool that he donated to the San Diego Wild Animal Park in 1973.

PARADISE FOUND

SUNSHINE YEAR-ROUND, miles of white-sand beaches, laid-back friendliness, history, Hispanic culture, and family-oriented outdoor entertainment at SeaWorld and the world-famous San Diego Zoo are enough to draw 14 million visitors annually to "America's finest city." But there's more than meets the eye here. If you look beyond the obvious, you'll discover why many longtime vacationers eventually become residents, and why residents have a hard time ever moving.

San Diego, occupying the southwest corner of California, boasts an almost perfect year-round climate. Most days are sunny, averaging 70°F, and humidity is low. The cool coastal climate is ideal for the area's most colorful industry—flower growing. Summer temperatures frequently reach 100°F inland, particularly at the Wild Animal Park near Escondido; even so, nights are cool enough to make it a good idea to have a sweater or jacket handy.

San Diego is a big city, where locals take pride in its small-town feel. With more than 1 million people living within the city limits, San Diego is second only to Los Angeles in population among California cities and ranks as the seventh-largest municipality in the United States. It also covers a lot of territory, roughly 400 square mi of land and sea.

Central San Diego is delightfully urban and accessible. You can walk the entire downtown area—explore the exciting and trendy Gaslamp Quarter, stop and shop at whimsical Horton Plaza, dine Italian, hear a rock band, attend a play, take a sunset harbor stroll, picnic in the park, or visit a historic building. Downtown you can catch the trolley or take the bus to the Balboa Park museums and the zoo, Old Town historic sites, Mission Bay marine park, Qualcomm Stadium, diverse urban neighborhoods, and Tijuana.

To the north and south of the city are 70 mi of beaches. Hiking and camping territory lie inland, where a succession of long, low, chaparral-covered mesas are punctuated with deep-cut canyons that step up to savannalike hills, separating the verdant coast from the arid Anza-Borrego Desert. Unusually clear skies make the inland countryside ideal for stargazing.

You'll find reminders of San Diego's Spanish and Mexican heritage throughout the region—in architecture and place-names, in distinctive Mexican cuisine, and in a handful of historic buildings in Old Town. The San Diego area, the birthplace of California, was claimed for Spain by Juan Rodríguez Cabrillo in 1542. The first European community, Mission Alta California, was established here in 1769, when a small group of settlers and soldiers set up camp on what is now called Presidio Hill. Franciscan Father Junípero Serra, leader of the settlers, celebrated the first Mass here in July of that year, establishing the Mission San Diego de Alcalá, the first of the 21 missions built by Spanish friars in California. San Diego, along with the rest of California, ultimately came under Mexican rule before entering the United States as the 31st state in 1850.

In 1867 developer Alonzo Horton, who called the town's bay-front "the prettiest place for a city I ever saw," began building a hotel, a plaza, and prefab homes on 960 downtown acres. The city's fate was sealed in 1908 when it was included among the 20 ports of call on six continents visited by the U.S. Navy's Great White Fleet—16 brand new battleships—during a 14-month round-the-world demonstration of American sea power. The military continues to contribute to the local economy, operating many bases and installations throughout the county; San Diego is home to the largest military complex in the world.

San Diego has taken an orderly approach to inevitable development with the adoption of a general plan to run through the year 2020. More than 50 projects are under way or on the drawing board for downtown. The most recent opening was a new ballpark for the Padres.

Links between the the city and south-of-the-border communities of Tijuana and Ensenada continue to strengthen. More than 140 million border crossings take place at San Ysidro annually, indicative of San Diego's two-nation nature, and Tijuana has grown into one of the biggest, most exciting cities in Mexico in recent years. If you go, you'll discover a sophisticated, pulsating place marked with excellent restaurants, trendy bars and discos, chic boutiques, discount malls, sports-betting parlors, broad boulevards congested with traffic, and new high-rise hotels.

Without question, San Diego is one of the warmest and most appealing destinations in the United States. As you explore, you'll make your own discoveries that will lead you to agree with most locals that this corner of California is just this side of paradise.

–Bobbi Zane

BOOKS & MOVIES

Books

There's no better way to establish the mood for your visit to Old Town San Diego than by reading Helen Hunt Jackson's 19th-century romantic novel, *Ramona,* a best-seller for more than 50 years and still readily available. The Casa de Estudillo in Old Town has been known for many years as Ramona's Marriage Place because of its close resemblance to the house described in the novel. Richard Henry Dana Jr.'s *Two Years Before the Mast* (1869), based on the author's experiences as a merchant sailor, provides a masculine perspective on early San Diego history.

Other novels with a San Diego setting include Raymond Chandler's mystery about the waterfront, *Playback*; Wade Miller's mystery, *On Easy Street*; Eric Higgs's gothic thriller, *A Happy Man*; Tom Wolfe's satire of the La Jolla surfing scene, *The Pump House Gang*; and David Zielinski's modern-day story, *A Genuine Monster.*

Movies

Filmmakers have taken advantage of San Diego's diverse and amiable climate since the dawn of cinema. Westerns, comedy-westerns, and tales of the sea were early staples: *Cupid in Chaps, The Sagebrush Phrenologist* (how's that for a title?), the 1914 version of *The Virginian,* and Lon Chaney's *Tell It to the Marines* were among the silent films shot in the area. Unlike many films in which San Diego itself doesn't figure in the plot, the screen version of Helen Hunt Jackson's novel *Ramona* (1936), starring Loretta Young as the title character, incorporated historical settings (or replicas).

Easy-to-capture outdoor locales have lured many productions south from Hollywood through the years, including the following military-oriented talkies, all or part of which were shot in San Diego: James Cagney's *Here Comes the Navy* (1934);

Errol Flynn's *Dive Bomber* (1941); John Wayne's *The Sands of Iwo Jima* (1949); Ronald Reagan's *Hellcats of the Navy* (1957, costarring Nancy Davis, the future first lady); Rock Hudson's *Ice Station Zebra* (1968); Tom Cruise's *Top Gun* (1986); Sean Connery's *Hunt for Red October* (1990); Charlie Sheen's *Navy Seals* (1990); and Danny Glover's *Flight of the Intruder* (1991).

In a lighter military vein, in *Francis in the Navy* (1955), in which a very young Clint Eastwood had a bit part, the famous talking mule hit the high seas at Coronado. The Tom Hanks–Darryl Hannah hit *Splash* (1984), *Spaceballs* (1987), *My Blue Heaven* (1990), *Hot Shots* (1991), *Wayne's World 2* (1993), and Ellen DeGeneres's *Mr. Wrong* (1996) are other comedies with scenes filmed here. The city has a cameo role in the minihit *Flirting with Disaster* (1996), and one of the best comedies ever made, director Billy Wilder's *Some Like It Hot* (1959)—starring Marilyn Monroe, Jack Lemmon, and Tony Curtis—takes place at the famous Hotel Del Coronado (standing in as a Miami resort).

Other movies including San Diego as either a co-star or surrogate for fictional locales include *Jurassic Park: The Lost World* (1997); *Pearl Harbor* (2001); *Traffic* (2000); *The Scorpion King* (2002); *The Antwone Fisher Story* (2002); *Bruce Almighty* (2003); and *Anchorman* (2004).

The amusingly low-budget *Attack of the Killer Tomatoes* (1980) makes good use of local scenery—and the infamous San Diego Chicken. The producers must have liked what they found in town, as they returned for three sequels: *Return of the Killer Tomatoes* (1988), *Killer Tomatoes Strike Back* (1990), and—proving just how versatile the region is as a film location—*Killer Tomatoes Go to France* (1991).

Television producers zip south for series and made-for-TV movies all the time. The alteration of San Diego's skyline in the 1980s was partially documented on the hit show *Simon & Simon*. Other productions that have filmed here include *Silk Stalkings*, *Baywatch*, *High Tide*, *Renegade*, and *Nip/Tuck*.

INDEX

Cover Photo (Mission Beach): *Giovanni Simeone/Fototeca 9x12.* F6, *Richard Cummins/viestiphoto.com.* F7 (left), *Richard Cummins/viestiphoto.com.* F7 (right), *Jeff Greenberg/age fotostock.* F8, *Johnny Stockshooter/age fotostock.* F9 (left), *Corbis.* F9 (right), *Richard Cummins/viestiphoto.com.* F12, *Richard Cummins/viestiphoto.com.* F13, *Jeff Greenberg/age fotostock.* F15, *Corbis.* F16, *Corbis.* F17 (left), *John W. Warden/age fotostock.* F17 (right) *Richard Cummins/viestiphoto.com.* F20, *Joe Viesti/viestiphoto.com.* F21 (left), *Richard Cummins/viestiphoto.com.* F21 (right), *Richard Cummins/viestiphoto.com.* F22, *Werner Bollmann/age fotostock.* F23 (left), *Doug Scott/age fotostock.* F23 (right), *Corbis.* F24, *Corbis.*

ABOUT OUR WRITERS

Former Fodor's staff editor **Andrew Collins** lives in Santa Fe, New Mexico, but has written about San Diego for many years in *Fodor's Gay Guide to the USA* and several newspapers and magazines. He contributes regularly to *Travel & Leisure, Sunset, Frommer's Budget Travel,* and *New Mexico Magazine,* and he teaches travel writing for New York City's Gotham Writers' Workshop.

Lenore Greiner grew up in San Francisco but transplanted herself to San Diego 16 years ago after vacationing in Coronado. She spends a lot of time on the road writing for other Fodor's guides, including Fodor's Las Vegas. Her travel articles have appeared in *Newsday,* the *San Francisco Examiner/ Chronicle,* Delta Airlines' *Sky,* Air New Zealand's *Pacific Way, Woman,* and *Healing Retreats & Spas.*

Recipient of the prestigious Pluma de Plata award for writing on Mexico, **Maribeth Mellin** lives in San Diego near the Tijuana border in a home filled with folk art and photos from Latin America—including a snapshot of the 140-pound marlin she caught in the Sea of Cortez. She has authored travel books on Mexico, Costa Rica, Argentina, and Peru.

Dining writer **David Nelson** has known San Diego since childhood and has lived there for more than 27 years, virtually all of which have been spent writing about the local culinary scene. Respected for his extensive knowledge of food lore, cooking techniques, and the restaurant industry, he was a columnist for the former San Diego edition of the *Los Angeles Times* for a dozen years. He now writes restaurant reviews and travel pieces for a number of Southern California publications.

Longtime southern Californian **Bobbi Zane** makes her home in the mountain hamlet of Julian. Bobbi's byline has appeared in the *Los Angeles Times,* the *Los Angeles Daily News,* and the *Orange County Register.*